THE FATE OF THE
ENGLISH COUNTRY HOUSE

THE FATE OF THE
ENGLISH COUNTRY HOUSE

David Littlejohn

Photographs by Sheila Littlejohn

New York   Oxford

OXFORD UNIVERSITY PRESS

1997

Oxford University Press

Oxford   New York
Athens   Auckland   Bangkok   Bogotá   Bombay
Buenos Aires   Calcutta   Cape Town   Dar es Salaam
Delhi   Florence   Hong Kong   Istanbul   Karachi
Kuala Lumpur   Madras   Madrid   Melbourne
Mexico City   Nairobi   Paris   Singapore
Taipei   Tokyo   Toronto

and associated companies in
Berlin   Ibadan

Published by Oxford University Press, Inc.,
198 Madison Avenue, New York, New York 10016

Oxford is a registered trademark of Oxford University Press

Library of Congress Cataloging-in-Publication Data
Littlejohn, David, 1937-
The fate of the English country house / David Littlejohn; photographs by Sheila Littlejohn.
p. cm.   Includes bibliographical references and index.
ISBN 0-19-508876-X
1. Country homes—Economic aspects—England.
2. Country homes—Remodeling for other use—England.   I. Title.
NA7620.L48   1997
728.8'0942—dc20   96-34084

9 8 7 6 5 4 3 2 1
Printed in the United States of America
on acid-free paper

To Robert Chase Littlejohn,

A true gentleman,

With happy memories of our own country house.

CONTENTS

ACKNOWLEDGMENTS

I first got the idea of writing about this subject towards the end of a four months' sabbatical leave in Oxford in 1991. I had finished reading proofs of a book and, as the chill of late autumn settled in, found I couldn't quite settle down to read, as I had planned to do. Visiting country houses—something I had been doing since my first trip to England in 1957, and continued with more method during extended stays in 1977–78 and 1986—was all very well. But like many writers who travel in search of aesthetic (and other) adventures, I become frustrated at simply playing tourist. In any case, most country houses, I found, were closed to tourists after October.

So I developed the notion of writing an article on "The Stately Home Industry," which in time grew into this book, primarily as a means of gaining access to country houses I wanted to visit, and meeting their owners. My visits with the owners of three historic houses in Oxfordshire, visits I repeated three years later, form the basis of the opening chapter.

My wife and I made an unusually busy six weeks' trip to England in the summer of 1994, during which we saw and she photographed a great many country houses (including some turned into hotels, schools, conference centers, and the like), and I conducted the interviews which lie at the heart of this book. People I was unable to visit, I interviewed by telephone. Many others have answered my questions by mail.

I would like to thank the Earl of Shelburne, William Proby, Terry Empson, and Peter Sinclair at the Historic Houses Association in London—and Lord Shelburne for his hospitality at Bowood House on two occasions; Lord Chorley, Ian Bollom, Patricia Barr, and other members of the staff at the National Trust headquarters in London; Lord Montagu (who also entertained us at Beaulieu), Sir Jocelyn Stevens, Stephen Williams, and June Prunty at English Heritage; Lord Rothschild, chairman of the National Heritage Memorial Fund—and now of the affluent Heritage Lottery Fund—as well as master of Waddesdon; Heather Wilson, of the Museums and Galleries Commission; Chris Smith MP, formerly Shadow Secretary of State for Heritage; and a number of individual experts on the English country house—John Cornforth, Hugh Massingberd, Rodney Melville, James

Lees-Milne, and the late Gervase Jackson-Stops—who kindly agreed to assist a beginner. I offer my special thanks to Mark Girouard and Norman Hudson, who generously read a draft of the entire manuscript and made many valuable suggestions.

For welcoming us into their or their employers' homes, hotels, and other establishments, and submitting to my questions, I would like to thank in addition the Earl of Arundel (Arundel Castle, Sussex); Patrick Cooke (Athelhampton, Dorset); David and Malvina Donen (Aynhoe Park, Oxford); the late Duchess of Beaufort (Badminton, Avon); the Duke of Marlborough (Blenheim Palace, Oxford); Lord Brocket (Brocket Hall, Herts.); Lord Saye and Sele (Broughton Castle, Oxford); Richard Wheeler, of the National Trust (Chastleton, Oxford); Colonel Alistair McLeod Matthews (Chenies Manor, Herts.); Robin Hudson (Chewton Glen Hotel, Hants.); Antony Jarvis (Doddington Hall, Lincs.); Rosalind Ingrams (Garsington, Oxford); Paul Henderson (Gidleigh Park Hotel, Devon); Kit Martin (Gunton Park, Norfolk); Richard Broyd (Hartwell House Hotel, Bucks.); Ian Malcolm, of the National Westminster Bank (Heythrop Park, Oxford); the Earl of Leicester (Holkham Hall, Norfolk); Jonathan Richie (Horsted Place Hotel, Sussex); Viscount and Viscountess Scarsdale (Kedleston, Derby); Judith (Mrs. Patrick) Phillips (Kentwell, Suffolk)—and Mr. Phillips, for his detailed written response to my earlier questions; Sir Thomas Pilkington, Baronet, and Lady Pilkington (King's Walden Bury, Herts.); Lord and Lady Sackville (Knole, Kent); Christopher Buxton, of Period and Country Houses, Ltd.—an exceptionally gracious host (Kirtlington, Oxford); Lord Cobbold and John Hay (Knebworth House, Herts.); Joanna Oswin and Graham Jackson (Leeds Castle, Kent); the Marquess of Bath (Longleat, Wilts.); Sir Richard Hyde Parker, Baronet, and Lady Hyde Parker (Melford Hall, Suffolk); Robert Spencer-Bernard (Nether Winchendon, Bucks.); Simon Scrimgeour (Parham Park, Sussex); Lord Courtenay and Tim Faulkner (Powderham Castle, Devon); the Earl and Countess of Yarmouth (Ragley Hall, Warwick—Lord Yarmouth's father, the Marquess of Hertford, had earlier answered questions by mail); Brian Ludford of the National Trust (Saltram, Devon); Nigel Nicolson (Sissinghurst Castle, Kent); Samuel Whitbread (Southill, Bedfordshire); The Hon. Ann Gascoigne (Stanton Harcourt Manor, Oxford); the late Bob Payton (Stapleford Park Hotel, Leics.); Brigadier William Le Blanc-Smith (Sudeley Castle, Gloucs.); and John Humphris and Rosemary Tupper (Sutton Place, Surrey). Alan Shrimpton waited in vain for me at Bryanston School, Dorset, on a day when I was unable to get there.

On occasions when my visits could not coincide with the owners' or managers' presence, or I was unable to get to the house, people patiently and helpfully answered my questions by phone. For these telephone interviews, I would like to thank William Hughes (Broadlands, Hants.); Lady Victoria Leatham (Burghley House, Lincs.); The Hon. Simon Howard and Paul Nicoll (Castle Howard, Yorkshire); the Duke of Devonshire and Roger Wardle (Chatsworth, Derby); Lord Apsley (Cirencester Park, Gloucs.); Lord Hesketh (Easton Neston, Northants.); David Pinnegar (Hammerwood Park, Sussex); Susan Lantz and Jan Beckett (regarding Harlaxton, Lincs.); Robin Brackenbury (Holme Pierrepont, Notts.); the Marquess of Cholmondeley (Houghton Hall, Norfolk, and Cholmondeley

Castle, Cheshire); the Earl of Derby (Knowsley, Merseyside); Jack Eyston (Mapledurham, Oxford); Jane Bence, of the Maharishi University of Natural Law (Mentmore, Bucks.); Sir Nicholas Bacon, Baronet (Raveningham Hall, Norfolk); Sir Thomas Ingilby, Baronet (Ripley Castle, Yorks.); Charles Cottrell-Dormer (Rousham, Oxford); the Earl of Scarborough (Sandbeck, Yorks.); Lord de Saumarez (Shrubland Park, Suffolk); the Earl of Cardigan (regarding Tottenham House, Wilts.); Sir Francis Dashwood, Baronet (West Wycombe Park, Bucks.); and Lord Howland (Woburn Abbey, Bedfordshire).

Both in 1991–92 and again in 1994–95, a number of people took the time and effort to answer my detailed questions by mail—though I fully respect the Marquess of Salisbury's response to my prying questions about Hatfield House: "I regret I am not willing to satisfy your curiosity with matters I consider to be my personal affairs."

Fortunately for me, others were less circumspect. Among my more generous correspondents—in addition to those I have also met in person, or talked to on the phone—have been Michael Farr (Allerton Park, Yorks.); The Hon. John A. Evans-Freke (Alnwick Castle, Northumberland); Earl Spencer (Althorp, Northants.); Sir Richard Carew-Pole, Baronet (Antony House, Cornwall); the Marquess of Zetland (Aske, Yorks.); Eiler Hansen (Berkeley Castle, Gloucs.); Lord Middleton (Birdsall House, Yorks.); James Hunter Blair (Blairquhan Castle, Ayrshire, Scotland); George Lane Fox (Bramham Park, Yorks.); Caroline Weeks (Brympton d'Evercy, Somerset); Charles Clive-Ponsonby-Fane (formerly of Brympton d'Evercy); Susan Cunliffe-Lister (Burton Agnes Hall, Yorks.); John Chichester-Constable (Burton Constable Hall, Yorks.); Lord Faringdon (Buscot Park, Oxford); Sir Humphry Wakefield, Baronet (Chillingham Castle, Northumberland); the Earl of Onslow (Clandon Park, Surrey); Sir Ralph Verney, Baronet (Claydon House, Bucks.); the Marquess of Downshire (Clifton Castle, Yorks.); Alan Swerdlow (Compton Verney House Trust, Warwick); the Marquess of Northampton (Compton Wynyates, Warwick and Castle Ashby, Northants.); the late Lord Methuen (Corsham Court, Wilts.); Andrew McLaren (Coughton Court, Warwick); Lord Croft (Croft Castle, Hereford); Lord Feversham (Duncombe Park, Yorks.); James Hervey-Bathurst (Eastnor Castle, Hereford); C. J. E. Spicer (Euston Hall, Norfolk); Nicola Wright (Eyam Hall, Derby); Katharine Burnett (Finchcocks, Kent); Viscount Hampden (Glynde Place, Sussex); Lord FitzWalter (Goodnestone Park, Kent); David Legg-Willis (Goodwood, Sussex); Lady Willoughby de Eresby (Grimsthorpe Castle, Lincs.); Jane Fry (Groombridge Place, Kent); Gerald Long (Harewood House, Yorks.); Sir Marcus Worsley, Baronet (Hovingham Hall, Yorks.); D. Len Peach, IBM UK Laboratories Ltd. (Hursley Park, Hants.); Francis T. Grant (Kingston Bagpuize House, Oxford); the Earl of Radnor (Longford Castle, Wilts.); James More-Molyneux (Losely Park, Surrey); Lady Morrison (Madresfield Court, Worcester); Lord Palmer (Manderston, Berwick, Scotland); Robert Hesketh (Meols Hall, Merseyside); John Manley, Sussex Archeological Society (Michelham Priory, Sussex); Robin Compton (Newby Hall, Yorks.); Peter Britton, of Jackson-Stops and Staff, Chipping Camden (sale agents for Northwick Park, Gloucs.); Lord St. Oswald (Nostell Priory, Yorks.); James A. Sellick (Pashley Manor, Sussex); Lord Egremont (Petworth House, Sussex); the Marquess of Anglesey (Plas Newydd, Anglesey, Wales); Colonel Michael Saunders Watson (Rockingham Castle, Leics.); Sir Richard Baker Wilbraham, Baronet (Rode Hall, Cheshire); Lord Hastings (Seaton Delaval Hall, Northumberland); Lord St. Levan (St. Michael's Mount, Cornwall); David Peake (Sezincote, Gloucs.); Simon Wingfield Digby (Sherborne Castle, Dorset); Jane Spier (Shugborough, Staffs.); the Countess of Normanton (Somerley, Hants.); John Warde (Squerryes Court, Kent); Annette Jacobs (Stanford Hall, Leics.); Lord Neidpath (Stanway House, Gloucs.); Andrew Rudolph (Stowe School, Bucks.); Lord Vernon (Sudbury House, Derby); Lord Clifford (Ugbrooke Park, Devon); the Earl of Bradford (Weston Park, Shropshire); Lord Forrester (Willey Park, Shropshire); and R. W. Stedman and Veronica Quarm (Wilton House, Wilts.). Among these are the owners or managers of some of the houses that I had hoped to visit in 1991 or 1994, but was forced to drop from my list.

The heads, librarians, or other staff members of a number of country houses that have become schools kindly sent me brochures, histories, and other information. Among them were representatives of Ampleforth College Preparatory School (Gilling Castle), Yorks.; Ashridge Management College, Herts.; Bearwood College, Berks.; Benenden School, Kent; Bryanston School, Dorset; Caythorpe Court (De Montfort University), Lincs.; Cheltenham College, Gloucs.; Cobham Hall, Kent; Harlaxton (the University of Evansville), Lincs.; Heath Mount School, Herts.; Kimbolton School, Cambridge; Kingston Maurward College, Dorset; Langley School, Norfolk; Milton Abbey School, Dorset; Moyles Court School, Hants.; Prior Park College, Avon; St. Mary's University College, Strawberry Hill, London; Scarisbrick Hall, Lancs.; Stonyhurst College, Lancs.; Stowe School, Bucks.; Westonbirt School, Gloucs.; and Wroxton College (Fairleigh Dickinson University), Oxford.

Commercial establishments that supplied me with information included Alton Towers, Staffs.; Cameron Hall Developments Ltd., Wynyard Park, Cleveland; Center Parcs Ltd., Longleat, Wilts.; Discover Britain, Inc., Worcester; Elvetham Hall Conferences Ltd., Hants.; Hever Castle, Kent; James Longley & Co. Ltd, Sussex; and Warwick Castle. The architectural firms Donald W. Insall & Associates and Rodney Melville and Partners sent me information regarding their country house restoration projects.

Lady Ryder kindly answered my questions about the country houses that have become hospices used by the Sue Ryder Foundation. The National Union of Teachers sent me information about their use of Stoke Rochford Hall, Lincs., and the Police Staff College about theirs of Bramshill House, Hants. The Country Landowners Association supplied their 1995 policy paper on British rural areas. From Wolsey Lodges and the Landmark Trust I obtained catalogues of their respective properties. John Walsh, director of the J. Paul Getty Museum, Malibu, California, helped explain the complicated negotiations regarding their attempted purchase of Antonio Canova's *The Three Graces*, a statuary group formerly at Woburn Abbey. The National Trust for Historic Preservation, the Preservation Society of Newport County (Rhode Island), and the Biltmore Estate (North Carolina) sent me details on some American country houses open to the public; La

Demeure Historique and the Caisse Nationale des Monuments Historiques provided similar material for France.

Of great help to both of us has been my wife's brother, Max Hageman of Berkhamsted, Herts., who not only provided us with aid and comfort during our travels, but also served as a mail-drop, communications center, and clipping service before, during, and after our visits. The success of our English travels also owes a good deal to the help and hospitality of dear friends: Harry and Mary Judge in Oxford, John and Hilary Lawrence in Gloucestershire, and Joyce Hird in Dorset. Although it is better known as an opera venue than a country house, a visit to Glyndebourne has now become a regular part of our tours, and I would like to thank Helen O'Neill and (in 1994) Mark Kay for making this possible and so pleasant. I would also like to pay tribute to the exceptional welcome offered by the owners of three smaller country houses where we stayed as paying guests: Kay Morgan at Old Cloth Hall in Cranbrook, Kent; John and Gillian Dilley at Chilvester Hill House in Calne, Wiltshire; and John and Susan Murray at Lewtrenchard Manor near Okehampton, Devon.

In the United States, I express my gratitude to the Academic Senate Committee on Research as well as other units of the University of California at Berkeley, for grants which first paid for my transportation to England in 1994, and then enabled me to hire three student assistants who undertook different portions of my library research. I must also thank those three students—Alison Hydorn, Ann Keary, and Pamela Johnson—for fetching and carrying books; finding, assessing and copying articles; scanning thousands of pages of *Country Life* magazines and Pevsner's *Buildings of England* guides; locating country estates on Ordnance Survey maps; helping me track the changing value of the pound; and doing so many of the other niggling chores one loves to push off on someone else.

When Oxford University Press asked me for the names of people in this country to whom they might show my proposal, Peter Stansky of Stanford University kindly came up with a list of American authorities. I don't know who the chosen ones were or what they wrote, but whatever they wrote worked, so I thank them, as well as Peter.

This book would not have been possible without the help of the man to whom it is dedicated, or that of my wife. Sheila not only took some 700 photographs, from which we culled those you see here. She also had to race with me about her native land at a time when my own strength was not quite equal to my over-ambitious plans, which turned what I hoped would be a working holiday into a considerable ordeal.

D.L.

In addition to the hosts and friends my husband has named, I would like to express my thanks to Sandy Sher and Dwight Collins at Studio One in Oakland for their help, and to my friends Christin Audo, Gerda Mathan, Miriam Ciochan, and Margaret Rhodes for their encouragement.

S.L.

NOTES ON THE TEXT

Two complex (and ultimately unanswerable) questions—"Just what *is* a country house?" and "How many country houses are left?"—are dealt with briefly in the appendix, entitled "Definitions and Numbers."

British prices and values, quoted in current pounds sterling, are as accurate as my sources permit. The dollar equivalents I give are rough estimates, based on the average pound/dollar values for the year in question. Pound/dollar values have been allowed to float freely for the past 25 years (from a high of $2.44 in 1971 to a low of $1.30 in 1985), so at the time of any cited sale, tax bill, etc., the actual rate may have differed from the annual average I have used. I have not tried to give dollar equivalents when a range of years is involved, or (as a rule) for historical cases. The further back in time you go, the less sense current "equivalents" make, unless you are able to factor in a great many social and economic changes.

I have confined my survey to English country houses, neglecting those of Scotland and Wales, as well as Ireland—both portions of which were a part of the United Kingdom until 1922—because I have visited too few country houses in the United Kingdom outside of England to do their story justice. From time to time I will make reference to country houses beyond English borders. But with all respect for the achievements of her neighbors, it is the houses of England I know best.

THE FATE OF THE
ENGLISH COUNTRY HOUSE

CHAPTER ONE

A Television Setting,
and Three Houses near Oxford

FOR MILLIONS OF PEOPLE in the English-speaking world, the now-standard image of the British country house is Brideshead Castle in Wiltshire: the domed and doomed Baroque country seat of the Marchmain family in Evelyn Waugh's 1945 novel *Brideshead Revisited*, filmed for television some 30 years later.

In real life, the house used for the television series is Castle Howard, one of the largest and most opulent private homes in England, located on 10,000 acres of gardens, parkland, and woods in North Yorkshire. It was the first building designed by the playwright John Vanbrugh (with some help from Nicholas Hawksmoor and its owner, the 3rd Earl of Carlisle). Construction began in 1701, and was finished in 1713.

In his preface to the 1959 edition of *Brideshead Revisited*, Evelyn Waugh wrote, "It was impossible to foresee, in the spring of 1944, the present cult of the English country house. It seemed then that the ancestral seats which were our chief national artistic monument were doomed to decay and spoliation like the monasteries in the sixteenth century. Brideshead today would be open to trippers, its treasures rearranged by expert hands and the fabric better maintained than it was by Lord Marchmain.... Much of this book therefore is a panegyric preached over an empty coffin."

Brideshead, today, *is* of course open to trippers. According to The Hon. Simon Howard, who has lived in Castle Howard since 1984, "'Brideshead' had a great effect on our international posture. We estimate it increased our number of visitors by thirty five percent. We're still getting income from the series. It was filmed in the winter, when we're normally closed to the public in any case. They offered a very hefty rental"—which, in fact, Mr.

Howard's father was able to renegotiate upwards after a TV technician's strike. Although the television setting figured in their advertisements until quite recently, "We try to play down the 'Brideshead' connection now," says Mr. Howard. "It doesn't seem quite fair to Vanbrugh—or to the family, for that matter."

Simon Howard, born in 1956, and his wife Annette live in twelve rooms of the east wing. He is a six-times-great-grandson of Charles Howard, the Earl of Carlisle who built Castle Howard almost 300 years ago. It was Simon Howard's father George who, coming into possession of the castle as a young man in 1944 (his uncle got the title, his father the house), managed to stop the trustees from breaking up its contents and selling the house. George Howard—eventually made a life peer as Baron Howard of Henderskelfe, the year before he died in 1984—devoted much of the rest of his life to restoring Castle Howard. He opened it to the public in 1952, and in 1960 rebuilt the dome, which had burned down in a disastrous fire in 1940. The *Brideshead* contract helped pay for further restoration, including the new Garden Hall on the south front. It is here that Charles Ryder, the fictional artist-narrator of *Brideshead* (played for television by Jeremy Irons) is seen painting the new murals actually completed by Felix Kelly in 1981.

Simon Howard and his three brothers are the directors of a company called Castle Howard Estate Ltd., which was set up for tax purposes in 1949, and which actually *owns* the house and its dependencies, rents them out to filmmakers, and receives the take from day-trippers. Castle Howard—the actual house that Waugh had in mind was considerably smaller and less showy—now plays host to more than 200,000 paying visitors a year, who spend, on an average, 3.5 hours and £7 ($10.50) each. Castle Howard Estate Ltd. has invited "prestige" corporations like Rémy Martin Cognac and American Express to sponsor the rebuilding of individual rooms, roofs, and wings, the way other corporations sponsor museum shows and opera productions. The company farms about two-thirds of its 10,000 acres. Most people, Simon Howard is convinced, come—at least come for a second and third time—for the "Elysian Fields" aspect, the broad lakes and the rolling green Capability Brown-designed parkland, rather than for the house, which lies to the west of a five-mile-long, tree-lined, arrow-straight drive interrupted for two monumental gates and an obelisk. The more visitors can be dispersed about the grounds, the better Castle Howard Estate Ltd. likes it. A little elephant train ferries people who prefer not to walk from the parking lot to the entrance, which are about 1,000 feet apart. Weather permitting, boat trips on the lake are offered on a Victorian-style launch. The company provides cafés and gift shops, says Mr. Howard, because "people expect them. We have farms, a plant centre, fishing, a caravan site." Like a great many country house owners nowadays, they rent out rooms (the Long Gallery can seat 280, the Grecian Room 160) and lawns for corporate entertaining. In June 1992, a lakeside concert featuring José Carreras drew 18,000 people at £20 to £55 ($35–100) a head. The estate earned £3 million ($4.5 million) from the sale of a Bernini bust to the National Gallery in 1986, and another £10 million ($16 million) by selling two 17th-century Italian paintings and some antique sculptures in 1995. During three days in November 1991, they cleared out 1,800 lots of surplus antiques, household furnishings, and junk at what the British press called the World's Largest Car-Boot (i.e., garage) Sale. It attracted 12,000 curiosity seekers, 1,000 buyers, and earned the company more than £2 million ($3.5 million), which they used to help restore the East Wing from the fire damage of half a century before, and to carry out other essential repairs.

In 1993, the firm decided to close down the 18,000-item costume collection (the nation's largest such collection in private hands) because of maintenance costs, and to sell the theatrical costumes. Yielding to television-tourists' fantasies, they announced plans to open on the estate a "Brideshead Golf and Country Club," with two eighteen-hole courses and a hotel. This was later scratched, or at least deferred, when no commercial partner could be found.

The Howards and their company recently reroofed the central block, and have done considerable work on the rose gardens and woods. But they still need about £12 million ($19 million) to put the place in order, Mr. Howard estimates. The British government has started saying no to their grant requests. That, along with internal family pressures, has forced Castle Howard to begin selling off artworks and appealing to corporate sponsors.

·   ·   ·

The fellow who mans the side gate, at the dead end of the picturesque village high street of Woodstock, in Oxfordshire, tells me to drive on in. "Just park alongside the black Daimler in the court. His Grace is expecting you. In fact, he and the duchess got back from London just minutes ago."

I drive through the green park, alongside the artificial lake with its arched stone bridge, turn under the triumphal arch with its dedicatory inscription ("Under the auspices of a munificent sovereign this house was built for John Duke of Marlborough . . ."). Through the vast kitchen courtyard, to a paved court in front of the house three acres in size, deserted now except for a woman in a head scarf walking two yapping little dogs. I park my brown Renault alongside the ducal limo and a little red Ford—his Grace's secretary's car—and look up at the columned facade of the only nonroyal, nonepiscopal "palace" in England. Three hundred fifty thousand people a year troop through the house—another of John Vanbrugh's palatial piles—with its operatic entry hall and the long enfilade of essentially useless 18th-century state rooms, decorated in honor of the 1st Duke of Marlborough. (The house was Queen Anne's and Parliament's thank-you gift to John Marlborough for stopping the forces of Louis XIV at Blenheim, in Bavaria, in 1704.) Tourists also get to look at an exhibit of Winston Churchill memorabilia surrounding the room in which he was born—Churchill was a cousin of the 9th Duke—and buy things to eat and drink at a large terrace café over the water gardens, as well as gifts and souvenirs at a modern shop on the way out. Another 150,000 people pay just to stroll about the formal gardens, and at least part of the spacious grounds, redesigned in the 1760s—like the grounds of so many country houses in England—by Lancelot (called "Capability") Brown, the most influential landscape architect in history. A narrow gauge railway carries you 600 yards from the house to a herb and lavendar garden with its own shop, a butterfly house (which charges extra admission), a cafeteria, a maze, two giant chess sets, a putting green, and an "adventure playground." Another little train takes you out to Capability Brown's lake, where free boat rides or rowboats (for hire) are available. "The idea," says the duke, "is to make sure there's something to keep each member of the family occupied, and to encourage them to come back."

But this is off-season. Except for a few customers at the nursery (or garden center, as the British call it—it has since been shut down), the duke and I appear to have the place to ourselves, plus whatever gardeners and staff may be lurking about. John George Vanderbilt Henry Spencer-Churchill, the 11th Duke of Marlborough, and his third duchess, make their home in the east wing of the main palace, which can accommodate sixteen overnight guests. The rooms here are slightly less grand than those of the standard tourist circuit elsewhere in the house—which are still used for private balls, and hired out for corporate entertaining—but they are impressive enough. John Piper's paintings of the palace hang on the walls of the family wing, among more historic works of art and framed family documents, cartoons, and signed tributes from celebrity guests. I wade through two huge, thick polar bear rugs to a spacious study, where high windows between shelves full of leather-bound books look out onto miles of rolling green. In a three-piece navy pinstripe suit and red tie, the duke sits before one of two wide desks laden with papers, red leather folders, and a modern communications console.

We had both spent the day before in London, at the annual meeting of the Historic Houses Association—the lobbying and support group for more than 1,400 owners of private country houses in Britain, of which his is one of the largest. Most of the talk there had been grim: government support for privately owned historic houses was drying up; more and more great houses were being sold, or turned into hotels, or left empty to decay, their paintings and furniture sent to the auction houses to help pay tax and repair bills. Heirs didn't want the grief of maintaining them, thieves were carting off gigantic garden statues, ghastly new "theme parks" were competing for tourists, and the number of visitors was down.

Yes, the duke confirms, the last tourist season (we were talking in 1991) hadn't been good. "The recession in North America, the Gulf War—Americans tend to plan their holidays well in advance, and when things look bad they stay home. Our numbers were off twenty-five percent last summer, which was probably all due to the loss of North American visitors. And they're absolutely essential. We couldn't pay our maintenance bills without them. We plough every cent back into the house and grounds. Of course, Blenheim is unique and well known, which helps—and we are on the London-Oxford-Stratford circuit. I pity the owners of more isolated, less famous houses." Overall annual attendance fell by 6 percent between 1990 and 1993. In 1992–93, he blamed the weak dollar for continuing to keep Americans home. By 1994, he thought the numbers were looking up again.

The duke, born in 1925, looks like most dukes (there were 24 at last count, not counting royals): smooth skinned and ruddy faced, slightly overweight but tailored well enough

John, 10th Duke of Marlborough.

to disguise it; tight lips, gray-blue eyes, silver-gray hair brushed back from a high, broad forehead. Actually, most marquesses, earls, and viscounts I have met over the age of 40 look rather the same. For their photos in the guidebooks to their homes sold to tourists they tend to dress in country-check jackets and tan trousers, with colored shirts and ties. Their wives, who often look younger than they do, have well-brushed, shoulder length hair, and sit at their husbands' sides wearing cashmere sweaters and wool skirts. Children and dogs, when there are children and dogs, pose happily about them, either in a paneled library or on a garden terrace. The point is to persuade the visiting public that this is still a "family home," and not just a business or tourist attraction: a home lived in by people not unlike themselves.

We talk of the financial problems of owning and running an immense, archaic estate, designed for an age of unquestioned class privilege, grandiose entertaining, vast households and almost unlimited servants; a time before income, capital gains, or inheritance taxes had to be taken into account, before one had to open one's great gates to all those thousands (more than twenty million, altogether) of tourists out "Doing the Statelies" between Easter Sunday and the end of October.

On the whole, the duke professes not to be concerned. One authority on country house economics I had spoken to predicted that Blenheim Palace would last at most one more generation in private hands. ("Baloney!" scoffed the duke.) British newspapers enjoy reporting on the occasionally ignoble life of the duke's son and heir, the Marquess of Blandford, who was born in 1955. But the duke assured me he had everything under control, thanks to a foundation he set up to protect the estate in 1986. He may have to sell off some of his remaining 11,500 acres, and put the proceeds into the foundation. But that, along with the regular hordes of visitors (at about eleven dollars per adult head), income from the gift shops and cafés, profits from special events—all that should, he believed, guarantee sufficient cash flow to keep the place out of the hands of the government that gave it to his eight-times-great-grandfather in the first place. Major donors to the foundation were invited to a ball at the palace in June 1990. Benefactors are given busts of Churchill as mementoes.

The duke and his managers try to run the Blenheim estates like any other business, with the separate branches—the farms, the forests, the horses, the shooting parties, the lake fishing, the day-trippers, the mineral water, the corporate functions, the special events (horse trials, craft fairs, open-air concerts), the catering and gift shops—each meeting its own budget and paying its own way. The total turnover is more than £2 million ($3 million) a year. But no matter what they do, income after taxes from the property is never enough to cover the millions of pounds required for major restoration jobs, like dredging the lake, or rewiring the palace. The big job in progress in 1994 was restoring the 134-foot Column of Victory; the northwest block was scheduled for work in 1995.

Hence the Blenheim Foundation, which can earn money tax-free. The duke obtained repair grants from the government in the past ("this is the first time in years the house hasn't been covered in scaffolding," he said in 1991), but that source has suddenly dried up, in the face of rival claims on the public purse. He feels that new legislation to aid "historic house" owners would be unpopular today, whichever party was in power. "We don't have any special relationship with any particular government. Whatever happens in heritage legislation has to be bipartisan. There's no point in telling the government we need something which five years later, ten years later, is going to be overturned. Remember, the Socialists helped take care of the heritage, too. And we're grateful."

Under present laws, the house itself, the works of art inside it, and its adjacent garden and parkland can be handed on free of inheritance taxes—although with many strings attached. Until the summer of 1994, there was still the threat that the next Duke of Marlborough might have to pay millions of pounds in taxes on the farmland, livestock, rented

Blenheim Palace, Oxfordshire. Tourists in the Great Hall.

buildings, and other investments. There were also fears that Lord Blandford, the heir-presumptive, might not be the ideal person to run the estate.

But in July 1994, just before my return visit, an announcement was made that Blenheim Palace and its "parliamentary estate"—that is, the whole property given to the 1st Duke by a grateful nation—had been conveyed out of family hands into a new "Blenheim Parliamentary Trust." The High Court had accepted the duke's (and his trustees') request *not* to have the parliamentary estate pass to Lord Blandford if and when he succeeds to the dukedom, for fear that the priceless property—the only private house in Britain declared a "World Heritage Site" by UNESCO—might be endangered by his irresponsibility. As duke, Blandford would be allowed to live there, and to make use of the estate income; but not to sell, lease, or manage any of the property. After the official announcement by the trustees' solicitors, the duke had submitted to a BBC television interview in the rose garden at Blenheim. Asked about his elder son, he said, "I think that there is always a black sheep in all families. I do not think there is anything new in that. We've had some good 'uns and some bad 'uns"—which is certainly true, of the last eleven Dukes of Marlborough and their kin.

When I spoke to Marlborough a week later, he was unwilling to discuss the new arrangement, beyond the official statement the trustees had just released. But he assured me that nothing at Blenheim would change. On the larger question of the fate of country houses in general, he had said in 1991, "Even the National Trust has stopped taking any more houses, unless they come with a gigantic endowment. I see lots more house sales ahead, for hotels or what you like, and more and more sales of their contents—which can only mean a loss of valuable tourist assets." Three years later, though he still feared for the owners of smaller, lesser-known estates, he seemed less troubled by the idea of country houses going on the market. "There are always buyers around. That's the extraordinary thing. . . . Some of the new people who have bought these houses have restored them magnificently."

·   ·   ·

Located sixteen miles up the A423 from Blenheim, then two miles west of Banbury Cross, Broughton Castle is the moated, 14th through 19th-century home of the 21st Baron of Saye and Sele. It's remarkably picturesque, so much what one *wants* a romantic old country house to look like that Lord Saye and Sele has little trouble renting it by the day as a background for movies, TV series, and commercials. He tries to confine corporate functions, where guests can get sloppy, to a marquee on the lawn on the other side of his moat.

I drive in the gate and across the fields on a one-lane road, pass a steepled stone 14th-century church full of Broughton, Wykeham, and Fiennes family tombs—they really *have* lived here for almost 600 years—cross the moat on a little bridge, then go through a castellated gatehouse built in 1405. The 21st Baron, a genial, gray-haired fellow born in 1920, candid and unassuming, meets me at the kitchen door and invites me to sit with him at the breakfast table—out of season, they heat only the modernized east end, where the family lives—and pours me a cup of coffee.

The family was once incredibly wealthy, he admits. Although one 18th-century ancestor had to be paid a pension in order to afford his seat in the House of Lords, by 1800 the 14th Lord Saye was able to pay off the national debt. Unfortunately, a later family addiction to horses and gambling left the estate bankrupt. The best things in the house had to

Nathaniel, 21st Baron Saye and Sele (at right, portrait of 8th Baron).

be sold in 1837, including the swans in the moat. During the great agricultural depression of the late 19th century, they let go 4,000 acres in Lincolnshire, and mortga⸱ ⸱d the house. A more respectable heir, the 16th Baron, was able to make some repairs,   ⸱d to hire the fashionable architect George Gilbert Scott to Victorianize portions of the interior. The castle still retains a number of rooms, passages, and a private chapel from the 14th century, as well as memories of James I's visit and antimonarchist conspirators. In the Great Hall, 14th-century stone walls are warmly lit by high 16th-century windows, under a pendant plaster ceiling of the 1760s.

"We're not a wealthy family today. My parents lived in the whole house, with a Victorian-sized staff. We live in this corner, with no servants. There were fourteen gardeners in 1910, two and a half in 1950. I have one—a wonderful young man from Nebraska.

"But taxes are the real problem. I operate under 'Case I Schedule D,' which means that Broughton Castle is actually a 'leisure industry.' That allows me to set off the costs of gardening, decorating, and cleaning against income from visitors and teas, and I can deduct the VAT [value-added tax, a 17.5 percent national sales tax] I pay for such things. The Inland Revenue people wanted me to reclaim only two-thirds of it, since I show only two-thirds of the house. But I argued that the public *sees* all the outside of the house, and they gave in. The farm rents just about pay the cost of regular maintenance. That still leaves a gap each year of about thirty thousand pounds, which is why I'm delighted to have film companies in. The Disney people were here for three weeks in nineteen ninety [filming

Broughton Castle, Oxfordshire.

parts of *Three Men and a Little Lady*]. Our own living expenses come from my business world pension—you *have* to earn your own living elsewhere. We get about sixteen thousand five hundred visitors a year—I'd like to get that up to twenty thousand."

What does he think of 200 or 300 strangers trooping through his house and garden, 50-odd days a year? "Oh, we enjoy them. Or perhaps I should say we enjoy them greatly at Easter, by September not so greatly. We meet a lot of very nice, very well-behaved people. Including Americans, of course. Did you know that an ancestor of mine, together with

Lord Brooke, the Earl of Warwick's son, founded Saybrook, Connecticut, in the sixteeen thirties? My wife and I visited there some years ago. We were treated like royalty.

"Some Sundays we can escape. But it's hard not to be around. And people expect it. Did you see that family tree hanging in the corridor? I'd never had one, but the visitors insisted, so I had one drawn up. Unlike Marlborough, I'm never recognized. Sometimes I'll sit in a room and answer questions. People always presume I'm one of the attendants."

Actually, Lord Saye and Sele has no choice about letting visitors in, even if they barely pay the costs involved in receiving them. His father got a government grant in 1956, which paid for renewing the roof—but at the same time obliged him to let in the public. (The house had been derelict and leaking badly when his father first inherited it in 1948. By legally transferring ownership to his son fifteen years before he died, he was able to spare the current owner the burden of inheritance tax.)

"About nineteen eighty an architect in Oxford recommended that we do a survey of the whole property, and put in a request to the government for a long range program of essential repairs. We estimated it would cost about a hundred thousand pounds a year for fifteen years. We're now in our eighth year of renewing all the defective stone, the timbers, the slate floors, the window lead. We've spent seven hundred and fifty thousand so far; it will be over a million by the time the south side is done. Then there's the east end to do. I was promised a grant for forty percent of the cost, but now they want to cut that to thirty-seven point five. I have a wonderful sixty-six-year-old stonemason, who has a twenty-five-year-old apprentice. When it's finally all done, the house will be in the best shape it's been in five hundred years, and should be good for another two hundred. One point of doing the repairs now is that if my son doesn't want to spend *his* entire income on the house ten years from now he won't have to. If the house wasn't open to visitors, I couldn't afford to do the major repairs—that's where the savings come."

On the whole, Saye and Sele appears justifiably sanguine about the future of his 700-year old family house. English Heritage grants, and the tourists they oblige him to receive, seem to have assured the future of Broughton Castle. "I think owners bellyache too much about English Heritage [the body responsible for maintaining and supporting England's "built heritage," funded by but largely independent of the government]. They *must* be careful how they spend public money. But if your architect is meticulous and you're patient and flexible, they'll be understanding, I've found. I have no sympathy with these old-line families who still want their butlers, who refuse to change." In fact, his major concern when I first visited appeared to be his unmarried son's choice of a future partner. "Wives don't *want* to play fulltime hostess and caretaker in a country house nowadays; they have other things to do. And yet it matters so much if the wife-to-be is willing to help run things. I do hope that Martin marries the right woman."

When my wife and I stopped by again in 1994, it was mainly to gossip, take photographs, and look at the handsome walled garden behind the castle, now under the care of a new gardener. The major repairs were progressing on schedule. Film makers were still renting the house: it was one of the settings used for *The Madness of King George*. Franco

Zeffirelli had swept by with his entourage, scouting locations. Like his fifth cousin Ralph Fiennes, Lord Saye and Sele gets to perform himself, though only once a year. He plays the role of his own ancestor James Fiennes, the first 'Lord Say,' who loses his head in Shakespeare's *Henry VI, Part II*—as he did in real life in 1450—when scenes from the play are read in the Great Hall by a group of summer students from California.

. . .

Stanton Harcourt Manor is about sixteen miles southwest of Blenheim Palace—all three of these estates are in Oxfordshire, near to the ancient traffic-clogged, tourist-jammed university town. Except for a pair of square, flat-topped towers that rise above the village, the manor looks like a sprawling old stone farmhouse, which it is. In fact, the lady of the manor—The Hon. Ann Gascoigne, daughter of the second and last Viscount Harcourt—first met me at the door wearing corduroy overalls and Wellington boots, just in from tending her sheep.

Ann Gascoigne is almost aggressively unpretentious, but she still manages to let you know how important the Harcourts have been. Talking with visitors about the age of her family house, she is careful to say "Nobody but my family lived here since it was built," which seems to be about 1380. (The manor itself has been in the Harcourt family since the middle of the 12th century.) Unfortunately, very little is left of the 14th-to-18th-century house. The family moved out in 1688, and let the house decay. In 1755, they started building a new house nearby at Nuneham Courtenay, and tore down crumbling portions of Stanton Harcourt for the stone. (Nuneham Courtenay is now a conference center, its parkland a branch of the Oxford University Botanical Gardens. The family returned to Stanton Harcourt in 1948.)

What's left of the old house are a remarkable 14th-century kitchen, with remnants of wall ovens and an open fireplace, and a smoke vent in the octagonal roof; the 1540 gatehouse, incorporated into the 19th-century house the Gascoignes live in today, which is also open on visitor days; and one of those two towers I noticed (the other crowns the old village church, which lies inside the manor grounds), where Alexander Pope spent the summer of 1718 in an upstairs room finishing his translation of the fifth book of Homer's *Iliad*. Downstairs in Pope's Tower is the family chapel.

Over the mantelpiece in the comfortable library hangs a Godfrey Kneller portrait of Pope. Otherwise, the room looks like any cosy, middle-class English sitting room, with a television set, and magazines strewn about.

"It's all very lived in, which I think people like. There are grandchildren and dogs and toys and christening photos. I once overheard a little girl saying to her mother, 'I didn't know princesses watched the telly.' We have very little help, so we can't afford not to mix and mingle. On visitor days [31 a year at Stanton Harcourt; they get about 4,000 people a season] I sit in the little kiosk myself from two to six and sell tickets and programs. If they have questions, they can come back and ask me. The children are always saying, 'Mummy makes it all up.' I get in three extra workers to sit in the rooms and help park cars, and

Mrs. Ann Gascoigne.

another volunteer sells eggs and cream from the farm. I give them each a lamb for their deep freeze." As at most British country houses, of whatever size or age, the gardens—these were in fact built by her parents, after they moved back from Nuneham Courtenay—are at least as much an attraction to visitors as the house.

"But I don't play fine lady, I make no exceptions for visitors. This is the way we live. I'm always here. My day as a farmer starts at five-thirty. Animals don't know when it's a weekend. I have my lambing duties, the farm to watch over. I'm a church warden as well, which means I unlock the church at eight, serve Communion at the second service. It isn't all neat and clean, aesthetic and tidy like a National Trust house. I don't like what the National Trust does to their houses. I couldn't bear to have that happen here."

She doesn't have much sympathy for other public agencies or organizations either. "There was no possible way we could pay the death duties when my father died in 1979, so we reluctantly agreed to permit public access. It was very upsetting and frustrating—every item exempted from taxes must be kept available for the public to see! They tell you how many days you have to open, where you have to advertise. They simply ignore the fact that a house this size is *lived* in—there's nowhere for the family to withdraw."

She also had to sell some jewelry at Christie's, and give some Elizabethan miniatures to the Victoria and Albert Museum in lieu of additional taxes on Lord Harcourt's death. The family held onto enough prizes to make important loans to the 1985 *Treasure Houses of Britain* exhibition in Washington, including a set of Sèvres china especially made for King

Stanton Harcourt Manor, Oxfordshire.

George III—but then felt obliged, in June 1993, to offer for sale at Sotheby's 300 pieces of the family silver, most of it accumulated by Mrs. Gascoigne's four-times-great-grandfather, the 1st Earl Harcourt, ambassador to Paris from 1768 to 1772 (two silver wine coolers went for £254,500, or $380,000), as well as paintings and furniture from Nuneham Courtenay that had been in storage since 1948.

At the time, her son William Gascoigne explained that there was no other way the family could maintain Stanton Harcourt, in the face of the "clobbering" their agricultural income was taking from government policies and European market competition, and the hopelessly inadequate grants available from English Heritage. The sale also included a rare early 17th-century gold-and-enamel clock-watch that had been given to the 1st Earl by Queen Elizabeth of Bohemia; it went for £132,500, or $200,000. The Harcourt silver, and related family treasures, realized a total of £2,602,327 ($3.9 million)—about one and a half times the auctioneers' estimate.

"It was partly to finish paying off my father's tax bill," Ann Gascoigne explained the following summer. "But more importantly than that, we wanted to set up a trust fund. We had already created one, because I sold some jewelry, and I put all the proceeds of that straight into the fund. And so we put a large dollop of the money from the silver sale into the maintenance fund for all these buildings, which have to be kept up. And another considerable amount to educate the nine grandchildren, which we feel is one thing we can do for the future. The rest has gone as an investment fund to produce money, in case a little parcel of land comes up for sale in the middle of the farm. Our problem is that in 1922, when my grandfather died, everything was sold off here because they were living at Nuneham. All we were left with were the bits and pieces that frankly didn't sell. And so my father spent all his time trying to buy back the other bits and pieces as and when they became available, pieces that had once been part of the estate."

The family feels an obligation to contribute to the support of the historic parish church across the road, which has cost them more than £200,000 (over $300,000) in repair bills so far—on top of which they must pay VAT on the expenses, which outrages Mrs. Gascoigne.

The most devastating hit of all may have been a burglary in September 1990, in which thieves climbed a wall, broke into the chapel in Pope's Tower, and made off with antique furniture, pictures, and altar fittings worth between £10,000 and £20,000 ($17,000–35,000). Just two weeks before my visit the following autumn, heavy lead ornaments cemented and bolted down had been stolen from the garden. "When you're open to the public, you're more vulnerable. People can come on visiting days and learn where things are." The burglar, a local man who had been hitting a number of houses in the vicinity, was eventually caught at nearby Rousham, and much of the loot recovered. In 1994, most of the chapel contents were back in place. As we sat talking in the garden we could look across at the lead peacocks, home again on their bases at the foot of the tower.

· · ·

The economic condition of the English country house—in fact, the very likelihood of its survival—depends on a great many variables: the size of the house (and its surrounding estate); the wealth of the resident family (if there is one), landed and other; its location—is it on or off the tourist track, in an area sufficiently populous to assure a steady supply of both day-trippers and staff?; its historic connections and (less significantly) its aesthetic value; its need for radical repairs and restoration; the appeal of its contents, from Van Dycks, Turners, Titians, antique statues, and 18th-century French furniture to collections of dolls, dog collars, costumes, antique cars, and Victorian pots and pans; the attractiveness of its parks and gardens; the prosperity of its farms, forests, and other productive subdivisions; and the ability of its owners to market and exploit their property in any of several different ways.

In the pages that follow, I will consider the past and present significance of these large, anachronistic, often very handsome cultural symbols; the situations faced by their current owners and the options open for their future; and the implications—ethical as well as political—of any nation's trying to preserve so cumbrous and extravagant a "heritage" into the 21st century.

CHAPTER TWO

What a Country House Used to Mean

BETWEEN THE RESTORATION OF 1660 and the Reform Bill of 1867—two centuries during which England was essentially ruled by the nonurban, landowning classes—there were at least 5,000 country houses of all shapes and sizes in the country; possibly as many as 10,000.[1]

These included houses that had served as the seats of the aristocracy and gentry for many generations, the wealthier of whom (by the 17th and 18th centuries) also had town-houses in London, and (by the 19th century) alternative residences elsewhere for fishing and hunting. Supremely wealthy and powerful families had owned two, three, or more estates from the early 16th century on, the result of either royal largesse, their eagerness for territorial expansion, or carefully arranged interdynastic marriages.

The lesser squires may have been simply better-off farmers. But taken all together, these were the people who owned and ran rural England (as well as Scotland, Wales, and Ireland) up to the late 19th century, when their political power over the countryside was drastically reduced by democratic reforms, such as the establishment of elected county councils. In more isolated regions, the hold of the landlord over his provincial domain lasted into the 1920s, with the country seat serving as a kind of provincial capitol.

Before then, the squire, whether a peer, a baronet, a knight, or a landowning commoner, normally served as the local magistrate, often signing legal documents and dispensing local justice *from* his country house, as well as from special sessions in neighboring towns. This made these houses seats of power as well as the central family residence of what was often a very large estate: typically, from 1,000 to 10,000 acres of owner-managed and tenanted farms, woodlands, cottages, and villages, of which the mansion or manor house was the official, visual, and symbolic center, and on which almost everyone living for miles around was in some way dependent.

Readers unfamiliar with this decentralized, estate-based system of "squirearchical" power may be puzzled by literary accounts of it in action. In Fielding's *Tom Jones* of 1749, Squire Allworthy takes Jenny Jones into his study at Paradise Hall, and reminds her that he has the power to send her to prison for bearing a child out of wedlock. ("You know, child, it is in my power as a magistrate to punish you very rigorously for what you have done.") He later sits, again in his country house, as sole judge of the poor schoolmaster accused of being her seducer, and punishes him (unjustly) by firing him from his job.

One of the many sharp glimpses into late-19th-century English country life found in Flora Thompson's autobiographical *Lark Rise to Candleford* trilogy occurs when the heroine, called Laura in the book, takes a job as assistant postmistress in a north Oxfordshire village.

> . . . she must not so much as handle a letter or sell a stamp until she had been through some mysterious initiation ceremony which Miss Lane called being 'sworn in.' This had to take place before a Justice of the Peace, and it had been arranged that she should go the next morning to one of the great houses in the locality for that purpose. . . .
>
> The interview next morning did not turn out so terrifying as Laura had expected. Sir Timothy smiled very kindly upon her when the footman ushered her into his Justice Room, saying: 'The young person from the Post Office, please, Sir Timothy.'
>
> 'What have you been up to? Poaching, rick-burning, or petty larceny?' he asked when the footman had gone. 'If you're as innocent as you look, I shan't give you a long sentence. So come along,' and he drew her by the elbow to the side of his chair. Laura smiled dutifully, for she knew by the twinkle of his keen blue eyes beneath their shaggy white eyebrows that Sir Timothy was joking.
>
> As she leaned forward to take up a pen with which to sign the thick blue official document he was unfolding, she sensed the atmosphere of jollity, good sense, and good nature, together with the smell of tobacco, stables, and country tweeds he carried around like an aura.
>
> 'But read it! Read!' he cried in a shocked voice. 'Never put your name to anything before you have read it or you'll be signing your own death warrant one of these days.' And Laura read out, as clearly as her shyness permitted, the Declaration which even the most humble candidate for Her Majesty's Service had in those serious days to sign before a magistrate. . . .
>
> When she had read it through, she signed her name. Sir Timothy signed his, then folded the document neatly for her to carry back to Miss Lane, who would send it on to the higher authorities.[2]

Justices of the Peace, like Squire Allworthy in the mid-18th century and Sir Timothy in the late 19th, commanded both judicial and administrative power in the shires. They were appointed by the Lord Chancellor on the advice of the Lord Lieutenant of a county, who served as the sovereign's official representative and a key dispenser of local patronage. Until very recently, most Lords Lieutenant were local landowning peers as well.

As the appeal of the court and the London season grew, country gentlemen left more and more of the business of rural administration to middle-class agents, magistrates, and other full-time professionals. But theirs was still the most powerful voice in local matters such as elections, regiments and militias, church and land policy. It was from their numbers (or their families) that were drawn, well into the 19th century, most military officers, most prime ministers and their cabinets, most ambassadors and other high officers of state. The appointment of beneficed clergymen was in their gift. From the 1740s to the 1830s, more than a third of the seats in the House of Commons were essentially "owned" by the landed aristocracy; their control over the lower house grew immensely during these years.

· · ·

As Mark Girouard has explained, in *Life in the English Country House*, the size and grandeur of these houses and estates were symbolic as well as functional. From the Middle Ages on, the great land lords were expected to receive and entertain hundreds of people, which might require a staff of hundreds more. But much of the staff, like the house itself, its expensive furnishings and gardens, was a matter more of display than of function. It was a way of demonstrating to the surrounding population the extent of one's wealth, power, and connections.

Even after income from agricultural land ceased to be the primary source of wealth (and thereby power) in Britain, the great country estate remained the major way in which those possessing or aspiring to social or political power let the world know of their importance. Domestic staffs of fifty or more (not counting gardeners) were not uncommon in great houses, up to and beyond World War I. In memoirs of country life between the wars, an indoor staff of twelve or fourteen is presumed to be the minimum one could cope with in even a small-sized manor house. In 1847, Benjamin Disraeli's Conservative backers lent him money to buy an estate on which to rebuild a country house, on the presumption that no one would be accepted as Prime Minister without one.

After the coming of railways ended the self-sufficiency of the landed estate, and agricultural revenues declined again, British cities became the real centers of power. But many of the new rich—often the incredibly new rich—of the Industrial Age decided to build *new* (albeit old-looking) country seats, both to enjoy the amenities of life in the country, even if only on weekends and holidays, and to ape the lifestyle and status of their aristocratic predecessors. Several of them, in fact, earned or bought titles of their own in the process. Well into the 20th century the British aristocracy, old and new, continued to play the role of statesmen, and their "power houses"—places like Hatfield, Chatsworth, Kedleston, Houghton, Hughenden, to a lesser degree Waddesdon and Cliveden—continued to play a part in national politics.

Whatever the English country house means today, then, either to its owner or to the nation as a whole, in previous times it meant something considerably different. We may esteem country houses in terms of their aesthetic value, their contribution to the tourist industry, or their elusive significance as a "piece of the heritage." But in centuries past, country houses played a genuine as well as a symbolic role in the nation's affairs.

·   ·   ·

The story begins with castles.

Between 1066 and 1485, a large fortified dwelling in the open English countryside meant power absolutely, as a red light means Stop. Specifically designed to repel invaders and to protect those sheltered within its thick stone walls, such a building both equalled and expressed its master's hold over his domain to anyone who looked at it. Centuries after their historical raison d'être has dissolved, British castles, even in ruins, still convey a powerful shadow of this original significance. Because of the need for defense and protection in a warfaring island threatened by violent raiders along its borders and coasts, men who served the king well between the 11th and 16th centuries were given tracts of land. On this land, they were expected to erect fortified buildings in which to live and from which, when necessary, to do battle on his majesty's behalf.

Fortified manor houses, with a slight increase in domestic comforts, began to be erected in the 13th century; one had to obtain from the sovereign a "license to crenellate" one's house. About 40 such semicastles survive, most of them in southeast or central England, with the Hall and its central hearth usually at ground level, and kitchen and service rooms separate, often in wings enclosing a central court. By the 15th century, furnishings were still minimal and spartan, but larger windows were ventured, fireplaces with chimneys moved into the the walls, and bedrooms and sitting rooms were added. It was only in the 16th century that these defensive citadels began to be given the luxurious accommodations that made them suitable for the residence or visits of the demanding, imperial Tudor sovereigns.

As many historians have pointed out, wealth and power flowed from the court in the years between Henry VII and Charles I. The greatest families among the landed aristocracy were created by the sovereign, and owed whatever rank and power they possessed to him or her. Many of the great country houses built and furnished during the Tudor and Stuart years were paid for by court-earned fortunes, and were designed to receive or impress the sovereign, or one's rivals for the sovereign's favor. The building of country houses during these years has been estimated as "the largest capital undertaking of the period...the amount of country-house building in the fifty years between 1570 and 1620 far exceeded that of any subsequent half-century."[3] Great expanses of glass (a precious material in 1600) were used primarily to let people know one could afford it. Suites of "state rooms," with silk wall hangings, tapestries, and velvet upholstery, carved walls and overmantels, and canopied beds the size of small rooms, were kept in readiness for a state visit, to demonstrate one's worthiness of royal favor.

The two major periods of English royal largesse fall within the Tudor and Stuart reigns: Henry VIII's sale in the years after 1536 of the lands and buildings of some 800–1,000 monasteries, which he had ordered dissolved and then seized; and James I's ennobling and

Sudeley Castle, Gloucestershire.

enriching of his friends (through the agency of the devious Duke of Buckingham) in 1603–9. Any country house today that has "abbey" or "priory" in its name is likely to take its origins from one of Henry VIII's seizures and transfers to some trusted courtier. Many were unroofed for the value of the lead, or levelled to provide building materials for a new house on the grounds.

The building of "status" houses was very much a part of the deadly jousting for power and place that went on constantly among the leading courtiers and place-holders under Henry VII and Henry VIII. Of the so-called prodigy houses of the Elizabethans and Jacobeans (e.g., Longleat, Wollaton, Hardwick), Lawrence Stone has written, "Their sole justification was to demonstrate status, their sole function to entertain the sovereign on one of the summer progresses.... The other, unacknowledged, reason for extravagant building was in order to satisfy a lust for power, a thirst for admiration, an ambition to outstrip all rivals, and a wish to create a home suitable for the residence of a nobleman."[4]

. . .

If one's wealth and status depended on the favor and largesse of the Crown, one was expected to show oneself worthy of such gifts by returning the favor. This became especially challenging when Elizabeth I adopted the custom of quitting the capital every summer, to escape the heat and the noxious vapors of the Thames. She owned a number of summer palaces of her own, most of them built or acquired by her father or grandfather, from Richmond and Greenwich to Hampton Court and Windsor Castle.

But to travel beyond this limited circuit, Elizabeth, alone in her coach, with her train of several hundred courtiers, retainers, and servants on horseback or in carts, was obliged to depend on the hospitality of courtiers who owned houses big enough to accommodate them all. In *The Progresses and Public Processions of Queen Elizabeth* (1788), John Nichols refers to 65 different houses at which the queen stopped during the 30 summer "progresses" she made between 1559 and 1602.

After a state journey to France in 1572, she returned "in progress" (according to Nichols's account of her travels) to Essex, Kent, Hertfordshire, and Bedfordshire; then made her way back to London by way of Kenilworth Castle, Warwick Castle, Charlecote Park, Long Compton, Weston Park, Berkeley Castle, Woodstock Park, Reading, Windsor Castle, and Hampton Court.

Elizabeth's longest and most memorable progress was that of 1575, which lasted three months, and climaxed with an extended stay at Kenilworth Castle, which the queen had given to the Earl of Leicester in 1563. The queen stayed at Kenilworth (or "Killingworth"), her household at Warwick Castle. Twenty to thirty horses were required just to send messages back and forth. For nineteen days, the queen and her court were entertained by a bank-breaking series of feasts, dances, masques, hunts, jousts, picnics, music, and pageants.

She paid three visits to Kenilworth, five visits to Burghley. But her favorite out-of-town lodging place was Sir William Cecil's house at Theobalds near London, which she is recorded as having visited thirteen times. According to Francis Peck's *Desiderata Curiosa*, published in 1732–35, each visit cost Cecil "two or three thousand pounds; the Queen lying there at his Lordship's charge sometimes three weeks or a month, or six weeks together. Sometimes she had strangers or embassadors came to her thither, where she has been seen in as great royalty, and served as bountifully and magnificently as at any other time and place, all at his Lordship's charge, with rich shows, pleasant devices, and all manner of sports that could be devised, to the great delight of Her Majesty and her whole train…"[5]

It has been suggested that both Elizabeth and her father Henry VIII sometimes dropped in on loyal subjects with the express intent of impoverishing them, and thus keeping them dependent. Both sovereigns knew well how to advance the interests of the Crown by gifts, sales, loans, or seizures of property. Forcing courtiers to build, accept, or relinquish great houses played a major role in their strategy. Setting the queen's expenses against those of her hosts, Lawrence Stone estimates that "she was more or less living free." Sir Thomas Wilkes wrote Sir Robert Sidney, on June 18, 1591, "Her Majesty hath been known often-times to mislike the superfluous expence of her subjects, bestowed upon her in times of her Progresses."[6] One has the feeling she might have misliked even more a display of excessive thrift.

·   ·   ·

It is impossible to calculate the sums made available to his friends and favorites by James I, the most extravagant king in English history, during his 23-year reign (1603–25). This is partly because many of their receipts took the form of bribes, kickbacks, and other forms of "undeclared" income they were able to obtain as a result of their position as officers of the court. Lawrence Stone has estimated the total capital value of the king's gifts at nearly £3 million, the equivalent of at least £200 million ($350 million) in 1990.

A vast amount of this newly distributed wealth went into the building of country houses. "No kingdom in the world spent so much in building as we did in [King James's] time," wrote one of the king's early biographers.[7] This pretty much ended in 1625, for a variety of reasons—mounting public resistance to the Stuart court and its excesses, the end of royal progresses, a growing distaste for medieval-style households, and above all the ruinous costs. After that year, few prodigy houses were built. Many of the largest ones were either torn down or, like Audley End, reduced to a fraction of their original size.

The only way such opulent houses could have been built and maintained was by way of court-earned fortunes, often earned in ways the modern world would consider corrupt. Lawrence Stone tells the story, in *Family and Fortune*, of one of the greatest and most "corrupt" builders of all, Robert Cecil, the 1st Earl of Salisbury (1563–1612), whose profits from political office—bribes, payoffs, kickbacks, the sale of offices and honors, wardships and gratuities, profitable deals with foreign powers—vastly exceeded anything he could have earned from a landed estate. His account helps to explain how palaces like Hatfield came to be built.

At a time when the greatest landed income in England amounted to £7,500 a year (and an ordinary workingman might be earning £10–15), Salisbury—Secretary of State, Lord High Treasurer, Lord Privy Seal, Chancellor of the Duchy of Lancaster, Master of the Court of Wards—was earning up to £50,000, most of it illegally. Even so, because of his building mania, and the lavish entertaining he felt obliged to undertake to maintain the king's favor, his debts often exceeded his income. "He found himself caught up in a world of fiercely competitive conspicuous consumption that reached its apogee during his time," writes Stone. "As a leading figure in one of the most recklessly extravagant courts in Europe, he had little option but to compete in the race, although it could be argued that in one key aspect, that of building, he compulsively over-built on a scale that defies rational justification."[8]

His father, Sir William Cecil, 1st Lord Burghley (also Secretary of State, Lord High Treasurer, Master of the Wards, etc.), had built not one but two of the most lavish houses in England before he died in 1598: Theobalds in Hertfordshire (where he kept 180 domestic servants in livery) and Burghley in Lincolnshire, which had gone to his elder son Thomas. Pressured by the king, who took a liking to Theobalds, Salisbury gave it to him in exchange for the manor of Hatfield in Hertfordshire (along with seventeen other manors) in 1607–9, where he commenced building an even grander house. As Stone writes, "The loss of Theobalds spurred Salisbury into the most astonishing building programme of the age, a programme so grandiose in its scope as to overshadow even his gigantic financial resources. At one time he was building simultaneously two country houses, Hatfield House in Hertfordshire and Cranborne in Dorset, Salisbury House in the Strand, and...the New Exchange, also in the Strand....It was this fantastic orgy of building which caused the soaring debt, the mere interest charges on which were running at about £4,000 a year....Cranborne House and Hatfield survive to this day to bear witness to the architectural ambitions and financial recklessness of the greatest builder of an age which was itself the greatest period of country house building in English history."[9]

One could tell similar, only slightly less dramatic stories of the building of Audley End, Hardwick, Knole, Longleat, Woburn Abbey, Montacute, Blickling, and a number of other "prodigy" houses of the Tudor and Stuart era, any one of which might have kept hundreds of masons, bricklayers, and fine craftsmen at work for years. It has been argued that Henry VIII used his grants of land, with the concomitant restrictions and obligations these entailed, as a means of keeping his courtiers in permanent debt to the Crown. The lavish houses they felt compelled to build, like Roman Baroque churches, were often far more costly and elaborate than any use could conceivably require. Their ornate excess was designed as an unmistakable expression of prestige and power; but the prestige and power displayed were ultimately those of the king.

·   ·   ·

The outbreak of Civil War in 1642 halted most building of new country houses for eighteen years—as well, of course, as the years of royal largesse and entertaining. Buildings still fortified and made use of by royalist troops or their supporters stood a very good chance of being either demolished or "slighted"—i.e., damaged so badly they could no longer serve as fortresses. England, Scotland, Wales, and Ireland are filled with ruined (or restored) castles that were if not leveled, at least partly blown up at the hands of Cromwell's men. Corfe Castle and Wardour Old Castle—both popular ruins today—were among those destroyed. Sudeley was left a shattered hulk, not to be restored till Victorian times. Arundel, Berkeley, Bickleigh, Bolsover, and Powderham Castles, Hoghton Tower, Aynhoe Park, Coughton Court, and Otley Hall were among the many royalist strongholds badly damaged during the war, although subsequently repaired.

Hatfield House, Hertfordshire.

A few country houses or castles belonged to supporters of the Commonwealth cause—notably Broughton Castle (a haven of Parliamentary conspirators) and Forde Abbey (the home of Cromwell's Attorney General). A very few new houses were built by antiroyalists, such as Thorpe Hall in Northamptonshire, now a hospital, and Coleshill in Berkshire, destroyed by a fire in 1953. But by and large the war years were not a good time for country houses or their owners, so long identified as the creations and creatures of now-despised kings. Some owners (like the Stuart heirs) fled abroad, leaving their property ripe for plucking. Sir Ralph Verney, of Claydon House in Buckinghamshire, wrote from exile, "I confes I love Old England very well, but as things are carried heere the gentry cannot joy much to bee in it."

Many of the old squires who remained in England suffered for their royalist sympathies. They either found themselves imprisoned, had their properties seized by the Commonwealth, were assessed large sums to aid the Parliamentary cause, or were forced to "lend" to the government similar sums, which were never repaid. More than 300 owners were spared legal seizure of their property only by "compounding"—that is, offering a substantial share of its value as the price for retaining it. For the first time until the attacks of David Lloyd George and the rebellious Irish 250 years later, great houses became in the eyes of a large portion of the British population a symbol not of legitimate authority, continuity, and prestige, but of arrogance, waste, and oppression.

.   .   .

The pacific interlude of 1660–88—from the Restoration to the second rejection of the Stuart kings—saw the introduction of a compact, rigorously symmetrical country house in what is sometimes called the "Christopher Wren" style, although Wren actually designed very few. Each of these dignified, foursquare brick blocks edged in stone was topped by a single hipped roof, underlined by a broad, crisp cornice. The all-sheltering roof was punctured by high dormers that accentuated its slope, crowned by a classical balustrade and (frequently) a central cupola on the ridge, and flanked by stately chimneys. Matching, symmetrical ranks of high windows surrounded a simple doorway, topped by a small pediment or flourish of carving, at the end of a short flight of iron-railed steps.

Coming between the extravagances of one age and those of another, this generation of neat Restoration houses—often handsomely decorated inside, with intricate wallcarvings and fine plaster ceilings—remains a beau ideal for many lovers of English country houses at their most refined. I'm not sure what this style reveals about the national psyche or cultural climate: perhaps a politic (or exhausted) retreat from Stuart excesses; perhaps a reassertion of Protestant virtues and values; perhaps nothing more than the singular influence of two of England's greatest architects, Inigo Jones and Christopher Wren, who helped to create what remains to this day a standard "English country house" image. It is a simplified version of this house form, foursquare, hip-roofed, and pedimented, that forms the symbol on the brown road signs that direct tourists to country houses today.

.   .   .

It was long part of the legend of Whig historians that the Glorious Revolution of 1688, by rejecting for good and all the Divine Right of Kings—William of Orange, after all, was *invited* to the throne by Parliament, as was George I a generation later—set Britain firmly on the path to democracy.

That may be true, but at the beginning of the 18th century no less than at the end, democracy was still a long way off. As James Lees-Milne has written, "The Glorious Revolution of 1688 established the power of the territorial nobility in Britain and marked the passing of authority from an absolute monarchy to a Whig oligarchy. A very significant sequel was the immediate spate of country houses on a monumental scale."[10]

The new oligarchs—twelve new dukes were created between 1688 and 1715—assembled vast estates of their own, which they ruled over like German princelings, in addition to running the country. They crowned their broad acres with spectacular palaces, visible symbols of their own princely power. With their triumphant, spreading facades, their walls and ceilings painted all over by showy, second-class masters, display-houses like Boughton, Chatsworth, Blenheim, Grimsthorpe, Kimbolton, Burghley (Elizabethan in origin, but totally redecorated between 1681 and 1700), Petworth, and Castle Howard declared the prestige and power not of King William or Queen Anne, but of the proud and interrelated band of Whig aristocrats who now owned much of and ruled most of the soon-to-be United Kingdom. The builders or rebuilders of these eight particular houses were, respectively, the new-made Dukes of Montagu, Devonshire, Marlborough, Ancaster, and Manchester (the last duke was related to the first); the 5th Earl of Exeter (a close relation of the first two dukes); the 6th Duke of Somerset (profitably married to the Duke of Montagu's stepdaughter); and the 3rd Earl of Carlisle.

Of Chatsworth, Lees-Milne wrote, "It looks, and virtually is, the capital of a principality."[11] Even today, one can drive for miles without leaving the Devonshire lands. All of these houses contained grand suites of State Rooms, and frequently entertained royalty. But the State Rooms were intended more as an expression of their owners' grandeur than as a deferential temptation to a no longer absolute monarch.

It would be wrong to think of all the great English country houses built in the 18th century—let alone the hundreds of lesser ones—as symbols of national political power, or as the places where major political decisions were made. Parliament and the chief ministers still met in London; politically, London was the place that mattered. Most of the grandees who ran the country spent more time at their lavish townhouses than at their rural estates. And yet it was still assumed—at least until the time of "great commoners" like the William Pitts, junior and senior—that it was these estates that provided the basis for their power, and the houses built upon them that displayed their stature to the world.

Increasingly through the century, "learning" and "taste" rather than the straightforward display of wealth and power came to dominate the design of country houses, as architects, furniture makers, decorators, and landscape designers grew in professional stature. Many books have been written on the "style history" of 18th- century English country houses, in which architects and other designers count for more than the landowners, politicians, and occasional merchants and bankers for whom they worked. These include people like Colen Campbell, Giacomo Leoni, and the Earl of Burlington, three interpreters of the style of Andreas Palladio, the 16th-century Italian master; William Kent and Henry Flitcroft; the indomitable midcentury trio of Robert Adam, Lancelot ("Capability") Brown, and Thomas Chippendale; in the regions, architects like (John) Carr of York and (Francis) Smith of Warwick; James Gibbs, Sir William Chambers, James Paine, James and Samuel Wyatt, and Sir John Soane.

Into the creations of such fashionable architects historians frequently read the attitudes and values of their wealthy and powerful employers. But in the absence of more direct evidence, I am never sure how far to carry this. Some 18th-century aristocrats were probably influenced by aesthetic considerations, or by an urge to express sentiments more refined than blatant display: an admiration for Greek and Roman ideals and art, perhaps; or an innate preference for balance, symmetry, and refinement as reflections of an ordered, Cartesian universe.

But my suspicion is that the majority of landowners commissioning new country houses during this century were just showing off, like their Tudor and Stuart predecessors and their Victorian successors, trying to keep up with the latest fashion by hiring currently chic architects, decorators, and landscape artists. They filled these houses with the paintings and sculptures they brought home from their continental Grand Tours—tours which had become de rigeur for the sons of the English aristocracy, paintings and sculptures which inevitably fell into the categories of what one was told to admire.

Despite their aesthetic, neo-Roman pretensions, most of the greater country houses of "the aristocratic century" were still primarily embodiments of the owner's political power and social prestige. Sir Robert Walpole, the first Prime Minister in all but title, who ruled Parliament for 21 years, built his sumptuous and costly seat at Houghton Hall in Norfolk to outdo his brother-in-law Viscount Townshend at nearby Raynham. But Houghton soon became a kind of presidential retreat, where the most powerful man in the country gathered twice a year with political allies and local cronies to hunt, drink, and plan his strategy for another parliamentary season.

Houghton Hall is astonishingly lavish. The exterior is faced with finely carved blocks of stone shipped down from Whitby. No house before it had made such free use of imported mahogany, then more costly than marble. The owner and his family are celebrated in carved coats of arms, portrait medallions, and Garter stars carved in the walls and ceilings. William Kent's throne-like chairs are upholstered in green and red Genoese velvet, with wall hangings to match. Much of the carved mahogany and ceiling plaster is gilded. The art collection was the finest assembled by any Englishman in the century. Mark Girouard explains the socio-political significance of this remarkable setting: "The greater part of the government went down to Norfolk during the summer or Christmas recess, and spent a week or more plotting politics in the interval of hunting, feasting and boozing with the local gentry. These congresses were perhaps the first important examples in England of country-house gatherings attended, in conditions of relative equality, by large numbers of people not related to the owner. They were considered a phenomenon at the time [1721–42], but by the end of the century better transport had made the political house-party a common enough event."[12]

These social gatherings took place not in the grandiose state rooms (which is perhaps just as well), but in the more informal rooms downstairs. "Here, as Lord Hervey, one of the guests described it, they lived 'up to the chin in beef, venison, geese, turkeys etc. and generally over the chin in claret, strong beer and punch.'"[13]

As with the Whig leaders earlier in the century, one can identify certain key power-brokers and ministers of state of the later decades with new country houses: the Duke of Newcastle with Vanbrugh's rebuilt house at Claremont, for example; his brother Henry Pelham with Kent's Esher Place, near neighbors in Surrey. The Duke of Bedford, an active Whig politico, was at home out of session at Woburn Abbey, rebuilt and enlarged in 1747–62; the Marquess of Rockingham, leader of the chief dissident Whig faction, at Wentworth Woodhouse in Yorkshire; the Earl of Shelburne, the peace-making Prime Minister of 1782–3, at Bowood in Wiltshire; the Earl of Stanhope at Chevening in Kent, now once again a cabinet minister's retreat. One genuine "power house" of the later century was Stowe in Buckinghamshire, where the political faction that eventually displaced Walpole gathered around the Grenville family.

Later in the century, the Whig dominion was threatened not only by divisions in its own ranks but by a resurgence of the Tories, favored by George III. Among the great Tory houses of the later century, newbuilt or remodeled, were Brocket Hall, Worksop, Wardour Castle, Badminton, Thorndon, and Sandbeck.

Local rivalries kept playing a part, as they had in northwestern Norfolk, where Holkham tried to outshine Houghton, which was built to outshine Raynham. Kedleston in Derbyshire was erected by Nathaniel Curzon to rival the nearby, already old-fashioned palace of the Dukes of Devonshire at Chatsworth. The Wentworths (Earls of Strafford) at Wentworth Castle in Yorkshire so despised their uppity cousins the Watsons (Marquesses of Rockingham) six miles away at Wentworth Woodhouse that they kept trying to outdo them in overbuilding. The Watsons ended the game by stretching the main facade of their house out more than 600 feet, creating what is still the widest, if not the largest house in England—"already, in 1750," writes Christopher Hussey, "out of date by its vastness."[14]

The lesser landlords and Justices of the Peace, however—the real-life counterparts of the fictional squires of Fielding and Smollett—were content to live the old country life, comfortable in their old-fashioned houses, attended to by their servants, lording it over their tenants, living for their hours in the saddle.

Successful merchants, as well as London bankers, began during the 18th century to buy their way into country houses, estates, and occasionally titles. Harewood House in Yorkshire is the monument to a Barbados fortune. Gerard Vanneck, builder of Heveningham, was the son of a merchant banker of Dutch ancestry, who made money in the French tobacco trade. Robert Clive—"Clive of India," the virtual conqueror and master of the subcontinent—invested some of the spoils of his lucrative office in tearing down Newcastle's house at Claremont and building one of his own. Stourhead and Southill, two of the great houses of the closing years of the century, were created for the banker Henry Hoare and the brewer Samuel Whitbread.

· · ·

The turn, not surprisingly, came at the crest: not since the Stuart era had wealthy Englishmen built so lavishly, or lived so extravagantly, as they did in the 1870s. But this time the wealth was their own, not theirs by grace of a sovereign. It was their share of the fabulous wealth of the British Empire at its broadest and most prosperous. In the 1870s, the rich in England—if not in the same league as their American cousins—could be very rich indeed. The houses they built and occupied, the number of servants they employed, the ways of life they lived all bear witness to this.

But after 1879, with the onset of the great Agricultural Depression, the landed aristocracy and gentry—which included most country house owners—began seeing the value of their holdings decline year after year. By 1885, what political power they had left was rapidly passing out of their hands. By the early 20th century, new-money men were displacing them at the top of the wealth ladder—and many of the new-money men had little interest in country houses, or the country house way of life. Mark Girouard notes a steady rise in the building or remodeling of country houses after 1850, which reached a record high around 1870, only to collapse almost immediately thereafter.[15] The idea of joining the landed gentry was beginning to lose its appeal.

As the relative wealth and power of the landed classes declined, the centuries-old significance of the country house declined as well. If it is not the visible capital of a great territorial landlord, not the seat of regional power and affluence, its "meaning" begins to shrink to the aesthetic, nostalgic, or touristic significance it carries today. Once a large country house is no more than a rich man's home—perhaps even his *second* home— and the setting for a socially fixed round of leisure, sport, and entertaining—its historical (if not its artistic) significance begins to disappear. As it happened, through the second half of the 19th century, the artistic significance of the English country house declined markedly as well.

Many of the bigger or better known Victorian country houses were in fact built or rebuilt for members of the old aristocracy, who were either restoring, adding to, or replacing earlier seats. Two ducal castles, Alnwick and Arundel, were essentially rebuilt in the late 19th century. Eaton Hall, the grandest Victorian of them all, was built in the 1870s for the richest landowner of them all, the Duke of Westminster: the second duke's third wife, Loelia, has written a grim account of the stifling life she and her difficult husband lived in this mammoth and extravagant spread, lost in hundreds of rooms, attended by hundreds of servants. Alton Towers, Bestwood, Bryanston, Cliveden, Holker Hall, Madresfield Court, Thoresby, Trentham, Welbeck Abbey, Worsley Hall, Wrest Park—all huge, once-famous Victorian piles—were among the many new houses built for dukes or earls, some with titles much older than the Duke of Westminster's.

But houses equally grandiose were built for a great many rich bankers: all the opulent Rothschild houses; the new Lord Overstone's huge Overstone Park ("A terrible bastard Renaissance house," Girouard calls it[16]); Baring family houses, Drummond family houses, Glyn family houses. Beer dynasties still recognizable from the names on labels and pubs (Bass, Coope, Buxton, Combe, and of course Guinness) settled into new-built country mansions as they grew rich. Thomas Brassey, the superrich railway contractor, built Normanhurst in Sussex, then bought and restored Heythrop Hall in Oxfordshire as well. Bear Wood in Berkshire, after Eaton Hall possibly the most grandiose of all Victorian mansions, was built for the owner of the London *Times*.

One city manufacturer who definitely set up as a country gent after making his fortune was Frank Crossley, the son of a poor weaver of Halifax who had built up a prosperous carpet factory, which employed 4,400 people by 1869. Frank and his two brothers, dedicated radicals and unpretentious Methodists, became the chief philanthropists of the town. But after Frank Crossley was made a baronet in 1863 he bought Somerleyton, a pretentious pile in Suffolk with 3,200 acres, the former home of a millionaire contractor who had gone bankrupt. After he died in 1872, his socially ambitious wife broke all ties with Halifax and the carpet factory. Their son was educated at Eton, entered Parliament as a Conservative and became, in 1916, the 1st Lord Somerleyton.

Sir H. W. Peek, Baronet, of Peek Frean's Biscuits, built a sprawling "Old English" house in Devon. Wealthy glove makers built Stokesay Court in Shropshire, and rebuilt Sudeley Castle in Gloucestershire. In *The Victorian Country House* (1971), Girouard traces commissions for large new seats in many different styles to Lancashire "cottentots," Middlesborough iron masters, arms manufacturers, hosiery manufacturers, an ostrich feather merchant.

But other than as a place of private reward and retreat, either during or after one's business career, it is difficult to find much historical meaning in these large, busy, hard-to-love places. Girouard fantasizes the ambitions of their builders: ". . . to the English merchant or industrialist, working twelve hours a day, disciplining and denying himself, fighting for survival in the commercial jungle, there was increasingly present the vision of a quiet harbour at the end—an estate in the country, a glistening new country house with thick carpets and plate-glass windows, the grateful villagers at the door of their picturesque cottages, touching their caps to their new landlord, J.P., High Sheriff perhaps . . ."[17] But he also acknowledges that a large number, perhaps a majority, of the new commercial and industrial men of wealth never made the effort to transform themselves into country gentlemen.

Even more interesting, few of those who did settle in the country—with the exception of some old banking and brewing families, like the Barings and the Guinnesses—founded active "dynasties" that lasted more than two or three generations, with sons and grandsons who could increase or even hold on to the family fortune. Unless they were willing and able to invest a great deal of energy both in the family business and in their new agricultural estates (as, say, the Rothschilds in Buckinghamshire and the Whitbreads in Bedfordshire managed to do), house, land, and fortune were all to likely to pass out of the family.

For most observers, the continuing interest of the larger Victorian estates lies in the intricate, self-enclosed social structures within their walls, the highly regulated lives led there by family, staff, and visitors. Like other students of Victorian architecture and society, Girouard is fascinated by the ways in which the ever-more-complicated designs and constantly changing styles of such houses reflected the antiquated social rituals and attitudes of their builders. But neither Ruskinian "style wars," nor the owners' and architects' anxieties over such things as how to keep housemaids away from footmen (and both of them away from guests) can give these overized, almost instantly out-of-date piles much more than passing significance to anyone but a dedicated scholar of Victorian taste and class behavior.

. . .

Many histories or memoirs of the English country house way of life describe the period between World War I and World War II as the "Indian summer" of this social phenomenon, a time when a false warmth and a fading glow, a last parade of people in evening dress going down to dinner served by liveried footmen allowed house owners and their guests, whether of ancient lineage or new-made wealth, to pretend that nothing had changed.

Actually, something very fundamental had changed. For many country house owners in the early years of the 20th century, these giant buildings or building complexes were no longer "home," but simply weekend and summer retreats. Rich people lived and worked and socialized through the week in London (or other prosperous cities), then fled from Saturday to Monday to their "country places" to enjoy, or pretend to enjoy, a legendary spell of hunting and shooting, croquet and parlor games, rich meals and gossip and walks and adultery with a dozen or two like-minded friends of their own class, waited on by a similar number of servants. Victorian house parties demanded complex arrangements by train and carriage, which usually meant that one was invited to spend a week or more. The introduction of the automobile made the shorter weekend visit possible, even at considerable distances—and also marked an end to the fiction of a "leisured" country class, since a weekend visit implied a weekday job.

But without any genuine, rooted country connection, those who simply weekended or summered outside the city could as easily have been at Biarritz or Capri—and when fashions changed, and new modes of transport made it possible, that is where they went. Against the centuries-old traditions of the great county families, hanging on in their old historic rooms, surrounded by their ancestors' parks and acres, still playing at High Sheriff and Lord Lieutenant, there now existed the spectacle of the fashionable new rich of 1890–1930, buying or building a great rural mansion in one generation (Bryanston, Polesden Lacey, Castle Drogo, Elveden Hall) only to sell it, tear it down, or give it away in the next. Even after the threatening, radical attacks on "unproductive" landless wealth made by Chancellor (later Prime Minister) David Lloyd George in 1909—and the new taxes that followed—few people enjoying the "country house way of life" before World War I could have realized how near to extinction they were. As late as 1908, the future president of the Royal Institute of British Architects could write, "probably more country houses are being built and more money and thought expended on them, than perhaps at any time since the days of the Stuarts."[18]

During these years, people who built or bought country houses, however immense and expensive, rarely bought more than a few hundred acres of land around them. Sometimes as few as ten or twenty acres would do. And that land often had nothing to do with agriculture. After the 1870s, it became decreasingly likely that farming alone would pay the upkeep on a large country house. The land new people bought in 1890–1930 was more what real estate agents today call "amenity land"—parkland to set off the house and impress visitors with the vistas; clumps of trees to form a picturesque setting and block other buildings from view; enough space for a long entry drive and outings on horseback; a fashionable garden; enough scrub and woodland for shooting and hunting. When one of the new men, the brewer Arthur Guinness, created Lord Iveagh in 1891, bought himself 15,000 acres around his house at Elvetham in Suffolk, two-thirds of it was devoted to scrub and woodland for raising pheasants to shoot. The cost of his outdoor staff (including 70 in the game department) was far greater than his acres could ever have earned as farmland.

But few nouveaux riches wanted an estate the size of Guinness's. As landlords grew increasingly anxious about the unprofitability and insecurity of property, they or their trustees allowed their domains to be broken into smaller and smaller pieces. This practice assumed runaway proportions after World War I, when millions of acres of land were sold, often to tenant farmers.

Although one can trace to the High Victorians (or to rich Americans of the Gilded Era) the notion of what we now label "society"—wealthy people who entertain one another according to set rituals, without any particular connection to politics or power— this phenomenon reached a dizzying height under two "society"-conscious Princes of Wales. The stylish, extravagant, leisurely ways of Edward VII and his grandson, briefly Edward VIII, in the years before and after their respective accessions, focused attention on the country houses they frequented not as "power houses," in the old manner of Houghton in the 18th century or Hatfield in the 17th or 19th, but as "social houses," like that kept by Mrs. Greville at Polesden Lacey. The hosts and fellow guests of these sovereigns and sovereigns-to-be might own large country houses and entertain lavishly, but they were as likely to be arriviste Americans or South Africans, City speculators, or yacht-owning retailers as members of old landed families.

A great deal has been written about the life led by the "smart set" in such places during these years. But to me it seems almost devoid of historical significance. So, therefore, seem the houses themselves. The thousands of grouse shot, the jolly chases after foxes, footmen in archaic costumes, liaisons in the guest wing, billiards for the gentlemen, endless costume changes for the ladies, after-dinner charades, croquet on the lawn, "Anyone for tennis?": it has become the stuff of a thousand light novels and West End plays. But at this point, the English country house loses its vital connection with English history, and becomes little more than a setting for an increasingly irrelevant mode of upper-class social life, of which its royal visitors are the figureheads.

The architectural styles and decoration of such houses tended to be artificial and fashionable, no more "rooted" in contemporary culture than this year's cut of a Paris tea gown: make-believe Tudor, faux-French chateau, imitation Jacobean, like the houses of the rich in turn-of-the-century America. They lacked even the dogged energy, the search for a meaningful style of the eclectic, uncertain Victorians, who at least believed there was some kind of moral significance to muscular neo-Gothic. The interior-decorated, over-

gilded rooms of Polesden Lacey, Manderston, and Luton Hoo are as notorious for their surfeit of luxe as the garish interiors of the Brobdignagian "cottages" of Newport, Rhode
Island. Eventually, after a brief twenties vogue for neo-Tudor, and a few feints toward
organic near-modernism, a safe brick neo-Georgian became the rule in country house
design. The rule still applies.

The last time a large English country house was identified by the press as a serious center of power was in 1936–39. It was in 1936 that a left-wing journalist named Claud Cockburn decided to label as the "Cliveden Set" a colorful assortment of politicians, publishers,
and writers who gathered at Waldorf and Nancy Astor's Victorian/Edwardian palazzo in
Buckinghamshire for big weekend house parties, where they enjoyed talking politics from
Saturday to Monday.

Cockburn introduced the theory—which was rapidly picked up by the pro-Churchill
press—that the Astors and their reactionary upper-class friends were secretly running
British foreign policy, and pushing Neville Chamberlain (by way of his foreign secretary
Anthony Eden, a Cliveden regular) toward appeasement with Hitler. "Subscribers to *The
Week* [Cockburn's newspaper]," he wrote, "are familiar with the pro-Nazi intrigues center-
ing on Cliveden and Printing House Square"—the address of the London *Times*. He wrote
of the "Germanophile plans...of Lord Lothian, [with] the Astors, Mr. Barrington-Ward of
The Times, and its editor Mr. Geoffrey Dawson at the head of it."[19]

Editors and political leaders in London, New York, and Washington took seriously
Cockburn's imagined cabal of powerful press leaders and cabinet members, meeting in
secret at an English country house. Within weeks, dozens of papers in both Britain and the
U.S., senators on the floor of Congress, public lecturers, and cabaret entertainers were
denouncing the dangerously fascist "Cliveden Set." David Low, the most popular British
political cartoonist of the time, published in March 1938 a caricature of a brownshirted
Lady Astor at Cliveden taking the Nazi salute from a parade of fools identified as Lothian,
Grigg, Dawson, J. L. Garvin (the *Observer* editor)—and George Bernard Shaw, another
frequent guest at Cliveden, who had accompanied Lady Astor and Lord Lothian on a trip
to Moscow in 1931. In February 1938, a Labor MP declared in the House, "The foreign
policy of this country is no longer settled by the Cabinet in Downing Street but at the
country house of Lady Astor at Cliveden."[20] Anthony Eden felt obliged to resign, and
Nancy Astor was vilified as a fascist traitor by Howard Nicolson, Upton Sinclair, Stafford
Cripps, and others.

This group of supposed conspirators, led by Lady Astor (who, like her father-in-law the
1st Viscount Astor, was born in the United States, and who was elected to her husband's
seat in Commons when he succeeded to his father's title in 1919), included, among political peers, Philip Ker, 11th Marquess of Lothian, a leading Liberal politician, who served
as ambassador to the United States in 1939–40; Lord Halifax, former Foreign Secretary,
named by Winston Churchill to succeed Lothian in Washington; Lord Cranborne, heir to
the Marquess of Salisbury; and Lord Milner, the arch-conservative former High Commis-
sioner of South Africa. The group also included, on a more or less regular basis, the editors

Cliveden, Buckinghamshire. The Shell Fountain.

of both the *Observer* (which Lord Astor owned) and the *Times* (which his brother largely owned); Harold Macmillan, Sir Edward Grigg, Robert Brand (Nancy's brother-in-law), Lionel Hitchens, the cabinet secretary Dr. Thomas Jones, and the Oxford publisher and bookseller Basil Blackwell.

Among this floating house party of politically minded friends there *were* a few arch-appeasers, who believed that any concessions to Hitler were preferable to war: Lord Lothian, who had never quite forgiven himself for what he regarded as the anti-German unfairness of the 1919 Treaty of Versailles, a treaty he had helped to draft; Geoffrey Dawson, the *Times* editor; Dr. Jones; and the Astors. Charles Lindbergh, who was convinced that Hitler was going to win, was a guest at Cliveden in 1938. But others among them were far more apprehensive of Hitler, and willing to go to war to defeat him.

The Nazis were "loathsome, of course," Lady Astor later wrote in her own defense. But war, she believed, would be far worse. She despised France ("nothing but one big brothel"), dreamed of the superior moral hegemony of an Anglo-American empire, and defended German rearmament, surrounded as the misunderstood Germans were by "hostile Roman Catholic powers."[21] Both Lord Lothian (in 1934) and Lady Astor (in 1936) had met privately with Baron von Ribbentrop, the German ambassador: he at Blickling, his beautiful country seat in Norfolk; she in London and at her "little" house at Sandwich on the Kentish coast. It was at one of her luncheons, in May 1938, that Chamberlain proposed yielding the Czech Sudetenland to Germany—before Hitler had even asked for it. Even after Hitler had invaded the Sudetenland, Lady Astor had the arrogance to suggest, on the floor of Parliament, that as the Czechs fleeing from his armies were probably all Communists, they were unworthy of Western sympathy or support.

At the time, Nancy Astor wrote to Supreme Court Justice Felix Frankfurter (one of her many high-placed American friends), "with regard to the 'Cliveden Set'...there is not one word of truth in all this propaganda. . . It is the attempt to create suspicion and a class war [and] is now being used by the Communist, Socialist, and Liberal opposition to bring down the Government."[22] It is possible, as one of her biographers has written, that "for Socialists of all denominations it was convenient to be able to ascribe all the guilt of appeasement"—which was not only the position of the government of the day, but probably the position of a majority of the population—"to a small group of people meeting in the country house of a Conservative millionaire, and of his wife who was a Conservative MP."[23]

After Hitler's armies marched into Prague on March 15, 1939, Nancy Astor and her friends, like many shocked Europeans, fell in line behind Churchill and the Allies. But the taint of "appeasement" has hung over the Astors, Lord Lothian, and Sir Charles Barry's huge, innocent house—now a posh hotel owned by the National Trust—ever since. It may well have represented a growing national hostility to the pretensions of the "country house crowd" in general, which was to encounter in the first Labor Party government in 1945 a degree of enmity it had not encountered since the dire days of David Lloyd George.

When a second Cliveden scandal, involving the next generation of Astors, a teenaged prostitute, a cabinet minister, and a suicide, hit the papers in 1963, everyone in Britain reporting it resurrected the "Cliveden Set" legend, keeping the malign magic of country houses before the public eye.

CHAPTER THREE

Tearing Them Down

MANY OBSERVERS TRACE the contemporary "cult of the country house" to a provocative exhibition mounted at the Victoria and Albert Museum in London in 1974, called *The Destruction of the English Country House*. In this exhibition, curators Roy Strong and Marcus Binney estimated that there were between 5,000 and 10,000 substantial country houses in Britain in 1874. Of these, they believed, between 1,200 and 1,400 had been demolished in the century preceding the exhibition. Binney has since upped his estimate of losses to almost double that number.[1] What had happened during these hundred years to wipe out so substantial a portion of the nation's architectural past?

· · ·

Although the reforms of the preceding 40 years had removed certain political powers from their hands, the leading country families still had reason to feel secure in their wealth and position as late as 1870. Within a few years, however, a deep agricultural depression had set in, which was not to reverse course for more than 60 years. Since most country houses depended on income from their farms and tenant farmers, a number of older estates had to be sold. In the process, many old houses were lost. Although large new Victorian mansions continued to be built, a number of fine Georgian houses had been demolished at the turn of the century, partly because the style had gone out of fashion. Many older castles and manors had been abandoned and left to decay. Strong and Binney count 63 important houses lost in the 45 years before 1918.

The major demolitions in their register, however, begin after World War I. For a num-

ber of coincident reasons—the continued depression in farm prices; the increasing difficulty of finding enough servants to run the houses, as better jobs became available in
cities; the death of heirs in the war; and the growth to record levels of income and inheritance tax—at least 458 substantial British country houses, for which new owners or uses
could not be found, were demolished between the two wars.

"They were enormous," Mark Girouard wrote of the Victorian country houses, "complicated, and highly articulated machines for a way of life which seems as remote as the
stone age, served by a technology as elaborate as it is now obsolete. They have become, too
often, stranded monsters, with abandoned gasworks, abandoned billiard tables, the gigantic boilers and miles of pipes rusting in the basement, the long rows of bells rusting in the
back corridors, the butler's pantry, brushing rooms and laundries empty, or occupied, in
this new society, by typists, nurses, schoolgirls, or delinquents." In 1935, Osbert Sitwell
had written, "What country houses of any size, one wonders, can hope to survive the next
fifty years?"[2]

For a while, Sitwell's fears seemed prophetic. Another 629 country houses, by Strong
and Binney's count, bit the dust in the 30 years after World War II, partly as a result of the
brutal treatment many of them received when taken over for wartime use. Of the more
than 90 country houses recorded in Shropshire in the 1870s, at least 35 had disappeared
by 1952.[3] In 1955 alone—a record year for demolitions—75 country houses were torn
down. (More recent estimates put all these numbers much higher. John M. Robinson, in
The Country House at War, sets the number of country houses demolished in the ten years
after 1945 alone at "nearly a thousand."[4])

Charles Ryder, Evelyn Waugh's fictional narrator, made his living and his reputation
doing paintings of country seats between the wars. He presumed—as did Waugh—that
they were doomed by the 1930s. Revisiting Brideshead as the captain of an army brigade
on maneuvers during World War II, Ryder describes the ghostly decay of the near-empty
house, its trashing at the hands of his own troops. "It doesn't seem to make any sense," says
his working-class, wave-of-the-future sergeant major. "One family in a place this size.
What's the use of it?"[5]

The romantic feeling that grew up around English medieval and Tudor houses in the
late 19th and early 20th centuries allowed most of those still intact in 1900 to survive—
although this was only a small fraction of those that had been built. But scores of significant (and insignificant) large houses of the 16th through 19th century began to disappear
after 1900. Although the National Trust had accepted, and thereby helped to save, its first
important country house as early as 1931 (Montacute in Somerset), it was not until 1949
that a private country house owner—the 6th Marquess of Bath—got the idea of exploiting
his own house as a tourist attraction, something Waugh could not possibly have foreseen
five years before. In the meantime Britain had lost a great number of important houses in
every corner of the country.

· · ·

The catalogue of losses from the 1974–75 V&A exhibition shows Samuel Wyatt porticoes, Palladian domes, Thomas Wright plasterwork, columned entry halls. The government itself tore down (not unreasonably) James Wyatt's additions to Chiswick House, Lord Burlington's neoclassical jewel box just outside of London. Trentham Hall in Staffordshire, designed by Sir Charles Barry for the Duke of Sutherland in the 1830s—a house larger and grander than Cliveden—was torn down in 1911. The Deepdeene in Surrey, a monumental Victorian remodeling job (also of the 1830s), was demolished in 1969. Dawpool in Cheshire, designed for the owner of the White Star Line by Norman Shaw, stood for just 42 years, from 1884 to 1926. Immense, even palatial country houses, obviously intended to stand for many generations, were lucky to make it through three or four.

Agecroft Hall in Lancashire—a 15th/16th-century house—was moved stone by stone to Richmond, Virginia, in 1926. Woburn Abbey, which the 13th Duke of Bedford was to turn into one of the most popular country houses on the tourist circuit, was greatly reduced in size as late as 1950. Bowood House in Wiltshire today attracts 150,000 paying visitors a year. But what these visitors see is simply an annex to the big house, which was redesigned by Robert Adam in the 1760s, and torn down in 1955. The walls and ceiling from Adam's Saloon at Bowood now surround the 11th-floor Committee Room in Lloyd's of London's stainless steel and glass headquarters on Lime Street.

Roy Strong, who had just assumed the role of director of the Victoria and Albert Museum in 1973, insisted that this, his first major exhibition, was intended to be "utterly objective." But the tone and presentation of both the exhibition and its catalogue were unrelievedly grim. Extrapolating from the curators' ever-increasing figures of country houses lost, decade after decade, persuaded by the bleak rhetoric of their presentation, the viewer or reader could not be blamed for believing that the end, in fact, was very near:

> In many cases a new generation has inherited, often with less inclination than the post-war owners to dedicate their lives to the often thankless task of maintaining an historic building and caring for its contents, gardens and parkland. Sheer acreage alone can no longer be coped with in the face of no help. The disappearance of gardeners, of living-in staff, of the estate carpenter and the odd-job man often spells the end of a house as a practical place to live. The family retreat into a wing, the gardens are turfed over, decay sets in. Opening to the public may bring some tax relief but it also brings problems, and some owners have been forced to shut for the simple reason that they cannot afford the insurance necessary to remain open....
>
> Few owners can now meet building and repair costs that rocket at the rate of 15 to 25 per cent per annum....Death duties, and capital gains tax, let alone the threatened forms of Wealth and Inheritance Taxes, spell the final ruin of these most precious works of art. Created lovingly over the centuries, they will be slowly eroded to meet the demands of the Exchequer.[6]

In his catalogue essay, James Lees-Milne picks up the thread: "The English country house is as archaic as the osprey. The few left fulfilling the purpose for which they were built are inexorably doomed." A year earlier, posing the rhetorical question *Country Houses in Britain: Can They Survive?*, John Cornforth concluded, "There is the distinct possibility of destruction on a scale not seen in this country since the 16th and 17th centuries...It is a future that looks full of gloom, and made all the worse because of the sense-lessness of bringing it about: no one will be any better off, and the nation itself will be greatly the poorer."[7]

· · ·

Anyone observing the scene since 1974—when strict new regulations put an end to the demolition of historic buildings of any consequence—will realize that these gloomy predictions have not come to pass. In fact, for all the apocalyptic rhetoric of the 1970s heritage lobby, the history of the English country house has been a history of demolitions. If we take the end of the Wars of the Roses in 1485 as our starting point, it becomes clear how many of them were built only to be torn down. As Maurice Howard notes, "Today little remains to demonstrate the character and splendour of Henry VII's and Henry VIII's works. Of the sixty or so houses for which the early Tudor kings had some degree of responsibility, only two survive with any substantial evidence of Tudor work both outside and inside the building, namely the palaces of Hampton Court and St. James's."[8] Among the royal houses long since disappeared are three of the grandest ever built: Richmond Palace, in what was then the rural outskirts of London; and Nonsuch Palace and Oatlands Palace in Surrey, on which Henry VIII spent £23,000 and £16,500, respectively, at a time when the pound was worth (in general purchasing power) perhaps one percent of its value today, and in terms of luxury building a good deal less. Henry VII's grand manor at Woodstock (1494–1503) was razed in 1710, to clear the park for Blenheim Palace.

The Earl of Leicester's vast Kenilworth Castle—scene of the three-week-long party he gave for Queen Elizabeth in 1575—is now a popular ruin near Stratford, which attracts 80,000 tourists a year. No trace is left of Theobalds, the splendid estate in Hertfordshire where William Cecil so often, and at such cost, welcomed the queen and her retinue, before being obliged to give it to Henry VIII. "Too large to be adapted to eighteenth-century use, or too closely associated with the Crown to survive the Commonwealth, most [Elizabethan palaces] have been demolished," Ian Dunlop writes.

> By the end of the Commonwealth, the England of Elizabeth had been to a large extent destroyed. A whole host of buildings, stained-glass windows, paintings and manuscripts had been swept away before the tide of triumphant Puritanism...Theobalds, acquired by the Crown in 1607, was among the first to go. "Our fathers saw it built," lamented Fuller, "we behold it unbuilt." For years its mutilated carcass lingered on, leased out for tenements or left to pilfering hands and eroding elements. By the time that antiquarian interest was fully aroused, nothing significant was left.
>
> Before the end of the Commonwealth the fate of Richmond, Greenwich, Oatlands, Woodstock, Kenilworth and Holdenby was likewise sealed. But in spite of the Restoration the destruction continued. In 1685 Nonsuch fell. The house that had been the architectural sensation of its age was sacrificed to the financial needs of the Duchess of Cleveland, and its passing was hardly noticed. No longer wanted, it was sold to brokers and gradually demolished. Whitehall, purged of its "superstitious pictures," survived a little longer, but fire was to destroy what bigotry had spared, and by the end of the century Hampton Court and Newhall were the only Tudor palaces to survive in anything like their entirety.[9]

The Strong and Binney list of country houses torn down between 1875 and 1975 is impressive and sobering. But my point is that one can compile an even more impressive list of great houses demolished *before* 1875, during centuries when no one regarded such demolitions as a cause for concern.

In early days, as Maurice Howard makes clear in *The Early Tudor Country House*, the pre-existing building (whether a castle, an earlier house, or—after 1539—one of the many monastic institutions that had been seized by the Crown) was often not so much levelled as swallowed up. Of 267 notable early Tudor houses Howard has discovered, nothing, or nothing but ruins or fragments, remains of almost half. Only a handful, like Compton Wynyates, Haddon Hall, Sutton Place, and Cotehele, stand more or less intact. Most large houses of the early 16th century were incorporated, in whole or in part, into newer houses built later on, as their owners felt the need for more space, comfort, or prestige. Progress was progress; a man's castle was his home.

Here stands an old wing, surrounded by newer wings; an old window or fragment of wall, incorporated into the newer fabric. We pass into a 17th-century brick mansion by way of a high old stone 16th-century gatehouse. Knole, the great house of the Sackvilles in Kent, kept evolving from 1456 on, until it spread over seven acres, seven courtyards, and (it is reputed) 365 rooms. Penshurst Place, a few miles to the west, grew organically out from its Great Hall of the 1340s to a gallery of the 1820s, surrounded by gardens restored in our own time to something approximating their Tudor state. Forde Abbey in Dorset contains the chapel, undercroft, dormitory range, and one cloister walk—now a conservatory—from a Cistercian abbey that stood on the site from 1150 to 1539; a Great Hall of 1520, with 17th-century paneled walls; and major additions built by Cromwell's attorney general during the Commonwealth of 1649–1660. But this sort of tear-down-and-add-on approach was the ruling pattern for most country house building well into the 19th century.

Alnwick Castle in Northumberland contains a compact history of English architecture in one large complex of buildings. Beginning with the remains of a 12th-century motte-and-bailey castle, it adds 14th-century towers and a 15th-century barbican over the moat, which is a small castle in itself. Inside, Robert Adam remodeled the state rooms in 1778. But then his work was swept away in a lavish redecorating job of 1850–90. Most of 12th- and 13th-century Arundel Castle was destroyed in the Civil War, after which the remnants were abandoned for 70 years. The "medieval" castle one sees at Arundel today is partly a Regency creation of 1795–1814, and even more a Victorian fantasy dating from 1875–1900.

Many of Robert Adam's great 18th-century creations were built on or carved out of earlier houses. Underneath Kenwood in north London and Saltram in Plymouth lie the brick carcasses of unfashionable predecessors. Osterley Park House west of London (1761–77) totally encases the house visited by Elizabeth I in 1576; only the Elizabethan stable block (now a tea room) retains its original aspect. At Newby Hall in Yorkshire, Adam completely disguised a Wren-era redbrick house of 1705 under his elegant improvements and extensions of 1767–76. His spectacular interiors for Syon House on the Thames (1762+) were fitted into a quadrangular 15th-century convent that had been given to the Duke of Northumberland in 1552, and first "improved" by Inigo Jones in the 17th century.

·   ·   ·

The first Duchess of Marlborough aroused no great hue and cry when she ordered that the remains of Woodstock Manor—"not in themselves a very agreeable sight," the Marlboroughs declared—be demolished so as not to mar the vista from the windows of Blenheim Palace. Such demolitions and replacements were, in fact, the rule rather than the exception for new-built houses of the 17th through 19th centuries, whenever builders chose not to incorporate fragments of old houses into new ones, or to add on wing after wing.

The list of country houses that stand on the sites of earlier houses that were leveled before 1875—either accidentally or on purpose—includes several of today's best-known tourist destinations. Of the 747 English country houses listed in the V&A catalogue as destroyed between 1875 and 1975, at least 36 fall into this category: houses that were demolished by fire or the hand of man, but subsequently replaced. One might also want to subtract from that total some of the 68 houses listed as "partially demolished," considering that it includes names like Bowood, Chiswick, Euston, and Peover—which, despite their losses, remain impressive country houses by anyone's standard; and others such as Gunton Park (Norfolk), Dingley Hall (Northamptonshire), Lees Court (Kent), and Middleton Park (Oxfordshire), which have been successfully transformed into multiple residences.

·   ·   ·

All that granted, the demolition of English country houses since the 1870s, and more especially after World War II, has proceeded at a rate far beyond that of past centuries. In the great majority of more recent cases, demolition was *not* done to clear a space for a newer, grander, more up-to-date or commodious house. Houses were torn down because they had ceased to serve any useful domestic function, or had become too costly to maintain. According to John Harris, Gautby Hall in Lincolnshire, torn down in 1872, was one of the first country houses to be demolished for economic reasons, rather than for replacement or because of the deleterious effects of a fire or an overlong period of neglect.[10] "Before the 1870s, it was very rare indeed for country houses to be sold or demolished. Most families were extremely tenacious in retaining the mansion and grounds, and devised elaborate methods of transference if the male line died out. And houses that were pulled down had usually been accidentally damaged beyond repair, or were being demolished so that something more modern and more grandiose might be put in its place. But gradually from the 1880s, and more markedly from the First World War, these trends…were put into reverse."[11]

Why were so many great houses torn down, beginning in the 1870s and 1880s? Although there is no necessary link between the fate of titled folk and the fate of country houses, one can draw some clues from David Cannadine's *The Decline and Fall of the British*

Aristocracy, which specifically deals with the period of 1880–1939; or the final chapters of books dealing with the British upper classes in the 19th century.[12]

The great theme of Cannadine's book is that in every demonstrable setting, the English landed aristocracy—which had held the reins of national power since 1688, of local and regional power since more than a century before that, and of imperial power since the empire began—*lost* power, not only relatively but absolutely, between the 1880s and the 1930s. In Parliament, after thirty years of increasingly bitter public attacks on the unelected hereditary upper house, most of the residual power of the Lords was ended in 1910–11. David Lloyd George, the Welsh firebrand who served as Prime Minister from 1916 to 1922, and perhaps the most ardent adversary the British aristocracy had ever known, introduced in 1909 (as Chancellor of the Exchequer) the so-called "People's Budget," which was clearly designed to take from the rich—by means of increased death duties, a surtax on large incomes, and a new tax on the unearned increase in land values—in order (among other things) to give to the poor, by way of old age pensions. It was, in fact, their outraged and unprecedented rejection of this budget that led to the castration of the House of Lords.

As the landowning classes were losing any legislative power of significance in the House of Lords, they were also losing their hold on the House of Commons and on cabinet posts. "Rotten boroughs" and "safe seats," which had long allowed the gentry to pack the House of Commons with their friends and relations, were abolished, and the buying of votes made illegal. Of 652 MPs returned in the general election of 1880, 394, or over 60 percent, were noblemen, baronets, landed gentry, or their close relations. Sons of prominent peers had been all but guaranteed safe places in Commons. When their fathers died, the elder sons moved simply across the lobby to the Other House. But these numbers and this tradition declined abruptly after the turn of the century. The Liberal Party landslide of 1906 reduced the 'country house contingent' to one-fifth or less. After 1920, Conservative members who could claim connections with the once-dominant landowning class never counted for more than ten percent of the House.

Similarly, one can trace the decline of aristocrats among Prime Ministers and cabinet members, from clear dominion to token representation to near-invisibility, despite the notable reign of the reactionary 3rd Marquess of Salisbury. Lord Salisbury was called on three times to serve as Prime Minister: 1885–86, 1886–92, 1895–1902. Not only his seat at Hatfield House, but also Bowood, Chatsworth, Kedleston, Knowsley, and Garrowby retained at least a vestige of symbolic power during these years, as their Conservative masters—as well a number of Salisbury's close relations—were given prestige positions in government.

But, as Cannadine notes, such country house notables had been effectively marginalized by the arrival of David Lloyd George as prime minister in 1916. He did not want anything to do with them, nor they with him. Most of those that remained in office were assigned to honorific or secondary posts of little significant power. Even his Foreign Secretary, the once-formidable Curzon of Kedleston, was virtually ignored, as Lloyd George conducted his own wartime and postwar foreign policy, leaving Curzon to feel like "a valet, almost a drudge."[13]

Two other patricians, the Earl of Rosebery (who owned three country houses, a London mansion, and a yacht) and Arthur Balfour (a nephew of Lord Salisbury's, and heir to 87,000 acres) held the reins of government in Britain in 1894–95 and 1902–5; William Ewart Gladstone, four times Liberal PM between 1868 and 1894, was himself a country squire. But Lord Salisbury—whose distant Cecil ancestors had served as chief ministers to Elizabeth I and James I—was the last peer, last head of a great dynasty, last master of a great country house, to serve as Prime Minister. Although journalists wrote glibly of the "Hotel Cecil" as a power house from the 1900s to the 1920s, by the end of that time, writes Cannadine, "Hatfield was more the home of lost causes than the centre of power."[14]

Cannadine traces, with relentless rigor, a similar diminution in the participation or power of the landed classes in every field they once controlled: the civil service, the foreign service, the army and navy, the established church, and the legal profession. He cites evidence from their own memoirs and diaries to define the dying old guard in these fields in terms of the welcome and freedom they enjoyed to spend weekends and weeks at their friends' country houses. Lord Lyons, Britain's Ambassador to France for twenty years, "spent his summers at Arundel, Chatsworth, Knowsley, and Raby." But, as Cannadine also points out, quoting Algernon Cecil, it was "no longer enough to know, as Lord Lyons always knew, what were the views held at Chatsworth, Knowsley, Hatfield, and Bowood; the whole country counts."[15]

Open civil service examinations, changes in the legal profession, the abolition of purchased army commissions, and the greatly reduced power of lay patrons to appoint their choice of clergymen all conspired to bring in a new breed of dedicated, hard-working professionals, who displaced the leisured gentlemen. As their representation in the "honorable professions" decreased, gentlemen unable to live off their estates (or allowances granted them by the head of the family) were forced to turn to the City (or cities) or to travel abroad, in search of primarily decorative positions in business, public administration, or the cultural establishment, where their titles and connections were still regarded as assets; or to genuine jobs in business or commerce, in which a few of them prospered. In either case, the old role and function of a "country seat" came to mean less and less. In the end, they often became useless liabilities to their harassed owners. "An estate now comes to be regarded solely as a burden and hence the willingness to dispose of it," wrote Henry Durant in 1936.[16]

A number of struggling patricians took overseas postings—which came with tax-free salaries, travel and entertainment allowances, and official mansions furnished and staffed at government expense—in order to escape the mounting cost of maintaining their country seats and servants at home. The Marchioness of Hertford begged the Prime Minister (in vain) for a colonial governorship for her husband, since they had been forced to let Ragley Hall, and found themselves homeless for three years. The Marquess of Lansdowne quit a rising career in national politics to become Governor General of Canada, then

Viceroy of India, from 1883 to 1894, specifically in order to hold onto the family estates. As he wrote to his mother, "India means saving Lansdowne House for the family. I should be able while there not only to live on my official income, but to save something every year. If I can let Lansdowne House, I might by the time I come home have materially reduced the load of debt which has become so terrible an incubus to us all, and in the meantime I shall be doing useful work for my country, instead of living in a corner of the house in England, perpetually worried by financial trouble, and perhaps increasing instead of decreasing the family liabilities."[17]

As local government was taken out of the hands of the squires and given to elected local councils, the country house lost its role and significance as a regional seat of justice. Although many great county families continued to dominate both local affairs and parliamentary elections well into the early 20th century, after 1888–89 (when county councils were first established) more and more of the duties of regional government were taken over by middle-class professionals. "In political representation as in landownership," writes Cannadine, "five hundred years of patrician history was reversed in fifty. Country politics was no longer an essential outwork of country house life."[18] The countryside was more and more managed by full-time bureaucrats and elected councilmen and aldermen, much to the distress of some of the tradition-minded gentry, who contrasted the "devotion, sacrifice, and character of the English squires" with the "untried and uncertain hands of those elected by popular vote."[19]

The squire in his country house continued to serve, for many generations, as Justice of the Peace, the chief local magistrate. Nominated by an aristocratic Lord Lieutenant, JPs were likely to be men of his own class. But increasingly after 1870, self-made, middle-class, town-bred men were being appointed to the bench. By the 1900s, they represented more than half the JPs in England.

· · ·

Like most historians of the period, Cannadine traces the beginning of the end of aristocratic power to the "sudden and dramatic collapse of the agricultural economy, partly because of the massive influx of cheap foreign goods from North and South America and the Antipodes.... the worldwide collapse in agricultural prices meant that estate rentals fell dramatically, and that land values plummeted correspondingly. As a result, the whole territorial basis of patrician existence was undermined."[20]

A country house was, by historical definition, the visible capital of a prosperous agricultural estate. As the estate declined precipitously in value (land prices fell by at least 30 percent between 1870 and 1890, and continued to fall into the 1930s; the price of wheat, and arable agricultural incomes generally, were less than half in the 1890s what they been had in the 1870s), the great house at its center lost not only the revenues required to staff and maintain it, but also its fundamental raison d'être—as the imperial palaces of Vienna ceased to have any social or political significance after the Hapsburg Empire disappeared in 1918. Many of the great British country estates, moreover, were so heavily encumbered with debt that their owners were at the mercy of bankers and other middle-class, town-dwelling men.[21] Country houses as historic and important as Houghton Hall and West Wycombe Park were put up for sale by aristocratic owners desperate for cash.

After the Third Reform Act of 1884–85, which doubled the size of the electorate, and finally allowed the working-class majority (including city dwellers and farm workers) to dominate elections, political pressures grew throughout England, Scotland, Wales, and especially Ireland—until 1921, a part of the United Kingdom—to force great landlords to sell off farms to their newly-enfranchised tenants, sometimes at disastrously low prices. "Were there any effective demand for the purchase of land, half the land of England would be in the market tomorrow," the Duke of Marlborough wrote to the *Times* in 1885.[22]

Faced with the threats of antilandlord rhetoric and budget proposals in the early years of this century, many owners sold out in fearful anticipation of new taxes or hostile legislation. Others did so in order to pay off mortgages or obtain funds for new and better investments. The burdens of taxation increased dramatically after World War I. Taxes on rental incomes as much as trebled, and the maximum death duty was raised to 40 percent on estates valued at more than £200,000. (There had been cries of "robbery" and "confiscation" in the House of Lords when death duties were first introduced, at a maximum of eight percent on estates over a million pounds, in 1894.)

It has been estimated that a quarter of the land of England—some six to eight million acres—changed hands, usually from large holders to small holders, between 1917 and 1921: the largest permanent transfer of land in the country since Henry VIII seized the monastic properties in 1539–41.

· · ·

Selling off land and houses—even at depressed prices—did not necessarily leave their owners broke, unless (as was true in a few cases) they were utterly overwhelmed by taxes and debts. In 1919—the same holds true today—the owner of a large agricultural estate might in fact improve his situation by selling off land, paying off his mortgages, and reinvesting the surplus in urban property, or securities yielding double or more the agricultural return.

But this process involved a transfer of wealth and attention from the great house and its contents to stocks and shares, from the country to the City. After the 1880s, more great houses were demolished than were built. New country houses continued to be built up to and beyond 1930, although at a far slower rate than before 1875, and generally on a far smaller scale. But many more were sold or torn down.

When Stowe was sold for a school in 1921, the *Estates Gazette* wrote, "It seems improbable that any family, however rich, will ever again build a house nearly a thousand feet long, surrounded by a garden of 4,000 acres."[23] Hundreds of important houses were sold between the wars, either to pay taxes, to reduce mortgages, or to realize capital for investment elsewhere. But in the case of houses for which no buyer could be found, demolition (or abandonment to eventual ruin) was the typical outcome. The large London town mansions went first, until very few were left by World War II. But the losses in the country were far more numerous. As we have seen, Strong and Binney account for 63 houses demolished between 1874 and 1918, and at least 458 more between 1919 and 1939. Their destruction was usually a direct result of declining family fortunes—what *Estates Gazette* called the "concurrent decay of the class which once thought them necessary."[24]

. . .

What really destroyed the stately homes of England was the Second World War. Mount Edgecumbe in Devon was gutted by German incendiaries in 1940, apparently by mistake; it was later reconstructed, at the expense of the War Damage Commission. Sandley Park in Kent was bombed in 1943, and the remaining shell demolished two years later. Appuldurcombe on the Isle of Wight was already in an advanced state of decay when it was blown up by a landmine during the war. It was deroofed in 1952, and is now maintained by English Heritage as a picturesque ruin. A number of houses (Penshurst, Knole, Syon) suffered from indirect hits, which blew out windows or knocked down parkland trees.

But the major destruction was wrought by the British government itself. During the First World War, a number of country house owners had offered their properties for use as hospitals and convalescent homes for wounded soldiers—the first time some of them had ever entertained working-class guests. The 5th Earl of Harewood offered—as his son was to offer in the next war—accommodation for wounded officers only, perhaps feeling that they would best appreciate his Adam ceilings and Chippendale chairs, his Turners and Venetian old masters.

During World War II, it was no longer a question of country houses being offered. They were demanded, requisitioned, taken over—almost all of them. These takeovers may well have aided the war effort. But in the end they were devastating to an already fading cultural and architectural institution.

Why did the government order virtually every country house owner to hand over his house? First, because of the general presumption that London and the big provincial cities would be severely damaged by aerial bombardment immediately on the declaration of war, and that these large houses could be used as a refuge for urban children and others. Secondly, because large, sheltered spaces were needed to accommodate millions of British, colonial, and (later) American soldiers and airmen, both those defending the British Isles and those preparing for air raids against and the final invasion of the German-held continent.

On the first presumption—which was only partially realized in 1944—the War government decided to evacuate from the major cities of Great Britain, and from certain coastal areas regarded as endangered (1) all young children; (2) all essential government offices; (3) members of the royal family, although most of the latter decided to stay at Windsor or Sandringham; and (4) works of art, rare books, and valuable documents from national collections.

Decision (2) was to have a serious secondary effect. As important government offices and bureaus were moved out of London into areas deemed less vulnerable to attack, many of them were rehoused in large boarding schools in the outlying areas. This meant that the schools, in turn, with all their students, staff, and facilities, had to find safe quarters elsewhere for the duration of the war. Very often, these quarters were found in country houses.

From the point of view of the War Office, British country houses had three great advantages: (1) they were big, and could accommodate large numbers of people; (2) they were scattered all over the country; and (3) they tended to be readily accessible to roads, railroads, and towns. Someone in London made up a list of desirable houses, but it was kept secret until long after the war. So country house owners were often unprepared for the requisitioning notices they received in 1939 and 1940. A few owners sold up quickly, afraid of the damage and decrease in value that a government takeover would cause. A few others, blessed with a firm manner or high-placed connections, were able to lay down stipulations. The house was to be occupied by schoolchildren, not soldiers—and preferably by girls; or, as at Harewood, by wounded officers, or (Cliveden) wounded Canadian soldiers. Smoking was to be forbidden (Woburn Abbey), in an island that had suddenly become a nation of smokers. The government was to be responsible for boarding over the paneled walls and protecting the floors (Parham Park, Audley End, Attingham). Field Marshal Montgomery-Massingberd pulled every possible string to keep the RAF from ripping up the trees and grounds of his estate at Gunby for an airfield.

The Earl of Beauchamp, perhaps fearful for his own valuable properties, tried to get the various governmental agencies involved in taking over country houses to agree to "memorandum of understanding" he had drafted early in the game: "Everyone will agree that (1) Large houses have played an important part in our history, (2) Many of them beautify the countryside, (3) Most of them should be preserved for ever, but (4) In a national emergency, they must be made the best possible use of. . ." [25]

Nothing came of his first three provisos. In 1939–45, no one had yet undertaken the now-essential process of "listing" buildings of unique architectural or historical importance, so no country house owner without friends in high places could expect special treatment.

Some owners, caught totally off-guard by their requisition notices, were furious. Ralph Dutton (later Lord Sherborne) was apoplectic over the sudden arrival of 40 girls from Portsmouth at Hinton Ampner in Hampshire, which he had just spent a decade remodeling. Hurrying to move his valuable artworks and furnishings out of their reach, he felt "a moment of intense bitterness . . . I found it difficult to comprehend that I was being turned out of my house." [26] In September 1939, some 750,000 children and 100,000 of their teachers and aides were evacuated from what we now call "inner cities" and dispersed in country houses all about Britain. When the anticipated 1939 bombing and poison gas attacks—the so-called "phony war"—never materialized, most of the children were sent home again. But during those first months, many of the evacuated children as well as their often recalcitrant hosts had been made thoroughly miserable: the children by their sudden displacement into totally alien surroundings, often in huge and unheated houses; the owners by these swarms of what they saw as filthy, lice-ridden, ill-behaved urchins from the city slums. One group of boys from the East End of London locked up the owners and proceeded to strip the walls, in order to redecorate them with obscene graffiti. Forty children from Manchester took over Lyme Park in Cheshire, while Lord Newton retired to the library with his dogs and a blazing fire. Most of the children still left in country houses were sent home by summer 1942 to make room for the 1.5 to 2 million GIs newly arrived in England. Many children—especially those from certain parts of London—were evacuated to the country once more, bewildered and unhappy, during the Blitz of 1944–45.

A relocated school, in many ways, was the gentlest form of occupation, and several owners hurried to make arrangements for this relatively safe means of doing their bit. James de Rothschild's Waddesdon Manor became a residential nursery school for 100 London children. Scone Palace and Drumlanrig Castles, Chatsworth, Elton, Crichel, Longleat, Duncombe, Knebworth, Longstowe, and Castle Howard all opted for the genteel and secure housing of displaced girls' boarding schools, "in the hope that this would provide the least damaging type of occupation."[27] Unfortunately, this did not always prove to be the case. Because of either an electrical fault or a soot-choked chimney (no one has directly blamed the evacuated girls, whose school in Scarborough *was* in fact destroyed by enemy bombs), Castle Howard caught fire early in the morning of November 9, 1940, and kept on burning until half of the south front was gutted; the great central dome had collapsed and the Pellegrini frescoes under it were destroyed; the roof over six state rooms had caved in; and all the mirrors in the Long Dining Room and the Garden Hall had cracked. The Howard family, which was only able to move back into "Brideshead" in 1953, is still trying to complete the damage repair.

A Welsh public school took over Chatsworth when its own quarters were requisitioned; the Royal School at Lansdowne moved into Longleat. In both cases, the girls and their teachers learned how wretchedly cold unheated great houses could be without an army of servants on hand to keep a hundred fires stocked and lighted. Water froze in bedside jugs, girls made their way through these "caves of ice"—as James Lees-Milne called the country houses of the 1940s—wrapped in blankets and quilts. Four hundred boys from Malvern College moved into Blenheim Palace for a year, before doubling up with the boys at Harrow when their place at Blenheim was taken by intelligence officers. Huge as it is, Blenheim was not entirely prepared. Not only did the art treasures and historic surfaces have to be locked up or boarded over; new kitchens, gas lines, and showers had to be added, and a bank of 60 "portaloos" built alongside one wing. Other boys' public and prep schools moved to the country houses of their wealthy Old Boys (i.e., alumni) or school governors. Catholic families took in convent schools. In a few cases, the family, exhausted by the war and the ordeal of renovating afterwards, ceded the terrain to the occupying school, which has remained in possession of the premises ever since.

It has been estimated that as many as 3,000 houses were taken over for hospitals by the Ministry of Health—not only for convalescing soldiers, but also for civilian patients evacuated from endangered cities. Caroline Seebohm, in *The Country House: A Wartime His-*

tory (1989), lists eight houses ceded to the Red Cross, after being relinquished by the War Office in 1940. Brocket Hall, Battlesden Abbey, Stockwood Park, Stockeld Park, and Farnley Hall became maternity hospitals for city evacuees. Thousands of additional patients were moved out of London to country houses during the Blitz of 1944–45. Among the larger houses turned into military hospitals were Harewood, Hatfield, Carlton Towers, Leeds Castle, Capesthorne, Corsham Court, Somerleyton, Cliveden, and Stapleford Park.

A number of historic houses became strategic military or intelligence headquarters, a few becoming even more historic in the process. Bletchley Park in Buckinghamshire ("a late Victorian house of limited interest") had already been purchased by the government between the wars for its Codes and Cypher School. The house became a piece of legend when its staff managed to break the Germans' "Enigma" code, and was retained by the government after the war. A huge map of the cross-Channel invasion area is still in place on the drawing room wall of Southwick House in Hampshire, headquarters of the Strategic Air Command under Eisenhower in 1943. Wilton House—one of the most beautiful and historic of all English seats—became the headquarters of the Southern Command. D-Day operations were planned under the eyes of Van Dyck's royals and aristocrats in its Double Cube Room. Montgomery's troops trained for their part in the Normandy landings at Merton Hall in Norfolk. Blenheim housed MI5, the top-secret intelligence unit. RAF photo-intelligence moved into Nuneham and Medmenham Abbey in Buckinghamshire. Churchill worked out of the operations room of Bentley Priory (headquarters of the RAF Fighter Command) during the Battle of Britain.

Perhaps the most written about wartime headquarters takeover of a country house, after Bletchley, was transfer of the Foreign Office's intelligence unit to Woburn Abbey for the duration of the war: first to the 1786 Henry Holland riding school and stables wing, plus outbuildings on the estate; then, when the old Duke of Bedford finally died, into the big house, the occupiers now numbering several hundred. After the Holland wing was finally vacated, its timbers were found to be so riddled with dry rot that it had to be torn down.

Almost all of these uses were, in the end, damaging. Hundreds of schoolchildren and teachers, patients and nurses, or army clerks and planners occupying a private house (however spacious) for five or six years inevitably left the rooms—walls, floors, furniture, facilities—much the worse for wear, as James Lees-Milne noted during his tours around country houses on behalf of the National Trust during and after the war.

But no use was more potentially disastrous than occupation by troops, which could reduce the stateliest of homes into a common barracks. "Their final tenants," wrote the architect/antiquarian Sir Clough Williams-Ellis, "our own British army, too often reduced them to virtual ruin."[28] The Grenadier Guard took over Stourhead, the RAF Signals Corps Hughenden; the Royal Naval College moved from Dartmouth to Eaton Hall, the Duke of Westminster's massive pile in Cheshire.

It is hard to get a handle on exactly how many soldiers had to be accommodated—the number obviously varied from year to year during the war, and many were housed in existing bases or in tents. The unanticipated evacuation from Dunkirk in 1940 suddenly threw

335,000 more Allied soldiers back on British soil. By 1941, space had to be found for up to two million British and colonial troops; then, after 1942, for almost as many more Americans. General Patton and the U.S. Third Army occupied Peover Hall in Cheshire with such vigor that the large Georgian wing had to be torn down after the war—reducing the house, to the delight of some antiquarian critics, back to its Jacobean dimensions.

The problem was not, as a rule, deliberate vandalism, although there was plenty of that. The main problem was that no one had foreseen the folly of billeting hundreds of soldiers in large houses without central heating, most of them with inadequate water supplies and negligible bathing facilities. When in domestic use, most prewar country houses—except those recently built or modernized—depended on a large number of servants to keep coal fires stocked and burning in all rooms in regular use. Bathrooms with hot running water were comparatively rare, by contemporary (or American) standards. Take away the servants, take away the fires and hot water, reduce the lighting and electricity to blackout and wartime shortage levels, let the pipes freeze in winter, and these buildings could become very nearly uninhabitable.

Many troops finding themselves in these circumstances tore out wooden fittings (wall paneling, stair railings, even floorboards) and furniture for firewood. Worse still, they built large fires in small fireplaces drawn by long-unswept chimneys, in houses filled with ancient dust, straw insulation, and hundreds of cigarette smokers. The result, according to John Martin Robinson in *The Country House at War* (1989), was that at least 25 country houses were burnt down *by* resident troops during the war. Sunderlandwick, in Yorkshire, made it to the bitter end, only to be set on fire by RAF airmen during a V-J Day celebration in May 1945. Mary, Duchess of Buccleuch, described what happened to Bowhill, one of her family's several seats: "The army moved into Bowhill . . . with not a thing put away. The officers' sitting room was where all the Van Dycks were. It was terribly badly used; the army did terrible things to the house, all the proverbial things that troops are supposed to do—hacking down the banisters to make firewood, and throwing darts at the pictures. They couldn't have done more harm, and ended up by nearly burning it down twice."[29]

In addition to houses actually burned down by troops during World War II, Robinson lists a dozen more so badly damaged by their wartime tenants that the owners abandoned or tore them down after the war was over. As he writes, "Many more were left in such poor condition in 1945 that they proved incapable of restoration. The thousand or so country houses demolished in the decade after the end of the Second World War were nearly all delayed war losses. The destruction of the country house brought about by its occupation and hard usage during the Second World War, while not as thoroughgoing as the dissolution of the monasteries in the sixteenth century, can only be paralleled in English cultural history by the architectural losses of the Reformation."[30]

At Great Glenham House, the 4th Earl of Cranbrook's country house in Suffolk, Caroline Seebohm writes, "One merry night the soldiers turned on all the bidets and bathtubs upstairs and everything flooded. The water seeped into a cornice over the drawing room, and water remained in this cornice throughout the war, so the whole of one wall suffered dry rot."[31] After a second wave of Yanks moved in in 1943, banisters were ripped away, the roof began to leak, damp and resultant rot started seeping into the Drawing Room, the floors were wrecked, and the parkland was ploughed. "We never thought we'd go back," said Lord Cranbrook. In the end they reduced the size of the house, sanded the floors, let out flats, and reduced a staff of six to a staff of one: classic postwar survival techniques.

The recorded "horror stories" of troop vandalism may be more exceptional than typical. But they are impressive nonetheless. At Marston Hall in Somerset, American troops apparently held jeep races up and down the shallow, cantilevered great double staircase, which collapsed as a result. A car knocked off the balustrade of Adam's bridge at Compton Verney in Warwickshire. "A favourite ploy," writes Robinson, "was to drive straight through a pair of closed iron gates at speed."[32] Canadian soldiers at Dunorlen Park in Kent cut the heads off all the garden statues. Other troops carved their names into James Paine's bridge at Brocket Hall—a fairly common way of signaling one's temporary presence at a historic monument, then as now. Americans stole the ormulu rosettes off the Adam door handles at Kedleston, and machine gunned the conservatories at Alton Towers. Italian prisoners of war ripped off the silk from the walls of Rufford in Nottinghamshire, and Free Czech refugees destroyed the mural decorations at Philip Sassoon's elegant Edwardian establishment at Port Lympne in Kent. At Langholme Lodge in Scotland (another property of the Duke of Buccleuch), the army washed down the hardwood floors as if they were decks of a ship before the arrival of each new contingent of troops. The resultant flooding and lack of airing led to rampant dry rot, to the point where it was impossible to save the house. At Blickling, already a prized National Trust property, RAF airmen crashed in the locked door of Bonomi's 18th-century mausoleum in the park in May 1942, and broke open the tomb of the Countess of Buckingham in search of jewels. Throughout his tours on behalf of the Trust, Lees-Milne kept coming across instances—at Culverthorpe, in Lincolnshire; at Hauduroy and Netley Park in Surrey; at Coleshill in Berkshire—of walls wilfully smashed, mirrors cracked, windows broken, wallpapers and historic color schemes painted over. Visiting Lady Dunsany's Slebech Park in Wales, Lees-Milne wrote in his diary for April 13, 1945, "A fresh unit of troops was trying to clean up the appalling mess left by the last. Since January water has been allowed to seep from burst pipes through the ceilings and down the walls. Most of the stair balusters have disappeared. Mahogany doors have been kicked to pieces. Floor boards are ripped up. All rooms mottled with and stinking of damp. I imagine dry rot has set in everywhere."[33]

In addition, gardens, parks, and pastures—two million acres of them, by June 1940—were ploughed up under national orders to raise edible crops, or destroyed for encampments, airfields, tank training, or artillery practice. Driveways were chewn up by heavy trucks and tanks, lawns and gardens abandoned to jungle-like growth. At Wentworth Woodhouse in Yorkshire, Earl Fitzwilliam and his family stayed on in residence, happy at first to entertain the troops. But within a year they grew dismayed at the destruction their new guests were causing. Lord Fitzwilliam complained about "the army creating havoc within and open cast mining encroaching from without." The enforced destruction of

Humphry Repton's parkland by open-pit coal mining, together with the mess left of this gigantic house by army occupation, led the 8th Earl to move out and let most of the house for educational purposes.

Finally allowed, after the war, to return or have access to the long-occupied portions of their houses—those that remained standing—many owners came upon the kind of dispiriting sight that faced the new Duke of Bedford at Woburn Abbey in 1947. (See page 88.) In many cases, they were not permitted to return until several years after the war. Certain regiments, government offices, and even schools had grown accustomed to their new quarters, and put up a considerable fight when asked to leave. It took Major Allington until 1953 to get back Crichel Down. Southwick Park in Hampshire, and Trent Park near Barnet were lost (against the owners' protests) to compulsory purchase orders. The Royal Observatory decided it wanted Hinton Ampner in Hampshire, but Ralph Dutton put up such a fuss that they settled for Herstmonceaux Castle in Sussex instead.

My opening question—why were so many country houses torn down?—is easiest to answer for the years *after* World War II, when somewhere between 629 (Strong and Binney) and 1,000 (Robinson) were demolished. First, making good the damage of six years of often careless occupation could be a costly and major undertaking, rarely repaid by the government's inadequate War Damage Compensation. Secondly, no house—least of all very large houses centuries old, fragile in every part of their fabric—could last out six or more years without regular inspections, maintenance, and repair: roof gutters went uncleared, so roof timbers soaked and rotted, roofs began leaking and walls began rotting; ancient window frames went unpainted and uncaulked and broken frames unreplaced, with similar results; stonework flaked and crumbled, brickwork mortar turned to mush. It happens all the time. But now, for six years, there had been no one to notice and make repairs. Rigmaden Park in Westmoreland, cited by Robinson, is a classic example. The gutters had been neglected, the new roof was a wreck, dry rot had invaded the walls. The owners abandoned the house, which decayed into a crumbling shell in a jungle of undergrowth.

And now, trying to clean and clear a few rooms so that they might move in and begin to clear six or more years of deferred maintenance, country house owners found that the postwar government refused to let them. Building materials were rigorously rationed. Annual expense on 'non-strategic' construction was limited to £100 (then $400) a year, which would not begin to cover the broken window panes alone. On July 5, 1945, Lees-Milne wrote with some bitterness of the repair restrictions in the case of Aylsham Old Hall in Norfolk, a National Trust property: "The army have derequisitioned it, and given us £450 for dilapidations, out of which we are allowed to spend £100 if the work is undertaken before August 1st. After that date only £10 p.a. is allowed, which means that no one can possibly inhabit large houses after troops have been billetted in them for six years. It would be quite acceptable if the army, on clearing out, were allowed to reinstate what they had spoilt. As it stands the regulation is unfair and absurd."[34]

A few owners went ahead despite the restrictions. Some (like Ralph Dutton at Hinton

Ampner, who did his rebuilding by night) got away with it; others (Earl Peel at Hyning, the Duke of Bedford at Woburn Abbey) were severely fined for trying to repair their own houses in excess of the stringent cost limitations.

By 1945, in addition, under Attlee's postwar Labor government, both property taxes *and* death duties were set at all-time highs. Paralleling the experience of the First World War, houses that had lost both an owner and his heir in a relatively short period of time were once again faced with a double, nearly confiscatory burden of taxes. The most notorious case was that of the Duke of Devonshire, whose father had died in 1950, and whose elder brother, heir presumptive to the dukedom (who had married John F. Kennedy's sister), was killed in the war. That left Andrew Devonshire, the 11th and present duke, with a double tax bill of 80 percent (more than £12 million—$33.6 million—in the end), which took him seventeen years to settle. He did this by handing over to the government Hardwick Hall, selling nine major artworks, plus a great number of rare books and 64,000 acres of land. In 1981 he had to turn Chatsworth, the great remaining family house, over to a charitable trust, declaring that "no individual can own anything these days."

But not all country house owners had secondary mansions, museum-quality art collections, and surplus thousands of acres to sell, or to offer in lieu of tax bills. Even without the added blow of inheritance taxes, the cost of repairs and deferred maintenance—when the authorities permitted one to undertake them—was often more than their resources permitted. Rationing of any number of essential materials (including gas and electricity, petrol, food and clothing, as well as building materials) continued in Britain for much longer than in most of the "victorious" Allied countries. And by a continuing natural process of demographic dispersal to other occupations, the pool of estate and household workers necessary to maintain even the most modernized and efficient of great houses dried up to a puddle.

If one could sell, one sold: to what few nouveaux riches were still interested in great houses; to any school, seminary, convent, private hospital, nursing home, civic body, corporation, or government agency that could still make use of and pay for the conversion and upkeep costs on these oversized white elephants.

But in the hundreds of cases where one could not sell, there was nothing to do but tear down, or abandon to decay. As the National Trust declared in its 1951–52 Annual Report, "Buildings on which our greatest architects and sculptors and painters have lavished their genius, and which stand high among our country's achievement, are today literally falling down; their irreplaceable contents, brought together by successive generations, are being dispersed; their gardens are overgrown; and the surrounding parklands of which they form the central and essential feature are becoming derelict."[35]

CHAPTER FOUR

To the Rescue

The National Trust

THE NATIONAL TRUST—officially, the National Trust for Places of Historic Interest and Natural Beauty—was established in 1894 in order to save endangered open space in England from the inexorable spread of Victorian building developers and railroads; "to provide" (as one of its founders put it) "open-air sitting rooms for the poor."

Less than a century later, the National Trust had become the largest private landowner in the United Kingdom (there's a separate National Trust for Scotland), the nonprofit proprietor of huge stretches of land and protected coastline, and more than 200 once-private houses and gardens (about 110 of them sizeable country houses in England), almost all of them now open to the public.

At the beginning, in the National Trust's own words, "country houses were in need of no one's help. Supported by their estates, tended by many servants, still the principal source of rural employment and initiative, the country houses of England in 1895 were enjoying their heyday."[1] The Trust did acquire and begin to restore a small country house in Somerset in 1907 for £11,500, then the equivalent of $56,000. But they had to wait until 1920 before they found a tenant willing to complete the restoration and furnishing. The experience put them off acquiring any more big houses for a number of years. The great Elizabethan house of Montacute, also in Somerset, was put on the market in 1929, after having been owned by ten generations of the same family. As no one bid on it, it seemed doomed to demolition until the grandson of Thomas Cook (of the travel agency) bought it in 1931 and presented it, via the Society for the Protection of Ancient Buildings, to the National Trust—denuded, unfortunately, of furniture and paintings, which it took the Trust another thirty or forty years to acquire.

About the same time, a number of interested observers began drawing public attention to the large number of country houses that had been demolished since the end of World War I. They included valiant cultural conservatives like the writer and aesthete Osbert Sitwell; the historian G. M. Trevelyan; the architect Sir Clough William-Ellis; Christopher Hussey and John Cornforth at *Country Life* magazine; and Nancy Astor's good friend the Marquess of Lothian. For perhaps the first time, people began to articulate the notion that these houses, even in private hands, were an essential part of the nation's cultural heritage, and deserving of public support. The ideas of tax exemptions and other special considerations for their owners, in return for guaranteed public access, began to be proposed.

At the annual meeting of the National Trust in July 1934, Lord Lothian—an active Liberal politician, Ambassador to the United States during the early years of World War II—warned that "most of these [country houses] are now under sentence of death, and the axe which is destroying them is taxation, and especially that form of taxation known as death duties....I do not think it an exaggeration," he said, "that within a generation, hardly one of these historic houses, save perhaps a few near London, will be lived in by the families who created them. Yet it is these 400 or 500 families who have for 300 or 400 years guided the fortunes of the nation."[2]

He specifically begged the Trust to step in and save them, by becoming "a landlord on an ampler scale." When the heirs of great houses found themselves faced with impossibly high death duties—which had climbed in some cases as high as 80 percent—he proposed that the Treasury accept their houses as a settlement of the tax bill, along with their lands and contents. Income from their estates, he hoped, would serve to maintain them. The Treasury would then turn them over to the National Trust. This double transfer would spare former owners any future inheritance or property taxes on their gifts. In return, the Trust could allow the donors and their families to continue living in the houses they had given, and the public to visit them at specified times. "What matters is that these houses, except perhaps the most monumental, should be lived in by people who care for them and also are prepared to make them not merely private houses, but places of hospitality and converse."[3]

At the time most English country house owners resisted the loss of status and independence this property-transfer implied (as many still do), and the Treasury rejected the idea of "tax breaks for the rich" (as it still does). Not even all the members of the National Trust—there were 3,400 at the time—were sure they wanted to get into the stately home business. Some of the Trust's directors feared, correctly as it turned out, that the organization would be no better able than were many of their private owners to afford the upkeep of large, unendowed country houses, even if they came accompanied by extensive agricultural estates.

But in 1937 Parliament made Lord Lothian's idea feasible, by enabling the National

Trust to earn income from its properties; to accept from house donors additional property, cash, or securities (with no tax obligation on either side), which could serve as income-producing endowments; and to allow donors and their families to continue to live in their houses as tenants, at whatever rent the Trust chose to charge. Three years later, Lord Lothian (who was unmarried and childless) put his property where his mouth was, and bequeathed the National Trust Blickling Hall in Norfolk, one of his four ancestral homes, along with its contents, more than a hundred houses and cottages, and 4,700 acres of woodland; it became National Trust property in 1941. Badly worn and vandalized during the RAF's wartime occupation, Blickling finally opened to the public in 1947, still sadly underfurnished. Twenty visitors showed up on opening day, at a shilling a head.

By the end of World War II—a war that made the parlous state of these large, archaic houses all the more apparent—the Trust owned 23 country houses, including notable estates such as Wallington; West Wycombe Park; Cliveden, which Waldorf Astor gave with a £200,000 ($800,000) endowment; and Polesden Lacey in Surrey, part of an even more generous bequest from Margaret Greville, the wealthy society hostess.

By 1950, it owned 42. The first five years after the war, which were especially hard times for owners, had brought the National Trust—in some cases by bequests or gifts, in others after prolonged negotiations—the following properties: Brockhampton (the big house, stripped of its contents, is now leased to an insurance company); Charlecote Park near Stratford, the occasion of some of the Trust's most trying negotiations; Knole, still one of the most important National Trust houses; Lyme Park, which it leased from 1947 to 1994 to the city of Stockport; Attingham Park, used for forty years as an adult education center; Cotehele, the first house to come via the National Land Fund; Petworth House, most prized for its contents, and Stourhead, most prized for its gardens; and Ham House and Osterley Park near London, in the transfer of which local and national authorities also played a role.

As the houses kept coming in, James Lees-Milne, indefatigable secretary to the National Trust's Country Houses (later Historic Buildings) Committee, had to remind himself of his priorities. "I have to guard against the collector's acquisitiveness," he wrote in his diary for June 1, 1945. "It isn't always to the advantage of a property to be swallowed by our capacious, if benevolent maw."[4]

By the time of the Victoria and Albert exhibition of 1974–75, the National Trust held a total of 90 country houses, and had 463,000 dues-paying members. One of the Trust's most important acquisitions during these years was Hardwick Hall in Derbyshire, which the Duke of Devonshire was obliged to hand over in order to pay the inheritance tax bill he was presented on his father's death in 1950. During the postwar years, the National Trust also began accepting nationally important gardens, like Hidcote (1948), Bodnant (1949), and Sissinghurst (1967)[5], while allowing the donors to retain possession of the houses attached.

Behind the transfer to National Trust ownership of each of these houses and estates lies a different, often a fascinating story. Some are stories of largesse and generosity; others of

Blickling Hall, Norfolk.

bitterness and desperation; still others of self-serving duplicity. Fourteen of them have been told by Lees-Milne in his book *People and Places: Country House Donors and the National Trust*, published in 1992. As in the celebrated diaries he kept during the years when he was the National Trust's chief negotiator with potential country-house donors, Lees-Milne is astonishingly candid in his character sketches of the landed gentry of the time and his evaluations of their houses:

> The present owners are impoverished. They have one indoor servant. The house is incredibly shabby, dirty and primitive. The porch room ceiling fell when Norwich was bombed and the débris has been left on the tables and chairs.... The walled garden is an absolute wilderness. It is pathetic

how within three years country people, who are unable to travel, become blind to the squalor to which they have become reduced. In spite of the terrible *délabrement* among which they live, these ladies with their long Plantagenet pedigree, their courtesy and ease of manner, were enchanting.[6]

We found Attingham a scene of Russian tragedy. Lady Berwick was hollow-eyed and miserable. Once or twice I thought she was in tears. They are fast selling contents and clearing out of the house . . . They will withdraw into the small east wing. Lord Berwick was wheeled up to us in a chair. He is a shrunken, almost inhuman bundle incapable of moving hand or limb. He speaks lower and slower, and is most piteous.[7] [Lord Berwick died two weeks after Lees-Milne's visit, leaving his widow to confront the problems of probate, death duties, and the remaining clearances and sales.]

Lord Newton came to see me about Lyme Park (Cheshire). I have seldom met a man more beset by domestic tribulations and worries over what to do with a vast house. He looks and behaves like a dazed, elderly hare watching the pack of beagles close in. . . . Lord Newton is hopeless. The world is too much for him, and no wonder. He does not know what he can do, ought to do or wants to do. He just throws up his hands in despair. The only thing he is sure about is that his descendants will never want to live at Lyme after an unbroken residence of 600 years. I am already sure that he will not see out his ownership. . . . [Lady Newton] is as languid and as hopeless as her husband. Both said they would never be able to reconcile themselves to the new order after the war. They admitted that their day was done, and life as they had known it was gone for ever. How right they are, poor people.[8]

All of them seem hopelessly defeatist, anti-Government, anti-people, and anti-world.[9]

In his judgments of houses, Lees-Milne was adamantly opposed to anything bogus; he could spot at once fake-medieval timbers, or 19th-century chimneypieces pretending to be Jacobean. "The house is a hideous, pretentious, genteel, over-restored fake, just like its inhabitants. A horrible property. I hope it gets bombed." His committee turned down Hever Castle as "a gross fake," unworthy of the Trust.[10]

A founding member of the Georgian Group, he also tended to be repelled by anything too grossly Victorian, or too flashily Edwardian. "The Hall, once Elizabethan, was dreadfully altered about 1850 and is not suitable for the Trust." "A terrible, Victorian, yellow brick villa, and the property unworthy of us. We should never have accepted it." "A terrible house . . . 1862, haphazard, bulky, inelegant, and of no merit." "A hideous red brick edifice of 1869." "A really ugly dark-red brick villa of 1902." "[Cardiff] Castle proper is, inside and out, the most hideous building I have ever seen."[11]

In describing the protracted wrangling over Charlecote Park, he admits that his and his committee's misgivings were due as much to the Victorian fakery of it all as to their problems with the Bad Baronet. In 1945, the committee agreed to an exhibition of the house's "treasures," "so long as the public were not led into supposing that the nineteenth-century exhibits purported to be of historic interest or artistic merit." Writing some 45 years later, Lees-Milne admits that this intransigent anti-Victorianism would be out of fashion today. Even at the time, he made exceptions. Cliveden—although its interior "has very little distinction"—was, he concluded, "well worthy of the Trust." James de Rothschild's palace at Waddesdon—"an 1880 pastiche of a François Premier chateaux" (which came with an endowment so generous the Treasury grew suspicious, and wanted to tax it)—was, he

decided, "a better Cliveden...by no means contemptuous." He even found himself growing fond of Mrs. Greville's Polesden Lacey, decorated "in the expensive taste of an Edwardian millionairess."[12]

His five volumes of diaries provide glimpses into the private lives, wartime privations,
and outspoken opinions of Lees-Milne's own upper-class/aesthetic London set, as well as
those of the country aristocracy and gentry, many of them then eccentric, superannuated,
and in dire financial straits. During these years, he made endless trips about England, at
first by train and bicycle, then driving not always dependable National Trust cars, often
staying in ill-heated rooms and being offered inedible food. Looking over country houses
under the watchful eyes of their owners, he had to decide whether they (or their contents,
or their lands) would be appropriate for Trust ownership; and if so, how to persuade their
proud proprieters to part with them. During one eleven-day motoring trip he made with
Harold Nicolson and Vita Sackville-West in October 1947, they stopped at and
inspected—whether welcome or not—more than 40 country houses, in addition to
churches, cathedrals, and towns.

His diaries afford an invaluable reminder of what country houses were like in these early
days of the National Trust's involvement with their fate, when the glory years of private
ownership were obviously past; when some houses were indeed in falling-down condition;
when the government offered very little help; and when many resident owners were
bewildered by the present and afraid of the future.

In some cases, Lees-Milne simply voted no—or at least persuaded his committee to
do so:

> We walked through the gardens to Knebworth House. It is undeniably hideous. The old house was
> rebuilt by Bulwer Lytton in 1847, and if only Lord Lytton had not recently removed the gargoyles
> from the absurd turrets and the heraldic animals from the terrace, it would be a perfect specimen
> of a Disraelian patrician's Gothic mansion. The whole outside is stuccoed in a base way. The
> Jacobean grand staircase and the Presence Chamber upstairs are terribly shoddy....At present the
> Froebel Girls' College is installed in the house, which becomes them....I told [the heirs] what I
> had not dared tell Lord Lytton, that I thought it doubtful the committee would accept the house
> on its own merits . . .[13]
>
>   The house [Luton Hoo] is terrible, outside and in. Built by Adam in the 1760s for Lord Bute, it
> was burnt down in 1840 and rebuilt by Smirke. It was deliberately gutted in 1903 and reconstituted
> for the Wernhers by Mewes & Davis, architects of the Ritz Hotel. The outside walls are still more
> or less Adam, but in 1903 a top storey with a mansard roof was added. The roofline is very untidy,
> with odd chimneys and unsightly skylights. The interior, or as much as I could see of it, for it was
> boarded up to eye level, is opulent Edwardian and Frenchified. Walking down the cavernous base-
> ment passages is like being in a tube station.[14]

Looking back in politically corrected retrospect, some recent critics have found much
to criticize in the attitudes and arrangements of the early National Trust (and those of
James Lees-Milne in particular), particularly in regard to their dealings with country
houses and their donors.[15] Each family the Trust negotiated with tended to have different

Knebworth, Hertfordshire.

ideas concerning their house and its proper maintenance, the nature of their own continued tenancy and their involvement in estate management, just how much they were willing to part with and on what terms, and how much public access they were willing to
grant.

In each case, a separate and unique arrangement had to be made, involving the tax
authorities and (in the case of bequests) the Court of Chancery as well as the donor, his
heirs, agents, and attorneys. Negotiations could drag on for a decade. The Trust frequently

made use of the nonbinding device of a "Memorandum of Wishes" (to which both parties were morally, but not legally bound), in order to circumvent the statutes which hold that a donor may receive no tax breaks from a charitable donation if it involves a contracted benefit in return—for example, a rent-free tenancy in a house you have given away. Under the circumstances, some donors drafted Memoranda of Wishes that were unusually generous—to themselves. They might ask, as one did, for three generations of rent-free tenancy, and the right to keep the profits from timber on the estate. They might demand that the Trust pay the wages of eleven indoor servants, and the insurance and conservation costs on furniture they had kept for themselves. They might insist on sufficient funds from the Trust for a new house, living expenses, and the education of their children. They might press for a restricted number of open-to-the-public days—none on weekends, for example, or during the pheasant-shooting season. Some managed to obtain long lease-back privileges, total control over furnishing and decoration, and the right to run the house openings themselves. The more canny retained ownership of the contents of their houses, which left the National Trust at their mercy in subsequent negotiations.[16]

Conrad Rawnsley, a grandson of one of the three founders of the National Trust, turned bitterly against it in 1967, after being fired from his job as a fund-raiser. "Excessive donor privileges" was one line of his comprehensive and venomous attack. Paula Weideger, an American critic, picked up this line again in 1994. The very idea of family members being allowed to live rent-free in a property they have given away seemed to her unfair. She criticized Lees-Milne and his boss, Viscount Esher, for not being more tough-minded in coming to terms.

In her book *Gilding the Acorn: Behind the Facade of the National Trust*, Weideger implies that Sir John Carew Pole was cheating the Trust when he handed over Antony, his house in Cornwall, in 1961, by pretending to be poorer than he was. She criticizes his son today for allowing visitors to tour what is still his family house (it has no "private wing" to retire to) for only three afternoons a week, seven months a year. "Antony," Weideger declares, "belongs to the Nation."[17]

In point of fact, it does not. It belongs, thanks to an arrangement they have made with the Carew Poles, to the National Trust—a large, independent registered charity—which is a very different thing.

She seems irked that Lord Sackville is not obliged to open his private garden at Knole more often, because of a deal his uncle worked out in 1957. (The Sackvilles are annoyed that they have to open it at all.) And she appears morally outraged that West Wycombe Park is never open from September through March—a part of the arrangement the Dashwood family made with the Trust so that they could invite their friends in for shooting parties during pheasant season. "This was the National Trust's idea of a compromise," she writes. "West Wycombe would be open for a total of twenty-eight days between 1 May and 31 August."[18]

In fact, although most National Trust properties of its size and importance *are* open five days a week, six or seven months a year, West Wycombe Park was open to the public from

2:00 to 6:00 P.M. for 65 days during the summer of 1994, and the gardens for another 22 afternoons in April and May. But Weideger seems to believe that a £20-a-year member should have equal rights of access with family members, even if the latter have endowed the house generously, and are still paying a large part of the operating costs.[19]

This seems to me, when all the facts are in, to be a nonissue. The National Trust took on houses in order to preserve them and, when possible, to help families retain historic connections to their houses and land. Public access was part of the deal; but it was never, at the time, their highest priority. The National Trust's priorities have changed in recent years. But given the number of visitors its properties attract, the condition in which they are maintained, and the reasonably good relationships they are able to maintain with most resident-donor families, it seems petty to carp about bargain tenancies and limited hours of opening.

As Simon Jenkins wrote in a review of Lees-Milne's *People and Places*, "Each deal was fragile. In less sensitive hands, all these negotiations might have foundered. Without trust, owners would have despaired and handed their estates over to the auction houses, the ever-present vultures of the tale. Certainly they would have done that before ceding them to any agency of Whitehall. In return for winning tax relief from the Treasury, the National Trust took upon itself heavy obligations.... In return they could offer the owners only a tenancy, and the unquantifiable benefits of genteel treatment and continued association with the property. It is hard to imagine a relationship more vulnerable to bruised feelings, bloody-mindedness and eventual collapse."[20] On the other hand, as Robin Fedden bluntly put it in an earlier history of the National Trust, "Without such agreements, the houses could usually not have been preserved, but where they are in force time is a ready ally. Donors are mortal, circumstances change."[21] In other words, if a tenant-donor is acting troublesome, just wait a bit: he or she will soon die.

When, in 1945, James Lees-Milne was first shown around Kedleston—the greatest of the great Robert Adam houses—by the mother of the 2nd Viscount Scarscale, he wrote, "I am convinced that this wonderful house is a doomed anachronism." When the 4th Baron Sackville found himself forced to cede his huge and historic house to the National Trust, he was sure that "no one after Eddy" (his son and heir, who only outlived him by three years) "would be able to live at Knole."[22]

In fact, the Scarscale family was still living at Kedleston in 1996, as the Sackville family was living at Knole—with what feelings towards their National Trust landlords we shall learn in Chapter Ten. The Trust's Country House Program clearly enabled a great many houses and house owners to survive the decades of doom around World War II even better than its early leaders and donors foresaw.

The Beginnings of Government Assistance

Beyond the ultimate gesture of giving up one's house to the National Trust (if they would have it), what other recourse was there for the private owner of a great country house—

oversized, heavily taxed, and too expensive to maintain—in the grim years after World War II? Many owners saw demolition as the only way out, until demolition ceased to be an option. Others sought out institutions like hospitals and schools willing to take the prop-erties off their hands.

But what hope was there for owners who didn't *want* to give up their historic houses, either for demolition, for sale, or to the National Trust?

Up to now, the British government may have seemed the villain of this story—and from the point of view of many country house owners, it was. However patriotic a view one may try to take of it, it is difficult to regard the uncompensated damage done to so many occu-pied houses during the war as anything less than confiscation. The refusal to permit more than minimal, Band-Aid repairs for several years after the war seems in retrospect remark-ably shortsighted. Death duties—particularly in the rare but devastating cases of "double death duties," when the owner and the heir died in close succession—could indeed be considered, as they were often called, "ruinous."

The postwar Attlee government frightened both Conservative country landowners and the National Trust with its moves toward nationalization. At one point the Trust feared its own properties were in danger of being taken over. Among 1945–51 Labor policies per-ceived as unfriendly, or at least unhelpful, were its increase in the maximum death duties to 75 percent; its persistence in continuing open-pit mining by the now-nationalized coal industry on private estates; its extension of the "lifetime gift" period (by which an owner could avoid death duties by handing over property to an heir) from a minimum of three years before one's death to a minimum of five years; and new laws that made it difficult or unprofitable to sell off surplus land for development.

Harold Wilson, in 1964, mocked his opponent Lord Home as the "scion of an effete establishment," and warned that if the Conservatives won, "Britain will still be governed from the grouse moors." By the 1960s, being a 14th earl with a country estate had become a political liability. ("After all, I'm the fourteenth Mr. Wilson," his egalitarian adversary had pointed out.) In power again from 1964 to 1970, Labor introduced a capital gains tax of 30 percent, which, given the inflationary climate of the period, led to unprecedented tax bills and resultant land sales; extended the lifetime-handover provision to *seven* years before death; set up a Land Commission with unlimited power of compulsory acquisition; and began taxing "unearned" increments in the value of farmland which had been granted planning permission for development. All these policies cut into the profits (or closed the tax loopholes) of country landowners.

On the next Labor victory, in February 1974, the victors promised that the new Budget would be intentionally designed, in Denis Healy's phrase, to "squeeze the rich until the pips squeak." "It was the first time in the twentieth century," writes Madeleine Beard, "that landed society in England was faced with policies aimed specifically at the redistribution of wealth."[23] Healy, as Harold Wilson's first new Chancellor, was especially eager to end the provisions that enabled wealthy people to circumvent death duties—which were already being cynically dismissed by some observers as a "voluntary tax": that is, a tax paid only by those without attorneys and estate planners sufficiently astute to find them the requisite tax shelters.

The 1974–79 Labor government began by abolishing death duties altogether, and substituting a Capital Transfer Tax at the same rates (then 60–70 percent at the top), payable *every* time property was transferred. (Exceptions were made for charitable donations, small-scale gifts, and husband-wife transfers.) This effectively ended—at least until the next change of government—the tax-escape route of a "lifetime handover," and precipitated the forced sale of many country houses, their contents and estates.[24] The setting up of discretionary trusts based overseas in order to avoid British taxes was no longer legal—unless you, too, moved out of Britain, as a number of landowners did. Even domestic trusts were now subject to taxation at ten-year intervals. So although they still offered relief from the sudden shock of death duties, they no longer represented the secure tax shelter they once had.

A number of other new policies of the 1974–79 Labor government were regarded by the Country Landowners Association as inimical to their 25,000 members: for example, their assurance of long-term security-of-tenure to tenant farmers and their families, as well as to cottagers, which made it impossible for a landowner either to evict them or to raise their rents; and their denial of tax breaks on let farmland (which represented the great majority of landed estates) comparable to those granted on owner-occupied farms.

But the most explosive threat of all was the threat to impose a new annual tax not just on one's income, but on *all* of one's "wealth." This, it was feared—though it has become common in other European countries—would have had a disproportionate and disastrous effect on country house owners. Their houses, furniture, art works, and acres might seem to be worth millions in the eyes of government assessors. But even if agricultural estates sometimes turned a profit, historic houses very rarely generated actual income. In fact, unless and until they are sold, they are almost always more a liability than an asset. They cost far more to maintain than they could possibly ever "earn." The proposed Wealth Tax, it was argued, could be paid only by those with substantial and negotiable holdings off the estate, or by selling off one's property piece by piece.

This, of course, is what many families had been doing for generations, in order to pay death duties. If the new annual Wealth Tax became law, they might have to do it every year. In a House of Lords debate in June 1974, Kenneth Clark (who kept his own great art collection at Saltwood Castle in Kent) argued that "a wealth tax on the contents of English country houses, large and small, would in a very short time lead to their extinction." Lord Montagu famously insisted that historic houses (like his own highly commercial enterprise at Beaulieu) were "not wealth, but heirlooms over which we have a sacred trust."

In fact, the proposed Wealth Tax never *did* become law—although the idea has not entirely died out among Labor Party leaders. House owners leagued in the new Historic

Houses Association, which joined forces with the larger and older Country Landowners Association to help lobby the proposal to death, with the help of more than two million signatures gathered from visitors to their country houses during the summer of 1974.

. . .

But not all the news from Whitehall and Westminster was bad. First of all, in the intervals between Labor governments—barring the war years, when no one was able to help much—their Conservative successors of 1951–64 and 1970–74 often did what they could to undo the leveling, anti-landowner legislation Labor had installed. Even more important were some government policies—instituted by Socialist as well as Conservative governments—that had long-lasting and beneficial effects on the fate of the English country houses.

The most important precedent was set by Hugh Dalton, Attlee's Chancellor of the Exchequer, when he announced, soon after Labor's victory in 1945, his intention of making use of the government's ability to accept houses and land in payment of death duties, and then to transfer such properties to the National Trust when appropriate. "It seemed to me desirable and appropriate...," he was later to write, "to set aside money so that, by various means, the beauty of England, the famous historical houses, the wonderful stretches of still unspoiled open country, might be preserved for the future, and increasingly become part of the heritage of us all."[25]

To make this possible, he created in the 1946 budget a new "National Land Fund" with a capital of £50 million ($200 million), derived from the proceeds of the sale of war surplus stores. The purpose of the fund was to acquire for the nation land and buildings of historic importance as a war memorial "to the memory of our dead and the use of the living for ever." Grants of up to £200,000 ($800,000) from this fund could be transferred to the Treasury, to compensate it for the money it had to forego whenever a house was accepted instead of cash, in payment of taxes owed. The houses were then given to the National Trust. This new policy helped the Trust acquire fourteen of the 38 houses it took on during the next fifteen years, including such properties as Cotehele, Melford Hall, Croft Castle, Ickworth, Beningborough, Hardwick Hall, Shugborough, Dyrham Park, Saltram, and (in Wales) Penrhyn Castle. After 1953, similar tax-transfers were allowed for works or art and other historic contents, which were often worth a good deal more than the houses in which they were found.

By 1957, the capital of this fund had grown to more than £60 million ($168 million in U.S. terms: the pound had been devalued in 1949), but only a small amount had been disbursed. One of the reasons cited was the low valuations government assessors put on properties offered. Owners felt they could do better selling on the open market, even after paying tax on the proceeds.

The National Land Fund was not authorized to contribute toward the endowments the National Trust required, in order to ensure the maintenance of any house given to it. Instead, the government grudgingly agreed to make up any deficit the Trust incurred in running and repairing houses transferred to it by the Treasury. But subsequent govern-ments reneged on this agreement, which left the National Trust burdened with "gifts" of great houses it could not afford to keep up. In time, the Trust refused to accept any more houses, whether from private owners directly or through National Land Fund grants to the Treasury, unless they came adequately endowed. The impasse was dramatized by the situa-tion of Heveningham Hall, a large and important 18th-century house in Suffolk which the owners gave up to pay a £300,000 ($600,000) tax bill. Although the National Trust agreed to manage Heveningham for the government, they refused to accept it unendowed, and it was put back up for sale in 1981.

However good Hugh Dalton's intentions may have been, the National Land Fund was always at the mercy of H.M. Treasury, which seemed loath to use public moneys to acquire private properties, however historic. (Parliament had no say in how this money was to be spent, since the Fund's assets had not come from "voted" income sources.) In 1957, Peter Thorneycroft, the Conservative Chancellor of the Exchequer, declared the entire fund to be simply a part of the Treasury's assets, and at a pen-stroke reduced its working capital to £10 million ($28 million)—an action that many blamed for the government's inability (or refusal) to buy Mentmore Towers the following year. This is often cited as evidence that the Conservative Party is no more to be trusted with the long-term welfare of England's country houses than the Labor Party—perhaps less, in view of Labor's creation of the Land Fund, the Gowers Committee, and "conditional exemption."

· · ·

On December 10, 1948, Sir Stafford Cripps, the Labor Chancellor of the Exchequer, appointed a committee "to consider and report what general arrangements might be made by the Government for the preservation, maintenance and use of houses of outstanding historic or architectural interest which might otherwise not be preserved, including, where desirable, the preservation of a house and its contents as a unity." In 1950, after 26 meetings, nineteen visits to country houses, interviews with eighteen private owners and the representatives of 23 groups, the committee submitted its findings and conclusions in an 80-page report. The chairman was Sir Ernest Gowers, best known as the author of *Plain Words* (a guide to the avoidance of bureaucratese) and the editor of *Fowler's Modern English.*

The first portion of the report stated, with a sober, conservative eloquence one can probably attribute to Gowers, the major reasons—aesthetic, historical, educational, eco-nomic, pragmatic, political, and moral—for preserving the country houses in question: "They are a constant reminder of that grace and dignity which gave place a century or more ago to the ugly and squalid sprawl of our industrial towns and the mean and haphaz-ard growth of many of our villages. Their presence is an encouragement to the recreation of beauty where it long seemed to have been lost.... In short, our concern is to see how we can best save something of a great national heritage, an embodiment of our history and traditions, and a monument to the creative genius of our ancestors and the graceful serenity of their civilisation."[26] Adding up the combined threats of destructively high levels of income and estate tax, the impossibility of finding adequate staff, the damage done during the war, and the soaring costs of repairs and maintenance, the report concluded that "we are faced with a disaster comparable only to that which the country suffered by the Dissolution of the Monasteries in the 16th century.... Sooner or later the house becomes decrepit and the garden runs wild; the park timber is cut down and the beauty of the setting destroyed. Eventually the house itself is sold (if a purchaser can be found) and it may either be put to a use that ruins its remaining features of interest, or broken up for the sake of the lead, timber and fittings of value it contains. "[27]

The report then proceeded to analyze the weaknesses of the existing situation in terms of government support, and concluded with a number of carefully reasoned recommendations. These included:

1. The establishment of Historic Buildings Councils, one for England and Wales and another for Scotland, appointed by and responsible to the Chancellor of the Exchequer, with power to list designated houses and contents as "historic" (the actual inventorying of historic buildings and monuments had begun in 1947); to make grants or loans for their repair or upkeep; and to buy or hold houses when necessary until new owners could be found.

2. The offering of relief from death duties on designated houses, listed contents, and amenity lands, as long as they remain unsold. This relief, the committee proposed, should also apply to any property left in care of trustees for the purpose of maintaining a historic house or its contents.

3. The offering of income tax relief on approved, owner-paid repairs and maintenance on designated houses and their contents. "No injunction can stay the course of decay," the committee argued, "and no compulsory order can force the owner of a house to spend money that perhaps he has not got." The case for what might otherwise seem inequitable tax relief to a favored group was stated almost syllogistically:

   That it is in the public interest for houses of outstanding architectural or historic interest to be preserved is implicit in our terms of reference. That the owner of the house is almost always the best person to preserve it was the unanimous opinion of our witnesses, and is our own firm conviction. That taxation is the chief cause of his being unable to do so is notorious. . . . What from one point of view may be described as making contributions out of public moneys to the living expenses of individual citizens might from another be called making reasonable provision out of public moneys to ensure that a national asset shall be preserved in the most appropriate way.[28]

4. If financial aid is given, whether by grant, loan, or tax relief, the house should normally be be shown to the public under appropriate circumstances.

• • •

The Gowers Committee's recommendations for tax credits and exemptions for what was perceived as a "privileged" (and largely Conservative) class of owners were anathema to many Labor politicians then in power—although the committee had tried to anticipate such objections. It was not until the Tories were returned to power in 1951 that a draft bill was introduced, incorporating some but not all of the Gowers proposals. After two years of acrimonious, class-oriented debate, the House of Commons passed the Historic Buildings and Monuments Act in October 1953.

One of its primary concessions was a provision for essential repair grants to listed build-ings. Three Historic Buildings Councils (HBCs) were established—one for England, one for Scotland, and one for Wales—which were enabled to make grants to owners of listed properties for essential repairs, up to the limit of whatever annual allocation they obtained from the Treasury. In 1953–54 the HBC for England made 87 individual grants for build-ings of all sorts, totalling £265,000 ($742,000). By 1975, its annual grant allocation had reached £1.6 million ($3.55 million).

At the start, it was presumed that the bulk of these sums—in light of the special focus of the Gowers Report, and of subsequent discussions in parliament—would be devoted to country houses in need. But the Historic Building Councils were set up to make repair grants for all sorts of buildings: historic churches and cathedrals; old town halls, railway stations, theaters, and town houses in London and other cities; historic barns, windmills, lighthouses, etc.

Throughout the lifetime of the HBCs, the majority of repair grants were for less than £10,000 (about $28,000); but taking into account the inflation in repair costs to historic buildings, which have increased about 2000 percent in 40 years, this was sometimes enough in early days to repair a rotting roof and preserve a house from decay. Antony Jarvis believes that Doddington Hall, his family's fine Elizabethan house in Lincolnshire, was saved from collapse by one of the HBC's earliest grants. At the time, £12,000 ($33,600) covered three-quarters of the cost of repairing the leaking roof and downpipes, the collapsing foundations and chimneys, the eroded window frames. "What now seem quite small grants," wrote John Cornforth in 1974, "were often equally crucial in enabling a family to battle on."[29]

In its first twenty years (1953–73), the English HBC had made more than 400 grants to country houses—National Trust, privately occupied, and institutional—totalling more than £3 million (about $8 million). These included major contributions for repairs at Knole (which received a total of £400,000, or more than a million dollars, in grant aid), Ragley Hall, Castle Howard, Lyme Park, and Wardour Castle. Most of the houses that were transferred to the National Trust during the 1950s and 1960s came with HBC repair grants, which allowed them to be put in shape before they were opened to the public.

Some country house owners refused to apply for repair grants, however dire their need. "My family has *never* requested a grant," I have been firmly told by several owners. For many, it was a matter of principle. Either they did not want their affairs looked into—a kind of "means test" was obligatory—and their activities regulated by government officials; or they were too proud of their station and independence to ask for state aid.

Others were unwilling to open their houses to the public, which the acceptance of a repair grant would have entailed. Still others could not come up with their share of the costs—particularly as the standard of repair required on listed buildings grew more and more stringent. (Although there were a few generous exceptions, HBC grants typically covered 35–50 percent of repair costs, and were paid only after the work was completed.) However helpful or even essential these grants may have been for basic repairs, they were never given for "improvements" (e.g., rewiring, central heating); as a contribution toward regular maintenance costs; or for the rehabilitation of private living quarters.

Some owners regarded the HBC inspectors and bureaucrats as alien and unsympathetic, as some owners regard their English Heritage counterparts today. Requests for even small amounts of aid, they complained, could take years, and require repeated submissions and site visits before they were considered.

. . .

As early as 1928, conservation advocates had proposed making a list of the nation's most precious country houses, those that should be preserved at any cost. Even before the National Trust was empowered to institute its "Country House Scheme" in 1937, James Lees-Milne had drawn up a list of 250.

The Town and Country Planning Act of 1932 enabled local authorities to prevent the demolition of "any building of special architectural or historical interest" without their consent, but little use was made of this provision for the next 30 years. Statutory listing of such buildings was introduced through regional surveys that began very slowly in 1945, to provide guidelines for local authorities in the exercise of this power. A methodical survey of every region in Britain was carried out over the next 40 years, in which buildings deemed of special historical importance were listed—according to the current, slightly revised categories—either Grade I (which today represents the top 1–2 percent of listed buildings), Grade II*, or "two-star" (the next 5 or 6 percent), or Grade II (all the rest)—a total that has now grown, by way of extensive resurveys in 1986–89 and thereafter, to more than 500,000 individual buildings.[30] A provision was added in 1947 which obliged owners to give two months' notice before proceeding to alter or tear down a listed building, in order to give local authorities a chance to issue a Preservation Order if they wished to do so. But even with these new powers, local authorities rarely intervened. It was not until teeth were added to this policy by subsequent Planning Acts in 1968 and 1971 that demolition of listed buildings effectively came to a halt.

After 1968, the owner of any listed building had to obtain written consent—from the local authority for Grade II and II*, from the national authorities for Grade I—not only to demolish it, but even to alter or extend it.[31] Under constant prodding from heritage lobbyists, amenity groups, and local ad hoc pressure groups, local and national authorities have, since the early 1970s, made it next to impossible to tear down a listed country house. Even alterations or extensions to buildings in the two top categories—which include several hundred surviving country houses—are subject to prolonged and sometimes futile attempts to obtain permission from local and national authorities.

So the somber roll call of country house demolitions, played over and over in the opening hall of the 1974 V&A exhibition, has come to a halt. But there is still no way to assure that those that remain will remain intact and in use. They may still be destroyed by clumsy conversions, or abandoned and left to decay.

· · ·

Along with the more painful provisions of the Finance Act of 1975 came what is now known as "conditional exemption." For the first time, so-called heritage properties could be exempt from taxation altogether, on being passed from one owner to another. (Officially, the taxes are not waived but deferred, against the eventuality of a possible future sale.) The properties exempted include not only houses judged historic, but also "any object which in the opinion of the Treasury is historically associated with such a building," and the land which "adjoins such a building and which in the opinion of the Treasury is essential for the protection of the character and amenities of the building." Other provisions of the 1975 act, achieved only after persistent lobbying and debate, offered further reliefs to the owners of "heritage" properties in Britain.

William Proby, then deputy president of the Historic Houses Association, wrote in 1989, "It is difficult to overestimate the importance of those reliefs ... they represented an acceptance by government (and a Labour government at that) that country houses had an important part to play in the cultural life of the nation, and that their survival should be actively encouraged. It therefore changed fundamentally the political climate towards country houses."[32]

The basic conditions attached to conditional exemption were three. First, public access (under terms acceptable to the government) had to be granted to any property so exempted. Houses and gardens had to be opened for a specified number of days a year, which may be anywhere from 30 to 150. Exempted paintings and furniture had to be visible to the public. Rare books, documents, and drawings had at least to be viewable on request. Secondly, all exempted property had to be kept preserved and in good repair, with its historic character maintained. And thirdly, if and when any exempted property was sold, the government would not only impose capital gains tax on any profit involved, but also have the right to "claw back" any transfer or inheritance tax the owner had been forgiven in the first place.

· · ·

In order to encourage the recovery of agriculture after the war, the Labor government instituted a series of policies to help farmers. These included income tax rebates on farm improvements, relief from capital gains tax whenever profits from the sale of development land were reinvested in agriculture, and death duty reductions on agricultural land. These policies, or others like them, have generally been continued by governments of both parties ever since. Some country house owners have been able to benefit from this fact by getting more "actively" involved in farming—at least temporarily, as a tax shelter—than they might otherwise have done.

Another important piece of Labor legislation, dating from 1976, enabled the setting up of "Maintenance Funds," in order to protect estates from the possible ravages of Capital Transfer Tax at the time of a death. An estate liable to this tax at the highest rate could have found itself wiped out, and obliged to sell off virtually everything. In order to prevent this, the new law enabled all or part of the estate to be transferred *free of tax* to a Maintenance Fund, even though the fund would still have to pay normal income and capital gains taxes thereafter. The estate could still be held liable for the original tax if strict conditions regarding the use of such funds were not met.

·   ·   ·

A last, indeed an ultimate way in which the British government came to the aid of endangered country houses in the years after World War II was to become itself their legal owner and protector. In addition to the houses it accepted in place of taxes and then passed over to the National Trust, the government now owns a few on its own, under the aegis of The Historic Buildings and Monuments Commission for England—a statutory but independent authority now known as "English Heritage" established in 1983, which took over functions previously carried out by the Department of the Environment or the Ministry of Works.

Most of the 400 "historic properties" administered by English Heritage today are in ruins—prehistoric ruins (like Stonehenge—its most popular site), Roman ruins, ruined castles, ruined abbeys. But for a variety of reasons too complicated to explain, the national government also ended up the proprietor of a number of intact country houses. These include Osborne House, Victoria and Albert's little getaway place on the Isle of Wight; Audley End, a historic 17th-century house in Essex, once much larger than it is today; Lord Burlington's perfect Palladian casino called Chiswick House, now surrounded by west London traffic; Robert Adam's Kenwood House in north London (which has its own Vermeer), a gift of the Guinness brewing family; Marble Hill House in Twickenham; Brodsworth House in Yorkshire, a Victorian period-piece first opened to the public in 1995; and a handful of others, dating from 1570 to 1815.

One reason the national government owns so few historic houses itself, compared to many other European countries (royal palaces are a different story), is that, by the terms of the 1913 Ancient Monument Act, which have never been revoked or superseded, neither national nor local authorities can become the "guardians" of any inhabited building. Once they *do* become official guardians, the building cannot be resold, which means it can never be lived in again. Hence the Department of the Environment's unwillingness, in 1980, to take permanent control of Heveningham Hall, when the National Trust turned it down. "Once the National Trust's country house scheme got under way in the late 1930s," wrote John Cornforth, "this presented a more adaptable solution to the problem of country houses [than government acquisition], and, in its turn, it explains why the system of Treasury transfers through the Land Fund was developed in the 1950s."[33]

In addition to the National Trust and the national government, civic and regional councils bought or accepted a number of surplus country houses for use as museums, schools, or community centers. By 1974, Birmingham, Leeds, Barnsley, Halifax, Manchester, Scunthorpe, Bristol, Swindon, Ipswich, Chorley, and Bolton had acquired valuable properties and parklands in this way—many of them estates that had lost their appeal to landowners, as they saw their grand houses gradually engulfed by suburban or industrial sprawl.

A number of other local councils lease unendowed (or underendowed) country houses from the National Trust, which they then repair and maintain as civic amenities, often for their precious open space or earning potential. Unloading Lyme Park on the Stockport Borough Council was, James Lees-Milne decided in 1947, the perfect way to dispose of a house that came to the National Trust with no furnishings and no endowment. (In the end Stockport gave up, and the Trust took Lyme Park back in its care in 1994.) Tatton Park in the same county is also owned by the National Trust, but financed and managed by the Cheshire County Council. It is immensely popular with local tourists—150,000 or more people each year visit either the house, the farm, or the Old Hall. Shugborough in Staffordshire, managed by that county's council for the Trust, is even more popular, although the attractions of its gardens, parks, farm, and special events outweigh those of the house.

The Stately Home Industry Begins

After the National Trust and certain limited forms of government assistance, the third (and most highly publicized) modern means for "saving" an archaic, no longer self-supporting country house has been for the owner to turn it into an tourist attraction, by opening it to the public for a fee—originally half a crown, or about fifty cents as the pound was then valued—at designated times and seasons. This has become such a commonplace of British day-tripping, such a staple of British holidays in the country and the circuit of foreign tourists, that it is sometimes hard to realize that the whole business only began—as a business—in 1949.

Of course, great country houses were open to visitors long before 1949. As far back as the time of Henry VIII and Elizabeth I—the latter a fairly active country house tourist herself—most royal palaces had people on the staff whose job was to escort distinguished visitors around, for a fee. Accounts of foreign travelers indicate that the same thing was true of the great new houses of the sovereigns' chief courtiers. Later in the 17th century, people like the diarist John Evelyn began visiting country houses in order to view their collections of paintings, carvings, and other curiosities. As early as 1710, the first Duchess of Marlborough complained about the large number of strangers wandering around Blenheim Palace before it was even finished. Memoirs, diaries, collections of letters, and travel guides published in the 18th and 19th centuries are filled with anecdotes of the author's descent on some noble lord's country seat, where his (often her) party was shown about the grander rooms by the housekeeper, and invited to admire the works of art and the gardens. It was on such a visit to "Pemberley," in Derbyshire, that Elizabeth Bennett and her relations (in *Pride and Prejudice*) accidentally bumped into its formidable owner.

One of the more engaging early English travel-diarists is Celia Fiennes—niece, cousin, and aunt to three subsequent Lords Saye and Sele. An unmarried lady who stayed either in inns or with genteel relatives scattered about England, she was an indefatigable traveler in the 1690s and early 1700s, when she made dogged, detailed, room-by-room accounts of every country house she stopped at.

Celia Fiennes had no interest in wooden Tudor houses, which she found depressingly old-fashioned. She was delighted to see so many brand-new houses going up all over the island; her jaunts about England coincided with the early years of the country-house-building boom in the generation after 1688.

Other than praising the latest fashion, Celia Fiennes has no sense of style or period, but contents herself with a kind of verbal floor plan, counting steps and windowpanes, noting "good paintings" (but never the painters), paneling and tapestries, climbing up to the "cupelows" to look at the "vistos," and taking special pleasure in fountains and gardens and parks:

> . . . the hall [at Burghley] is a noble roome painted finely, the walls with armory and Battles, its lofty and paved with black and white marble; you go thence into parlours dineing rooms drawing roomes and bed-chambers, one leading out of another at least 20 that were very large and lofty and most delicately painted on the top, each roome differing, very fine Carving in the mantle-pieces and very fine paint in pictures, but they were all without Garments or very little, that was the only fault, the immodesty of the Pictures especially in my Lords appartment . . . the great variety of the roomes and fine works tooke me up 2 full hours to go from on roome to another over the house . . .[34]

Her diaries include naive walk-through inventories of the rooms and gardens at twenty other country houses, including her own family home at Broughton, as well as passing references to a great many others she rode by or walked around. She managed to look through the Earl of Chesterfield's house at Bretby Hall—including the bridal bedchamber—while a wedding reception was in progress, and was offered a glass of wine in the garden room. A modern tourist would be in heaven.

Arthur Young and Daniel Defoe wrote extensive topographical surveys of Great Britain in the early 18th century, based on their own travels, in which a good many country houses are described. Like Celia Fiennes, Defoe was impressed by Burghley, but more for its collection of Italian masters ("of more value than the house itself, and all the park belonging to it") than for its naughty frescoes or "blew velvet beds with gold fringe."[35] Private travelers such as James Boswell and Samuel Johnson, Fanny Burney, and Augustus Hare were sometimes invited guests at the houses they described; but they often simply dropped in to have a look around. An indefatigable and unusually knowledgeable 18th-century country-house tourist was Elizabeth Percy, first Duchess of Northumberland, whose detailed and critical accounts of the houses she visited have proven a boon to architectural historians.

As early as 1726, the practice of country house visiting had become so common that specialized guidebooks to individual houses and their collections were being printed, in some cases by the owners themselves. In *A Country House Index* (1979), John Harris lists nearly 140 British country house guides and catalogues of their art collections published between 1726 and 1880, at least 32 of them available before 1800.

In her own history-guidebook of Chatsworth and in the visitors' brochure, which she also wrote, the present Duchess of Devonshire points out that "The house has been open for people to see round ever since it was built." The Howards at Castle Howard make the same claim. "In the 18th Century the family lived mostly in London," the duchess adds, "but the housekeeper had instructions to show people round, and when the Fifth Duke and Georgianna were here there were 'open days' when dinner was even provided." At Kedleston, Lord Curzon built an inn "for the accommodation of such strangers as curiosity may lead to view his residence."[36]

Not all 18th-century owners were so hospitable, nor all 18th-century visitors so well received. "I am tormented all day and every day by people who come to see my house, and have no enjoyment of it in summer," Horace Walpole wrote from Strawberry Hill to his friend Horace Mann in 1783. "Coaches full of travellers of all denominations," wrote Lord Lyttleton, of Cobham Hall in Kent, in 1778, "and troups of holiday neighbours, are hourly chasing me from my apartment and strolling about the environs keeping me prisoner in it; the lord of the place can never call it his during the finest part of the year." In 1785, John Byng, son of Viscount Torrington, found himself denied entrance at Wroxton, the seat of the Earl of Guilford. "Very rude this and unlike an old courtly earl!" he wrote. "Let him either forbid the place entirely or else fix a day of admission; but for shame don't refuse travellers who have come twenty miles out of their way for a sight of the place." One woman on the road in 1772—an MP's wife—was outraged that the Earl and Countess of Buckingham pretended not to be in when she dropped by unannounced, and kept scurrying from room to room to avoid her.[37]

Many house owners had stopped the gracious practice of keeping open house by the early 19th century—perhaps because the number of visitors was becoming a burden, as transportation grew more convenient. Others cited acts of vandalism and theft. But the hospitality at Chatsworth continued unabated: "The Duke of Devonshire allows all persons whatsoever to see the mansion and grounds every day in the year, Sundays not excepted, from 10 in the morning till 5 in the afternoon. The humblest individual is not only shown the whole, but the Duke has expressly ordered the waterworks to be played for everyone without exception. This is acting in the true spirit of great wealth and enlightened liberality."[38] (In fact, the gardeners at Chatsworth often demanded extra tips for turning on the fountains.)

By 1840, an inexpensive coach took tourists direct from London to the gates of Penshurst Place—a three hour trip—three times a week. When, in the summer of 1849, a railway line was extended from Derby to a village three miles from Chatsworth, the house was visited by 80,000 people—which would be an impressive number for a country house open to the public today. The first organized tour brought a group of 500 people up on the new train line that June, where coaches and carriages were lined up to drive them (at sixpence a head) the three miles from train station to house. There they were taken about free, in groups of twenty—and the servants were apparently forbidden to accept tips. "I dare say they will bring down the floors some day," the 8th Duke of Devonshire is reported to have said. "But I don't see how we can keep them out." With luck, visitors to Chatsworth might even spot the duke.[39]

Hampton Court Palace, opened free to the public by Queen Victoria in 1838—without even a housekeeper to tip—was attracting 122,000 visitors a year by 1840, and more than 350,000 in 1851 and 1862, the two exhibition years. As a royal palace in a huge and popular riverside park near to London, Hampton Court was a special case. It was a place that all classes of Englishmen had come to regard as "public property," just as they regarded historic churches and cathedrals. But as Adrian Tinniswood points out, its immense popularity with working class visitors from London "could be said to have inaugurated a new era of popular tourism," in which more and more people of all social orders took it as their right to walk through great houses and gardens.[40]

The difference between country house visiting before and after 1949 is that the earlier custom was the result of noblesse oblige, and to some degree of a great landowner's desire to maintain "the county interest." The modern form is at heart a business, designed (originally) to help pay the bills or taxes at unprofitable inherited estates, and to raise money for the upkeep and repair of oversized and old-fashioned houses. Eighteenth-century visitors were expected to tip the housekeeper who showed them around, a sum in most cases more than equivalent to today's admission charge. Horace Walpole grumbled that his housekeeper was growing rich at his expense, showing the visitors who so annoyed him around Strawberry Hill. Before railroads allowed the middle and working classes to travel more freely, most country house visitors were people of relative leisure and affluence themselves, who traveled with a post chaise and servant. At a few over-visited houses, advance tickets—although free—began to be required. A few that had been open—Haddon, Kedleston, Harewood, Woburn—closed in the early 20th century, under the pressure of increasing numbers. In 1908, the 9th Duke of Devonshire *did* begin charging for admission to Chatsworth, but the proceeds went to a local hospital—as did the fees paid to see the picture collection at Corsham Court in Wiltshire. By the 1920s, a number of great houses were charging sixpence or a shilling per visit. Even so, according to Tinniswood, "Profit was not the dominant motive behind this widespread adoption of admission charges and regularized visiting hours.... It was the desire to maintain social control in the face of a rapidly expanding demand . . ."[41] Before 1949, the landed gentry and aristocracy of England were not expected to need public assistance in order to maintain their inherited estates and ways of life—let alone do anything so crass as to collect money from visitors for their own benefit.

This was all changed by the situation many country house owners found themselves in after World War II. In 1945, the Marchioness of Exeter, chatelaine of Burghley, opened her house to the public, and advised her fellow war-damaged owners to do the same. But she still described it more as a matter of aristocratic duty and state-assisted survival than as a profit-making enterprise: "I am sure that none of the 'privileged' will object to the increasing demands made upon their time and what is left of their income. All they ask is that they may be permitted to continue to serve and that the scales shall not be too unfairly weighed against them.... owners, impoverished by taxation and increased costs as they are, desire to open their houses again to the public ... if the country as a whole wishes its treasure houses to be maintained by their traditional and rightful guardians, not as museums but as homes with a soul and atmosphere—the result of loving care given by successive generations—the necessary assistance must be forthcoming somehow."[42] Both the Duke of Marlborough at Blenheim and the Duke of Devonshire at Chatsworth opened their houses to paying visitors in 1950. By 1951–52, guides to country houses open to the public were able to list and describe 104 houses—48 of them still privately owned; 34 in the hands of the National Trust; the others the property of cities, government bodies, or other institutions.

·   ·   ·

By far the best known stately home entrepreneurs, the founding fathers of a branch of the British tourist industry that now attracts millions of paying customers each year, were three peers who went on to become celebrity showmen, not unlike theatrical producers: the 6th Marquess of Bath, who opened Longleat in Wiltshire in 1949; the 3rd Baron Montagu of Beaulieu, who opened the Palace House at Beaulieu (Hampshire) in 1952; and the 13th Duke of Bedford, who opened Woburn Abbey in Bedfordshire in 1955.

All three attracted as much attention for their novel, highly personal forms of showmanship and self-promotion as for their houses. Beaulieu is really a fairly minor house, most of it built to designs by the Victorian architect Sir Arthur Blomfield between 1871 and 1874. It contains interesting family portraits and memorabilia, but no art or furniture of major museum quality. The exterior of Longleat is historic and important, its parkland setting splendid, and some of its contents impressive. But most of its state rooms were radically rebuilt in a fussy, "Italianate" style by the fashionable interior decorator J. D. Crace in the 1870s and 1880s. Of the three, only Woburn Abbey can claim high marks for architecture, landscape, and collections—and a large portion of it was torn down in 1949–50.

There is no question that it was the salesmanship, the secondary tourist attractions, and the attention-getting stunts of these three pioneers, even more than their Titians and Canalettos, their monastic gatehouses and Elizabethan great halls, their parks designed by Capability Brown or Humphry Repton that laid the foundation for the "stately home industry."

·   ·   ·

In 1946 Henry Thynne, the 6th Marquess of Bath, born in 1905, inherited both his title and Longleat—the first important building of the English Renaissance, designed by Robert Smythson and built between 1541 and 1580. Educated at Harrow, he had served as a Conservative MP for Somerset (long a part of the family's political domain) and a member of the Prince of Wales's council in the 1930s. He was a major in the Royal Wiltshire Yeomanry during World War II, during which he was wounded at El Alamein. *His* father, the 5th Marquess, had been Undersecretary of State for India, and a regional grandee of considerable power: Lord Lieutenant of Somerset for 46 years, chairman of the Wiltshire quarter sessions for 33, and chairman of the Wiltshire County Council for 41. He owned 55,000 acres of land, had twelve church livings at his disposal, and, before World War I, employed eight gamekeepers and 40 house servants. By the end of his life, however, the 5th Marquess was living alone in Longleat with a butler and a housekeeper—and 300 girls from the Royal School near Bath, who had moved in for the duration of World War II, and didn't move out until 1947.

His son, taking over the house just afterwards, and faced with a heavy burden in death duties and restoration, decided to sell off some 45,000 acres of land, and convert Longleat into a tourist attraction. As David Cannadine notes:

> . . . the idea of turning the family mansion itself into a money-making venture, by opening it to a mass public, was the most significant innovation of the period. The pioneer was the sixth Marquess of Bath, who inherited the dilapidated, 118-roomed mansion of Longleat, and £700,000 worth of death duties in 1946. He was obliged to sell off much of the land, and in April 1949 opened the house to the public as the showplace of the West Country, the first stately home to admit visitors on a regular paying basis. Within a year, 135,000 people had paid to come to look at Lord Bath's home and heirlooms, and by the mid-fifties, the figure was topping a quarter of a million. Soon, Longleat was open every day except Christmas, and Lord Bath was employing as large a staff as his ancestors had known in the nineteenth century—albeit for rather different purposes.[43]

The 5th Marquess had opened Cheddar Caves on family land fifteen miles away in Somerset as a tourist attraction in the 1920s, which gave his son the idea of opening Longleat on a similar basis. Cheddar Caves attracted 500,000 visitors a year—at a shilling a head, for a turnover of £25,000 ($100,000). "I realised I could never live at Longleat unless I did something about it. I had to pay the death duties when my father died, and then I had the brainwave—why not open it like Cheddar Caves to the public . . . ?"[44] He announced his plans at a press conference, and hoped to get 50,000 people to go through the house that first summer at two shillings sixpence a head. Greeting the first-comers on the front steps himself, he ended up attracting 138,000. In 1964, with a series of Sunday pop concerts, he increased the number to 150,000. In 1966, in partnership with circus-owner Jimmy Chipperfield, he added a drive-through safari park called "The Lions of Longleat" on the grounds (charge £1—then $2.80—per car), which quickly became a far greater draw than the house. When once asked, "Does it worry you that people are more interested in the lions than the Van Dycks?" Lord Bath candidly replied, "No, I am not all that

Longleat, Wiltshire.

interested in pictures myself, although I love possessing them." In the same interview he said, "When people leave the lion reserve they have to pass the house, so they pop in and see it—at least a good many of them do. It is awfully hard to decide or make up one's mind where to draw the line…When does a stately home become unstately? To my mind the lions definitely have not reduced the stateliness of Longleat—I think the lion is a very stately animal. But the whole object really is to make the thing pay…. you must have something else to attract them, something to keep them interested, apart from just a stately home."[45]

Lord Bath never lived in the house after he divorced and remarried in 1953. He allowed his son and heir Alexander (who had run his father's parking lot as a teenager) to use

Longleat, however—when he was not living in St. Tropez—partly so he could create his notorious mural paintings on the walls of the west wing. In 1958, he handed over most of the estate to Alexander in the hope of avoiding another round of inheritance taxes, by taking advantage of the lifetime-handover rule. The marquess retained ownership of the house itself and its surrounding 700-acre landscape park, although he himself lived in a modern mill house nearby.

When his father died at 87 in 1992, Alexander, who was then 60, and who had culti-vated a reputation as an artist, a political radical, and a ladies' man, succeeded as 7th Mar-quess. He has since completed a deal with a Dutch entrepreneur, who installed a 600-chalet holiday village in Longleat Forest, to help keep the up the flow of visitors and cash. He now has plans to build the world's largest collection of mazes, and erect a replica of Stonehenge (called "Thynnhenge") to serve as a new tourist magnet and a setting for out-door concerts.

In 1993, you could buy an all-inclusive ticket to Longleat; or pay separate admission charges for the house, the safari park (which now contains camels, giraffes, and rare white rhinos as well as lions), the grounds and gardens, and a dozen other attractions. Among the exhibits are 60 watercolors by Adolf Hitler, the skin of the first lion of Longleat (named "Marquess"), and the brightly colored, orgiastic "Kamasutra" murals painted by the present Lord Bath in his private apartments, visible to adults only for an extra £1.50, or $2.25. He has turned the upper floor of his private wing into a series of futuristically decorated rooms, which he is considering renting out for private parties.

The 7th Marquess, while admitting that titles "are good for business," goes by simple Alexander Thynn, the name he used when running for Parliament on the Wessex Region-alist ticket in 1974 and 1979. Over lunch in his untidy private apartments, he explains his passion for autonomous regional governments for Britain and the rest of the world, within a nest of continental parliaments and a global "Assembly of Equals." In Alexander Thynn/Bath's Utopia, all education would be public and free, all incomes would be limited to a middle-class average, and all hereditary titles and inheritances—like his own—would be banned.

A series of his paintings hangs around the dining room: big primitive cartoons carved out by his fingers in a thick impasto made of sawdust and paint, depicting major events in the history of Wessex. They are explained to a surprised group of tourists who are shown through the room midway in our meal.

The marquess himself looks and acts like no other marquess I have ever met. Father Christmas-sized, with long matted gray hair and beard, he wears colorful hippie rags, goes barefoot, drinks red wine from the bottle, and throws leftover bones onto the carpet for his dog. But he is clearly no fool, as his £85 million ($127.5 million) deal with Center Parcs (the holiday village entrepreneur) makes clear. Even with 9,600 acres of farmland and 150,000 visitors to Longleat each year, he believes that the 400-acre Center Parcs devel-opment and his other projects in planning are essential to maintain the house and estate. "What I've done with Center Parcs is lease the land to them for eighty years for a nice

Longleat, Wiltshire. One of Lord Bath's mural paintings.

sum. And each year they pay a rental, which is recalculated every five years according to set methods. So that if the thing goes up, we get more. The more profitable they are, the better we do. And of course everyone who stays there is within a bicycle ride of Longleat. Cars aren't permitted in the village—which is part of its appeal—but we've also got an agreement going that we'll send buses down and hive them off here. So I don't think there will be any way to stop them coming to Longleat." His regionalist Utopia, with its fixed income limits, will have to wait.

·　·　·

In part because he has been so active and articulate a spokesman for the stately home industry; because he started young and remains in control; because he and his advisers have proven themselves ingenious entrepreneurs and businessmen; and because one of his secondary attractions—the National Motor Museum—is a well-run enterprise of genuine merit, Edward Montagu, 3rd Baron Montagu of Beaulieu, has become the best known and most respected of the three founding fathers.

By means of a carefully pruned family tree printed at the back of the £1.95 ($3) Beaulieu Palace House brochure, one learns that, although he is but a baron, Lord Montagu counts among his ancestors at least six dukes (Montagu, Buccleuch, Manchester, Marlborough, Argyll, and Queensberry) and the Stuart kings of England. He can trace his family's ownership of this property back fourteen generations, to 1538, when Beaulieu Abbey—one of the monastic properties seized by Henry VIII—was bought by Sir Thomas Wriothesley, later 1st Earl of Southampton and grandfather of Shakespeare's good friend. It came into the Montagu family by marriage in 1667, and became the property of the present Lord Montagu's branch of the family 200 years later. It was then, in 1867, that his great-grandfather, the 5th Duke of Buccleuch, who was married to the daughter of a Marquess of Bath, gave Beaulieu as a wedding present to his second son, Lord Henry Scott. (Lord Montagu is also related to his other fellow pioneer. One of the two daughters of the 4th Earl of Southampton, his nine-times-great-grandfather, married a duke of Montagu; the other a duke of Bedford.)

Lord Henry, created 1st Baron Montagu in 1885, enlarged the medieval gatehouse-turned-hunting lodge into the comfortable Victorian house the 3rd Baron inherited in 1951, on his 25th birthday. His father had died when he was two, at which time most of the family capital went to pay the death duties. Trustees ran the estate in the intervening years.

The ruins of the 13th-century Cistercian abbey that had once been the soul of the estate, along with a small museum, had been open to the public since 1908, and attracted up to 40,000 people a year at a shilling a head. After considering giving away most of the house to a religious or educational institution, Edward Montagu decided to sell part of the property to pay for repairs, and then—like Henry Bath—to open his house to the paying public as well, in the hope that their shillings and half-crowns would cover the cost of maintaining it.

Apart from the abbey ruins and a favorable location (in the New Forest and near to Bournemouth—two popular holiday destinations) the house had little to recommend it to tourists. So he hit on the idea of capitalizing on his father's early career as a propagandist for horseless carriages by establishing a "Montagu Motor Museum," a drawing card comparable to Lord Bath's menagerie. To begin, he had only a 1903 De Dion Bouton that had belonged to his father, along with books, photographs, and other memorabilia. He managed to persuade British car manufacturers and collectors to donate or lend a number of other vintage machines, and installed three of them in the front hall of the house. A former journalist and a professional public relations man, Lord Montagu managed to get a great deal of national press space in advance of his opening in April 1952—including a celebrated photograph in the *Sunday Pictorial* ("It's Enough to Bring a Peer to His Knees!") of his lordship in his shirt sleeves scrubbing the floors.

He continued to generate publicity and attract tourists, largely by means of the antique cars, and ended the season with a total of about 70,000 visitors. Unlike his rival at Longleat, Montagu lived in the house himself from the start, and has always made his and his family's own presence one of its selling points. He lets visitors into the family apartments, in Blomfield's Victorian wing, when the family is away. He spent the off-season in 1952–53 learning more about public relations in New York (Montagu has always credited American marketing and management techniques for much of his success), then took a three-month tour of the United States, lecturing on "The Stately Homes of England," displaying his Coronation robes, and showing a film of Beaulieu at each stop. In 1954, aided by Coronation-year visitors and the popularity of the movie *Genevieve* (its plot is built around the annual antique car race from London to Brighton), the visitor count rose to 110,000.

He kept adding more "veteran" (pre-1918) and "vintage" (1919–30) cars to his collection—there were 100 by 1959—as well as early bicycles, motorcycles, trucks, and trams. In 1956, then again in 1959 (by which time attendance had risen to 200,000), he added larger new buildings to house the collection. Every new attraction or publicity stunt—motorcades, car auctions and jumble sales, river regattas, a huge model railroad, overseas tours, running the London-to-Brighton race himself with a movie star at his side—made the papers and magazines. A series of jazz concerts on the grounds beginning in 1956 kept growing in popularity, until the disruptive behavior of drunks in the crowd led him to end them in 1961.

He offered medieval banquets in the surviving abbey building, rented out the house and cars for films and TV, and began reconstructing an 18th-century shipbuilding village nearby to serve as a second supplementary attraction. In 1968 he had turned the car collection—now the *National* Motor Museum—into a charitable trust, which allowed him to raise donations for a new and larger building, housing 200 vehicles, which opened in 1972, the same year he opened a large full-service restaurant.

By 1975 Beaulieu (which the British pronounce Bewley) had become one of England's prime tourist attractions, drawing more than half a million visitors a year. Over the next twenty years, Montagu's major problem was thinking up new attractions to keep people coming back, especially in view of the many competing attractions that had grown up around him. He began to fear that too many open country houses might be competing for a limited pot of tourist money.

Meanwhile, as a prolific writer and lecturer (on antique cars, stately homes, and the museum business), as founding president of the Historic Houses Association, president of the Union of European Historic Houses, and (later) chairman of English Heritage—bully pulpits all—Lord Montagu has constantly argued for professional management and commercial exploitation of historic properties, and done a great deal to enhance public awareness both of the "stately home industry" in general, and his own enterprises at Beaulieu in particular.

Does he feel that he has become the national spokesman for the private country house? "I think that over the years I have taken on this role," he says, "and it's very difficult to shake it off. People do look up to me a little bit, especially in the House of Lords, expect me to speak up for them."

Still ruddy and fit at 68, Lord Montagu, just in from a hot drive down from London, swims a few laps before joining us for lunch (including fresh seagull eggs from the estate), which his butler serves at a poolside table hidden away not far from the milling crowds heading off to look at the cars. Over lunch, he bristles at the idea that his house is less important than his motor museum. "We have a very comprehensive tourist complex here, and the house is part of it." Even without the museum, he reckons he would be getting at least a quarter of a million visitors. "We're in such a good geographical location, here in the New Forest. We were getting fifty, sixty thousand a year before we even opened the house, just for the abbey ruins."

But would Beaulieu have maintained itself in the top league if it was just the house, and nothing else? "Not in the top league, no. But it would certainly have had very respectable figures of visitors. When I say that, I totally accept that the Motor Museum is the biggest attraction at Beaulieu. But I can tell you there are seventy motor museums in the country, and a lot of them are going broke. They get pathetic attendance figures. It's the house and abbey which give that extra dimension."

He thinks that Henry Bath made a terrible mistake separating out the wild animal park from Longleat, and letting his partner market the animals independently. "Chipperfield was getting people to the safari park who couldn't care less about the house. It all became 'The Lions of Longleat,' and people forgot about Longleat. Until recently, there were separate tickets for everything. We kept advising Longleat to have an all-in ticket, but only two or three years ago did they accept our advice."

Lord Montagu insists on our going through the Palace House to see his latest innovations—costumed attendants (who do a reasonably good job of answering my questions 'in character,' perhaps because the boss is beside me); and a fairly low-tech computer-generated quiz game for children, in which they—or their parents—answer questions about items in each room in order to win some sort of prize.

"As long as we carry on running Beaulieu in a businesslike, sensible way, thinking ahead all the time, seeing where the trends are in tourism and what people want, we shall be all right. We believe that involvement of the public in visiting houses is tremendously important. That is why we set up the 'Go Club' for children, that is why our interpreters are actors acting out certain roles. The cavalcade of motors in the afternoon, the carol singing at Christmas—all these things the public love. We've never had guided tours here. We never will."

·   ·   ·

For many years Ian Russell, 13th Duke of Bedford, attracted the greatest amount of personal publicity of the three industry pioneers. This was partly because his exaggerated antics were intended to do precisely that; but also partly because he was, after all, a duke. Not counting royals, there are only two dozen British dukes left. Whatever the excesses of their ancestors may have been, in the 1950s dukes were expected to behave—well, ducally.

But Ian Russell, who was born to the courtesy title of Lord Howland in 1917, was not brought up or educated as heir to a dukedom, and from the day he succeeded to the title in 1953 (the estate remains in the hands of a private company set up by his grandfather, controlled by an independent board of trustees), he was determined to do things his way. "I do not know how dukes are meant to behave, but apparently I do not conform to what people expect....I suspect some of my fellow peers disapprove of my behaviour and approach, but frankly I couldn't care less....I have been accused of being undignified. That is quite true, I am. Fortunately, I was never brought up as a gentleman, so I have never had the consequent limitations."[46]

In his self-defensive autobiography, A *Silver-Plated Spoon* (1959), the Duke of Bedford describes his bizarre and loveless upbringing, followed by a scrambling, impecunious series of jobs, which in a perverse way may have "freed" him from any sense of aristocratic propriety. He never even saw his grandfather, the cold and lordly 11th Duke of Bedford, or realized who he was, until he was invited to spend one miserable day at Woburn Abbey at the age of sixteen. By that time his grandfather and his father, the Marquess of Tavistock— by all accounts a reclusive, unfeeling crank—had already drawn up the deed of trust that would forever keep the family estates out of his grasp. "You must succeed to the dukedom but you do not succeed to anything else," his grandfather warned him in 1938. Educated at home or farmed out to tutors (his father, bullied at Eton, had lost his faith in schools), he was sent at nineteen to live in a London hostel with an allowance of £98 (less than $400) a year, then cut off without a penny when, two years later, he married a divorced woman thirteen years his senior. At the time Ian Howland wrote to a cousin, "My father is a notorious eccentric and is a complete failure so his wishes are beneath consideration. Even my grandfather is gloomy about the prospect of what is going to happen to Woburn when my father inherits." When he protested his treatment, his father coolly replied:

> I consider that the enjoyment of a substantial unearned income can only be justified if the recipient spends the money wisely and performs some real service to the community which, often at great sacrifice, provides the money. Your grandfather and I, according to our lights and in our different ways, have tried to show ourselves not wholly unworthy of our privileges . . .
>
> You, however, to my great sorrow and disappointment, have, in spite of your opportunities, done absolutely nothing in the way of social service and you have shown yourself, so far, completely destitute of any sense of honour or responsibility in this matter. . .
>
> Yours affectionately,
> Daddy[47]

Ill-educated and something of a social sponge, Lord Howland took a job as a rent collector in Stepney. His grandfather's death in 1940 made his father 12th Duke, now responsible for £3,100,000 (about $12 million) in death duties, and Ian the new Marquess of Tavistock, but not a penny richer. He worked for a few happy months as a reporter for Lord Beaverbrook's *Sunday Express* at £10 ($40) a week. He was declared physically unfit for military service, and, after his first wife died a suicide in 1945, he remarried—this time more appropriately, in his father's eyes, to a baron's daughter nearer his own age. In 1948 he moved with his wife and eight-year-old son Robin to South Africa and began a career as an apricot farmer.

None of this prepared him for the day in October 1953 when he learned that his father's body had been found on his estate in Devon, shot to death by his own gun—a hunting accident, it was declared, although his son and heir suggests possible reasons for suicide. Faced with £5 million (then $14 million) in inheritance taxes—plus the still-unpaid half of the £3 million bill due on his grandfather's death, and an unfriendly board of trustees who officially owned (and owed) everything—the new Duke of Bedford, at 36, determined to hold on to Woburn Abbey at all costs. "To me the whole future of the family and indeed its right to exist in the second half of the twentieth century were bound up with the reopening of Woburn. Insofar as I am able to concentrate on anything, it became an obsession with me."[48]

The trustees sold off large chunks of the Russell family estates to help pay the tax bill, and would have preferred to hand over Woburn to the National Trust for the same purpose so that they could concentrate their attention on the family's valuable real estate in the Bloomsbury district of London. But despite their misgivings, the new duke was determined to restore the great house, which had been left a shambles by wartime occupation, the 1949–50 demolitions, and its subsequent abandonment by his father. He persuaded the trustees to lease to him Woburn and forty of its 13,000 acres, for a rental (in 1970) of £30,000 ($72,000) a year. "The Abbey looked as if a bomb had fallen on it," he wrote, describing his first inspection of the place in 1953, after thirteen years away:

> The building which had housed the indoor riding school and the tennis court, connecting the two Flitcroft stable blocks, had disappeared; so had the whole of the east front, together with at least a third of the north and south wings, where it had joined them. There were piles of stones and building materials lying in a haphazard fashion all over the place . . .
>
> The interior was freezing cold and desolate. It looked as if it belonged to a series of bankrupt auction rooms. There were piles and piles of linen baskets in the front hall, right up to the ceiling, mounds of furniture lying everywhere, most of it without dust sheets. There were beautiful Louis XV chairs with kitchen table legs straight through the seat, the walls and cornices were peeling, and everything was covered with dust and filthy. The whole house reeked of damp.[49]

He and his wife Lydia, together with a few hard-working servants, set to the Herculean task of clearing, cleaning, and repainting one room at a time of the important 17th- and 18th-century state rooms, all of which remained. "Gradually the wave of filth and decay began to recede. We used to work all day, camping out in this vast house, boiling up water for morning coffee in an electric kettle, and then going out to the Bedford Arms in the village for a warm meal in the evening."[50] (The kitchen had been in one of the demolished wings.)

With no family tradition to respect, the new duke and duchess were free to furnish each room as they wished, striving to make them all look "lived in" (which, at the time, they were not) with their choice of the remarkable collection of 17th- and 18th-century furniture, tapestries, china, glassware, and paintings they found piled around the rooms, and silver and gold plate from the family vaults in London. They discarded the second-rate art and the heavy Victorian and Edwardian furnishings of his father's and grandfather's day, and concentrated on fine French and Georgian furniture, family portraits, and the best of the paintings—which included a set of 21 Canaletto views of Venice commissioned by the 4th Duke, excellent works by Rembrandt, Van Dyck, and Reynolds, and George Gower's "Armada Portrait" of Queen Elizabeth I. They discovered on the floor of one of the stable blocks a 183-piece hand-painted set of Sèvres china given in 1763 by Louis XV to an earlier Duchess of Bedford, whose husband (the 4th Duke) had been Ambassador to France, and decided to wash every piece themselves.

As the April 1955 opening day came closer, they added new access roads and parking lots, a tea room in one of the stable blocks, paddle boats in one of the lakes, ropes and carpet-covers, and a children's playground and petting zoo. A unique collection of rare deer, European bison, Mongolian horses and other animals already roamed about the park. The 11th Duke, who may have loved animals more than people, had been president of the Royal Zoological Society.

The Duke of Bedford was determined that people were going to have a good time at Woburn—something he felt was not always the case at other open houses, where owners looked down on tourists as an annoying intrusion, tolerated only because they helped pay the bills. From opening day, Bedford walked round the house himself, smiling, answering questions, signing autographs, fully aware that most visitors were even more excited about seeing a real live duke than they were about seeing his house. The first year, he says, he attracted 181,000 visitors; in 1956, 234,000; in 1957, 372,000; in 1958 and 1959—now opening on winter weekends, and adding new attractions every year, including special weekend events (scooter rallies, traction engine races) and yet another wildlife park—— more than 450,000. "I have made it my business over the years," he wrote in 1959, "to see that there is always something new to offer in the grounds. We are in a competitive business, and as in any other commercial undertaking, half the battle is publicity. Unless you draw attention to yourself and your wares, people will take no notice of you."[51]

The Duke of Bedford regularly found new ways of drawing attention to himself. In imitation of Lord Bath, he joined forces with Jimmy Chipperfield to open his own drive-through safari park in 1971, featuring rhinos and elephants as well as monkeys and lions. He sat behind the counter in the gift shop himself, walked around the house regularly during open hours, invited a convention of nudists to camp at Woburn, performed in a skiffle group, danced the twist on television, joined Lord Montagu in singing Noël Coward's "Stately Homes" on BBC's *Tonight* show, appeared in documentary films, auctioned off his butler's services to Americans, and invited tourists to have dinner with a real live duke and duchess, then enjoy bed and breakfast at a genuine stately home, for a bargain 50 guineas (later raised to £90, or $250) a head.

In 1974, though—just three years after writing, "the place only partly belongs to me; but I belong wholly to the place,"⁵² Bedford either tired of the game, or of British income taxes, and left with his third wife for Paris, then for Monaco, turning Woburn and all its treasures over to his elder son Robin. Born in 1940, the latest Marquess of Tavistock had been working contentedly as a stockbroker in London, and had all along presumed that it was his son Andrew rather than he who would become the next master of Woburn. "What could I do with fourteen sitting rooms, half a dozen galleries and the rest?" he complained in exasperation at the time. "It was different from the past. They used to have endless country house parties, people moving in flocks from one to the other. Today, most of us are working."

Whatever his and his wife's initial feelings, however, the Marquess and Marchioness of Tavistock fell to the task of keeping Woburn alive and in good repair with energy and flair, despite ever-spiralling costs and competition. Henrietta Tavistock, a professional horse-breeder, reopened the Bloomsbury stud at Woburn, and in 1975 bought a celebrated mare—her lifesize bronze statue stands just outside the house—that produced ten national champions.

In 1988, Lord Tavistock suffered a near-fatal stroke. By 1991 he had made a substantial recovery, but he was forced to relinquish a good deal of control to his wife, his eldest son Andrew (Lord Howland)—now a professional horse dealer—and the Woburn trustees. Together they run not only "Britain's largest drive-through safari and leisure park," but also a 40-shop antiques center in the south stable block, two restaurants, two gift shops and a garden center, a pottery, a campground, and two eighteen-hole championship golf courses. The Duke of Bedford's ventures into weekend events on the grounds back in the 1950s have now burgeoned into a list that includes dog and horse shows; craft, doll, and antique fairs; sheepdog trials; car, truck, and bus rallies; antique airplane fly-ins (his great-grandmother was a hardy pioneer pilot lost over the channel in 1937), swap meets, rock concerts, and so on.

If, as at Longleat, the fine house itself is "often ignored," as one writer put it, "in favour of baboons and hippos," it cannot be denied that the Tavistock family, like their notorious patriarch, is trying very hard to give visitors what they want. Until a few years ago, they were still holding annual pop concerts (Neil Diamond, Tina Turner, Dire Straits) for 60,000 people on the grounds, but those seem to have been put on hold. So have plans, once proposed, for a giant new theme park and a full-scale race course. Lord Howland admits that "people have a lot more choice what to do on a Sunday" than they did when his grandfather and Jimmy Chipperfield first opened the Woburn zoo in 1971. In 1993, they bought out Chipperfield and poured another million pounds into the Animal Kingdom, with apparent success in terms of visitor numbers. At about age thirteen, Howland believes, children lose interest in wild animals and start looking for "white-knuckle rides." But he isn't prepared to add those to Woburn just yet.

· · ·

By 1975, when the country house was declared in immanent danger of death, more than 160 private owners had opened their doors to tourists as a means of survival; some seven million people were trooping through their state rooms and wandering about their gardens between Easter and October each year. The aggressive, fun-fair, all-out tourist industry approach of Henry Bath, Edward Montagu, and Ian Bedford was never wholeheartedly adopted by what Montagu called "The Gentlemen" (as opposed to "The Players"—the analogy is to cricket matches in which genteel amateurs challenge vulgar professionals). Among the latter Lord Montagu included himself, of course, as well as Bedford and Bath, the Duke of Norfolk at Arundel, George Howard at Castle Howard, the Marquess of Exeter at Burghley, the Marquess of Hertford at Ragley, and the Earl of Leicester at Holkham. Some of these houses have since been handed on to descendants or charitable trusts. The house of one of Montagu's imaginary 1967 teammates—the Earl of Warwick—has since become the property of a leisure corporation; that of another—Lord Gretton—is now an upscale hotel.

The Gentlemen, wrote Montagu, "are owners of essentially amateur status, usually the occupiers of naturally attractive properties, but with no inclination for the cruder aspects of professionalism. Like their sporting counterparts . . . they are a dying breed."[53] In 1967, his list of Gentlemen included the Dukes of Devonshire (Chatsworth) and Marlborough (Blenheim Palace); the Duke of Rutland (with two houses, Belvoir Castle and Haddon); the Dukes of Argyll (Inverary Castle) and Atholl (Blair Castle) in Scotland; the Marquess of Salisbury at Hatfield; the Earl of Harewood at Harewood, the Earl of Pembroke at Wilton House; Sir Harold Wernher at Luton Hoo; Sir Walter Bromley-Davenport at Capesthorne; and Captain R. G. Berkeley at Berkeley Castle. Although some of these houses have also since passed on to heirs, or are officially owned by charitable trusts, they are all still "family houses": the one loss has been Lord Astor's Hever Castle, which, like Warwick Castle, now belongs to a leisure-industry corporation.

Whether all their owners—and those of the hundreds of other English country houses who now try to pay part of their maintenance and repair bills by opening their doors to tens or hundreds of thousands of tourists every year—would be classified by Lord Montagu today as "gentlemen" or "players" I have no idea. What is clear is that the most successful among them—including several of those on his original "Gentlemen's" team, or their heirs—have learned a great many lessons from the three founding fathers. See the posh gift shop, the miniature railway, the rental boats at Blenheim; the elaborate new restaurant and "duchess's own" delicacies for sale at Chatsworth; the imitation-Tudor kitchen and audio-visual time trip at exquisite Wilton House, "incorporating the very latest technology of wrap-around sound and video laser disc."

The stately home industry may have been born out of simple desperation, by young heirs familiar with the business world who found themselves suddenly hit by death duties and strapped for operating cash. They may have begun hoping that tidying up the rooms, stringing up ropes, adding parking places and toilets, engaging a few room attendants, and opening the doors would be enough for common folk who—like the country house trav-

ellers of earlier centuries—would be happy to catch a glimpse of How the Other Half
Lived. But the cannier ones learned quickly that more than that was wanted, and began
opening cafés, shops, zoos, museums, and amusement parks, throwing in special events,
offering themselves as well as their family portraits as exhibits. What England has ended
up with, in the most commercially successful cases, are historic houses surrounded by
ancillary, non-historic tourist attractions.

An exaggerated image of this phenomenon is Alton Towers in Staffordshire, a fabulous
palace built between 1811 and 1840 for the 15th and 16th Earls of Shrewsbury—at one
time the largest private house in Europe. It passed out of the hands of the Earls of Shrewsbury in 1924, and was taken over by the Army as a training center during World War II
and left a near wreck. Because of the dilapidated and dangerous condition of its roofs and
timbers, it was gutted in 1951. It now stands as a picturesque, empty shell at the heart of
the most popular fee-charging tourist attraction in Great Britain, still called Alton Towers:
a Disneyland-type theme park with spectacular thrill rides (Nemesis, The Beast, Thunder
Looper, The Runaway Mine Train, The Congo River Rapids) and a hundred other attractions set in the splendid Shrewsbury gardens, which plays host to two and a half million
people a year.

CHAPTER FIVE

The Country House Owner Today

Challenges and Problems

IMAGINE THAT YOU ARE THE OWNER of a substantial English country house. You and your family still use it as a home, with at least some of its original furnishings and acres. Let us say that it has been in your family since it was built, whether in 1300 or 1915—or at least for several generations—and that you still feel closely attached to it.

There are many people in Britain who think that your house should *not* be torn down for something newer, something more rational, compact, and convenient; that it should remain intact with its furnishings and its surrounding acres, as part of a mystical thing called the National Heritage, a piece of the national past that should be handed on through the present to the future. Many of these people, moreover, would like to see your family continue on as the owners or at least as inhabitants of the house. That, they believe, is part of its historic essence and appeal. They may even assert—a most un-American notion—that it is the government's responsibility to help you do so.

Let us say that you, the homeowner, agree. What challenges are you likely to face in trying to retain and maintain your house? And what can you do to meet them?

· · ·

The most monumental challenge, for the owners of big old houses in the country—and the challenge grows exponentially the bigger and older the house—is the cost of maintenance and repair. It has been estimated that the cost per square foot of maintaining a listed historic house is from four to five times that of an ordinary modern house.

Retiling a roof with old slates can cost three times as much as doing the same job with new concrete tiles. Replacing the layer of lead and boards underneath those old slates will cost six times the price of the felt underlayer typical of a modern roof. To cut out and renew a single 42-inch stone mullion may cost £125 ($220), compared with £21 ($35) for the same piece in wood. Cast iron guttering will cost you seven times the price of plastic.[1] "The cost to repair stone is just horrendous compared to brick," says Sir Nicholas Bacon at Raveningham Hall. "And the cost of stone tracery windows is just mind-boggling."

In 1992, Norman Hudson estimated the average cost of restoring a historic house (after a fire, for example) at £300–500 ($530–880) a square foot. Taking Lawrence and Jeanne Stone's figures of 5,000 square feet as the minimum size for a "proper" country house, and 10,000 square feet as the average for one built between 1540 and 1880, we are looking at a minimum full-scale rebuilding cost of £1.5–5 million ($5–9 million).[2] The recent restoration of the south range of Wilton House cost almost £3 million ($5.1 million). Lord Northampton figures he recently spent over £2.5 million ($4 million-plus) restoring and redecorating Castle Ashby. A limited survey undertaken for the Historic Houses Association in 1995 suggested that routine repairs and maintenance on a typical large country house could run about £63,000 ($95,000) a year; that this sum still fell considerably short of what the owners thought they ought to be spending; and that, in many cases, hundreds of thousands of pounds' worth of major repairs remained to be done.[3]

Much of the added cost comes from the archaic luxury materials that must be used. One is not allowed to substitute less expensive, more readily available modern materials—however adequate, even undetectible—in the publicly visible portions of listed buildings. If inspectors conclude that more than half of "the architectural interest" of a listed house remains after a fire, owners can be ordered to restore it to its historic pre-fire condition, using original materials and highly skilled craftsmen.

Another reason for the high cost of repairs, of course, is the need to find and pay such craftsmen. Over the past two decades, the wages of specialized building-trade workers have increased at about double the rate of inflation. Their meticulous work—restoring tattered silk wall hangings, replacing eroded stone mouldings, carving new balusters for a worm-eaten stair rail—may take weeks instead of days, months instead of weeks. The owner of a country house in Worcestershire was in the middle of restoring the painted chapel on which Evelyn Waugh modeled the family chapel in *Brideshead Revisited*. "We need specialists for this work who have not only to be paid quite a lot," he complained, "but need to be fed and put up for two weeks as well."

A few building firms in Britain have grown into multi-million-pound enterprises by playing latter-day Renaissance craftsmen, with large crews of apprentices learning how to carve stone cartouches and finials, slip steel pins and plates into ancient wooden beams, give new-made wall paneling the luster of centuries, and restore stained glass windows so they look as good as old. "Over the years our craftsmen have perfected the techniques used by medieval carpenters and joiners," boasts one firm of timber restorers.

Most country house owners I talked to could draw up lists of several hundred thousand, even millions of pounds' worth of repairs—repairs to walls and roofs primarily, but also to furniture, paintings, and tapestries, to heating and electrical systems—that "must" be undertaken soon; but for which there was no income or capital available.

At Badminton, the Duchess of Beaufort flicked half a dozen switches at the door to the Great Hall, in order to let down and illuminate the magnificent tiered chandelier. But what it revealed—in addition to the empty wall-space where the Badminton Cabinet once stood—was the shabby, almost threadbare condition of the upholstery on the Georgian chairs that stood around the walls. The stonework at Woburn Abbey needs constant refacing, poisoned as it is by the sulfur spewed into the air by three nearby brickworks. Old houses really do crumble, Lord Scarborough explained to me of Sandbeck. "Sulfur dioxide in the air works on the limestone and simply turns it to powder."

Like Lord Saye and Sele at Broughton Castle, the Earl of Arundel was nearing the end of a long-term series of major repairs at Arundel Castle in 1994. These had been in progress for about seven years, and would cost him about £100,000 ($153,000) this year. He felt fortunate to be living in what was, for all practical purposes, a relatively "modern" house (despite its 12th-century outer defenses, Arundel Castle was completely rebuilt in the 1880s), rather than a really "old" house like Chatsworth; one, moreover, built within some fairly solid walls. But that still left him all the other estate buildings to keep up. "We had a mass of repairs to carry out. All the lodges in the park have cost a hundred thousand to repair. We just finished the last one last year, the walls, the iron, the wood, the storm cave. So we were in a very precarious financial positiion. But now we're level. One little ambition I have is to repair the park wall, which goes the whole way round the park, five and a half miles. So far, in the last twenty years, we've repaired about three miles of it. Two and a half miles to go. And as you can imagine that is costing a lot of money. But that's a little ambition I have, to repair it before I die."

Antony Jarvis describes a particular case at Doddington Hall. "We've got two full rooms of seventeenth-century tapestries hung up by the Georgian-improving landowner, and we've had quotes—a hundred and fifty thousand pounds for the two rooms—that are ten years old. And they're not very exciting tapestries. . . . But that is an unimaginable scale of expenditure for a house like this, which just about makes ends meet. These are bills we can never pay. . . . We've got four very fine, very splendid George the First Spanish-mahogany-framed chairs, which had to be completely reupholstered. We spent thirty-five hundred pounds on those chairs. And they're not even embroidery. We used wool damask, which is the nearest thing we can get within our budget."

The primary reason for regular annual maintenance—repainting walls, repointing bricks, cleaning gutters, resurfacing drives, and so on—is to avoid the far greater cost of major repairs, which become necessary when such jobs are left undone. It was the lack of such regular maintenance for six years, even more than damage done by billeted troops, that doomed so many houses after World War II. For the same reason, houses left unoccupied and uncared for more than a couple of years can end up costing millions to put back in service.

Arundel Castle, Sussex.

In August 1993, Geoffrey van Cutsem, Britain's best-known country house salesman, put the annual cost of running a medium-sized historic house on ten acres of land (including one gardener) at about £30,000 ($45,000) a year, which included maintenance, taxes, heating, lighting, and gardening—presuming the house was in good shape to begin with. "If you buy a place that's falling down," he said, "then all bets are off."[4] After the Duke of Gloucester and his family were forced to leave their country house in 1995 because they could no longer afford it, one British reporter estimated that "the bottom line for maintaining the most modest of historic houses is roughly around £100,000 ($160,000) a year."[5]

A 1994 sampling of 120 owners of listed houses revealed that they planned to spend an average of £7,000 ($10,700) on repairs and improvements over the next year—five times the national norm.[6] In most cases they planned to do what most homeowners plan to do, from time to time: replace windows, improve insulation, refit kitchens, improve security, repaint inside and out. The difference is that these jobs cost them a good deal more than they cost the average homeowner.

However carefully you keep an eye out for fresh leaks and signs of dry rot or subsidence, trying to avert disasters before they occur, a large old house will still need major renovation at least once or twice a century: stonework renewal, a new roof, total rewiring or plumbing, complete interior repainting; the removal and replacement of dangerously rotted wood. These are the six- or seven-figure jobs that can lead, in great mouldering old mansions, to selling off the Beccafumi drawings or the development land near the motorway. The Constable that was sold off from Sudeley Castle in 1990 for £10 million ($17.8

million) went partly to offset death duties; but also for reroofing, rewiring, and renewing the stonework. Houghton Hall was shut in 1994–95 so that every pipe in the house could be replaced. Lord Leicester estimated he had spent several million pounds on the estate in the twenty years he had been running Holkham Hall, more of it on estate cottages and outbuildings than the great house itself. "But then, of course, these enormously high interest rates came along, and it just seemed idiotic to go on paying seven hundred thousand pounds a year on the loans. So we sold sixty-six old master drawings to clear the decks. It seemed sensible to me. After all, we've still got two hundred and forty left."

· · ·

For all the grief of maintenance, the 1994 survey referred to above found that "the cost of repairing a listed home is the second rather than the first gripe of owners. Red tape and bureaucracy in the guise of planning constraints is the main disadvantage of owning an historic home."[7] The report prepared for the Historic Houses Association in 1995 cited instances of what owners regarded as tedious and costly delays, English Heritage inspectors' "over-purist" standards, and a general lack of flexibility or sympathy. The Earl of Shelburne, in one of his *Historic House* editorials, wrote that "The extension of listed building regulations over the past twenty-five years has assumed that most owners are either idiots or vandals. . . . Many owners whose link with a property goes back to its conception find this interference hard to bear . . ."[8]

Homeowners the world over have to deal with building inspectors telling them what they can and cannot do. But the terms of Britain's Town and Country Planning Acts give national and local inspectors dealing with "heritage" properties an unusual amount of arbitrary power. Current law states that no alterations or extensions "which would materially affect the character" of a listed building may be made without permission. Owners of such buildings may be penalized if they do not keep them in good repair. But this leaves open to discussion what the "character" of a building is, or ought to be; what kinds of changes would "materially affect" it; what "good repair" implies; and whether permission should be granted or not. In the case of a Grade I-listed house, the 1994 survey pointed out, "even the size, shape, and type of nails used to repair a shelf would have to be approved."[9] Which may explain another of the pollsters' findings: only 31 percent of the owners of listed houses who had made repairs to their houses in 1991–93 bothered to ask for official consent.

House owners claim that building inspectors become petty and academic when it comes to particular decisions regarding repairs and alterations; that they show far too little flexibility regarding the convenience and comfort owners seek to introduce, or the expenses they are obliged to undergo. Some feel they are forced to deal with badly trained, narrow-minded young university graduates in architectural history who haven't a clue about the realities of either the past or the present. Others believe they are up against politically hostile apparatchiks who disapprove of the very idea of private families living in grand houses today.

"The sometimes blindly purist and strictly preservationist attitude of local conservation officers and English Heritage has continued to cause difficulties," wrote Norman Hudson in 1991. "While nothing should be permitted that is fundamentally damaging to buildings of historic or architectural integrity they must, as most have done to meet the requirements of previous generations, be allowed to evolve in order to permit their continuing habitability and economical survival. Faced with English Heritage opposition, even to a proposal supported by eminent architectural historians and conservationists, an owner may feel the odds stacked against him."[10] He described the circular trap in which an owner, frustrated by the intransigence of his local planning authorities, appeals their decision to the Secretary of State for the Environment. The Environment Secretary then turns for advice to the local English Heritage officer—who is likely to be the same person whose opinion persuaded the local authorities to make their unwelcome decision in the first place.

Even in cases where owners appear to have the best interests of the building and the "heritage" at heart, there is often a fundamental difference between their attitude and that of those who must approve any alterations to their house. The owner and his family want to *live* in the house, frequently to maintain a family tradition many generations old. In the past, family members could take it for granted that modernizing, redecorating, enlarging here, contracting there, adding their own touch or trace to an ever-evolving home were simply evidence that a house was still lived in by human beings. Local planning inspectors and English Heritage officers, on the other hand, tend to see themselves more as guardians of a fixed and timeless heritage, like museum conservators on a grander scale. Their job is to assure that the piece of the heritage called Althorp, or Kentwell, or Doddington Hall remains just as it was when it was first listed, first declared a national treasure. They are not particularly interested in where the children of the family are to play, or whether the house is too cold, or the cost of restoring a fallen battlement in the same Normandy stone it was built of in 1602.

Patrick and Judith Phillips, who salvaged and restored Tudor Kentwell Hall in Suffolk, tell the tale of an unusually frustrating battle with English Heritage over their request to enlarge the family kitchen in 1990. (Their household of eight tended to use the kitchen as a "family room.") The first young woman from English Heritage who looked over their proposal, says Patrick Phillips, "obviously took the view that we should not, indeed nobody should, be living here anyway." Judith Phillips was outraged when this woman—"who could not have been more than twenty-seven, twenty-eight!"—presumed to tell her how to run her household. She shouldn't be letting her children do their homework in the kitchen, she was told.

Despite the support of local councilors, the local preservation society, and the Historic Houses Association, and the Phillipses' argument that their proposed extension was "a continuation of numerous small extensions which had taken place in the wing over the years," a series of intransigent EH inspectors continued to impose delays and demand plan alterations. For a year and a half they refused their consent. In the end, the Phillipses' request was forwarded to the Minister for the Environment—who (precisely as Norman Hudson describes) then referred it back to English Heritage, who sent it to the very inspector who had rejected it in the first place. "The problem as I see it," wrote Phillips, a London attorney and a Queen's Counsel (QC), "is that there is no control whatsoever over the Inspectors, which is the level of official with which we all have to deal. Their word is law. . . . The Inspectors' advice can only be challenged by the time consuming and costly route of a public hearing of one sort or another, which process may not be completed in much less than 3 years." He complained about the inspectors' lack of professional experience; the tedious approval procedures required for even the most minor alterations; the absolute, dictatorial power put into the hands of ill-trained local functionaries; and a system that allows them to play the role of both prosecutor and judge when their decisions are appealed. Three years later, English Heritage was still demanding detailed profiles of every cabinet molding in the proposed kitchen extension before they would give final consent.

As many owners point out, some of the most interesting features of their houses would never have been created if Historic Buildings Council or English Heritage regulations were in force in earlier times. Houses now admired for their mixture of styles and their overlay of centuries would have been frozen like Sleeping Beauty's Castle at whatever moment the officials did their listing surveys. Robert Spencer-Bernard, who owns a wonderful jumble of a house called Nether Winchendon near Aylesbury, enjoys pointing out the confused genealogy of his Drawing Room. The basic structure may have been part of a medieval

Nether Winchendon, Buckinghamshire.

monastery. The carved frieze on the walls and ceiling dates from the 1520s. The 17th-century oak paneling was painted a cream color in the 1820s, when the whole house was encased in stone and romantically gothicized. In the adjacent Great Hall, similar wall panelling was left unpainted. Today, Spencer-Bernard could get permission neither to strip the 19th-century paint from his Drawing Room walls (to return them to their "authentic," earlier state), nor to paint the walls of his Great Hall, in order to match them to the style of the rest of the interior. "They're fossilizing it," he says. "This house would never have been as it is if that attitude prevailed in centuries past."

Patrick Cooke at Athelhampton, much of which had to be rebuilt after a disastrous fire in 1992, is one owner who sides with English Heritage. "Ninety-nine times out of a hundred, those horror stories you hear occur when people are doing things they probably shouldn't be doing, trying to change the look of something, trying to convert the interior

Athelhampton, Dorset. Great Hall.

to a different use. Extensions, modernizing—that's where all the problems come from." Cooke, in fact, was allowed to replace carved wall paneling destroyed in the fire with Gothic-style wallpaper found in the house. But he agrees that the building as it is today could never have been completed under current English planning codes. "You've got a Tudor Great Hall—there was a Solar [a 16th-century term for a sunlit chamber] at the back there, but that's been demolished. The Great Chamber is Elizabethan. Then there's a Georgian structure, you've got a Victorian gable and tower in the corner here, and two sets of buildings as late as the nineteen thirties. So whether the planning authorities would have allowed all six extensions to be built over the last five hundred years is an interesting question. I'm sure they'd have stopped us somewhere."

Cooke is, however, one of very few owners I talked to who remain sympathetic to the all-powerful inspectors with whom they must deal. Over and over I heard from frustrated owners of their griefs in having to deal with intransigent local inspectors, whom they regarded as petty, ill-informed dictators ordering them to do what they had no wish to do, and forbidding them to do what they wanted. "On its record to date, so far as the private property owner is concerned, English Heritage has actually been a menace," declared Lord Hesketh of Easton Neston—himself a former Undersecretary for the Environment. "They're an absolute pain," said Lord Apsley at Cirencester Park. "They want buildings in every part of the country to look the same." The Marquess of Northampton at Compton Wynyates called his dealings with English Heritage "more frustrating a relationship than any other aspect of the stately home business."

Lord Montagu of Beaulieu, who served as Chairman of English Heritage from its creation in 1980 until 1989, admitted in 1994 that their complaints may have been in part justified. "It is true that when I was first there they did tend to turn up in sandals, with beards, late, and say, 'You can't do this, you can't do that.' You do get the very young inspector, just out of school, and they get very nervous—'Oh no, no, no, you can't do that!' I don't deny the complaints; I'm afraid it's all true. But I think you'll find it's got better. Takes time to get these people moving on. After all, they are civil servants."

· · ·

Far fewer country houses depend, as the great majority once did, on the income from an agricultural estate. But those that do have suffered grievously in recent years from the decline in agricultural prices and rents. The period between 1983 and 1991 was one of extraordinary depression in English farming, usually attributed to subsidized overproduction—with resultant surpluses and low prices—during the previous, prosperous decade. To this was added the effect of record interest rates, and, more recently, fears that new international market policies would reduce the price-support subsidies on which so many British farmers depend.

After a steady, state-supported growth in value since 1950, and a City-financed boom in the late 1970s and early 1980s, land values began falling in 1983, and continued to plummet for the next eight years. During this time most English farmers operated at a loss every year. Institutional investors began bailing out; the average price per acre of English farmland fell from £2,000 an acre to £1,500 ($2,700 to $2,000) in the second half of 1984. Thousands of farms folded, tens of thousands of farmers left the land. Between 1987 and 1990, annual declines of more than 20 percent in average farm incomes and average values per acre left both at their lowest levels since the war. Farm debt grew from £3 billion ($7 billion) in 1980 to £7 billion ($12.5 billion) in 1990. Although agriculture still takes up 77 percent of the total land area of England, its contribution to the Gross Domestic Product fell from 2 percent in 1981 to only 1.4 percent ten years later. In 1991, the president of the National Farmers' Union declared that "British agriculture is now suffering the worst recession in more than 50 years."[11] This situation—which has had a disastrous effect on many country houses—only began to turn around in 1992, with the devaluation of the pound and the reform of the European Community's Common Agricultural Policy.

In the long view, the decline of English agriculture began far before 1983. Between 1880 and 1976, the great agricultural estates of England and Wales shrank in size by 76 percent, which reduced most of them well below what now seems to be a minimum "house-supporting" size of 10,000 acres. At Holkham Hall, seriously hurt by the slump in farm prices after World War II, the Marquess of Cholmondeley's grandfather—the name is pronounced 'Chumley'—sold off half the 8,000 acres of his estate—which had already been reduced from 17,000 acres in the previous century.

Today, more than half Britain's farms are owner-occupied rather than leased, and a few large estates do seem to be profitable. But Robin Brackenbury at Holme Pierrepont insists, "There is no future in farming. The policy of all British governments has been cheap food. There's no future, no long-term future in farming. Oh, there may be, for a few very big, very efficient farmers." The Earl of Arundel agrees. "I don't believe there's any way you can keep an agricultural estate and a big house going on agricultural rents and profits alone. Those days are gone. You've got to diversify into other areas of potential income. I believed that from Day One, from the time I was eighteen. My son is six, and the last thing I'd want him to do is go to [The Royal Agricultural College at] Cirencester. Because there'd be no future." From Sandbeck Park in Yorkshire, with 5,000 acres, to Powderham Castle in Devon, with 3,500, owners told me that agricultural income is nowhere near enough to maintain the house, as such estates were once expected to do. On the other hand, estates such as Sandbeck and Powderham were once a good deal larger.

One of the most publicized recent cases of agricultural collapse took place at Bowood in Wiltshire, where Lord Shelburne, former president of the Historic Houses Association, cried poor with eloquence and persistence. In 1985–86, he announced, he had made a profit of £7,300 out of a total farm income of £1.2 million. In 1992, when he announced the conversion of a large part of his estate into a golf course, he explained to the *Times* that his agricultural income (largely from food grains) had been cut in half over the past ten years. In 1986–87 his return from farming was only slightly above that of the previous year—about 1.7 percent. "Obviously we could not go on like that," he told the reporter. His temporary solution was to have sheep graze on the poorest grade land, let the rest to

Bowood, Wiltshire. Staircase.

short-term tenants, and contract the dairy operation out to independent farmers. "Although costs have been significantly reduced, none of the Bowood enterprises produces the income needed for the upkeep of the house and grounds. 'So what do you do?' Lord Shelburne asks. 'The only way is to sell off capital assets, and that is why I am very despondent about the future.'"[12]

.   .   .

Less serious economically, but of considerable importance aesthetically, is the exceptionally high cost of maintaining the extensive and elaborate gardens and parklands that were typically a part of any historic country house, given the labor-intensive nature of garden maintenance, and the shrinking pool of trained gardeners. Almost every substantial country house owner whose family has lived in a house for three or more generations tells a version of the same tale: "Of course, my parents [or grandparents] had an outdoors staff of seven [or five, or ten, or twenty] in those days. Nowadays, we have to make do with one very good young man [or young woman, or one and a half, or a boy from the village]."

Some couples do all the gardening themselves, until advancing age makes it impossible. It is the rare private house owner today who can afford—as can Fred Koch, at Sutton Place in Surrey, which has one of the finest gardens in England—a brilliant head gardener like John Humphris, who directs a full-time staff of ten. Sissinghurst has eight gardeners for just six acres, which allows the National Trust to replace 5,000 plants every year, and maintain every square inch in impeccable order. At Cragside in Northumberland, the National Trust decided in 1963 to reinstitute Lord Armstrong's Victorian carpet gardens, intricately geometric patterns made up of foliage plants rather than flowers. "It was still very showy, a status symbol and obviously very labour-intensive," says head gardener Andrew Sawyer, who maintains the garden with two assistants. "But the Armstrongs employed hundreds of gardeners and wanted everybody to know it." One 655-square-foot bed required 12,400 separate plants.

The standard ways to cut labor costs in a country house garden are to dispense with the greenhouses and kitchen gardens; to abandon the process of "bedding out," in which thousands of flowering annuals were moved from the glass houses into prepared beds every few months, in order to maintain a year-round feast of fresh color; to replace them with hardy perennials, or even shrubs; or in the end simply to turf over much or all of one's garden, and maintain it as lawn. The great stretches of lawn that once took platoons of men hundreds of hours each month to weed and mow can now be kept in trim once every week or two by a single worker astride a giant power mower or pushing a tractor-driven cutter, with blades that can cut a swathe as wide as seventeen feet.

Even when one can afford them, the problem of *finding* trained and willing gardeners remains troublesome to many country house owners, particularly those in remote parts of the country. To add to all these problems, the great 100-mile-an-hour hurricane winds of 1987 and 1990 wiped out tens of thousands of trees, and many garden buildings, on estates throughout southern and western England.

· · ·

The last ten years have seen ever-increasing and more brazen thefts of art objects from historic country houses—not just portable paintings and objets d'art, but carved chimneypieces, stone and bronze garden statues, wrought iron gates, roof lead, whole windows, things no one regarded as particularly vulnerable before. In the summer of 1992, police traced four vanloads of objects—more than 1,000 pieces of antique furniture, paintings,

Sutton Place, Surrey.

ornaments, clocks, and porcelain—that had been stolen from country houses in Gloucestershire to five separate storage facilities in London. But 92 percent of the more than 1,000
objects reported stolen from private country houses between 1990 and 1995 have never
been recovered. In the summer of 1994, an entire £30,000 ($45,000) glass conservatory
went missing. A house in Norfolk lost its fireplaces, stained glass panels, shutters, paneled
doors, and staircase balustrades, as well as its kitchen sink and central heating system. The
two most famous country house burglaries occurred at Russborough House in County
Wicklow, Ireland, the home of the late Sir Alfred Beit, heir to an immense South African
diamond fortune. It was from here that one of the last three Vermeer paintings remaining
in private possession was first stolen in April 1974 as an IRA protest, then recovered
within a week; then stolen again in May 1986, only to be discovered—along with several
other paintings taken at the same time—seven years later. This gives Lord Cholmondeley
reason to hope that the precious little J.-B. Oudry painting, *The White Duck* (1753), which
was stolen from Houghton Hall in 1992—with the Longleat Titian, the most important
country house theft in recent years—may still eventually turn up.

   The astonishing increase in burglaries from country houses in recent years is not only
distressing in itself. It also leads to far more costly and specialized insurance coverage, by
insurers who require owners to install ever more intricate and expensive security systems.
As the value of all sorts of historic art objects has leapt since 1980, and museums and gal-

leries have become more sophisticated in their security installations, the art-burglary industry has concentrated increasingly on the vulnerable, unprotected, and often pub-lished collections of country houses and churches. And the adversary, today, is nothing less than an industry: an intricately organized, highly professional international business with a current take of perhaps $7 billion worth of unrecovered objects every year. Specialists in the theft of garden statuary, iron gates, and outdoor furniture—a major growth industry in Britain since the late 1980s, when single stone urns began fetching £500 ($750), and gar-den statues £20,000 ($30,000) or more—now come prepared with crane-equipped trucks, tractors, blocks-and-tackles, and high-powered blow torches; concentrate on houses located near motorway escape routes, where they have already managed to survey the grounds and access paths; drill through or smash doors, lever locks, squeeze through holes, and scramble up walls; and make advance arrangements with overseas shippers, who can have these difficult to trace items sealed in dockside containers, or even out of the coun-try before the owners are aware they are gone.

At the lower end of the market, burglars have discovered the high resale value of sal-vaged architectural fragments, which puts any unoccupied period house at serious risk. "Empty buildings are particularly vulnerable to these opportunist thieves, who will actually destroy two or three historic chimneypieces in the rush to rip out one that they can sell to an architectural salvage company for a couple of hundred pounds," says Philip Davies, chairman of the Council for the Prevention of Art Theft.[13]

Sir Thomas Ingilby, who founded a security "hotline" for country house owners after his own house was burgled in 1988, tells of a case in which Northamptonshire police raided a house on suspicion of drug sales in 1994:

"One of the things they found in there—which they certainly hadn't expected to find—was a huge stone water trough, weighing the better part of three-quarters of a ton. When they made enquiries, it turned out to have been stolen off a farmhouse thirty miles away that same morning, three hours previously."

"How did they do that?" I asked.

"Well, yes. Good question. They claimed they had bought it at a local car boot sale." He described another group of suspected burglars who were found in possession of a stately home guide in which they had listed details of the garden statuary at fifteen different houses.

Many owners, insurers, security advisers, and police authorities presume, nowadays, that designated works are stolen to order by what they call "commission burglars," people with a network of eager buyers who are well-informed about the latest security systems almost before they are invented. I have read minutely detailed explanations of the "progressive layers of defense" that one should install: motion detectors and beams inside rooms; high quality locks and alarm contacts on all doors and windows; radio alarms and vibration sen-sors underneath garden statues; and "perimeter protection" around the house and estate walls—microwave detection systems, underground pressure sensors, even closed circuit TV backed by infrared and floodlighting. Were my interest in the subject other than academic, I might be well on my way to devising means to get around all these obstacles. As Jonathan David points out, "However hard you try, you will not beat a determined professional thief who knows what he is looking for."[14]

Quite apart from burglary protection, insurance on a historic house will cost a good deal more than that on a comparable modern dwelling, because of the legal obligation to repair damage (in particular fire damage, but also damage caused by floods, storms, or ground subsidence) to the full level of a listed house's original condition. "We are keen that private owners should have enough insurance to rebuild in the same style, rather than rebuilding in modern materials," says a spokesman for English Heritage.[15] As repair costs at listed houses can average from four to five times those at unlisted houses, this premium will be reflected in the cost of insurance. James Sellick has had to insure Pashley Manor in Sussex for "between 2 and 2.5 times its market value," he writes, to cover what he would have to pay to replace its 16th-century wood paneling in case of fire. Most insurers demand 100 percent coverage on an entire house in order to obtain 100 percent repayment on a partial loss, and require regular revaluations of the entire building and contents. Others may insist on annual chimney-sweeping, elaborate fire-prevention systems, or the presence in the house of professional staff or "house sitters" at all times. After maintenance and repairs, the cost of fire-prevention and burglar alarm systems, plus fire and theft insurance, are likely to be the largest single items of expense in a country house.

· · ·

Taxes are a burden on almost everyone who earns an income or owns property, and complaints about them are as common as complaints about the weather. In terms of income tax, one could argue forever about the justice of different tax rates for different income levels, the exemption of certain kinds of income, and the ability to deduct certain kinds of expenditures from a tax liability. In any case, the top level of income tax in England dropped by half (from 80 percent to 40 percent) during the fifteen years after the Conservative victory of 1979. Most home and estate owners at the level we are discussing are wise enough to hire good accountants and attorneys to help them sort their way through the frequently changing British tax codes. There are almost always legal ways to maneuver, by means of incorporation, the setting up of trusts, having one's house declared a business, "one-estate election," and so on. "You don't want to be *too* honest," one owner told me.

Property taxes, in the American sense—what used to be called "rates" in Britain—were replaced in 1993 by local council taxes, or (in the case of houses run primarily or partially as tourist businesses) by business rates. These are set by local political jurisdictions, so it is difficult to assess in any general terms the burden they create on country house owners.[16]

Agricultural income, as a legacy of the wartime attitude that farming was an essential and "patriotic" industry, still benefits from income tax concessions, capital gains relief, and deductions for expenses or losses that other forms of income do not. Although these were not enough to counterbalance the great depression in agricultural income between 1983 and 1991, in good years these privileges may benefit those whose capital exists largely in the form of land. The really scandalous tax-avoiders, country landowners are convinced, are City speculators who know how to mask or roll over income, or hide their assets off-shore. A huge 18th-century house and 5,000 acres of farmland can't be spirited away to Liechtenstein or the Seychelles.

Many European countries levy an annual Wealth Tax—typically 1–2 percent—of the sort the Wilson government proposed (and abandoned) in 1974. Country house and land owners remain apprehensive that a future Labor government might try to resurrect the idea. I asked Lord Courtenay at Powderham Castle whether such a tax would really make all that much difference. "If your whole investment is in something like this," he replied, sweeping an arm around the castle courtyard from our table outside his café, "you don't even *earn* one or two percent. Under Capital Transfer Tax, if you were paying at the top rate, it did in fact work out to thirty percent every thirty years, or one percent a year; and a lot of places did pay that. On a place like this, that is every bit as much as you earn; in other words, it's the equivalent of an income tax of one hundred percent."

The tax burden that country house owners protest most vigorously is the Value Added Tax, or VAT (pegged at 17.5 percent since 1991) they must pay on the very repair expenses (both labor and materials) they are obliged by law to make. This protest has long been a rallying cry of the Historic Houses Association, which is perhaps why almost everyone who brings it up uses the same example to demonstrate its unfairness: you pay no VAT when installing a new swimming pool (new construction is exempt); but are obliged to pay the full 17.5 percent when repairing a historic Tudor window!

Successive Conservative chancellors, under Margaret Thatcher and John Major, rejected the pleas of the Historic Houses Association, the Country Landowners Association, the National Trust, English Heritage, and others who have asked for VAT relief on listed building repairs, despite the recommendation of the government's own Select Committee on the Environment. Labor spokesmen have indicated they would at least be willing to consider it. Any changes in VAT today must be coordinated with tax policies in the European Union (which evolved out of the EC in 1993) generally, because of their effect on "common market" price equity. But it is still believed by historic house owners and their advocates that the EU could be persuaded to grant at least a reduced—say, a 5–10 percent—level of VAT on repairs to listed buildings.

Lord Hesketh—former Conservative Party whip in the House of Lords, and owner of Easton Neston in Northamptonshire—remains convinced that a reduced level of VAT for listed property repairs will never be granted, because the Treasury regard it as unpoliceable: there are simply far too many listed buildings. "Every slightly dodgy builder will produce an invoice saying it was a listed building even when it wasn't. If you've got all these thousands of houses, probability suggests there will be one or two who will abuse it. And you know what the British press is like. It's absurd to give tax credit to a whole class of buildings; it becomes a tax incentive to own an old house."

· · ·

The most serious challenge to the continued family possession of a historic country house—which is of course not quite the same thing as a house's "survival"—occurs when the time comes to pass it on from one owner or generation to another.

Inheritance taxes have been a part of British revenue policy since 1894, when the 5th Marquess of Lansdowne drew down the wrath of his fellow peers by proposing an 8 percent tariff on inherited estates. The rates steadily climbed to 18 percent, 40 percent, 65 percent, then peaked in 1949 at 80 percent on everything above the first million pounds. The deaths of an owner and an heir in fairly rapid succession—the father dying at 80, say, his 60-year-old eldest son only surviving him by five or ten years—could mean the by the time the next-in-line inherited, the estate had been reduced by as much as 96 percent.

Most major sales of country houses in the past century, or transfers from private to National Trust ownership, have been the result of capital taxes levied on estates at the time of death and inheritance. Variously known as Death Duties, Capital Transfer Tax, and Inheritance Tax, these at one time appeared to be killing for all time the traditional pattern of grand houses (financed by their own agricultural estates) being retained in the same family generation after generation.

Since the strict regime of 1945–51, various degrees of tax avoidance or relief have been made possible, by means of "lifetime handover" provisions, conditional tax exemption on designated heritage properties, and various forms of trusts. In nine national budgets between 1980 and 1994, the Thatcher and Major governments lightened the burden by lowering the top tax rate and expanding reliefs.

But in most cases the challenge remains: how is one to come up with 40 percent of the assessed value of a grand house, its valuable contents, and (after deductions for tax-free agricultural land) its valuable surrounding acreage—*without* selling acres, contents, or house? This is further complicated by the fact that, if you find yourself forced to sell things to pay inheritance taxes, you will be charged a capital gains tax on anything that was purchased for less than you get for selling it, with no account taken of inflation. You may also have to pay duties deferred earlier on tax-exempted items—duties that might be "clawed back" at current rates and valuations. And after all this, the regional assessor may set a value on your property far in excess of what you think it is worth, which can lead to years of costly litigation.

The obvious answer is to have a fortune in disposable wealth—stocks and bonds, urban real estate, perhaps a business partnership—entirely independent of your historic house and estate. If your historic estate is valued at a million pounds, let us say (above the tax-free limit of about £150,000, and tax-free agricultural land), and you have another million pounds' worth of saleable assets off the estate, you could then pay off a 40 percent inheritance tax bill by liquidating £800,000 worth of the latter—again, net of capital gains taxes.

Your job upon inheriting, then, as a conscientious new head of family, would be to build whatever external assets remain back up to a million or more before the time comes for *you* to hand over the estate, so that your heir can do the same thing. This may not, on the surface, seem all that difficult. Two hundred thousand pounds, earning 10 percent a year, will grow to a million pounds in seventeen years. Capital gains taxes, as well as living and maintenance expenses, may eat into this sum along the way. But many people in Britain have done as well or better.

Unfortunately, few of them have been traditional country house owners. Because they either have few or no external, off-estate assets to begin with; because they have little interest in or aptitude for the business world; or because what liquid assets they do possess are in supposedly "safe" or low-return investments, the traditional aristocracy and squirearchy, which depended for centuries on agricultural rents, are rarely major competitors in today's economic race. Fortunes sufficient to pay (or elude) every kind of tax that may be devised are being made all over Britain. But except for a few impressive cases, they are not being made by traditional country house owners. By and large, their assets tend to remain within their estates: and these are what they must sell to pay their inheritance taxes. "Only two owners of Hagley have died in this century," says Lord Cobham. "Each time the size of the estate has been halved, with a corresponding reduction in the income available to maintain the house."

The happiest country house owners tend to be those who not only *have* outside incomes or fortunes, but heirs with independent incomes as well. "I believe that future generations should be able to live here," said the owner of a fine Tudor house in the Midlands, which had been in his family since it was built—"*if* they've got other employment. Luckily, our eldest son-in-law is a successful young banker—and we've got two grandsons, which is great good news. We can look ahead a bit now."

One of the more morbid aspects of all this is that it obliges the owner of a historic house—one who is eager to keep it intact and in the family—to spend a major part of his life and energy worrying about its status after his death. Every investment, every tax deal, every sale of an acre or piece of furniture—one's place of residence, one's choice of career, one's decision whether to apply for a repair grant or to take out a loan—is made not in view of the family's (or the house's) present welfare, but of something that may happen to someone else, after you are dead. You may even feel guilty about becoming ill at an inopportune time, since—if your heir is to be spared the burden of death duties—the tax code obliges you to live at least seven years after you have given your house away. Had his father lived just three months longer, the current Duke of Devonshire would have been spared some £12 million ($33.6 million) in death duties. Some owners have taken out costly life insurance policies to guard against just such possibilities.

Samuel Whitbread, whose father gave him Southill to run when he married in 1961 (he was then 24), feels a bit of pressure to pass the house over to his son in turn. But, like Lord Cobbold at Knebworth, he wants to enjoy living a bit longer in the house he has devoted so much effort to restoring. "I guess in ten years time, when I'm sixty-five-plus, and he's forty-plus—if he wants to. He may say, 'Good God No, the last thing I want is a house like that!' My grandfather, and I'm sure my father thought that the next generation would be the last. They could see the pressures building up....I think from a tax point of view, my son will be all right because of the sale of some land. We managed to get some of it into a

Southill, Bedfordshire. Garden view.

trust for him before it was developed and therefore at a relatively low value. We have—touch wood—secured enough cash for him in his trust to be able to pay any Inheritance Tax for him on my death. That's the aim of the exercise. From the moment I came here thirty years ago, one was thinking about how one was going to hand it on. It becomes an obsession."

The Earl of Leicester agreed, when I put this same idea to him. "You're quite right. It's peculiarly... I was going to say 'dispiriting.' But it just does take a very great deal of one's time and one's money in dealing with professional advisers, lawyers, and accountants. And it seems an awful waste of good brains on really negative things. But we're a big estate, nearly twenty-six thousand acres. I can afford to hand over a certain amount to my son and still keep a certain amount for me to live on. So a great deal has gone to him; in fact, he's rather better off than I am."

William LeBlanc-Smith, who managed Sudeley Castle for Lady Ashcombe, described the endless complications and negotiations that he and the family went through trying to keep the estate healthy and intact for the next generation. "There are difficult periods, times when we question the whole thing, when we sit around the family table and say, you know, what are we doing here? And in the end the driving force, the one thing that makes it all worthwhile, is for the family to inherit it." (Lady Ashcombe's son Henry came back from America to take charge of the estate on his 30th birthday in 1996.)

·   ·   ·

A secondary problem involved with inheritance, which causes considerable worry to some country house owners, is the possible unfitness or lack of interest on the part of an heir. Most traditional owners I talked to felt reasonably confident (again, knocking wood) that their children and grandchildren would love the house as they did, would want to live on in it, when the time came, and make the effort to keep it going. Some thought that just growing up in a great house, having it as the setting for one's earliest memories, would create the required emotional ties, as the experience had done for them a generation before. But responses vary:

> As the Berkeleys have been here for 24 generations they are reasonably confident as far as the next 24 generations are concerned. (Eiler Hansen, Custodian, Berkeley Castle)
>
> If future generations can avoid drink, drugs, and general incompetence, I guess they will want to live here if they can. (Lord Middleton, Birdsall House)
>
> There is always the appalling prospect that my son may, when he inherits the house at the end of 2007, feel that the costs and problems outweigh the revenue and advantages. (Marquess of Zetland, Aske Hall)

Others insist that daughters-in-law are the real secret to success. Michael Saunders-Watson of Rockingham Castle, a former president of the HHA, once said that the two secrets to the survival of country houses were "not dying" and having your heir marry the right woman. "The fate of country houses is in the hands of the daughters-in-law," Roy Stong once said to the Duke of Richmond. When I asked Lord Cobbold whether he saw the next generation living in Knebworth, he replied, "Well, you'll have to talk to the next generation about that." After a time studying filmmaking in California, his eldest son was back living in the village with his American wife, and seemed at least willing to consider the idea.

But there are exceptions. As James Lees-Milne reminded me, "You've got to be dedicated. You can't expect father and son, father and son forever to want to manage a big house, and show the public round. You've got one who wants to live overseas, or is already a solicitor or a composer or something. He can't be bothered. It's not just the lack of money—it's other interests. It's no sinecure, owning a country house today."

"These large estates are businesses," says Nicholas Howard, "and not all eldest sons make the best businessmen." Nicholas is himself a second son; it is his *younger* brother Simon lives in and looks after Castle Howard today. Lord Montagu—who feels fortunate that his elder son takes a great interest in Beaulieu—said in his farewell speech as presi-

dent of the HHA, "Forget about taxation, forget about everything else; continuity of succession is the one thing you've got to worry about." "When a house is sold," wrote a
reporter for the *Economist* in 1984, "the reasons are rarely just commercial. A common
cause of closure is simply the passing of a house to an heir who cannot or will not give up
his job to run it."[17] Veronica Tritton's last years, according to her obituary in the *Telegraph*,
"were clouded by painful problems and uncertainties about the future of the house and
estate" at Parham, to which she and her parents had devoted their lives.[18] Her nephew and
godson, beneficiary of the Parham Trust, had no interest in living in the house; his cousins
have also been reluctant to move in.

The Marquess of Hertford made a point of letting his son Harry, the Earl of Yarmouth,
know that he would hand over Ragley Hall to him the minute he married. Lord
Yarmouth—who married and took over in 1990, at 32—sees that as a much more satisfactory solution than waiting until old age or death forces one to hand a house on. "All over
this country, you have parents in the big house, who have collected tons of stuff; and they
stay on and on and on. And the son who is due to inherit at some time goes out and gets
married and has kids. He and his wife set up home in a very comfortable house somewhere,
where they have their own life and they're educating their children. And Dad rings up one
day and says 'I'm moving out, I can't take it any more. I'm leaving next Monday, and you
can move in.' And it's, 'Sorry, Dad. But we don't actually want to.'"

Part of the reason for the passing of Kedleston from the Scarsdale family to the National
Trust was the fact that Lord Scarsdale's eldest son was *not* interested in living there, and
wanted his promised share of the estate in cash. A similar situation led to recent sales of
art treasures from Castle Howard. Much of the Blenheim Palace estate was locked up in a
trust in 1994, primarily because the Duke of Marlborough did not believe his eldest son
and heir could be trusted with running it. "I don't know a single English country estate in
which the inheritance has been straightforward," says Lord Arundel. "There are always
these terrible complications."

When Robin Davenport, the owner of a fine 1726 house in Shropshire, found himself
dying at 37 of a brain tumor, his wife told him she didn't want to go on living in the
house—which she couldn't afford doing in any case. Their son was only nine months old
at the time. So Davenport left the house to a trust, which currently rents it out to a catering and functions business, until the year 2013. At that time his son William, at 21, will
inherit Davenport House, with its 2,000 acres and heirloom contents, and he can decide
what to do next.

• • •

Some Possible Solutions

For each of these challenges to living in, maintaining, and handing on intact a historic
country house, there are possible aids and supports; to each problem, a possible, at least
partial solution.

Ragley Hall, Warwickshire.

English Heritage—the Historic Buildings and Monuments Commission for England—has, in the ten years since its formation in 1984, grown into a "quango" (quasi-autonomous nongovernmental organization) with about 1,600 employees, and an annual budget of £115 million ($184 million). While it remains the major source of public funds for repairs to historic buildings and monuments, it tends to worry more about its own properties-in-care, from Stonehenge and Dover Castle to what is left of Hadrian's wall.

English Heritage will consider paying a portion of the cost of essential repairs "which are beyond an owner's means" to buildings they "judge to be of outstanding national interest." They have always restricted their grants to buildings rated (or deserving a rating of) Grade I or II*—about 8 percent of all listed buildings—which leaves most country house owners out of the running.

But this general policy became somewhat academic, as the total amount offered for country house repair grants to private owners dropped from a high of £3.75 million ($6.4 million) in 1988–89 to less than a million pounds ($1.77 million) between 1990 and 1993.[19] With hundreds of house owners in need of help, all of them in competition with the owners of historic town halls, churches, cottages, factories, follies, and bridges (as well the National Trust), this means of salvation began to seem less and less likely, unless a house was in imminent danger of collapse.

As English Heritage's first chairman Lord Montagu pointed out in 1991, "Pressure has increased for the preservation of types of building which, a few decades ago, nobody would have thought of saving: these include mills, warehouses, barns and cinemas." His successor, Sir Jocelyn Stevens, repeated the message in 1992: "The definition of the word 'heritage' is widening to include types of building which have previously been neglected, for example, twentieth-century and industrial buildings and monuments."[20] EH's annual budget—which is always at the mercy of the current government's money men—has to cover the upkeep of its own 400 properties, which had a repairs backlog of £47 million ($72 million) in 1994; grants for town planning and "conservation areas"; and what is called "rescue archeology" at any one of 60,000 Roman and prehistoric sites threatened by farming or development.

When Samuel Whitbread realized, in 1989, how extensive the essential repairs at Southill were going to be (they ended up taking five years, and costing £4 million—about $7 million), he applied to EH not for a grant but for a loan, to cover the period before he was able to develop a part of the property. No, he was told: "'You have other assets you can sell: furniture, pictures, land.' And English Heritage was so limited. Their total grant budget for that whole year was just nine million. So we dropped it in the end and went to see the bank manager. We would have had to open the house until the grant was repaid. [The house is not normally open.] But we were prepared to grin and bear it for two or three years."

The percentage of repair expenses covered by grants varies from government to government: HBC subsidies as high as 60 or 75 percent under Labor have declined to EH grants of 40 percent or less under the Conservatives. Speaking of the grants his father obtained from the Harold Wilson government to restore Ragley Hall in 1964, Lord Yarmouth said, "The Conservatives took the attitude that we wouldn't touch you with a barge pole, because it would be like giving money to a dead donkey. The Labor party said, 'Well, if you show us your books, and they're honest—if you don't have a million stashed away somewhere—we'll see what we can do.'"

Some owners are loathe to apply to English Heritage for repair grants for the same reasons they dislike dealing with them over ordinary remodeling jobs. The trustees at Wilton House estimated that "the delays, frustration and extra work" imposed by English Heritage ate up at least 10 percent of their grant; others have put the extra costs resulting from special EH requirements as high as 40 percent. Several country house owners insist they will never apply for repair grants because of what they regard as the inflexible, unhelpful nature of the EH bureaucracy; the detailed "means test" to which they must submit; the expensive standard of work EH inspectors require; or the costly, long-term program of repairs to which a single small grant may commit you.

Several private house owners told me that they believe the current British government feels it has already "done enough" for their kind. They are reminded that they have enjoyed almost four decades of special favors, and told that they must now look elsewhere for help, while the government directs its attention to others in need. Something like this feeling does seem to have settled into Fortress House in Savile Row, English Heritage headquarters. One senses a prevailing attitude that they and their predecessors, the Historic Buildings Councils, may have been—by political standards—overly generous to country houses in the past. A majority of their repair grants nowadays goes to churches and cathedrals, together with other nondomestic listed buildings, many of them in cities and towns.

Lord Montagu of Beaulieu, chairman of EH in 1991 (and obviously a friend to the private owner), was stung by criticisms of his group made in an editorial written by the Earl of Shelburne, one of his successors as president of the Historic Houses Association. Montagu reminded Shelburne that the public perception of the "national heritage" continues to grow in scope; that English Heritage is now expected to help preserve a great many types of buildings—not just country houses; and that "there is never going to be enough public money to satisfy all demands."[21]

The other complaint frequently raised with regard to repair costs on country houses—the fact that they are burdened with VAT charges, whereas new building expenses are not—may be answered by a change of government. Chris Smith, my Labor Party informant, told me in October 1995 that lower-band VAT for repairs to listed buildings was "an idea we're certainly looking into—perhaps in return for the imposition of VAT on new build additions."

• • •

So far, the far larger resources available from the Heritage Lottery Commission—£260 million ($416 million) in the national lottery's first year of operation—have been restricted to public and institutional owners of heritage properties and collections. As of 1995, the only allocation from the fund made for the restoration of a country house (£2.65 million, or $4.2 million) had gone to Christchurch Borough Council in Dorset, to finish the job of reroofing and repairing Highcliffe Castle, which was left a wreck by disastrous fires in the 1960s and 1970s. But Chris Smith wrote me that "a Labour Government would make individual owners of historic houses eligible for funding from the National Lottery, provided that any added equity value can be recouped if the property is sold on."

The other important central funding body, the National Heritage Memorial Fund—

now also the channeling authority for National Lottery heritage grants—is also forbidden by its charter from giving grants to private owners. It tends to offer repair grants only when a house is in grave danger and is about to be taken over by the government in lieu of taxes. It then passes the house on to the National Trust (or another charitable foundation), by transferring the unpaid tax funds to the Treasury, and sometimes offers an endowment for maintenance as well. But this is no help to a struggling owner who wants to hold on to his house.

. . .

If agricultural estates were for a decade or more millstones around the necks of already battered country house owners, things have taken a turn for the better since 1992—although most country landowners do not expect CAP ("Common Agricultural Policy," a European Union arrangement) subsidies to last beyond 2000 at their current irrationally generous levels. It is satisfying to talk with a rare owner like the Earl of Leicester at Holkham Hall, where the cost of maintaining a magnificent country house, begun by his great-great-great-grandfather in 1734, is easily covered by a 26,000-acre agricultural estate:

> My philosophy has been to spend money on the estate while we were making money, get the estate in good order, clear off the overdraft, and get a sum of money in the bank the increment on which we could use during those years (which are bound to come) when we will need it. But at the moment, yes, certainly, the estate is self-supporting. In fact it makes a nice profit. But you're right: we are a big place.
>
> I don't mean to sound pompous, but I understand land, and I can make money out of farming it. I enjoy it, I walk over it, I shoot on it; it's something that I enjoy and understand, so therefore I've kept it. In fact, I keep buying new bits and pieces all the time.

Few owners opened their account books to me quite as freely as did Lord Leicester. But given the estimated size of their holdings, I expect that farming and farm rentals still turn a profit most years at estates the size of Alnwick, Chatsworth, Badminton, and Brocklesby Park, which range from 27,000 to 100,000 acres in size; and Garrowby, Mulgrave Castle, Longford Castle, Cirencester Park, Wilton House, Aske Hall, Woburn Abbey, Althorp, Hatfield, and Knowsley, all between 11,500 and 18,000 acres. The houses at Castle Ashby, Castle Howard, Longleat, Blenheim Palace, Raveningham, Sledmere, and Southill stand at the center of estates of at least 10,000 acres.

Income from even such extensive properties may not be sufficient to maintain a very large historic house. But, particularly if the property includes a roll of well-maintained houses and cottages for rent, it will probably make a major contribution. Several country house owners I talked to still regard themselves primarily, and proudly, as farmers. At least 38 present peers or their heirs were educated at the Royal Agricultural College, an indication of the seriousness with which some members of the landed gentry still regard their agricultural holdings and obligations.

Most owners of English country estates, in fact, take agriculture very seriously indeed.

Holkham Hall, Norfolk. Marble Hall.

Some of them talk more knowledgeably about price supports and crop yields, tractor mod-els and milk quotas than they do about fox hunting, grouse shooting, and equestrian events. It is notable that many of the remaining important houses that are *not* open regu-larly to the public, which means the owners have not accepted the kind of government grants or concessions that would oblige them to open, are surrounded by extensive agri-cultural estates.

•   •   •

One of the most potentially rewarding forms of off-estate income is urban property, as any-one who has ever played "Monopoly" can tell. This is the source of the wealth of Eng-land's richest landed aristocrat, the Duke of Westminster, whose family firm (Grosvernor Estates) owns a number of the prize West End spots on the game board—a total of more than 300 acres in Mayfair—which more than pays the bills for his out-of-London home, Eaton Hall in Cheshire. (Actually, Eaton Hall is not a "historic house" anymore; it was largely torn down and rebuilt in the 1960s.) A number of other country houses and estates are sustained in part on the high rentals obtained from property their former owners had the good fortune to inherit in places like Birmingham, Sheffield, Folkestone, Grimsby, Scarborough, Skegness, and of course London. Even more survive on rental properties, both residential and commercial, that lie within estate boundaries, which often include one or more villages.

The city of Cirencester has grown up around the Earl of Bathurst's extensive Gloucestershire estate, the parkland of which he opens up daily to local residents. But, says his son Lord Apsley—who has run Cirencester Park Properties since 1988, when he was 27—it is the real estate they own in the town that makes the major contribution to the company's income. "We've got a great diversity here. We've got commercial blocks in town, be it shops or factories, then on top of that the residential properties, then on top of that the agricultural side, then on top of that the forestry side." Large as it is, the 15,000-acre farmland has become what Lord Apsley calls "just a sideline."

There are other ways of making money out of cities than by owning substantial pieces of them. A significant number of country house owners today—even 21st barons—spend most of their working hours and years in London, where they earn their living as bankers, brokers, attorneys, tax consultants, film or television producers, estate agents, journalists, or business executives. Many country house owners I have met concede that it is their business or professional income—not that of their estate—that pays their family's living expenses, and often contributes substantially to the cost of maintaining the house.

One reason that houses such as Southill in Bedfordshire, Cowdray Park in Sussex, Thornton Manor in Cheshire, and Kings Walden Bury in Bedfordshire need not open to tourists is that their owners are heirs to industrial fortunes as well as country estates. Recent new owners of country houses and estates are primarily people whose fortunes and incomes came from sources other than land: attorneys and investors, entertainment industry leaders, British and foreign oil magnates.

I was impressed by Lord Arundel's argument—seconded by a number of other current owners—that the only dependable way to maintain and preserve a historic country house nowadays was to develop sources of income *off* the estate. Forced into outside investments by a straitened inheritance, he began a small propane and butane distribution company in 1979 for £18,000 ($38,000) in the East End of London, worked very hard at it, and ended up selling it to Esso nine years later. ("The eighties was a terribly lucky time to set up new businesses," he modestly says.) Now he has a waste-processing business in the North, which is also going well.

My line has always been, whatever money you're going to risk, whatever energy you're going to put into setting up that sort of thing, do it off the estate. Because what you're trying to do is preserve. My main thing now, my new rule is: Preserve Arundel. Preserve the castle, preserve the pictures, let as many people enjoy it as possible—as well as the family—and hand it on intact. And to achieve that, you've got to diversify into other things. And if you diversify off the place, you can very often get far better returns.

There's always a lot of investment opportunities around one, and sometimes I think people get carried away by thinking you must develop on your doorstep. And the reason that you go to your doorstep is that the land is free. But I think that's a great error. If it goes badly, you can't fold it up easily. If it goes well, you can't sell it to somebody else. But apart from that, you've got to compete in the real world. I mean, are golf courses really so profitable? If a thing's really profitable, it's got to stand up on its own two feet. You should write in the land at its proper value, and then see if the investment still makes sense.

As for his eldest son Henry (all of six years old when we talked): "What I want him to do is either set up in business and make a fortune to keep this place going, or to go and get a good job in the City or industry. Because you just aren't going to keep it going any other way."

"Luckily," Arundel adds, as in an afterthought, "we did also inherit a bit of Sheffield."

Sir Nicholas Bacon, of Raveningham Hall in Norfolk (the premier baronet of England, as Lord Arundel's father is the premier Duke and Earl; their titles date from 1611 and 1483), echoes these sentiments: "My overriding principle is that if you have inherited something, you leave it better than you inherited. If I can do that, if I can make sufficient money on the side in order to project the house and estate through the next generation here into the next, then that's good enough for me. I can't do much more than that.

"You've got to get out and make money elsewhere, not actually on the estate. In a way, you've got to *enjoy* your estate, and make money elsewhere."

Brewing, says Samuel Whitbread, is a more dependable source of income than farming. Like Arundel, he believes that too many owners grow fixated on thinking of their inherited house and grounds as their sole and only income source, and come to feel that their only hope of saving it is to exploit it. Out of this myopia comes the anxiety to sell off land for development—land which, once sold, you can never get back.

Robin Brackenbury, at Holme Pierrepont in Nottinghamshire, grows warm on this point:

The reason for the failures of such houses as Brympton d'Evercy and Pitchford was incompetence: the inability of the family to earn enough money to keep going. And that is a basic requirement. There are plenty of people in this country who've made a great deal of money in the last few years. There's never been a shortage of people who can make money....If you can make enough money—if you can earn three hundred thousand, half a million, a million a year, which plenty of people can do—you can run a fairly substantial country house.

If people are going to continue to live in these houses, they've simply got to have the earning ability. The agricultural estate is irrelevant. It's an amenity. Even before the war, a land agent told me, if you could make an estate break even, you were doing very well.

Most estates have been subsidized by selling off land, or by outside money. What has subsidized Somerleyton? Crossley's Carpets. What's subsidized the Duke of Marlborough? Vanderbilt money from America.

I bring up the successful businesses of Lord Arundel, heir to the Duke of Norfolk, and his hopes of reuniting the family estates.

"The Duke of Norfolk is the son of Lord Howard of Glossop, who was a very influential man in the City of London, because he had money. He became very rich, *because* he worked in the City of London. And his children went into the City of London also. The present Duke of Norfolk and his brother Mark worked in Fleming's Bank, which has been hugely successful. Professor, the landed property is an irrelevance, if it's purely agricultural. What you've got to have—every generation, at most every two generations—is the entrepreneurial skill to create wealth. Because a historic house is a depreciating asset, like your motorcar. You've got to pour capital into it every hundred years or less. Because every hundred years it has to have a new roof." He gossips about a few recently sold houses. In each case, he insists, the families failed not because of tax burdens, or because of Lloyd's losses, but because they lacked entrepreneurial skills.

. . .

There is one avenue for income tax reduction open to country houses—at least some country houses—that are regularly open to the public.

Such houses, if they can demonstrate from their account books that they are "managed on a commercial basis with a view to the realization of profits," can declare themselves businesses. This allows them to deduct a large part of their general maintenance expenses against visitor income, and to set off house-opening losses against overall income. As a rule, the tax people will not consider a country house a proper business if it attracts fewer than 15,000 visitors a year. Below that number, the tourist traffic is considered incidental. Expenses directly related to attracting and accommodating visitors may still be deducted from income—the cost of advertising, guides, car parks, repairing visitor damage, and the like. But house maintenance is then regarded as more a family than a business expense.

This also applies to Value Added Tax. The 17.5 percent tax on admissions, gift sales, and other earnings collected for the government can be set against a similar amount of VAT due from the owner on house-related expenses. At very popular houses, this can represent an enormous sum. "We get so much VAT to lap up we don't know what to do with it," says Lord Montagu at Beaulieu. "Reduced VAT would be very important to smaller houses, or houses not open to the public. But we certainly can't complain: we've got millions!"

There are so many possible avenues of inheritance-tax avoidance that it has, as I noted earlier, been labeled by critics and cynics alike as a "voluntary" tax, paid only by those patriotic or foolish enough not to have obtained better advice on tax shelters. This outrages left-wing critics today, as it outraged Denis Healy in 1974. "The trusts through which British wealth is sheltered as inheritance-tax avoidance scams should be legislated against. Inheritance tax should be unavoidable," wrote one such spokesman in 1994, railing against tax exiles and overseas-based trusts and the inequities of the class system. "This is undemocratic and unreasonable and shortchanges the Treasury from an important source of revenue."[22]

The most common means of avoiding inheritance tax on a large estate is a scheme I have already mentioned, whereby the owner hands over a substantial portion of his property to an heir during his lifetime, gambling that he will live for at least another seven years. If he *does* live the magic seven years, the transfer is exempt, and no inheritance tax will be due. The transferer would be wise, of course, to hold on to sufficient resources for himself—a comfortably furnished farmhouse, perhaps, a healthy pension or annuity—against the possibility of his designated heir suddenly turning into a Goneril or a Regan. Beyond that, the only crucial question is timing: at what age will you be willing to move out of your own ancestral home (or start paying rent to your son), while still feeling sturdy enough to survive the seven-year interregnum? At what age will your heir be able and willing to take it over? "The awful thing," says the Earl of Scarborough, "is the crystal ball gazing: how long am I going to live? I smoke like a chimney. But I don't want to go hat in hand to my son to ask for one or two thousand. It's all fairly ghoulish, you know."

·   ·   ·

"Conditional exemption" is the long-established policy, described in Chapter Four, whereby inherited pictures, books, and manuscripts, as well as houses and (after 1976) parkland determined to be a significant part of the "national heritage" could be exempted from taxation, as long as they remained unsold, were maintained in good order, and were made "reasonably" accessible to the public. (In general, this exemption is limited to houses listed Grade I or II*.) The public access requirement for conditional tax exemption, and the similar string attached to English Heritage repair grants, represent the main reason that so many British houses are open to the public. The majority of owners of open houses with whom I have communicated have said flatly that the *reason* their house is open is not to earn money—opening almost never pays; nor some feeling of cultural benevolence; but because they were obliged to grant public access as a result of tax concessions or repair grants.

Conversely, many owners refuse to ask for conditional exemption precisely *because* of the access requirement it implies. At Shrubland Park in Suffolk, Lord de Saumarez is trying to strike a deal with the Countryside Commission to grant him conditional exemption not so much on his house (which his mother now runs as a health clinic, and where visitors would get in the way) as on "the house in the landscape." The result, he hopes, will be that he need only grant access to his gardens, from which people could *look* at his house.

One of the first times the "Conditional Exemption" policy came into question was when it was made known that the former Earl and Countess of Spencer had quietly sold an estimated £2 million ($3.5 million) worth of heirlooms from Althorp—many of which had apparently been granted conditional exemption from death duties on his inheritance in 1975. When the Capital Tax Office learned of the sales of these items after Lord

Spencer's death in 1992, a spokesman insisted that if anything was found to have been sold on which tax had been deferred, the person judged responsible would have to make good the exempted tax.

The Conditional Exemption policy came in for some more nasty press in 1992 when it was discovered that not all owners of exempted property and art works were equally forthcoming regarding public access. "Secret Tax Deals for Landowners," headlined the *Observer*: "£150 Million 'Access' Scandal"; "Hoards of a Hidden Heritage," cried the *Guardian*: "A Little-Known Loophole in the Law."[23]

The crux of these reports was that many owners who had been granted conditional tax exemption on certain items made access to them so difficult—often simply by making it virtually impossible to learn which works of art were supposed to be accessible—that the public was no better off after the exemptions had been granted than before. The *Guardian*'s reporter drew a few prize remarks out of the Earl of St. Germans, over lunch at his country house in Cornwall. St. Germans had no intention of opening his house, he declared, in order to let day-trippers gape at his tax-exempted Rembrandt, Van Dycks, Reynoldses, antique furniture and silver. "I lead a life of opulent obscurity. Why should Mrs. Tiggywinkle come here on a Saturday afternoon out of mere curiosity?"[24]

On the whole, this struck me as the sort of artificial scandal which even responsible British newspapers enjoy stirring up. As with National Trust properties, *preservation* of places and objects of artistic and historic importance, preventing them from either decaying or being lost to the country, is more at the heart of such policies than the insistence that they be on ready and regular public display. Owners of smaller, wholly lived-in country houses are understandably reluctant to open their doors to all comers for the sake of one or two pictures they may have inherited free of taxation. Other owners fear that granting excessive publicity or access to their works of art, tax exempt or not, will only encourage thieves, and increase their security costs. Private owners of valuable works of art often keep their ownership secret, even when lending them to museums.

But the exposé sparked a parliamentary inquiry, which led to the Capital Tax Office's sending a letter to all owners of conditionally exempt objects in December 1992, laying out stricter regulations regarding publicity and access. "It takes detective work," the *Guardian*'s reporter had protested, "to find out who benefits from this tax loophole and what they own." Precisely. To protect themselves from thieves who know how to read, the HHA advised its members *not* to reveal their own names or addresses in association with items they owned, which are now registered on a computerized, easily accessed log; when feasible, to permit viewing of tax-exempted treasures only at places away from the house; and to verify the identity of anyone asking to inspect them.

·   ·   ·

A common means of inheritance-tax avoidance, in Britain as in the United States, is the establishment of a family trust. The property to be protected is then vested in the trust, which has the right to buy and sell and make investments (hence the term, "discretionary" trust). One names a designated beneficiary who may, upon inheriting, elect to extend the family trust for further generations.

Trust law in both countries is far too complicated (and too frequently changed) for me to understand or explain it. In the United Kingdom, the primary value of a setting up a discretionary trust seems to be that of sparing one's heir the sudden shock and burden of death duties. Since 1976, the capital assets of such trusts have been taxed at ten-year intervals. The result is that, over a statistically averaged "generation" of, say, thirty years, an estate will be taxed as much as it would be if inherited directly, although there may be some tax savings on capital gains.

But at least these taxes can be anticipated and prepared for. At Knole, where the tax bill on the Sackville family trust comes due every time the year ends in zero, Lord Sackville told me that at each round they pay the bill by handing over to the Treasury another piece of furniture or work of art—which then remains in the same place it has been in for centuries.

. . .

To be certain that your estate remains intact, if not precisely "yours," you can instruct your lawyers to try to set up a charitable trust. The trust—which may be a non-profit company—would then own the house (or, more often, lease it from you for 40 or 75 or 99 years) and be responsible for its maintenance. If you want to keep living in it yourself, you must then rent (or sublet) your family quarters from the trust at the market rate, and agree to pay for the decorating, repairs, and other expenses in your own rooms. You will also be expected to pay the going fee to use the public rooms, should you wish to celebrate Christmas in the chapel, or your son's coming-of-age with a ball in the Great Hall.

You can try, of course, to run the trust yourself, and stack its board of trustees with family and friends. But the British Charity Commissioners (who must approve the formation of such foundations) insist on an "arms length" rule, according to which the prior owner is expected to keep a certain ethical and economic distance from the running of the new institution. Any private benefit that accrues to the donor family must be "purely incidental." A majority of the (unpaid) trustees is expected to be wholly independent—although the donor and members of his family, as well as "safe votes" like the old family lawyer, may be among them.

The Knebworth House Education and Preservation Trust was established in 1984 when Lord and Lady Cobbold, who had moved into Knebworth in 1970, realized they simply could not pay the costs of restoring the house and gardens out of estate and tourist income. The trust was given a 70-year lease on the house and gardens, which currently cost about £275,000 ($420,000) a year to run, of which about £100,000 ($150,000) is for capital improvements. Manager John Hoy figures there are about £3 million ($4.5 million) worth of repairs still to do. Among the trustees were Lord Cobbold's mother and his eldest son, but also the mayor of the nearest town, and the chairmen of the local district and parish councils. When Knebworth returns to family ownership in the year 2040, all nicely restored, the heirs can then decide whether to renew the trust, or take possession them-selves.

According to the 1951 Act of Parliament that made them possible, country house char-itable trusts must be justified for reasons of "advancement of education or other purposes beneficial to the community," among which are included the "promotion of the study and appreciation of the house as a place of historic and architectural interest and the advance-ment of education in the arts." The trustees must demonstrate this public benefit—com-parable to that of a National Trust property—to the satisfaction of the Charity Commis-sioners, and be open to the public a minimum of 90 days a year. A substantial endowment will be required at the outset for maintenance and repairs, which means that the owner must usually donate art works, rental cottages, or development land for the trust to sell.

The Duke of Norfolk easily persuaded the trustees of Arundel Castle to take the route of a charitable trust when he inherited in 1975, because the endowment the National Trust demanded was five times greater than that required by the Charity Commissioners. The Duke of Devonshire sold (among other things) a painting by Poussin for £1.65 mil-lion ($3.3 million) to help endow the Chatsworth House Trust in 1981. In recent years, the National Heritage Memorial Fund (NHMF) has been willing to contribute to these endowments to help get a charitable trust under way—"a cost-effective alternative," says attorney Douglas Connell, "to the requirements of the National Trusts or English Her-itage." Major NHMF grants to Weston Park in Shropshire, Burton Constable in Yorkshire, and Hopetoun House near Edinburgh have made it possible for those houses to be suffi-ciently endowed to be transferred to private charitable trusts in the years since 1980.

The great advantage of a charitable trust is that it allows the estate to continue intact without the drain or threat of income or capital transfer or inheritance tax. Moreover, as any investments or property deeded to the endowment are also spared the bite of income and capital gains taxation, the endowment has a chance to grow more rapidly than a pri-vate fortune could. Unlike the National Trust, a charitable trust can run its own farms, and thereby—in good years—earn more tax-free income from an estate.

Lady Victoria Leatham at Burghley points out another advantage of living in what is, in effect, the property of a registered charity. She has been able to solicit donations to help restore the house and its contents from corporate and other donors—almost £100,000 in her best year—who might be less forthcoming for a house in private hands. "They know I'm not going to spend it on a good holiday."

From the government's point of view, one major advantage of putting a country house in the hands of a charitable trust is that the National Heritage Memorial Fund—which is to say, ultimately, the British taxpayer—will be thereby spared the huge expense of a des-peration "buy-out" from a private owner unable to pay his taxes. The Charity Commission and Inland Revenue inspect the accounts of each charitable trust every year, to be sure that their rules are being observed, and that any benefit to the family is truly "incidental." There are now perhaps thirty country house charitable trusts, including those that own (or lease) and manage—in addition to Chatsworth and Knebworth—Leeds and Arundel Castles, Allerton Park, Boughton House, Bowhill, Burghley House, Burton Agnes, Burton Constable, Grimsthorpe Castle, Lamport Hall, Luton Hoo, Parham Park, Stoneleigh Abbey, and Weston Park; as well as Hopetoun House, Mellerstain, Paxton House, and Thirlestane Castle in Scotland. Leeds Castle was left to a charitable foundation with a £1.4 million ($3.3 million) endowment on the death of its last owner, daughter of a Whitney heiress, in 1974—the first house so transferred. The stated objectives of the Leeds Castle Foundation are "to preserve Leeds Castle in perpetuity for the benefit and enjoyment of the public," which it has done very well so far; to host "significant national and international medical seminars"—two major medical meetings are hosted free each year, as well as diplomatic conferences and the like; and encouraging "other artistic and cultural events," such as the Pavarotti concert held in the grounds in 1993. Left a relatively free hand by their trustees, the Leeds Castle managers have interpreted these objectives rather freely, and converted the estate into one of the most popular tourist attractions and conference centers in Britain. Blenheim Palace was transferred to a charitable trust, for special reasons already discussed, in 1994. Lord Cholmondeley acknowleged, in 1995, that he might consider the charitable trust route for Houghton Hall, if he could talk the Charity Commissioners into what he regarded as a reasonable number of opening days.

The major disadvantages are the obligation to come up with a large amount of money to endow the house—unless the NHMF agrees to help out, as it did in the three cases mentioned above; the fact that (except in leasehold arrangements) you no longer own your own house; and that all management decisions must now be shared by outside trustees. For owners of smaller country houses, charitable trusts rarely make sense. The owner of a larger house transferred to a charitable trust may be able to hold on to all or some of the land and the contents, and continue to live in part of the house; but ultimate decision-making still passes out of his hands.

For this reason, some owners, however dire their present or future financial straits, don't like the idea of giving their house to an ad hoc charitable trust any more than to the National Trust. And a total transfer (as opposed to a leasehold) is irrevocable. Antony Jarvis is considering, but still resisting the possibility of the charitable trust solution for Doddington Hall. "It would keep it safe for all time, of course, and you might be able to get an endowment from the Memorial Fund. But fine though that might be for the future of the house, if it really came to the crunch, I still think I'd want my family to have to opportunity to sell this lot. I mean, the whole atmosphere of the heritage might change dramatically in twenty-five years, and this could be a major asset. I don't see why I should be persuaded to give it away into something that would remove it from ownership. I would simply be giving away half of my inherited wealth."

· · ·

The Historic Houses Association has for several years been lobbying to allow the income from another device, called a Maintenance Fund, to be exempt from taxation, as long as that income was entirely devoted to the maintenance and upkeep of a historic property.

A Maintenance Fund is a restricted (but revocable) fund operated by trustees and approved by the government—not *legally* a discretionary trust, but very like one—in which the house owner is allowed to vest some of the income-producing portions of his estate: income-producing farmland, for example, rented buildings, or financial investments, as well as property or artworks that may be sold for a profit. Such funds may be set up at any time, although they are often made as part of a will, or established by an heir upon his predecessor's death, because the assets then vested in them become exempt from inheritance tax. The trustees can do what they like with these assets—buy and sell shares, invest and reinvest. But all income derived from the trust's holdings must be exclusively devoted to the maintenance and repair of the historic property.

The assets contributed to a Maintenance Fund are exempt from inheritance tax. But as I write, the income on its holdings (or on the capital gains realized when they are sold) is still taxable, at the 35 percent (1994) rate on discretionary trusts. The trustees of such a fund are also trapped with regard to the possible sale of any "heritage" items they may hold which have previously been exempted from taxation. Once they are sold, the exempted taxes must also be paid, which may then force the trustees to sell still more. "At the moment," says Sir Nicholas Bacon, "there's no advantage at all in setting up a Maintenance Fund. It's taxed at the same rate as your other income, and you can't do anything else with it."

The Historic Houses Association has been trying for several years to alter these provisions. It is their position that exempting from income tax the earnings of such Maintenance Funds will make all the difference between allowing private owners to continue to own and maintain their historic houses ("for the nation," of course; "we regard ourselves only as unpaid stewards," etc.); and forcing them to sell them or give them away in lieu of taxes, which all too often involves commercial conversions or development of a sort the HHA deplores.

Lord Shelburne, president of the Association from 1989 to 1993, sent to the Chancellor of the Exchequer in 1991 a set of figures designed to prove that tax-exempt maintenance funds would end up *saving* the government £4 million ($7 million) a year. His basic argument went something like this. If the government permitted Maintenance Funds for historic houses to earn money free of income and capital gains tax, at least 700 house owners would decide to take advantage of their benefits. (This may have been a rash assumption, considering that only about 75 funds were set up in the first fifteen years they were permitted. But tax-free status would make them more desirable.) Setting imaginary average endowments and average incomes to each of these, Shelburne came up with a projected net "loss" to the Treasury of £3.7 million ($6.5 million) a year in taxes.

But, he argued—comparing imaginary future apples with genuine past oranges—the government had spent £85 million in the preceding eleven years, or an average of £7.7 *million* a year, in order to "save" or shore up historic houses at risk. His point—by which Chancellor Norman Lamont was not persuaded—was that if all those unfortunate owners who had to be bailed out by the government, like Lord Scarsdale at Kedleston, had been allowed to establish tax-free Maintenance Funds, they would never have gone under in the first place.

Whether or not one accepts the logic of this argument, whether or not tax-exempt Maintenance Funds are the road to salvation for private country house owners, Shelburne and his colleagues have made a persuasive case that, without some form of relief, the present they confront is bleak, and the future will be bleaker still. "The nation has to make up its mind [he argued in a series of *Historic House* editorials] whether it wants to retain a living heritage or whether it wants all our properties turned into a profusion of country house hotels and museums. . . . We are not seeking any personal benefit or special concessions. We must pay our taxes like every other citizen in the land. However, if an owner is prepared to endow his property with his own personal assets for the benefit of the building, it is surely not too much to ask that the endowment should be tax exempt."

Antony Jarvis remains convinced that the only way to persuade the government—any government—that owners are not obtaining undue personal benefit from tax-free Maintenance Funds is to tie them permanently and irretrievably to the house. If and when the house is sold, the fund goes with it, as much a fixed part of the place as a chimney or a porch. Anything less, he believes, would leave room for self-serving abuses, and justifiable suspicion on the part of both the Treasury and the public.

But most other country house owners are loathe to lock away assets in such a permanent, alienated fashion, even for the benefit of their beloved family house. To them, Jarvis's kind of Maintenance Fund seems no more than a narrowly focused Charitable Trust. "Charlie Shelburne used to think you'd get Maintenance Funds exempt if you made them irrevocable," said Alistair Macleod Mallison, at Chenies Manor in Buckinghamshire. "But a lot of the [HHA] members don't want to make them irrevocable. It's all very well to put down a million pounds and make it irrevocable if you're the Duke of Devonshire and have got a hundred million, or like Charlie's father [the Marquess of Lansdowne]. Then it's nothing. But if it's half your patrimony . . ."

Shelburne thinks that something like the Jarvis scheme will be essential if the HHA is ever going to persuade politicians and the public to accept tax-freedom for Maintenance Funds. But most HHA members, like Macleod Mallison, are leery of permanently locked funds. "When we canvassed our members as to whether or not they would accept Maintenance Funds that were inalienable in perpetuity," said Shelburne, "the consensus that came back was No, they would not. They would accept twenty-five years—a generation. So that was the remit I had to try to negotiate with the Treasury. But when I'm speaking personally, and not on behalf of the association, I say, 'Look: The only way we're ever going to persuade the man on the street to accept this deal—and it is a deal—is if the money is locked *inalienably* to the property. If the family have to leave their property, they wave that fund goodbye."

CHAPTER SIX

Five Ways to Pay the Bills

Sell the Contents

ON NOVEMBER 3, 1985, an exhibition of more than 700 objects, borrowed from some 200 British country houses, opened at the National Gallery of Art in Washington, D.C. By the time this exhibition, grandly called *The Treasure Houses of Britain*, had closed five months later—in time for many of these objects to be back in their proper places for the 1986 tourist season—it had become the second most popular show in the museum's history, and one of the top "blockbuster" exhibitions of all time. Extended for a month beyond its originally scheduled closing, it was seen, by April 13, 1986, by just short of one million visitors.

The exhibition generated or perhaps revealed in American museum-goers a remarkable interest in and enthusiasm for the great (and lesser) country houses from which these objects were borrowed. This, as far as its lenders were concerned, was precisely its purpose. "The agenda of the show is plain," wrote Robert Hughes in *Time*. "It is a fund raiser, aimed at drumming up more American support for that collectively unique, financially insecure, historically indispensible phenomenon, the Stately Home."[1] Gervase Jackson-Stops, the brilliant, indefatigable curator of the exhibition (who died of AIDS in 1995), made no bones about it. "That was absolutely open, really," he told me in 1994. "It was trying to put the English country house on the map as an international tourist attraction. And on the whole, I think that it did get the message across—that it isn't our museums, it's our country houses that are the great asset in this country."

The 1985 loans contained works of considerable historic and artistic value: contemporary portraits of Henry VIII (from Sudeley Castle), Edward VI (from Loseley Park), Mary I (from Compton Wynyates), and Elizabeth I (from Hatfield House); ancestral and family portraits ranging in time from the Cobhams of 1567 (Longleat) to the Marlboroughs of 1905 (Blenheim Palace). Artworks shipped home to England from Italian Grand Tours included a Raphael drawing from Wilton House and a Tintoretto from Longleat—the latter recently lost to burglars. A Velázquez, a spectacular Rubens, and a Titian were among the many treasures sent back to Kingston Lacy by a 19th-century connoisseur forced to spend the last fourteen years of his life in continental exile, in order to avoid prosecution in England for homosexual acts. There were glittering Canalettos of Venice from the collections at Woburn Abbey and Tatton Park, and pompous portraits of travelling milords by Batoni and Mengs.

One could admire 17th-century tapestries from Montacute and Hatfield, embroidery from Hardwick, suits of armor from Penshurst and Warwick Castle, old English chests and chairs from Arundel Castle and Cotehele, and a famous 1680 suite of table, looking glass, and candlestands from Knole ("truly hideous," *Newsweek* called them) covered with thick, lumpy layers of silver. Of the three old masters hardest to avoid in English country houses, the loans included Van Dycks from Weston Park, Petworth, Broadlands and Corsham Court; Reynoldses from Bowhill, Chatsworth, Woburn, and Castle Howard; and Gainsboroughs from Bowood, Bowhill, Houghton Hall, and Ickworth. On the walls hung respectable Dutch masters from a number of houses, and Constable's *The Lock*—since sold to the Thyssen Foundation in Lugano, Switzerland for almost £11 million ($19 million)— from Sudeley Castle in Gloucestershire. Elaborate gold and silver pieces—the most obvious "treasures"—were on loan from many houses (a 1710 silver wine cooler from Burghley House the size of a bathtub was hard to miss), as was a surfeit of hand-painted 18th-century china from both Europe and Asia. Some of the finest French 18th-century furniture outside of museum collections was on display, along with chairs and settees specifically designed by William Kent for a number of houses, and one of John Linnell's giltwood and damask sofas from Kedleston, whose legs are carved to represent mermaids and mermen wrapped around dolphins.

· · ·

It has been claimed that the country houses of England, taken all together, contain the most valuable and important collection of portable art in the world, and more great Old Masters—paintings dated before 1800—than in the rest of the world put together. That's an impossible claim to test, since many country house collections are neither catalogued nor visible to the public.

What is clear is that in no other country do private collections contain anything even close to the number or quality of works of premodern art one can find in English country houses—although both the number and the quality are diminishing rapidly.

My guess is that the English country house collections would beat any conceivable competition in terms of the number of works by British portrait painters—Reynolds, Romney, Lawrence, and company—popular with previous generations of aristocratic sitters and collectors. The Queen owns more Holbeins, and the Tate Gallery more Turners; but the house owners would probably win out on Van Dycks, which can be found in at least 28 country houses open to the public. Rubens is represented in at least 21 open country house collections; Claude in ten, Canaletto in nine, Turner and Rembrandt in eight, Poussin in seven, Giordano in six, and Titian and Tintoretto in five. Paintings in country house collections closed to the public would obviously increase these numbers.

Eighteenth-century British aristocrats making their Grand Tours were the first great foreign buyers of Italian, French, and Flemish masters, and many important works by these artists remain on their walls. British buyers got the chance to add more world-class masterpieces after the French Revolution, when many French aristocrats' estates were broken up. The great collection of the dukes of Sutherland (including five Titians, two Raphaels,

Holkham Hall, Norfolk. Statue Gallery.

and seven Poussins, many of them now on extended loan to the National Galleries of Scotland) is built around treasures once the property of the Duc d'Orleans, sold off between 1792 and 1800. Napoleon's occupation of Rome in 1798–99 led to yet another round of panic-selling, this time by Italian nobles. Once again, their British counterparts were more than willing to help. And from the early 19th century, British gentlemen began to buy heavily in Dutch painting of the "Golden Age," which was often undervalued at home. The long, one-way commerce in works of art across the Channel (there are relatively few works by British artists in continental collections) is more a tribute to the superior wealth, power, and stability of Great Britain between 1688 and 1918 than to the superior taste of its collectors.

Many of these purchases have since been downgraded by reattribution; it is astonishing how many Raphaels and Rembrandts people once thought there were. The very best have been given or sold to museums, often after passing through the hands of wealthy Americans. But impressive antique sculptures and old masters are still to be found in many country house collections.

No single institution could come up with as much fine porcelain, as much silver and gold plate (except perhaps the Church), or as much 18th-century French and English furniture as one will find in English country houses today. Non-European art is notoriously absent, with the exception of a few small-scale collections of works from India and other once-imperial outposts. After Constable and Turner, the high Victorians (recently returned to favor), and the Pre-Raphaelites, things pretty well grind to a halt. Of course, unknown modern or exotic treasures may lie behind the walls of houses *not* open to the public, including those owned by reclusive foreigners. Mereworth Castle in Kent, Britain's prize Palladian villa, is now owned by a Arabian billionaire-diplomat who may have the world's finest collection of antique silver and gold.

·   ·   ·

Almost as soon as they began serious art-collecting, English aristocrats began serious selling. For more than two centuries, the paintings, statues, furniture, and decorative art assembled in country houses by previous generations have represented a valuable asset to be liquidated in times of distress. Whatever the state of one's debts, the art works always went before the house; the house, if at all possible, before the land.

The first famous sale of an art collection from a great house was that of Sir Robert Walpole's from Houghton House in Norfolk—"certainly the most famous country house collection of pictures in Great Britain" of its time, Francis Haskell has called it[2])—which Walpole moved to Norfolk from his London house when he retired from politics in 1743. Just 36 years later, his grandson George, "eccentric to the point of insanity" and sinking under a burden of gambling debts, sold 174 of the best paintings in the collection to Empress Catherine the Great of Russia for £40,000. A single Guido Reni went for a record £3,500; two Rembrandts went for £300 each, a Velázquez and a Giovanni Bellini for £60—which gives some indication of the taste of the time.

The second most notorious sale of the contents of a country house was that of Stowe, the extravagant home of the even more extravagant dukes of Buckingham and Chandos. Completed in the 1770s by Richard Grenville, Earl Temple—then thought to be the richest man in England—the house and its contents passed first to his nephew George Grenville, then in 1813 to George's son Richard, created 1st Duke. Richard's son, the 2nd Duke, after declaring bankruptcy with debts of over £1.5 million (the equivalent of more than $50 million today), held an auction of most of the contents of the house—including what was called "one of the finest collections of manuscripts ever assembled"—in August 1848, and then fled to the Mediterranean on his yacht. During this so-called sale of the century, held on the premises, "an endless stream of visitors [came] to see an ancient family ruined, their palace marked for destruction, and its contents scattered to the four winds of Heaven. . . . [The Duke] is at this moment an absolutely ruined and destitute man."[3]

His son, the 3rd and last Duke of Buckingham, tried vainly to clear the remaining debts; then he too fled abroad. Finally the 3rd Duke's daughter, Baroness Kinloss—who inherited in the absence of available males—sold off not only the remaining contents, in 1921, but also the house itself, which became a new public school in 1923.[4]

The 2nd Earl of Warwick sold off a number of major works to pay off his creditors in 1804. The 3rd Marquess of Landsdowne cleared out paintings and antique busts from Bowood. Many of William Beckford's treasures at Fonthill—including Giovanni Bellini's *Doge Loredano*, Hogarth's *Rake's Progress* series, and paintings by Perugino, Watteau, Veronese, Canaletto, Memling, and Bruegel, as well as innumerable jeweled and gilded *objets de vertu*—were sold off in 1823, when he was faced with the ruin of his West Indian estates. Broughton Castle was stripped of its treasures (down to the swans in the moat) by the prodigal 15th Baron of Saye and Sele in an eight-day sale in 1837. In 1842, the fabulous collections of Horace Walpole, the Prime Minister's younger son (who had died in 1797) were sold from the neo-Gothic villa near London he had designed for himself.

A Titian *Venus* from Holkham Hall went in 1831. The great collection formed by Sir Robert Peel, prime minister in the 1830s and 1840s, was largely dispersed by the end of the century. Lord Northwick's sale of 1859, of the total contents of Thirlestane House in Cheltenham and much of those of Northwick Park in the Cotswolds, saw the prize European and British acquisitions of a great pre-Victorian collector dispersed into the avid hands of the Rothschilds and their rivals. Gerald Reitlinger called the 22-day, 2,516-lot, £100,000 sale "unquestionably the most magnificent sale of a single collection that has ever been held anywhere."[5]

After the Settled Land Act of 1882 (which allowed trustees to set aside a will in order to sell the contents of a house), Hamilton Palace in Scotland—which included the remaining prizes of Beckford's collection, by now the property of his grandson the 11th Duke of Hamilton—was emptied of its contents in 1882–83. With four Rothschilds now bidding, French furniture prices went through the roof. Three pieces bearing Marie Antoinette's emblem brought £24,300—a record for French furniture unbroken till 1926, when the pound had twice the purchasing power. Held over seventeen days, the Hamilton

Palace sale earned a total of nearly £400,000. A final clearing out in 1919 got rid of what was left at Hamilton Palace (including a Van Dyck, a Rubens, and a Raphael); the house itself was torn down three years later.

The historic library of the 3rd Earl of Sunderland (1672–1722), followed by a major collection of old masters (including Van Dyck's great equestrian portrait of Charles I, and a Raphael Madonna, both now at the National Gallery) was dispersed by the 7th Duke of Marlborough in a series of sales between 1881 and 1883. The 8th Duke was forced to continue selling off pictures, furniture, and china from Blenheim Palace: a Christie's auction in 1886 listed eighteen Rubenses and thirteen Van Dycks. The family fortunes were only restored by the 9th Duke's loveless marriage in 1895 to a Vanderbilt heiress, who came furnished with $4.2 million in American railroad stock. But Blenheim was never again to contain an art collection worthy of the house.

Between 1870 and 1930, agents like Bernard Berenson and art dealers like Joseph Duveen helped to build the collections of rich American collectors (Morgan, Frick, Huntington, Mellon, Kress, Gardner) with the treasures of British country houses. In some cases, prices were driven to unprecedented levels—prices many of these works would not bring today, even accounting for inflation—by the Americans' resources and avidity.

Country house owners benefited from an American craze for Rubens in the 1880s, and Van Dyck after 1906. Duveen managed to manufacture an extravagant, never-since-equalled market for Gainsborough, Lawrence, Reynolds, Romney, and Hoppner, to the immense benefit of country house owners who often owned more works by these artists than they knew what to do with. At least a dozen Gainsboroughs crossed the Atlantic before 1930 at prices ranging from £50,000 to £150,000—the latter the world-record price (over £5 million, or $7.5 million, today) Henry Huntington paid for the Duke of Westminster's *The Blue Boy* by Gainsborough, whose loss was regarded as a national scandal by the British press in 1910. Its companion piece on Huntington Library place mats and playing cards, Lawrence's *Pinkie*, went to California in 1926 for £90,000—then $375,000. Reynolds's *Sarah Siddons as the Tragic Muse*—another of the Westminster prizes—went to Huntington for £75,000 in 1925. He also bought three Reynolds portraits from Althorp that year for £50,000 each. Andrew Mellon paid a record £70,000 for the Bromley-Davenport Romney. Five-figure prices were paid by U.S. collectors for paintings by Giovanni Bellini, Mabuse, Mantegna, Titian, Whistler, Van Dyck, and Velázquez, all from British country house collections. British-owned works by Raphael, Rembrandt, and Titian—most of them now hanging in museums in New York, Washington, Boston, and California—all went for £100,000 or more between 1900 and 1929 (when the pound was generally valued at $4–5), the greatest "boom" period in international art prices before the 1980s.

In 1913, a committee organized by London's National Gallery reported that in the preceding few years 52 Rembrandts (or what were then thought of as Rembrandts), 29 Gainsboroughs, 21 Rubenses, eleven Holbeins, and seven Vermeers had left the country, most of them for the United States. In 1952, a similar committee reported that in the intervening years the following once-British-owned works had been sold overseas: 48 Gainsboroughs, 45 Rembrandts, 40 Rubenses, twelve Holbeins, ten Velázquezes, four Duccios, two each by Giovanni Bellini, Giorgione, Raphael, Titian, and Van Eyck, and one each by Correggio, Filippo Lippi, Mantegna, Signorelli, and Vermeer. If British country house collections remain impressive today, they were many times more impressive fifty and a hundred years ago.

• • •

So the phenomenon of the distressed English country house owner selling art from off his walls and floors—in fact, sometimes selling his walls and floors—to help pay the bills is nothing new. It has been going on so long and so actively that the wonder is there is anything left. Lord Brownlow, desperately trying to hold on to Belton House, sold old masters (Titian, Bellini, Rubens, Rembrandt), ancient marbles, silver, and furniture in 1923 and 1929; another major sale took took place at Belton in 1967. Thirteen masterworks from the great Petworth collection, including a Holbein, as well as 172 rare books, went in 1927–28. The sublime Wilton Diptych left Wilton House for Trafalgar Square in 1928. A major Titian from Alnwick joined it at the National Gallery in 1929. The 6th Marquess of Lansdowne sold off most of the remaining antique marbles his ancestor had bought for Bowood in 1930, for £63,000 ($306,000). Lord Lothian parted with the 10th-century Blickling Homilies in 1932. Lord Lytton sold off a collection of furniture and objets d'art from Knebworth in 1946, after the National Trust declined to accept the house.

From innumerable lesser houses, collections were broken up and sold in the years after World War II. After 1948, the prices of illuminated manuscripts rose to such absurd heights that many English owners rushed theirs to auction. A boom in the prices of Chippendale furniture led to many postwar sales. Many of the paintings from Woburn Abbey were sold by the trustees in 1951, before the 13th Duke of Bedford took over and began trying to restore both house and collections. During the fifties, Houghton Hall sold a Nicolas de Largillière, Harewood a Titian, and Longford Castle a Velázquez.

The major Chatsworth deacquisitions began in 1958. The Duke of Westminster sold off a record-price Rubens, the Altieri Claudes, a Titian drawing, and other treasures in 1959. From Berkeley Castle, a 168-piece 18th-century dinner service went to the United States for £207,000 ($580,000) in 1960, the same year that Lord Cowper handed over the large Rembrandt equestrian portrait known as the "Panshanger Horseman" to the National Gallery in lieu of taxes. In 1961, the Duke of Leeds got a record £140,000 ($392,000) for Goya's *Duke of Wellington*, subsequently stolen from (and recovered by) the National Gallery in 1965. The Astor sales and settlements at Hever and Cliveden involved the disposal of manuscripts, silver, china, paintings, and tapestries. The Earl of Derby's Rembrandt (*Belshazzar's Feast*) went by private treaty sale to the National Gallery in 1964 for a record £375,000 (more than a million dollars)—reduced to perhaps half that by his inheritance tax bill. The Spencer-Churchills and Harewoods both sold major collections in 1965.

Nor has the art drain abated since. By 1985, seven of the ten most expensive works of art ever sold at auction had come from English country houses; the hyper-inflated market for art objects of all kinds has made their sale an almost irresistable means of paying one's bills. In the decade since then, major works have departed from Chatsworth, Houghton, Holkham, Nostell Priory, Alnwick Castle, Longford Castle, Badminton, Floors Castle and Dalmeny in Scotland, Castle Howard, Stanton Harcourt, Raby Castle, Ripley Castle, and Luton Hoo. Four and a half million pounds worth of 18th-century silver and other objects were sold from Luton Hoo in 1995, to help clear a mountain of debt that had cast its shadow over the owner's suicide four years before. In December of that year Britain's only painting by Fra Bartolommeo left Firle Place in Sussex for the Getty Museum in Malibu (in exchange for £14.5 million, or $23 million), and two distinguished 17th-century paintings quit Castle Howard, adding an estimated total of £10 million ($16 million) to the house's repair-and-maintenance funds.

.   .   .

One major difference between previous sales of country house contents and those since 1980 is, quite simply, that of price. When *one* of your paintings, statues, or pieces of furniture—for example, the Sudeley Castle Constable, the Woburn Abbey Canova, the Badminton Cabinet—is suddenly declared to be much more valuable than your house, the temptation must be very great to decide that you and your heirs might possibly live without it.

Part of the increase in prices simply parallels inflation in other spheres, a phenomenon far less common before this century. It may cost you, as it would have cost your father or grandfather, the price of a Salomon van Ruysdael seascape or a Boulle commode to repair your leaking roof, even though that figure may have risen from £300 to £30,000 to £300,000 in just three generations. But sale prices on the art auction market since 1980 have risen far faster than the cost of most other things, especially in certain areas—such as old master paintings and good 18th-century furniture and silver—in which English country house collections were particularly strong. A Holbein portrait of Henry VIII was sold from Althorp to Baron von Thyssen by the 7th Earl Spencer in 1937 for £10,000. It would fetch tens of millions today. When he decided in 1966 to try to buy back for West Wycombe some of the furniture his father had sold, Francis Dashwood was able to get Chippendale and Adam consoles for £500–1,000 a pair. The same sets now might go for a quarter million. As late as 1978, Lord Brooke sold four of Canaletto's views of Warwick Castle for just over £1 million; comparable works have recently sold for £3–10 million each. (He also sold Warwick Castle.)

In a number of significant recent cases, works of art that country house owners decided to part with—usually to pay inheritance taxes, or to help with the upkeep of their houses—went to the British government or to public museums. One advantage of this kind of transfer (even though the government or museum may offer less than the market price) is the possibility of the owner's being spared at least part of the tax bite that would have been paid on the net profit of a sale at public auction. In the 1980s, a Jacopo Bassano from Weston Park, a Frans Hals from Elton, and two Hogarths (one of *Children playing at Easton Neston*, from the estate of the same name) all came to national museums via "tax sales," to assist their owners to pay the taxes due on the remainder of an inherited estate. In 1990–91 alone, more than £11.5 million ($20.3 million) worth of tax bills was satisfied by "payments in kind"—that is, by handing over works of art instead of cash—which the Inland Revenue then handed over to the National Trust or to one of several national museums, in return for the requisite sum. During these two years, taxes were paid by such things as four old master drawings, a collection of musical instruments, a Pissarro, a Corot, a Rubens cameo, and a Van der Weyden valued at £4 million, or $7 million (from Houghton Hall) that went to the National Gallery. At least three of these tax gifts were allowed to stay on loan in the houses they came from. Between 1985 and 1993, the total value (by the Treasury's evaluation) of art accepted in lieu of taxes came to almost £30 million.

After the Spencers began selling off treasures from Althorp in wholesale lots in 1976, the British Museum was able to purchase, for £1 million ($1.8 million), two silver-gilt wine coolers from the original Marlborough collection—"the most remarkable group of silver ever known to have been in one man's property," it has been called.[6] Paul Storrs's gold Portland Font (1797–98) from Welbeck eventually ended up at the British Museum—but the museum had to pay £1.25 million ($2.2 million) for a work that had earlier been offered to the government for less than half that amount. A collection of the 4th Earl of Chesterfield's silver vessels from Highclere Castle, sold to endow a maintenance fund, also made its way into national museums, after first being sold at auction. A Van Dyck double portrait from Broadlands and Lawrence's portrait of the 3rd Marquess of Londonderry from Bayham Abbey in Kent both came to the National Gallery, in 1987 and 1992, as the result of "tax credit" sales. Castle Howard, forever in need of cash for maintenance and repair, parted in 1986 with Bernini's marble bust of Cardinal dal Pozzo of Pisa (which had been in the Washington *Treasure Houses* show the year before) to the National Galleries of Scotland for £3 million ($4.5 million), one year after parting with fifteen other Howard treasures to the National Gallery. A large Roman silver dish dug up near Alnwick in 1735 (long in the British Museum) was judged to be worth £1.83 million ($2.7 million) in tax credits to the Duke of Northumberland in 1993. Other recent transfers from country houses to public collections include three large Poussins (from Knowsley Hall, Sudeley Castle, and Powis Castle—the latter only after an export license to the Getty Museum, which had offered £7.25 million, or $11 million, was held up for several months); a rare 15th-century Spanish painting by Bartolomé Bermejo (valued at £10 million, or $15 million) and an equally fine Altdorfer, both from Luton Hoo, and both now at the National Gallery; and Canaletto's historic *View of Old Horse Guards from St. James's*, formerly in Lord FitzHarris's house in Hampshire, which Andrew Lloyd Webber bought at auction in 1992 for more than £10 million ($18 million), and then placed on loan at the Tate Gallery.

When prize samples of the two greatest private British collections of master drawings went on sale in recent years, the government tried to hold up the export of a considerable number. But in the end most of them passed out of the country, generally to the United States. Seventy-one old master drawings were sold from Chatsworth in 1984 for a total sale price of more than £21 million ($28 million); the British Museum got Rembrandt's *View of the Amstel* for £668,000 ($900,000). But six other Rembrandt drawings escaped, along with three Van Dycks, two Rubenses, two Raphaels, a Holbein, a maybe-Titian, and a Mantegna—"one of the greatest artistic losses to this country in a century," declared the Art Export Reviewing Committee. The Devonshires had originally offered the lot to the British Museum for £5.5 million ($8.25 million), but the museum could not come up with the price. A sale of old master *prints* from the Chatsworth collection drew £3.6 million ($4.7 million) in 1985, but none went to public collections. More master drawings from Chatsworth (including two Rembrandts and a Veronese) were sold in 1987, and ended up abroad. About the same time, the Chatsworth trustees sold a Raphael and two Guercino drawings to public museums in Edinburgh, Oxford, and Cambridge.

The country had more luck with the 1991 Holkham Hall sale of old master drawings collected by the 1st Earl of Leicester, eventually acquiring eighteen of the 66 sold, after deferring export licenses on the ones they wanted. These included works by Annibale Carracci, Castiglione, Pietro da Cortona, Guido Reni, Poussin, and Guercino.[7] Although Leonardo da Vinci's Codex Leicester was sold to Armand Hammer in Los Angeles, five other rare 11th-to-15th-century manuscripts were transferred from Holkham to the Bodleian Library at Oxford in 1980. All of this went to help clear a huge inheritance tax bill dating back to 1976.

In 1992, what Sotheby's called "the greatest British picture still in private hands," Joseph Wright of Derby's powerful *The Iron Forge* from Broadlands (another prize of the 1985 *Treasure Houses* show), was put up for sale by the financially strained Lord Romsey, heir to the late Earl Mountbatten of Burma.[8] In the end, with the sweetener of government tax credits, the Tate Gallery got the painting—which the 1st Lord Palmerston had bought from the artist in 1772—for only £2,243,000, or $4 million.

The most expensive recent transfer to a national museum was Holbein's 21-by-15-inch *Lady with a Pet Squirrel and Starling* from Houghton Hall, which the artist painted during his stay in England in the 1520s, and which was thus regarded as an English "national" treasure. Christie's—whose spokesman called it "the most exciting picture to come on the market in Europe since Van Gogh's 'Sunflowers'"—had predicted a sale price of £15–20 million ($25–35 million) for this rare, tiny, perfectly painted portrait, a price assumed to be far beyond the government's ability or willingness to pay. When the predictable fuss arose over "one more loss from the nation's artistic heritage," the owner, the 6th Marquess of Cholmondeley, wrote to the *Independent*: "While I deplore the lack of Government funding for museums, I feel that owners of works of art should not be blamed for trying to achieve fair prices, especially, as in our case, when the proceeds will be used to preserve another, undoubtedly more vital part of the national heritage: one of the greatest historic houses, Houghton Hall in Norfolk and its collection of furniture and paintings."[9] But just before the auction, scheduled for April 1992, Lord Cholmondeley agreed to sell his Holbein—which had been at Houghton since 1780—to the National Gallery for "about £12 million" ($21 million) in a private treaty sale. Because of the tax concessions involved, this still worked out to a good deal for him.

In several happy instances, the government—or the museum involved—decides that it is in the British public's best interest to have the work it has just bought, or accepted in lieu of taxes, remain in the house from which it came. The most important such arrangement thus far was the first, made in the 1960s by John Wyndham, 6th Baron Leconfield and 1st Baron Egremont—he tends to use the latter name—heir to Petworth House in Sussex. The house had already been left to the National Trust by his uncle in 1947. Sixteen years later, after two intervening deaths and long negotiations, the Treasury agreed to accept the majority of the pictures at Petworth in settlement of the family's inheritance tax bill. But, most significantly, they also agreed to leave the pictures where they were. So now the nation owns most of the art works at Petworth; the National Trust owns the building and grounds; and the Egremonts still make their home in the house.

A 1618 portrait by Daniel Mytens of Thomas, 14th Earl of Arundel, pointing to his own historic collection of antiquities at Arundel House in London, and a parallel portrait of his wealthy wife Althea *should* by all rights hang in Arundel Castle. And so they do, although they have since 1980 been the property of the National Portrait Gallery in London. The same is true of two other portraits closely identified with Arundel's heirs, the Catholic Dukes of Norfolk: Gainsborough's portrait of the 11th Duke, and Millais's of Cardinal Newman, all of which were handed over to pay the 1975 death duties on the other, nonexempt contents of the castle. "The marvelous thing is we've gone through that death and ownership-handover without *anything* being lost from the place," says the present Earl of Arundel, who lives with his family in the castle. Since 1975, he declares with some pride, "We haven't sold a thing. Not a single vase or silver teaspoon. In fact we've collected, actually; we've bought back, in a minor way, little family things which came up for sale again." He cites a portrait of the 14th Earl's father-in-law, the 7th Earl of Shrewsbury, which he and his father, the Duke of Norfolk, were able to buy at auction in 1992, to fill a gap in Arundel Castle's almost unbroken series of family portraits.

Between 1987 and 1991, Viscount Cobham settled part of his tax bill by ceding to the Birmingham City Museum five portraits, five overmantels, several pieces of 18th-century furniture, pier glasses and tapestries—all of which were allowed to stay at Hagley Hall. The beguiling family portrait of *The Children of the 1st Lord Porchester* by Sir William Beechey was accepted by the government in lieu of taxes, but allowed to remain at Highclere, once the children's home. Guido Reni's powerful painting of *Joseph and Potiphar's Wife,* at Holkham Hall, has officially belonged since 1993 to the Fitzwilliam Museum at Cambridge, after the Government took it in place of £2.5 million ($3.75 million) in taxes. A gorgeous pair of Baroque bookcases (1740) made for Powderham Castle by John Channon was sold to the Victoria and Albert Museum in 1987, but can still be seen in the library at Powderham (or in the 1993 film version of *The Remains of the Day*).

Perhaps the most satisfying such arrangement since Petworth was the National Trust's decision (with the aid of a £6 million NHMF grant) to purchase almost all of the furniture that Thomas Chippendale had designed for Nostell Priory in Yorkshire, so that (a) the family could pay its tax bill, and (b) the furniture could remain in its Adam setting, since 1953 a property of the National Trust.

.   .   .

Most often, in recent years, art works from country house collections have been sold on the open market, either at one of the two great London auction galleries, Christie's or Sotheby's; by way of a "house sale," wherein the entire contents of a broken-up house are auctioned on the grounds; or by private, unannounced transfers. Among publicly announced sales, at least 32 works from British country house collections have been sold since 1980 to overseas buyers for more than £1 million, eleven of these to the young Getty Museum in California, which (blessed with the largest endowment of any museum in the world) is eagerly trying to fill its old master gaps. Among the more publicized overseas sales of the last fifteen years have been the following:

The Badminton Cabinet, sold at auction from Badminton House in 1990 for £8,580,000 ($15 million)—still the highest price ever paid for a piece of furniture. This huge Baroque fantasia of gilded ebony, bronze, and *pietra dura*, with inlaid pictures on every drawer and door, and ormolu figures sprouting from the top, was commissioned from the Medici workshops in Florence by the 3rd Duke of Beaufort in 1726. It is now in the collection of Barbara Johnson (a Johnson & Johnson heiress) in New York. It was offered to the Victoria and Albert Museum for less than half that price, but they could not afford it.

Fra Bartolommeo, *The Holy Family with the Infant St. John*, from Firle Place to the Getty Museum, 1995: £14.5 million ($23.2 million).

John Constable, *The Lock*, from Sudeley Castle to the Thyssen Foundation in Switzerland, 1990: £10,780,000 ($19 million).

Leonardo da Vinci, The Codex Leicester—a hand-written manuscript by the artist, containing many of his autograph ink drawings on the pages—from Holkham Hall to Armand Hammer of Los Angeles, 1980: £2,200,000 ($5.1 million). Viscount Coke—now the Earl of Leicester—sold this as well as 200 other rare books and manuscripts (and a faded Raphael cartoon) from the Holkham collection. Coke argued that the Codex Leicester had been kept in a sealed portfolio and unseen by the public since the 18th century. After the completion in 1990 of the Armand Hammer Museum in Los Angeles, the manuscript—renamed the "Codex Hammer"—was given a dark, vaulted chamber all its own. In November 1994, after Hammer's death, his museum found itself entangled in lawsuits, and put its prize possession up for sale. The purchaser was Bill Gates, the Seattle computer billionaire, who got the manuscript (the Codex Gates?) for $20 million.

Andrea Mantegna, *Adoration of the Magi*, from Castle Ashby to the Getty Museum, 1985: £8,247,500 ($10.7 million). The sale of this treasured painting enabled Lord

Northampton to purchase the fabled Sevso Silver collection, a horde of disputed origin and previous ownership that may now be worth as much as $75 million.

Michelangelo, *The Holy Family with the Infant Baptist at Rest on the Flight into Egypt*, drawing from Great Tew, Oxfordshire, to the Getty Museum, 1993: £4.18 million, or $6.3 million (record price for a drawing).

Nicolas Poussin, *The Holy Family*, from Chatsworth, 1981: £1,650,000 ($3.3 million). This sale, made jointly to the Norton Simon and the Getty Museums in California, was to endow the new charitable trust which assumed ownership and control of Chatsworth in 1981.

Raphael, two drawings from the 1984 Chatsworth sale: one to a New York dealer for £3,564,000 ($4,775,000), the other to the Getty Museum for £1,512,000 ($2,026,000).

Rembrandt, *Portrait of Johannes Uyttenbogaert*, formerly at Mentmore, later at Dalmeny House, Scotland, to a U.S. purchaser, and subsequently to the Rijksmuseum, Amsterdam, 1992: £4,100,000 ($7,257,000). The *Financial Times* warned at the time, "The appearance on the market of this important Rembrandt, with the strong possibility that it will sell to a foreign buyer, will intensify fears that the national heritage is disappearing abroad with increasing frequency."[10]

Peter Paul Rubens, *Forest at Dawn with a Deerhunt*, from Wynnstay, then Llangedwyn, Wales (Williams-Wynn collection), 1989: £3,300,000 ($5.4 million). Now at the Metropolitan Museum, New York.

Titian ("and workshop"), *Venus and Adonis* (a version of the Prado painting), from Somerley to the Getty Museum, 1991: £7,480,000 ($13,240,000).

J. M. W. Turner, *Seascape: Folkestone*, from the late Kenneth Clark's collection at Saltwood Castle, sold by his son Alan Clark in 1984: £7,400,000 ($10 million)—at the time, the highest price ever paid for a painting. The work was resold five years later for a reported £20 million ($33 million) to David Thomson of Toronto.

Anthony van Dyck, *1st Duke of Hamilton*, from Lennoxlove (Scotland), to the Prince of Liechtenstein, 1988: first offer £1,350,000, eventually sold after license deferral for £4,500,000 (dollar equivalents $2.4 million and $7.4 million).

As I write, there were fears for the sale abroad of art treasures from Alnwick Castle, after the death late in 1995 of the 11th Duke of Northumberland. British museum directors are also anxious to know what will become of the great collection of the current Duke of Sutherland (born 1915), when taxes fall due on his gigantic estate. Fortunately for England, a grant from the Heritage Lottery Fund enabled the National Gallery to acquire in 1996 the last Dürer oil painting in private hands, a tiny *St. Jerome in the Wilderness* at Raveningham Hall valued at more than £10 million, or $15 million.

. . .

In 1952, the British government established what are now called the "Waverly formulas," after John Anderson, 1st Viscount Waverly, who chaired the committee on art export controls. According to these formulas, a British-owned work of art must pass three tests to determine whether or not it is of sufficient "national importance" for an export license to be blocked: Is it so closely associated with our history and national life that its departure would be a misfortune? Is it of outstanding aesthetic importance? Is it of outstanding significance for the study of some branch of art, learning or history?

If a work of art offered for sale and sought by foreign buyers meets these criteria, an overseas export license can be forbidden for a "reasonable time"—typically three to six months, although the period can be extended—in order to enable a British institution (or, since 1990, a British individual) to come up with sufficient funds to match the highest overseas offer. Many of the major works listed above that have been sold out of the country in recent years have had "Waverly formula" sanctions imposed, only to have them lifted when no British buyer showed up able to match the best foreign offer. Whatever their feelings about a national "cultural heritage," Tory governments have not wanted to appear hostile to the ideal of an international free market, in works of art or in anything else. But neither have they sufficiently increased the acquisitions budgets of the national museums (which have been effectively frozen since 1985) to enable them to compete in this market.

The most extreme use of these sanctions to date has been in the case of the Antonio Canova sculpture group, *The Three Graces* from Woburn Abbey, which the Getty Museum thought it had bought for £7,600,000 ($12.5 million) in 1989—still a record offer for a sculpture. This elegant marble group of three embracing female nudes balanced on tiptoe is in fact a second version of the original, ordered from the sculptor by the 6th Duke of Bedford in 1814, when he saw and admired the first version Canova was making for the Empress Josephine, now in the Hermitage Museum in Russia. A special circular rotonda, with a dome and cupola supported on eight antique marble columns, was built in 1819 to house the work—the prize of the impressive Woburn Abbey collection of antique and modern marbles—at the angle where the Orangery and the Sculpture Gallery meet. As late as 1991, six years after it had gone, brochures advertising the availability of these rooms for corporate entertaining still showed a photograph of the three ladies in their sunlit little temple.

On being handed the estate by his father in the 1970s, Robin Tavistock and his trustees offered *The Three Graces* to the nation in lieu of some £1.2 million in taxes, but the offer foundered over questions of valuation and access. They then transferred title in the work for a reported £1.25 million (about $1.7 million) to Fine Art Investment and Display, a company registered in the Cayman Islands, even before it went on view (still identified as the property of Woburn Abbey) at the *Treasure Houses of Britain* exhibition in 1985, perhaps to showcase it for potential U.S. buyers.

After the Getty Museum made its first offer in 1989, the Reviewing Committee on the Export of Works of Art recommended a six-months' delay—the maximum till then allowed—to allow British museums a chance to match the Getty's offer. This was extended another three months, after the Victoria and Albert Museum (where the statue was temporarily displayed) failed dismally in an effort to raise the money by way of a public appeal. In February 1990, Lord Rothschild proposed that his newly inherited estate buy the statue and then cede it to the government in return for an equivalent tax write-off on his inheritance, but the Treasury refused his offer. Then two Scottish-born entrepreneurs even richer than Lord Rothschild, David and Frederick Barclay, offered to equal the Getty's figure, and leave the statue in the V&A, and the government changed the rules to make this possible. But the Barclay brothers backed off when the Cayman Islands company demanded five years' interest payments on top of the £7.6 million price.

The Rothschild and Barclay offers dead, Fine Arts Investment applied again for an export license in 1993, and the Getty renewed its original offer. In February 1994 Heritage Secretary Peter Brooke granted British museums yet another stay-of-export. This time, the V&A joined forces with the National Galleries of Scotland. By August, with some help from the NHMF, they had raised £5.8 million ($8.9 million). A new Heritage Secretary—they come and go—extended the deadline once more. At the last minute the collection-box was topped up by major donations from two foreign-born philanthropists, John Paul Getty, Jr. (son of the Getty Museum's founder) and Baron von Thyssen-Bornemisza of Lugano. By November 1994, the three nude daughters of Zeus were dancing in the grand foyer of the V&A. In August 1995, they moved to National Galleries of Scotland for a four-year stay. They will divide their time between London and Edinburgh after 1999.

The only people left unhappy are John Walsh, director of the Getty Museum, who remains convinced that the British system dealt with him unfairly; and a number of observers—including the Tavistocks at Woburn—who wonder whether a duplicate of a sleek Canova statuary group was worth all the money and fuss.[11]

· · ·

Even more significant than these sales of individual works may be the wholesale dispersals of the complete contents of a house when the estate itself is sold. Sayer and Massingberd, in *The Disintegration of a Heritage* (1993) list at least 28 such "house sales" since 1979, not counting cases where house *and* contents ended up in the presumably safe hands of either the National Trust, English Heritage, or a private charitable trust.

The most notorious of all such sales—at least in our time—was that held at Mentmore in 1977. Among the more substantial and important house clearance sales since Mentmore—the auctioneers simply move in and try to sell off everything in the house, down to the dishtowels and cruets—have been those at Great Tew, Oxfordshire; North Mymms, Hertfordshire; and Pitchford and Stokesay Court, both in Shropshire. Each of these realized more than a million pounds; each was described by the heritage lobby as a cultural disaster. In both 1993 and 1994, the big three auctioneers (Sotheby's, Christie's, and Phillips) held at least ten sales of the contents of country houses, usually occasioned by an end-of-the-line death, with no direct heir to take over the house; by severe losses at Lloyd's; or by the desire of owners to cash in and live more simply. These sales, all held on the estates, earned an average of about a million pounds.

I must say that, from the neutral outsider's point of view, such sales can be great fun. The auctioneers set up shop under large tents on the lawn, in view of the house, where champagne and strawberries may be offered to the bidders. Curious amateurs and knowledgeable dealers sit on folding chairs, the dealers towards the front. A glossy illustrated catalogue is sold. Over a number of days (following a number of days of in-house viewings), item after item is carried out and lifted into view. Lesser objects often sell for higher prices than they would fetch in London, if only because the amateurs in attendance (I speak from experience) are determined to bring home a souvenir. A Phillips auction spokesman, commenting on the phenomenon of country house sales, said, "The buying public is absolutely riveted by them. A lot of local people always turn up to the sales because they want to see the inside of the big house, and maybe buy something from it. The viewings are always packed. They can't get enough of it."[12]

The four-day Stokesay Court sale, in September 1994, attracted 8,000 people and the usual hyperbolic press attention. The wildly eclectic array of contents in this large, overwrought 1893 house—many of them gathered by the builder's son, who shopped manically at bazaars throughout Asia and Africa during the 1890s—had been locked away in the attics when the house was requisitioned by the army in 1939, not to be seen again until the builder's reclusive granddaughter—who lived in just three of the 37 rooms—died in 1992. It was only then that John Holden, a neighbor and fine art agent called in by her executors, discovered scores of tarpaulin-covered packing cases up under the bat-hung rafters, untouched for 53 years:

> In them lay the entire contents of Stokesay Court as it had been at the outbreak of the Second World War—paintings, furniture, glass, ceramics, and thousands of exotic objects brought back to the house by a previous owner, a Victorian millionaire, at the end of the last century. Holden had stumbled upon an historic timepiece, a slice of life preserved in mothballs, complete even to the frilly white Mary Poppins sun parasols and the sun-dried turtle-flipper that he found in a kitchen drawer. It was the stuff of which dealers, stylists, art and architectural historians dream. For years the house had appeared almost bare, yet all the time the roof had been stuffed with riches. . . . the cocoon of tarpaulins around the boxes had kept the contents in pristine condition. The textiles, in particular, protected from sunlight for 50 years, emerged with the colours extraordinarily vivid— bolts of cloth that had never been unpacked, Indian saris circa 1893, curtain tassles shining with gold thread, silk and satin ballgowns. Out of the attics came an astonishing 5,000 items. This was an Atlantis in the world of interiors; a huge collection created by the jackdaw instinct of successive generations of the same family.[13]

Sotheby's unpacked all the items and refurnished the house in something like its pre-1939 guise. Although the Allcroft collections at Stokesay Court did include a few valuable pieces—a Louis XIV Boulle chest, an 1862 Gillow marquetry cabinet, an Agra carpet, Victorian Royal Academy pictures (the sale earned the Allcroft heirs an unexpected £4.5 million, or $6.9 million)—viewers and bidders were at least as fascinated by the Victorian metal hot water jugs, a leopard-skin motoring rug, 1930s lingerie, a 1943 section of dried turtle (for making soup), the hats, the toys, the ostrich eggs, and especially the long-preserved Asian fabrics and souvenirs.

Sotheby's director James Miller, gloating over the success of the Stokesay Court sale, attributed the popularity of such sales to the large numbers of British country house fans who often travelled hundreds of miles to attend. ("You might call them groupies," he said, mimicking the villainous politician of TV's *House of Cards*. "I couldn't possibly call them that.") Other reasons cited were overseas phone buyers, the end of the recession, and the popularity of two British television series (*Lovejoy* and *The Antiques Roadshow*) that feature sales and valuations of antiques around the country. Moreover, Miller said, "People have become avid visitors to country houses. But they are frustrated because they cannot touch. Here you can pick it up and smell it.... You can't go into a National Trust house and pick up the curtains and say you fancy a pair of them yourself. And you can't experience the feeling of going into the silver vaults which probably no one, apart from the butler of the house, has seen before."[14]

.   .   .

In 1977, Sotheby's took seven days to auction off 3,739 lots from Mentmore Towers, for a record (quickly broken) of £6.4 million, then just over $11 million. Admission to the auction, held on the grounds of the mock-Elizabethan mansion in Buckinghamshire built for Baron Meyer de Rothschild in 1849, was by purchase of at least one of the five volumes of the auctioneer's catalogue, which sold for £30 ($52) the set. Each volume concluded with an advertisement reminding bidders that the house itself, with 660 surrounding acres (including a let farm and thirty houses and cottages), was also for sale.

Like almost all sales of country houses and their collections in recent years, the passing of Mentmore and its contents out of the Rothschild/Rosebery family was described at the time by some people in Britain as an irreparable loss to the nation's heritage. But I found the sale catalogues, as I find the house itself, disappointingly oppressive. The Rothschild cousins *did* know how to collect—particularly French furniture, along with many kinds of painted, carved, inlaid, and gilded objects. But Baron Meyer's collections at Mentmore, for all the prodigious display of workmanship and expense, add up to an assemblage far inferior to his cousin Ferdinand's collections at Waddesdon.

Fortune magazine, at the time, called the Mentmore auction "the greatest of all garage sales." *The Economist* wrote (the house had never been open to the public before), "Mentmore is a shabby disappointment, full of shredded taffeta, chipped cherubs, and cracked Sèvres," and thought the government had been wise *not* to have taken on this awkward, dilapidated house with its eclectic mountain of costly contents.[15] Other experts thought the same, despite the energetic "Save Mentmore for the Nation" campaign. The best paintings from the house were either sold off privately in advance of the sale (three Tiepolos, a David, a Titian), or retained by Lord Rosebery for his other house in Scotland.

All of which makes the catalogue of the most recent great English country house sale—that of selected works from Houghton Hall in Norfolk, auctioned off in just four hours on December 8, 1994, at Christie's in London—seem all the more refined. The catalogue itself, to start with, is a 361-page hardbound volume (price £30 or $50), which illustrates in impeccable color each of the 147 lots up for auction, describing each item and its history in the microscopic jargon of the contemporary connoisseur.

Lord Cholmondeley's main justification for selling these pieces—apart from his basic obligation to pay the costs of maintaining the *two* country houses he had inherited in 1990, at the age of 30—is that they were later additions, in the Victorian/Edwardian taste of the Rothschilds and Sassoons, rather than works native and original to Houghton. Cholmondeley's grandmother, born Sybil Sassoon (1894–1989), was the granddaughter of Baron Gustave de Rothschild of Paris. Her brother Philip (1888–1939) was a diplomat, collector, socialite, and tastemaker, and chairman of the National Gallery trustees.

The Rothschild/Sassoon items included numerous objects made of or mounted in gilt bronze—including seventeen porcelain potpourri vases, French furniture and bronzes, japanned desks, carpets and tapestries, and china from Baron Gustave's collection—all in the Mentmore style, if not in such suffocating quantity.

The big sellers, in the end, were Jean-François Troy's painting, *La Lecture de Molière* (five languid ladies and one gentleman lounge about a Paris salon ca.1730, pretending to listen to someone reading a book), which sold for £3,961,500 ($6 million) to a London/New York art dealer; two Louis XV green porphyry vases, each with a pair of gilt bronze lions climbing over the edges to serve as handles (£1,926,500, or almost $3 million); a two-sided Rubens sketch bought by the 3rd Earl of Cholmondeley in 1751 (£1,761,500, or $2.7 million); two sumptuous Louis XIV Boulle inlaid ebony coffers on stands (£1,541,500, or $2,358,500); and a pair of George II ewers of gold-enwrapped jasper, which sold for five times the estimate at £1,266,500 ($1,937,745). An elaborate Louis XVI cabinet of brass-inlaid ebony, designed to display a collection of shells, went for £903,500 ($1,382,500). Four little gold-topped 1740 perfume bottles, valued at £5–8,000, sold for £67,500 ($103,000). The total take, before commission, was £21,256,795, or more than $32 million. In July 1995, Lord Cholmondeley was still negotiating with the government to accept a few *other* pieces of furniture (which would then remain at Houghton) in place of the 40 percent capital gains tax bite on the sale.

By way of this and his earlier sales, Cholmondeley hopes to find some way to share his inheritance with his three sisters; to hold on to his ancestral home, Cholmondeley Castle in Cheshire; and to establish a maintenance fund that will help pay the extravagant costs of repairing and running Houghton Hall, which he estimates at from half a million to a million pounds a year. Unlike nearby Holkham Hall, Houghton—one of the finest, most truly historic country houses in England—has insufficient agricultural property around it, and no potential land for development. Like Holkham, it is located on an unfrequented corner of the north Norfolk coast, and attracts only about 10–15,000 visitors a year.

·   ·   ·

On the occasion of many of the sales referred to above, a great hue and cry has been raised about not only the loss of "Britain's Own" artistic heritage—a heritage that now includes a great many works purchased from previous owners in other countries when *they* were in need of funds; but also about the alienation of these works from their "proper" homes, i.e., the houses they have been in for a century or more. In the United States, a number of private houses, like the Frick Collection in New York and the Gardner Museum in Boston, have been converted into museums designed to contain and perpetuate their owners' art collections. Several important private collections in the United States (like the Sainsbury collection in Britain) have been housed in new museums of their own.

But in general, important American art collectors, after at most two or three generations of collecting and private possession, have either liquidated their holdings, or donated them to museums. Very rarely has an major American collector entertained the notion that it was imperative that his or her collection remain not only intact, but in situ. Those who have, like William Randolph Hearst, Dr. Albert C. Barnes, and Isabella Stuart Gardner, tend to be regarded as imperious, egocentric cranks; people who wanted to be accorded after their death the same kind of eternal respect expected by the founders of great British collections, in their resplendent country houses.

· · ·

Develop the Property

In addition to the traditional means of supporting a country house—living off the farms and forests, and the rentals from other estate properties—there are a number of other more or less natural income sources that can be generated from a country house and the acreage that typically surrounds it. One may try to develop, or sell to a developer, *some* of one's estate, as a way of supporting the rest—usually the manor house in the middle, and enough garden and parkland around it to maintain its distinctive identity. Permission to develop or subdivide must be obtained from local—and, for more historically important estates, national—planning authorities. This may be difficult to get, if the planning authorities believe that your proposal will degrade historic buildings or space, or if enough of your neighbors complain.

Not all of one's property can be casually developed, even if local planners give their consent. If you or your predecessors obtained a conditional tax exemption on so-called heritage land, selling this land breaks one of the conditions, and the deferred tax will have to be paid.

One attempt to develop a country estate that may have destroyed its owner in the process was that at Luton Hoo, the luxurious Wernher mansion in Bedfordshire. In 1982, Nicholas Phillips, the grand-nephew of the builder, conceived the idea of a top-of-the-line business park called "Capability Green," to be built on 85 acres of the 4,000-acre estate, part of which had been landscaped by Capability Brown. As the 85 acres in question had been sliced off from the rest of the estate by a link road to Luton Airport, planners agreed, after five years of appeals, that industrial development was a reasonable use. Phillips promoted the property—ten minutes off the M25 ring road—as near to both London and

Heathrow airport; promised to maintain the classical landscape by allowing building on only fifteen percent of the land; and hoped that its association with a well-known stately home would give it added cachet.

All planning hurdles finally cleared, building began in 1986. By 1989, Phillips had four major tenants. By 1990, the recession brought new building and leasing to a halt. Phillips was now more than £20 million ($35 million) in debt to the Swedish banks that had underwritten his project. In March 1991, at 43, he was found dead of carbon monoxide poisoning inside his car, the engine of which had been left running inside a closed garage at Luton Hoo. Since then, his widow has been able to clear the debts by selling major works of art from the Luton Hoo collection. As of May 1995 the business park itself, in other hands than the Phillipses', was finally flourishing.

A happier industrial development project was that at Wynyard Park in County Durham, a palatial mansion built by the 1st Marquess of Londonderry in 1822 out of coal-mining profits. A number of his successors entertained here, as they did in London, in a manner befitting their exceptional fortunes. In the early 1960s, after a period of disuse and decay, the 9th Marquess moved back into part of one wing of the house, which he turned into a fashionable gathering place for the gilded youth of the decade. But by 1987, the 5,400-acre estate was no longer generating enough income to maintain the huge house, so Londonderry sold off the estate, house and all, to John Hall, an up-from-poverty developer, for £3 million ($5 million). Hall had made a fortune out of his 1979 Metro Centre, a gigantic, American-style shopping center near Gateshead; he then poured a large part of the profits into resurrecting the football club at nearby Newcastle.

John (now Sir John) Hall, un-coroneted Duke of Tyneside, decided to restore the mansion and redecorate its rooms at a cost of £4 million ($6 million); his plan was to use one part of the house for company business, another to house cultural events, and a third as his family home. From Wynyard Park, Sir John and his son Douglas now oversee a 7,500-acre domain in which agriculture has yielded to a factory site for Samsung Electronics of Korea. In 1995, there were plans for more businesses, three golf courses, a hotel and country club, and 1,000 single-family houses scattered among landscaped green spaces, threaded by footpaths and equestrian trails.

Another notable success, financially, was the arrangement described earlier that the Marquess of Bath was able to make with Center Parcs, the Dutch-based leisure corporation that built a whole complex of 600 holiday cottages within the Longleat estate. One of three such villages in England, the £85 million ($127.5 million) Longleat Centre Parcs development, which opened in 1994, includes a glass-enclosed, swimming complex as well as other sports, shopping, eating, and entertainment facilities, all connected to the cottages by pedestrian and bicycle paths through the woods. Bath and his trustees leased the land for an adjustable rental which virtually guarantees Longleat a substantial income for many years to come. It will also, he presumes, provide a virtually "captive audience" for the house and its many ancillary attractions. Several other estates have been allowed to convert outlying properties into commercial or housing tracts. It was the sale of 26 acres of residential land by the Wilton House trustees in 1987 that enabled them to spend almost £3 million ($5 million) on a complete renovation of the historic south range.

At Broadlands in Hampshire, Lord Romsey was thwarted three times between 1985 and 1994 in his attempts to develop a corner of his estate, part of his effort to create income to maintain the stately, heavily mortgaged 85-room Mountbatten home—formerly the home of two Victorian prime ministers (Lords Melbourne and Palmerston), and thereby authentically "historic." He had made a £2 million ($3 million-plus) arrangement with Tesco to build a 28,000 square foot supermarket on the north edge of his property near to Romsey village, and planned another commercial development on a farm to the south. But village shopkeepers, fearful of straying customers, dug in their heels in opposition. "I am sure Lord Romsey has other options," said one. "If it comes to losing Broadlands but keeping Romsey vibrant and alive," said the secretary of the local chamber of commerce— "well, so be it." A year later, Lord Romsey decided to cut his losses by opening Broadlands to the public for two months a year instead of six. The chamber of commerce, now suffering from the loss of tourist trade, protested once again.

Lord Cobbold at Knebworth has been more successful with his planning applications over the years, in part because of some canny politicking on his part, and his ability to involve the city fathers of Stevenage, just across the motorway, in his projects and profits. What other country house owners most envy at Knebworth is Cobbold's ability to obtain not only his own motorway exit (Interchange 7 off the M1, just minutes from London), but also planning permission for a 103-bed hotel between the motorway and his house. The hotel, which opened in 1988, permits him to offer overnight accommodation to conference groups, and serves the city of Stevenage as well.

The long-term plan for Knebworth began in 1981, when the future of the estate was felt to be endangered by the financial crisis of the previous decade. It was then that the Cobbolds asked for and (three years later) obtained planning consent to develop six acres of housing on their estate across the M1, and to add fifteen houses and a new village green alongside the local pub (The Lytton Arms) in Old Knebworth village, just south of the house. That won them some friends in the village, and provided a £1.7 million ($3.4 million) endowment for the charitable trust, established in 1984, that now owns the house. The Cobbolds wisely designated the Mayor of Stevenage, the chairman of the local parish council, and the chairman of the North Hertfordshire District Council as members of their board of trustees. This, as Lord Cobbold points out, is not only likely to provide them with useful friends in office at any given time, but also supporters among former mayors and chairmen who have served on their board. After a three-year struggle with the district council (the land lies within a designated Green Belt, and a special exception had to be made) they won planning consent not only for the new hotel—part of the French Novotel chain—but also for a visitor center, museum, and a trailer park on a 50-acre plot alongside it. None of the latter has yet been built, but Cobbold and his trustees keep renewing their planning request in order to keep open the possibility of future development. In 1987 they made a tentative million-pound deal with BP Oil (for whom Cobbold then worked)

Burghley House, Lincolnshire.

for a motorway service station on the property, but were denied permission to build it by the Environment Secretary, who felt that Knebworth was no longer in the desperate straits that had justified its "Green Belt exception" of 1984. In 1991 they revised their planning request for the site to include a science park and research center, and a corporate head-quarters building, but failed on that occasion as well. By 1996, Cobbold and the Kneb-worth trustees were insisting that without permission to sell off and develop more of the estate, it would be impossible to restore or retain the house.

On a smaller scale, a number of country house owners have found ways of turning dis-used service or farm buildings to profitable ends, by converting them to what planning au-thorities regard as "sympathetic" uses. Lady Victoria Leatham at Burghley set a pattern by renting workshops in her old stables to "fine craftsmen"—so far she has a textile conservator, a bookbinder, a painting restorer, a stonemason, and a gilder—whom she then makes use of to help restore Burghley's own museum-quality contents, and who benefit from their presence as a community of artisans around a famous stately home. ("We would dearly love to have a furniture person, a clock person, and a porcelain person," she says.) Lady Ashcombe has done something along the same lines with the new workshops and exhibition center at Sudeley Castle, where reproductions of castle furniture are made and displayed. At Sudeley, as at other estates, uninhabited farm cottages have been turned into holiday rentals. At Hagley Hall, the owners found a number of profitable ways to reuse their redundant farm buildings. The conversion of the south stable block at Woburn Abbey into an "antiques supermarket" of 40 separate dealers was another such commercial and yet appropriate transformation. The Tavistocks also opened a tract of 42 new houses on a piece of derelict timberland on the Woburn estate. It is, as far as I know, a unique example; but the Duke of Richmond and Gordon (or rather, the "Goodwood Group of Companies") owns not only Goodwood House, but also the famous Goodwood racecourse—the house is closed to the public on racing days, when the family is likely to be using it to entertain guests. Other non-agricultural features of the 12,000-acre Goodwood estate include a classic motor racing circuit, an airport and flying school, and a golf course with its own 88-room hotel—each facility with a separate restaurant. In 1990, the duke was able to get an interest-free loan of £3.4 million ($6 million) from the state to rebuild and enlarge the historic grandstands, where private boxes now rent for more than £20,000 ($30,000) a year.

. . .

Golf Courses

In 1988, the Royal and Ancient Golf Club of St. Andrews, the Vatican of the golfing world, published a report claiming that, with a population of three million golfers—up from a million a decade before—Great Britain would need 691 new golf courses by the year 2000. By 1991, there were about 2,000 existing courses in Britain, 20,000 people on waiting lists for memberships, and 253 new courses under construction. Planning permission had been requested for more than a thousand more. By the end of the decade, 30 new links had been planned for Norfolk alone—which, one commentator wrote, would almost enable one to hit a golf ball uninterrupted across the county.

Country house owners had long before begun to look on their rolling green lawns as potentially profitable fairways—in effect, a subset of property development. In most cases, such conversions of parkland only took place after the house itself was transformed into a conference center, as at Leeds Castle or Brocket Hall, or a resort-and-conference hotel like Hintlesham Hall or Horsted Place. Other country house hotels offer nine-hole courses, putting greens, or miniature golf, and many have arrangements with neighboring courses allowing hotel guests to play. The grounds around Mentmore Towers, the Rothschild house turned Transcendental Meditation institute, were converted in 1992 into 36 holes of golf links (with adjacent new houses), partly with Rothschild money. Moor Park in Hertfordshire, a grandiose Palladian mansion of the 1720s with painted Verrio ceilings, has been for some years the most elegant clubhouse of any golf club in England, although the house itself still belongs to the local council. There's even a nine-hole course at Stowe, an amenity featured in the school's prospectus.

But a number of private house owners, notably the Sackvilles at Knole (where the fairways are nibbled by antlered stags, and the "rough" looks untouched since the Middle Ages), the Richmonds at Goodwood, the Scarsdales at Kedleston, the Pearsons at Cowdray Park, the Sitwells at Renishaw, and the Tavistocks at Woburn Abbey—who managed to carve two championship eighteen-hole courses out of their woodlands in 1976, and now have planning permission for a third—have been able to remain in residence, and transform a portion of their grounds into popular and profitable courses they like to think of as a natural part of the landscape.

Recently, however, a number of failed or "insensitive" golfing proposals on historic house landscapes—often as part of a hotel or conference center conversion—led to a backlash from the heritage lobby, which has begun to resist new applications to turn country house parklands into golf courses. A new golf course went up alongside Belton House in Lincolnshire, over the ardent objections of the National Trust, which now owns the house. Asil Nadir, the Turkish Cypriot entrepreneur who bought Burley-on-the-Hill, planned to build *two* eighteen-hole courses on the grounds, before his empire collapsed and he fled overseas. An interim owner/developer at Orchardleigh Park in Somerset began digging up the parkland for two golf courses, but went bankrupt halfway through and left the grounds an ugly moonscape of upturned trees and half-bulldozed hills.

In a report entitled *In the Rough* issued in June 1991 jointly by the Georgian Group, the Garden History Society, and the Association of Garden Trusts, it was argued that golf courses inevitably damage historic landscapes; that golf and historic parks do not fit well together; and that "golf development should be excluded from parks on the English Heritage register," with exceptions made only where the development would actually restore decayed landscapes and itself be unobtrusive. By that time, the owners of at least 50 of the 1,120 parks and gardens in Britain officially labeled "sites of special historic interest" had applied for golf course conversions, and the English Heritage Historic Landscapes panel was beginning to say no. As the *Times* noted, "English Heritage believes that the stately homes of England and parkland of historic interest are under threat as landowners and business consortia line up to send in the bulldozers to transform vistas that have been entwined into the natural landscape over hundreds of years."[16]

Near Highclere Castle in Hampshire, Lord Carnarvon sold off 250 of his 1,500 acres for a golf course in 1991, in order to repair the castle roof and renovate his follies. But he was then refused permission for the course by his local council, despite his insistence that "there would have been no earth moving, and not a tree felled.... The only difference is that there would have been 18 little red flags flying."[17] The land was, he insisted, impossible for house-visitors to see, and of no agricultural use. An even more significant rejection was that of a £40 million ($70 million) plan to convert the park around Warwick Castle into two golf courses and a hotel larger than the castle, which Environment Secretary

Michael Howard killed on appeal in 1992. Of course Warwick Castle, like Mentmore Towers, has long ceased to be a private home; and in neither case is the owner of the building the owner of the park.

The most-discussed golf course conversion has been that at Bowood in Wiltshire, where the Earl of Shelburne decided in 1987 that this was his family's last chance to save a historic house and estate where farming had ceased to be profitable, and tourism hadn't taken up the slack. Of the 2,000-acre park (part of a 22,000-acre estate) designed by Capability Brown, Hugh Massingberd wrote "[it] has strong claims to be the finest landscape park in England."[18] But the new golf course, Shelburne pointed out, would be implanted in a 200-acre corner of the property formerly used for agriculture, and have no effect on the Grade I "heritage" landscape. Existing views or riding paths would be retained, even made a feature of the course. Only seven trees would have to be removed, while another 60 beeches, oaks, and birches were to be planted. "For the past 250 years," Shelburne replied to his critics, "my ancestors have adapted the land use to the needs of the day. I'm simply continuing that policy." If Capability Brown were alive today, his press agent suggested, he would probably be designing golf courses.

Visiting the new course with some apprehension, country house maven Hugh Massingberd was won over. He found the new moundings, sculpted with earth from the estate, to be "surprisingly inoffensive." He was pleased to see the roughs seeded with wildflowers, the wide fairways blending into the landscape. Even the usual clash between the yellow gashes of sand bunkers and the mellow green of the lawns—a chief hate-target of the antigolf

Bowood, Wiltshire.

lobby—had, he wrote, been minimized by planting grass down the sides of the traps, and by using sand of a color that matched the local stone. Local stone, in fact, was also a feature of the new Bowood Golf and Country Club, which opened its Golden Gates (designed by Charles Barry in 1860) to players in May 1992. Both the clubhouse and the pro shop/restaurant were made out of converted 18th-century farm buildings of a handsome ocher stone. A 19th-century manor house overlooking the eighth fairway offered overnight accomodation.

On a dark day in December 1991, I drove on icy roads from Oxford down to Bowood in Wiltshire, where Lord Shelburne gave me a tour of his golf course-in-the-making. The greens were frosted. Estate workmen huddled about fires of burning scrub. Black deer leaped among the trees. Shelburne was obviously very proud, and very hopeful, and I must say it all looked quite handsome—even in the context of the sublime landscape of the nongolfing reaches of Bowood park, with its long 40-acre lake and cascade, its Doric temple and hermit's cave, its rose terraces and forest of specimen pines.

The whole enterprise cost £5 million ($8.8 million) of mostly borrowed money. Shelburne decided on a "pay as you play" scheme (£25 a round on weekdays, £40 on weekends—about $42 and $60) rather than a closed membership, as the mounting recession had reduced the popularity of costly share-owner clubs. At the same time, he hoped to attract at least 250 "cardholders" who would get priority booking and other special privileges for £875 (later £1,000) a year: $1,300–$1,500 at the time.

Despite a great deal of opening season publicity, his expectations were never realized. By the time the course opened the club had only 80 cardholders. Although in two years the number grew to just over 200, his revenue projections, Shelburne later admitted, turned out to be "wildly optimistic." At first he said he hoped to see 40,000 rounds played the first year, then scaled that down to 25,000; the actual number was just over 13,000. Summers saw healthy play, but in wintertime the greens and clubhouse were often empty.

The real culprit, Shelburne's controller conceded, had been the recession. New golf courses, a pipe dream of the booming Thatcherite 1980s, made less sense in the harsher economic climate of the 1990s. But Shelburne remained convinced that Bowood would remain in family hands—thanks to the golf course. "It was absolutely clear when I took over Bowood that this place didn't have a dog's chance of surviving unless we diversified into something which I thought had a chance of success," he told me in July 1994. "And I'm still convinced it was the right thing to do."

Even without the heritage protests, the Bowood experience suggests that the 1988 predictions of the Royal and Ancient Golf Club had been mistaken, and that the British golfing bubble may have burst. For all the widespread and growing popularity of the game, most country house courses (unlike Bowood) are designed for the upper end of the market, which often means businesses or business people able to pay six-figure membership fees and four-figure subscriptions; or for wealthy foreign visitors willing to pay £100 ($150) or more for a round. In times of straitened corporate and private budgets, such luxuries assume lower priority.

When I talked to him in 1991, Simon Howard was quite excited about plans for a new "Brideshead Golf and Country Club," including a hotel, at Castle Howard. Three years later, unable to find a partner willing to share the capital investment, he had put the plans back in a drawer. The Duke of Westminster (for reasons of security, not aesthetics) decided in 1990 to remove a 25-year-old golf course on the grounds of Eaton Hall in Cheshire, and restore it as a landscape park, grazed by a herd of deer. Perhaps this particular fantasy of a fresh source of income for the English country house has come to at least a temporary halt.

· · ·

The Functions Industry

Most of the larger country house owners now actively seek out "functions," as they call them—weddings and receptions, business meetings and conferences—which they find a more efficient means of making money than admitting streams of day-trippers at three or four pounds a head. "We had British Telecom here for the whole of May," wrote young Earl Spencer at Althorp, in 1994. "Apart from being a prestigious corporate event, the income was the equivalent of what we would get from being open every day for three years to the general public."

At a number of lived-in country houses *not* open to casual tourists—Carlton Towers in Yorkshire, Castle Ashby in Northamptonshire, Catton Hall in Derby, Moyns Park in Essex, Rossway Park in Hertfordshire, Sandon Hall in Staffordshire, Somerley in Hampshire—the owners will rent the house and grounds for acceptable functions (weddings, dinner parties, residential conferences) which take over all or part of the building. Since 1995, stately homes that meet registration requirements can legally be used as the setting for civil marriages in Britain, which has increased their share of the lucrative wedding reception trade. Henry Holland's famous 1789 Sculpture Gallery at Woburn Abbey (minus *The Three Graces*) is now reserved exclusively for private luncheons, dinners, and meetings. A few houses, including Castle Ashby, offer overnight accommodation to party- or conference-goers as well.

The managers of Leeds and Hever Castles aggressively seek and lavishly service the function and conference trade, in addition to daytime tourists. Gatherings that make use of the 25-bedroom Tudor Village at Hever (originally built in 1903 by William Waldorf Astor for his guests) get their own facilities for swimming, tennis, and croquet, as well as meeting, dining, and billiard rooms. Tudor banquets, with champagne and minstrels, can be laid on in the Castle Dining Room. Leeds Castle—"the perfect place for great minds to meet"—can offer a purpose-converted, motel-like conference center ("ideal for middle-to-senior management meetings or training courses") built around its old stable court, with sixteen bedrooms, plus meeting and dining rooms. "For main board or high level international meetings," Leeds suggests you may wish to book some of the nineteen bedrooms in the Castle itself (£235, or $360 per person, with meals), plus a flat £1,250 [$1,925] "facility fee" for the use of the private apartments, which are off-limits to tourists. Henry VIII's own banqueting hall, most of which was installed in 1927–28—and which tourists *can* see—rents for £2,000, or $3,000. Renting the big lawn at Leeds for an outdoor event would cost the father of a society bride, or a corporation offering hospitality to favored customers, a base rate of £5,000–9,000 ($8–14,000), depending on whether you invited more or fewer than 1,000 guests. That fee includes two days to set up your tables and tents and one day to take them down, plus car parkers and stewards. Catering, marquees, entertainment (and, in all of these cases, drinks and VAT) would be extra.

At some private houses, the owner offers to meet and mingle with the guests, which (especially if he or she is titled) may be a distinct selling point over a nearby hotel. Some owners have their own in-house chefs and kitchen staffs. The catering services at Hagley Hall and Knebworth have grown into such professional enterprises that they handle off-site jobs as well, including functions at *other* country houses. Other houses have set up elaborate businesses that can handle a customer's needs for invitations, flowers, wines, speakers, secretaries, audiovisual aids, and music, organize costumed theatricals or ghost hunts, shooting parties or balloon rides, and an after-dinner fireworks show in the garden. The resident potter at Woburn Abbey will craft personalized mementoes for your guests. More than a hundred English country houses, from relatively modest manors to palaces like Althorp, Blenheim, Harewood, and Castle Howard, advertise their available rooms and facilities in *Hudson's Historic Houses and Gardens*, an annual directory published by Norman Hudson which was originally aimed at the travel and "functions" trade, but which now serves the general tourist as well. Even Sandringham, the Queen's country house in Norfolk, rents out its grounds for rallies, fairs, and concerts, and its restaurant for other events. A few National Trust houses are available for meetings and parties, particularly those managed by other entities (Shugborough, Tatton Park). But in most cases such use is seen as conflicting with the Trust's primary obligations of preservation and public access.

A perusal of the Hudson guide suggests the extraordinary range of "functions" country house owners are prepared, even eager to host. On the questionnaire Hudson sends them, almost all owners seem to tick off fashion shows, archery, wedding receptions, and garden parties. Clay pigeon shooting appears to be a very popular diversion, from the number of houses that offer it. Most houses welcome such outdoor events, as well as open-air concerts and exhibitions, because they spare the house itself from the wear and tear of large numbers. Robin Compton, at Newby Hall, says, "We flatly refuse to host functions in the house, except occasionally for charity and good causes."

But many house owners will rent out their state rooms as well, for receptions, cocktail parties, lunches, banquets, balls, and corporate meetings. Almost anyone with a large enough medieval hall will do you a Medieval Banquet. Tatton Park in Cheshire, according to the Hudson guide, can offer the conference planner "Spotlights, catwalk, dance floor, full public address system, sailing, parkland, shuttle service and marquee hire. The pillar-less Tenants Hall [8,000 square feet] has 2 sources of 3 phase power, a scaffold tower and can seat up to 400 for lectures. Projector and screens can be provided. Independent telephones throughout." Stripped of its Rothschild furnishings, Mentmore Towers retains its spacious and opulent interiors, which the Maharishi's meditators offer for conferences and

Woburn Abbey, Bedfordshire. Estate potter.

other gatherings. "We can now offer 3 machine high-band editing," they advise, "including time-coded computer list editing. Cameras (Sony DXC3000PK), a prompter, and portable and studio high-band recorders are also available for hire."[19]

The real money comes from corporate functions of one kind or another, both business and social. The brochures and information kits published by country houses in quest of corporate business—Hagley, Goodwood, and Weston Park seem to be among the most aggressive, along with "dedicated" conference-houses like Brocket Hall and Leeds Castle—include long and impressive lists of their previous clients. Corporate functions include seminars, conferences, and training courses, which inevitably involve the need for at least coffee, a lunch, and a drinks break, served in some elegant space on the premises. "Product launches" are another very popular use of country houses. Automobile manufacturers regularly book them to introduce new models to their salesmen, which allows the cars to be driven about the grounds; but so do publishers and distillers. Commercial exhibitions are usually held outdoors, in marquees or temporary steel-frame structures on the lawns.

Most unusual, to an American unfamiliar with corporate mores, are the "morale-building" or "incentive" Company Days, which British firms regularly offer to their employees, grandiose company picnics which make use of both the interiors and the grounds of country houses. At the breaks between lunch, tea, cocktails—and if one is near enough to home or overnight accommodations are available, a banquet, even a dinner-dance as well—employees have their choice of a variety of country diversions such as archery, clay pigeon (or even game bird) shooting, falconry, tennis, croquet, river rafting, fly casting, and riflery on the estate. The more adventurous estate owners throw in "motorized activities," so that grown men (and women, I presume) can roar about the grounds in off-road vehicles or "quad bikes." Lord Lichfield's Shugborough Estate, owned by the National Trust and imaginatively run by the Staffordshire County Council, offers (among scores of other visitor enticements) Corporate Activity Days, in which "guests join in a fun packed day, choosing from a range of activities including clay pigeon shooting, rifle shooting, blindfold driving, hovercrafting, archery, karting and quad biking."

More adventurous still are treasure hunts, war-games, and "survival outings," designed to build team spirit among workers by challenging them to live rough in the woods for a weekend, like Scouts. Eastnor Castle in the Malvern Hills even provides a separate dormitory in the woods for "Survival/Team Building" participants, equipped with its own shower and kitchen, as well as the chance to ride over its rugged Land Rover test track with qualified instructors.

Rarer, but still available, are hot air ballooning, polo and cricket facilities, and horse riding and jumping facilities; even jousting. In its own promotional material, Somerley in Hampshire reminds businesspeople that the estate

> is not open to the public; the magnificently proportioned rooms with high gilded ceilings house a treasure trove of fine antique furniture, porcelain, paintings and objets d'art, and can be enjoyed by guests who visit to conduct business meetings, conferences, concerts, receptions, product launches and top level corporate hospitality. The house is 1¼ miles from the nearest road and although easily accessible, provides privacy for meetings demanding security and complete confidentiality. The 7,000 acres of parkland can be used for incentive fun days, promotions and Golf events. The high standard of service and cuisine (much of the food comes from the Estate and gardens) and the warm friendly atmosphere are very rarely found in a house of this size. The peace and tranquillity of the grounds are a sheer delight.[20]

·   ·   ·

Film and Television Locations

Like Simon Howard or Lord Saye and Sele, you can rent out your house and grounds as a location for advertising photos, feature films, television documentaries or dramas, or commercials. In 1995, the Historic Houses Association was recommending that owners charge fees of at least £500–2,500 ($800–4,000) a day for advertising photography; £1,500–2,750 ($2,400–4,400) a day for feature films using the interior of a house; £1,200–2,000 ($1,920–3,200) a day for TV dramas; and £1,500–3,000 ($2,400–4,800) a day for commercials. For major location work in a feature film, which can take several weeks, this can add up to a substantial piece of change. Individual owners sometimes ask for more. Francis Dashwood demanded, and got, £5,000 ($8,000) a day for the use of West Wycombe Park in the Clint Eastwood film, *White Hunter, Black Heart* (1995), which spent six days on location. Altogether, he figures, he has earned (and transferred to the National Trust) some £200,000 from film fees.

In conjunction with Norman Hudson, the HHA has prepared sample contracts for film location work—an idea that originated with George Howard, first president of the association, as a result of his experience with *Brideshead*. Hudson's 1995 revision of the HHA booklet, *Film and Photography for Historic Houses and Gardens*, and his lectures to country house owners, are full of warnings of the ways in which a film crew may damage your house, and how to guard against these by meticulously written contracts.

The desirability of actual country houses as locations in recent years—for feature films and episodes in television series, as well as TV commercials and upscale magazine advertisements—has become so important to the industries involved that a number of location-hunting agencies now work full time at seeking them out, and keep detailed logs of available houses and gardens. One such agent now has more than 6,000 houses—obviously not all of them stately homes—on her books. The British Film Commission also maintains a computerized list of thousands of houses (large and small, urban and rural) suitable for filming. The owners of many large country houses specifically invite inquiries from photographers and film makers. Groombridge Place in Kent (*The Draughtsman's Contract*) and Floors Castle in Scotland (*Greystoke*) boast in their advertisements of being used in previous films. The National Trust, once reluctant to permit commercial filming on its properties, changed its mind when visitor numbers at both Lyme Park (Pemberley, in the BBC's *Pride and Prejudice*) and Saltram (the Dashwood family's house in *Sense and Sensibility*) grew enormously during 1995. Several other National Trust houses have been rented out for movies or TV in recent years.

Quite apart from the value of using country houses in films because of the growing popular interest in them, as locations they offer filmmakers features either unavailable in or less expensive than studio built sets. Good modern mock-ups of the carved stone, wood, and plasterwork of historic houses can be terribly expensive, and are unlikely ever to capture the authenticity of the original, when a period setting is required. Genuine, centuries-old rooms, with their fireplaces and paneled walls, their shelves full of books, their tapestries and framed pictures—rooms opening through elaborate doorcases into similar rooms, or out French windows into authentic terraces and gardens overlooking acres of parkland—are unattainable in any purpose-built set. Actors, it is claimed, find it easier to "think themselves into" a period or setting when the setting is real. With luck, there will be no visible power or telephone lines, no noise from passing trucks or overhead air traffic routes, no nearby neighbors to fuss—and plenty of space for trailers, toilets, dining tents, cars, and people. The house may even (like Broughton or Stanway) have its own adjacent medieval church, and a spectrum of possible centuries to choose from; perhaps even an adjacent village free of TV antennas. Plastic cobblestones (or soil and grass) can always be laid atop the streets, and modern wires and signs taken down, as the citizens of Stamford learned during the BBC's recent filming of *Middlemarch*.

Through casual reading and conversation, and a few chance identifications while viewing, I have learned the names of the country houses used for more than 100 films or television series. There have obviously been many more, but location-finding agencies prefer not to identify many of the houses they represent—in particular houses not normally open to the public—for security reasons.

The major disadvantage to renting out one's country house as a film or television location is the extraordinary disruption it involves. Large trailers (for offices, costumes, makeup, props, toilets, artists, and equipment), immense power generators, and a dozen or more cars may be parked for days on the lawns or drives. A crew of 50 to 70 people may invade the premises from 7 P.M. to 7 P.M. each shooting day, to get the maximum use of their daily fees. Tons of camera, sound, and lighting equipment may have to be hauled or wheeled into the state rooms, threatening floors and walls; yards of cable will snake through the house and gardens. Frequently, full-scale metal scaffolding will have to be erected, on which to position lights and cameras. "They are so used to working in studios that they think nothing of standing on a Chippendale chair with their boots on to change a light bulb," wrote Lady Cobbold at Knebworth—which has been used for at least half a dozen films, "or getting out a paintbrush and touching up the eighteenth-century decoration around the doorways, changing doorknobs or taking out windows and putting in different glass. I watch in agony as the cameraman backs his camera to within inches of the ancestors on the wall.... You only need to lose one or two small valuable pieces to have lost any profit you might have made on the film, and things do disappear."[21]

Some owners are shattered by the experience, and flee. It is not, as one location agent put it, an undertaking for the house-proud, the meticulous, or the highly strung. Others frankly admit to enjoying the manic circus of having a film made on their property, and sometimes even end up taking bit parts. The owners of Peppard's Cottage, the house in Henley that stood in for *Howards End* in the Merchant-Ivory film, professed to love every minute of the six weeks of filming.

Most "open" houses (such as Castle Howard) arrange to have filming done during off-season, to avoid loss of visitor income. But Lord Yarmouth, at Ragley Hall, decided to let regular tourists (keeping "quiet on the set") continue going through the house during the two weeks in 1993 the BBC were filming the *To Play the King*, in which Ragley stood in for Buckingham Palace, and Ian Richardson played a particularly nasty Tory prime minister.

Allan Bennett, author of *The Madness of King George*, followed the film crew from location to location, and described their invasion of Broughton Castle:

Mentmore Towers, Buckinghamshire. Filming on location.

Broughton, a mile or two away [from Banbury], could not be in sharper contrast; the most beauti-ful of houses, medieval in a 16th or 17th-century shell with Gothic additions, entered across a moat and through a gatehouse, almost a standard kit for an idyll. There's a formal garden, great plush borders along the old ramparts and cows and sheep grazing in water meadows beyond.

On to this rural paradise the film unit has descended like an invading army. Twenty or so vans have ploughed up one of the meadows, 30 cars are parked under the trees; there are half a dozen caravans, two marquees and the sodden ground is rapidly turning into a quagmire. Churning up the edges of the perfect lawns, company cars ferry the actors to and from the location in the house where the sparks lug their lights and tripods down the superb vaulted corridors.

Seemingly unaffected by all this is the lady of the house, Lady Saye—really Lady Saye and Sele, only nobody is sure whether one drops the Sele in ordinary conversation. She's tall and cheerful and happy to show anybody round, the house as magical inside as out, handsome rooms lined with linenfold panelling and a splendid drawing-room overlooking the moat. My wonder at the place makes me foolish and I'm sure I gush, though it's partly to offset the unimpressed one-location-very-much-like-another behaviour inseparable from film crews, who congregate at the door having coffee and a cig.[22]

Most owners specifically ban smoking, eating, and drinking inside their houses. At Knebworth, Lord Cobbold insists on an advance bond, which is forfeited if anyone is caught smoking during filming, a policy the HHA now recommends to all owners. At Dor-ney Court near Windsor—a popular film location—Peregrine Palmer charges a £10 fine for every nail, tack or staple hole he finds in his 15th-century walls. Frequently, substan-tial alterations are made even to the finest country houses, to suit them to the needs of the film: ceilings are lowered, modern light fixtures or radiators removed, brick walls extended by polystyrene imitations, whole suites of new furniture brought in to replace what is there. For Disney's *Three Men and a Little Lady* at Broughton Castle, the carpets and curtains were replaced, and the family furniture in the Great Hall stored in the garage, to be replaced by masses of armour. Artificial ivy may be stapled to the walls to hide burglar alarms. Owners describe their surprise at seeing lawns spray-painted to look a better shade of green, or plastic flowers inserted alongside insufficiently colorful real ones. After having searched all England for a proper stand-in for Longbourn, the Bennett family's house, for their 1995 version of *Pride and Prejudice*, the BBC happened upon Luckington Court in Wiltshire. They then persuaded the owner to move into the nursery wing for three months; completely removed her furniture, heating system, and electric fittings; installed new walls and doors; and redecorated the house in appropriate Regency style, including specially printed new wallpaper. The garden was replanted with flowers more in favor in Jane Austen's time. But when it was all over, owner Angela Horn said, "I will miss the film crew. They really were awfully nice. They became like a family. I cried at the thought of them leaving. It was like a ghost town when they went but I cheer up by reminding myself that I now have enough money to re-roof the west wing."[23]

At one house in Gloucestershire, filmed in September for a margarine commercial, the producers wanted to persuade viewers they were looking at the garden in three different seasons. "For spring they cut off the tops of the flowers and planted plastic daffodils and tulips," said the owner. "In the summer scene they had an artificial sun on a crane standing by. In autumn we hit trouble. They imported hundreds of bags of leaves but the artificial snow wouldn't stick to the acacia tree and they put a ton of salt on the lawn on a polythene sheet. The trees were sprayed with artificial snow. The yew trees and the grass went brown. The mulberry tree hasn't recovered yet, nor has one of the yews."[24]

In every case the film maker agrees, of course, to return the house and garden to the status quo ante, and in most cases does. In a few especially fortunate instances, the film maker's alterations—a new carpet, a new paint job, undergrounded wires—are precisely what the owner wanted, and are allowed to remain as a bonus. As for more substantial damage, one reads stories of a painting melted by high-intensity lights, another poked through the canvas by a technician, carpets torn by cameras on tracks, the tip of a chandelier hacked off to keep it out of camera range. But as crews become more adept, and contracts more precise, such damage seems to have become rare.

Of course, not all country house owners may want to share in the "image" of a particular film or television show. The makers of two rival 1993 TV versions of the love lives of the Prince and Princess of Wales had difficulty obtaining stand-ins for Buckingham Palace, Kensington Palace, Windsor, Balmoral, Sandringham, and Highgrove. The originals were obviously unobtainable. The National Trust (to whom they turned first) thought it best not to get involved. The Queen Mother, for one thing, is honorary president of the Trust. Many private owners thought the whole enterprise a bit tacky.[25] In the end, the owners of Manderston in Berwickshire, Scotland (a reasonable facsimile of Buckingham Palace), nearby Duns Castle (for Balmoral), and Eastnor Castle in Herefordshire (for various other royal residences) were able to reconcile their monarchist consciences and their maintenance-bill needs.

CHAPTER SEVEN

Opening to the Public

Counting the Costs

IN 1994, JUST OVER 200 PRIVATELY OWNED and lived-in English country houses open to tourists, charging admission fees ranging from £1 to £7 ($1.50 to $10.50), were listed in the latest edition of *Historic Houses Castles & Gardens in Great Britain and Ireland*, long the standard visitors' guide. Another 60 or so, listed in the appendix (some of them obviously smaller than our working definition of a "country house") were open only by appointment.[1] Norman Hudson's *Historic House & Garden Directory* of the same year identified some 240 private country houses open to the public, out of a total of about 400, public and private, National Trust and corporate. In 1996, the latter guide, renamed *Hudson's Historic Houses and Gardens*, listed 195 large, privately owned country houses regularly open to the public; another eighteen open only by appointment; and ten available exclusively for conferences and other functions. All things considered, one might reasonably estimate that about 250 English homeowners occasionally permit strangers to pay for the pleasure of walking through their country houses.

. . .

Most country houses the average citizen or tourist has heard of are those open to the public, if only because their owners make an effort to publicize their existence. But a look at the figures makes it clear that the great majority of surviving English country houses are *not* open. If there remain (at a minimum) 1,500–2,000 country houses in private occupation, and only 250 of these are officially open to the public, it follows that at least 1,250 are not. Why not?

Samuel Whitbread at Southill in Bedfordshire—a great house rebuilt for an earlier Samuel Whitbread 200 years ago, which has never been open to the public—talked about friends of his who let strangers through their houses. "Most of them don't actually relish it. The only reason most people I know have to open their house to the public is that they've accepted a government grant." The Whitbreads, who have substantial outside resources, have never felt obliged to request a grant—although the family spent millions of pounds on structural repairs and interior redecoration during the early 1990s. "And the bottom line sometimes is not very attractive. We've looked at it obviously here as a possibility eventually, if we have to. But the cost of putting in the shop and the tea room and the lavatories you would have to do, and the cost of all the things you would have to do to conform with the health and safety regulations if you're charging people to come in just makes it very unattractive, I think—unless you're going to go all the way. The people who do it tell me that they're on a treadmill. Because it's no good saying that you've got a lovely house, come and see it. If you're going to get people coming back and back and back, you're going to have to give them something new every year."

Caroline, the late Duchess of Beaufort, admitted in 1994 that she was unlike her father, the old Marquess of Bath, who loved the crowds he and his lions attracted to Longleat. Although they lived alone in the house much of the time, the Beauforts still used all of Badminton for entertaining, primarily for hunting parties and the annual horse trials. She still showed small groups around on request. "But that snowballed, so I'm stopping." In any case, her insurers frowned on the practice. She felt that at Badminton (which has nearly 100 rooms), there would be nowhere for her to escape to if tourists were to start wandering through—"and then that stops it being a home immediately, doesn't it?"

Badminton *had* been open to the public, in the time of the last Duke of Beaufort—her husband's third cousin, who died in 1984—but only ten Wednesdays a year, between 2:30 and 5 P.M. "And there were never an enormous number of visitors. When the late duke and duchess owned it, they only lived in three rooms, over there. But now we really live in all of it. And so it makes it pretty intolerable, if you have to have it open. If we admitted the public, we'd have to put in proper lavatories, we'd have to have attendants in every room. Tea shops. And then the whole business is really too much."

Most owners who do not open their houses cite the loss of privacy as their primary reason—"the emotional strain of allowing strangers into one's home"—and the unrecoverable costs of opening as the second. Others worry about litter and theft. "It is extremely doubtful that we will be opening the house to the public in the foreseeable future because of its relatively small size," wrote the owner of a Tudor-plus-18th-century house in Wiltshire, whose Edwardian terraced gardens are open to visitors. "The advice of the Historic Houses Association has been *not* to open the smaller houses unless you absolutely have to." "The difficulty about opening," says the owner of an historic house in Yorkshire, "is that, unless yours is in the top league of historic houses, opening is not profitable and ties up capital resources in public amenities that would be best used elsewhere."[2]

Many owners of historic houses have no desire to get into the tourist business, which opening for more than one or two afternoons a week virtually obliges one to do. They would rather devote their time and energy to their primary profession, whether it be farming or banking or horse breeding—or (if they can afford it) simply live the traditional life of an English country family. Of Cirencester Park, his family's large house in Gloucestershire, Lord Apsley says simply, "Opening would kill it."

If you live in a house full of beautiful things—small objects and souvenirs you put out on mantels and table tops, as well as carpets and paintings and pieces of furniture you dearly love—one price of allowing strangers to walk through your house will be the obligation to put away all the smaller, more precious pieces every visiting day; to lay plastic mats over your carpets; to put up ropes on poles to keep people from touching your furniture and paintings; and—your insurance company may insist on this—to install sensitive and costly alarm systems, and engage attendants to sit in every room, keeping an eagle eye on the art lovers. Many people with handsome houses and "good things" are unwilling to disturb their way of life to this degree.

. . .

In 1992, partly as a result of parliamentary pressure to publicize places the public had a legal right to visit, English Heritage published a list of all properties to which it had given repair grants since 1984, along with the size of the grants and the public access requirements they entailed. The 1984–92 list included at least 160 private country houses to which access was obligatory, *because* of a government grant. The EH roster does not represent a complete list of open properties, or the extent of their accessibility. But it does give some idea of the way in which repair grants have forced private owners to let strangers into their homes. Grant recipients are obliged to advertise their opening times, which should normally "be within the summer months, and include the major Bank Holidays."[3] Of Nether Winchendon House in Buckinghamshire, owner Robert Spencer Bernard said, "It's not open to make money. It's purely because of that grant money ten years ago. There's no point in repaying that."

One hears versions of this explanation over and over. "I am obliged to have visitors, having received a grant from English Heritage which would be repayable if I closed the house." "English Heritage grants to repair massive dry rot in the 1980s included conditions for 30 days of mandatory opening." "We got government repair grants when repairing the main block . . . and therefore were obliged to open." "A moral obligation exists to show the public what was achieved by our grant." "A 1950s repair grant obliged us to open."

In addition, the granting of "conditional exemption" from inheritance taxes on certain prize properties—which can include paintings, furniture, and parklands as well as historic houses—carries with it an obligation to let the public see them.

At the start of the Stately Home industry, most country house owners who opened their doors to the public did so in order to make money. This is rarely the case today, when most private houses open to the public let in visitors only because they are legally obligated to do so. But complaints about the invading public tend to be similar, whether you open your house because you need the cash, or because a government agency orders you to. Only a relatively small number of owners—perhaps those who are extroverts and showmen by nature—appear to be wholeheartedly happy about opening.

The apprehensions regarding loss of privacy expressed by owners who have not yet opened their houses to the public are validated by a great many others who have. Those most distressed by strangers trooping through their houses tend either to be relatively shy and private people themselves; or people, like Ann Gascoigne at Stanton Harcourt, who have nowhere to escape to when the visitors come. (One of the nuisances of opening, said an owner in Sussex, was "being interminably nice to people when you don't always want to be nice.")

I heard numerous stories of tourists "crashing" into private quarters, no matter how many signs and barriers are put up to warn them away. Owners are spied upon sunbathing or changing clothes, interrupted at lunch. As Lord Sackville put it (quoting a particularly snoopy visitor at Knole), "They always want to see your 'private parts.'" Robert and Nicola Wright were obliged to open Eyam Hall in Derbyshire in 1992, as a result of inheritance tax concessions. "Now that the house is open," Mrs. Wright says, "it is quite difficult to lead a normal life. We have our own rooms, but have to share the stairs and hall with the public. With tours happening every twenty minutes, we have to plan every movement quite carefully. I tend to resent it less than the children, as I am working when the house is open; but they do get very resentful at times."

The young Brazilian-born Countess of Yarmouth told of the time she was driving her jeep back through the garden at Ragley Hall, only to be stopped by a woman visitor who told her, "You know, you really shouldn't be here." Every time she leads her daughter around the house on her pony, people stop her and ask when their children could have a ride.

Like several other current owners, Lady Yarmouth and her husband claim to enjoy the presence of satisfied tourists, or at least not to mind them. They decided to hold Gabriella's second birthday party in the Great Hall at Ragley, with all of her preschool classmates and their mothers on hand, on a day when the house—and the hall—were open to the public; the public, of course, was enchanted. Owners whose houses have been open to the public since their parents' or grandparents' day—particularly those who can retreat to a private wing or floor—insist they are "used to visitors." A few seem actively to relish the presence of happy day-trippers, clucking over their china and envying their delphiniums. The retired owner of an Elizabethan manor house in Buckinghamshire, surrounded by a series of flawlessly maintained gardens, enjoys sitting out in a shady pavilion two afternoons a week, receiving the admiring glances, nods, and compliments of British garden-lovers (mostly women) on their way to and from his tearoom.

Another "privacy" problem created by some country houses open to the public—particularly those located in or ajacent to small villages, rather than far off in the country—is that of neighbors who feel *their* privacy disturbed, their rural tranquillity invaded by tourists and their automobiles. In 1992, Andrew de Candole bought Groombridge Place in Kent—the 17th-century house and garden which were the stars of Peter Greenaway's mysterious film *The Draughtsman's Contract*. But when he made plans to open the gardens to the public, local planners received more than 100 letters of opposition from neighbors who expressed concern about the increased traffic his proposals would cause, as well as the "damage to the character" of their village. After the owner reduced and relocated his planned parking area, and settled for a country store/tea room in place of a restaurant, the good burghers of Groombridge were mollified. In his opening year, de Candole shared his gardens with 20,000 well-behaved visitors—twice as many as he or his neighbors had expected.

The major added element of cost, once a house is open to the public, is paying the staff: people to clean, people to sell tickets and direct traffic, people to work in the tea rooms and gift shops, above all people to work as tour guides or room attendants. Different owners find them in different ways. "We need more permanent staff, to begin with," said Lord Arundel, speaking of the castle whose name he bears. "Cleaning, security, the grounds, maintenance, you know. Plus about forty or fifty guides we can call on—at any given time we may have twenty on hand. From the town. They do it for love, not for money. Most of them are retired, they adore coming here, they're wonderful people. I'm afraid we don't pay them a fortune. We couldn't afford to. If I had nothing else to do, I'd love to stand in a room there. You learn more about history, you meet these interesting people."

At Powderham Castle in Devonshire, Lord Courtenay said, "I employ a young staff in the summer, mostly university students. They're young and fit and agile, and they can take people round the house and talk about things." At Doddington in Lincolnshire, Antony Jarvis said, "We have a host of part-time ladies of various grades and roles and responsibilities. One's also our housekeeper, another's a sister of my foreman, the other's his wife. Today they're both in the strawberry hut selling pick-your-own fruit." Patrick Cooke, at Athelhampton in Dorset, thought the tourist staffs demanded in popular country houses today weren't all that different from the masses of live-in servants of his great-grandfather's time. "There certainly were about twenty staff here at one stage, during the late nineteenth century. But when you take into account the people required to open the house at the moment, it's probably not that much different now."

In addition to hiring staff, opening to the public may require new fire and security systems, advertising and public relations expenses, brochures, tearooms, toilets, gift shops, and parking facilities. Some of these may actually create income on their own—but suddenly you're in business, like it or not, and the outlay, as in so many new businesses, can be formidable.

Opening a house for the first time can also be daunting in terms of the sheer physical and emotional demand made on the owners, who often start out trying to do everything themselves. Patrick and Judith Phillips—he a London attorney, she a school teacher—fell in love with Kentwell, a handsome moated redbrick Tudor house in Suffolk. "I gave up work in seventy-five," she tells the story,

Powderham Castle, Devonshire.

and we decided to open the house the following year. And we contacted the Tourist Board and they reckoned we'd have about five thousand visitors. Well, we got sixteen thousand the first year, and we were thrilled with that. And at the time I was earning about twenty five hundred pounds, which was quite a big salary. So we calculated if we got five thousand, each paying ten shillings, it was going to pay my salary. Instead we got sixteen, which was eight thousand pounds that first year, just through the door. And that was really without any outlay, except for the sheer organization of how you manage people once they arrive.

We used our dining room to serve people cups of tea. And they loved that. I was here, and a friend of my younger brother's—who was 'finding himself'—came and helped me keep the house clean and serve cups of tea on Wednesdays and Thursdays. And Patrick was here for the Sundays, when we were busier.

But then we felt that it wasn't really very satisfying just doing that. We wanted to do something a little bit more positive—and try to generate even more income. So we made the attraction our 'restoration in progress.' And of course restoration can go on forever. It was always very slow, because eight thousand pounds doesn't go very far at all. We're obviously still at it. But now we're adding new things as well.

Owners of private houses open to the public have typically felt in uneven competition with neighboring National Trust houses—Holkham vs. Blickling in Norfolk, for example, or Brympton d'Evercy vs. Montacute in Somerset. In each case, the private house was rarely able to attract half the number of visitors of the National Trust property next door. This is largely because the Trust's two million members feel that if they visit their "own" properties, they are getting in free. (In fact, they are paying £20 a year or more.) But another reason for the enmity, or at least envy, is that the private owner must either handle all his own administration and accounting, as well as maintenance, repairs, security, and visitor servicing—or else pay others to do it, out of taxed private income. The Trust, on the other hand, thanks to its base of endowments, bequests, donations, and memberships, can hire fulltime administrators and a huge backup staff, independent of house income. And as a registered charity the National Trust pays no taxes.

The additional "wear and tear" brought by tens or even hundreds of thousands of extra hands and feet in your historic house is likely to become apparent quite soon. Stone stairways and wooden floors that have shown relatively little visible wear after centuries of use by an ordinary household (including servants and guests), may soon begin warping and bowing under the pressure of hundreds of tourists marching through at once. The humid exhalations of several hundred people a day, crowded into an enclosed interior space, can cause major damage to paintings (especially wall paintings) and fabrics. Textiles are exceptionally vulnerable to the presence of tourists. At Brocket Hall, Lord Brocket found that even when they were not sitting on them, visitors could not keep from fingering the soft furniture, which meant that each piece had to be reupholstered every few years; so he replaced all the antiques with reproductions. Unless ropes are set up to force people to keep their distance, they will inevitably run their hands over priceless tapestries, draperies, and bed coverings, which can wear them to shreds even faster than sunlight—the sunlight that now shines through large windows into bedrooms and sitting rooms far more hours a day than in the past, so that afternoon tourists can see what they paid to look at. I have seen people running their fingernails over inlaid marquetry furniture, just to verify where one piece of precious wood ends and another begins.

The National Trust began to discover the destructive effects of mass tourism in the early 1990s. Their first response to the damage was simply to try to promote their more fragile properties less actively, in the hope that fewer people would come. When that didn't work, they had experts at the University of London study optimum numbers of visitors in terms of undue wear and tear, and began to institute a policy of "timed tickets," like that commonly in use at major museum exhibitions. This allowed them to limit the number of visitors per day—especially on Bank Holidays and summer weekends—at places (usually relatively small places) they thought especially endangered: Winston Churchill's house at Chartwell; the gardens at Sissinghurst and Hidcote; Calke Abbey in Derby; Cotehele in

Cornwall; Wightwick Manor near Wolverhampton. Even in Waddesdon Manor, which looks huge, the fairly compact show rooms can quickly become overcrowded. So timed tickets were introduced there when it was reopened in April 1994. When Chastleton—a house as fragile in its contents and quality as Cotehele or Calke Abbey—reopens under National Trust management, the plan is to keep visitor numbers under 20,000 a year.

Nigel Nicolson, who lives at and keeps an eye on his late parents' garden at Sissinghurst, thought the damage done by crowds there might have been exaggerated in 1991, after 200,000 visitors came in one season—3,000 on one September afternoon. Next year, on the National Trust's orders, their numbers were down to 150,000—"and almost nobody has had to wait at all! But the gardeners will notice if a tiny little flower has been trodden on. And I used to say to them, when they complained about the numbers, after a busy summer's day, 'Well, show me.' And they would take me round to an obscure corner: 'Look! *Pulsitilla palpitans*! Squashed!' Never mind that there were another fifty or sixty *pulsitilla palpitans* in the same place. But each one is their baby. And one has to listen to the gardeners, for they create the beauty that people come to see. And so we introduced the timed tickets two years ago, and it did cut the numbers down. And the gardeners say—well they would, wouldn't they?—that it has made all the difference."

Gardens are undoubtedly a major, perhaps *the* major draw of country houses, at least for repeat English visitors from the neighboring region, who account for the majority of visitors. Houses unpossessed of bright, attractive walled or formal gardens suddenly feel obliged to add them. Houses where gardens had been allowed to run down must put them back in order. Topiary, knot gardens, mazes, and kitchen gardens will all do. But most English visitors, being flower gardeners themselves, come to see if your flowers are more varied and impressive than theirs. And planting and maintaining a prize-winning garden of flowers, preferably one that can comfortably accommodate dozens of people at a time on its footpaths, is an expensive and time-consuming proposition. A few owners try to look after the gardens themselves, perhaps with some part-time help. But one or two fulltime gardeners is standard at many open houses. Ragley Hall, said Lord Yarmouth, now makes use of about two and a half. Patrick Cooke estimated he had the equivalent of five fulltime gardeners (counting part time and seasonal workers) at Athelhampton, where the gardens remain the major attraction. A recent *Guardian* photo—the sort of free publicity private owners dream of getting—showed Cooke himself up a ladder, shaping one of the twelve 25-foot-tall pyramids of yew in the Great Court.

Fears of theft and burglary, as we have seen, are part of the life of anyone who lives among valuable and portable—even not-so-portable—things. But once thousands of strangers start walking through your house and around your grounds each year, the danger multiplies a thousandfold. Anyone who wishes can now "case" the house during a tour, noting the location not only of prize targets for theft, but also of doors, windows, alarm systems, hinges, bolts, escape roads, etc. Country house burglaries tend to peak just after Easter, when houses first open their doors to the public. It has been estimated that 65 percent of thefts from country houses occur while the house is open; if the thefts take place

Athelhampton, Dorset. Topiary garden.

overnight, it is most often by someone who "toured" the house day before—and perhaps even stayed behind, hidden in a closet, after closing time. Among the most vulnerable objects for daytime thefts are pocketable items like medals, arms and armor, statuettes, and porcelains. Things that disappear overnight are mostly china and silver, although burglars are increasingly going after garden statues and urns, which are less likely to be wired to alarm systems, and relatively easier to sell.

Sir Thomas Ingilby, who established and still runs the "Stately Homes Hotline," which allows country house owners to contact one another (and the national police network) instantly when their suspicions are aroused or something is missing, has become all too familiar with the methods of country house burglars posing as tourists:

In one case where we were able to help two years ago, a visitor was seen at a house in South York-shire, looking at the outside of a house two or three times, taking notes. We spread the word over the Hotline overnight. And he was actually arrested at a stately home in Leicestershire the following weekend. He was caught breaking in. They waited till he went through the door, then went through and caught him with things in his pockets.

On another celebrated occasion, the police raided a house and found a floor plan of a stately home there. The only thing was, the floor plan didn't say which stately home it pertained to. It had simply every detail about the alarm system. It had the access routes, where the dogs were kept, where the pressure pads were. And inside each room on that floor plan it had an exact layout showing which paintings were where, and where the most valuable items were. The arrows actually said, for example, 'Punch Bowl, £4,500; such-and-such a painting, £20,000.'

We were able to circulate that, and we did actually identify the house where it came from. And that house was able to take new security measures, and we were almost certainly able to save that house a considerable amount of money. It was all done by someone going round the house: it was open to the public.

"You usually increase your security measures at the behest of your insurance company," Samuel Whitbread says, "when you renew your insurance." A daring series of country house burglaries had taken place shortly before we met, at Luton Hoo near his own home in Bedfordshire, and at three big estates in Scotland. "Most of the houses that have been burgled have been open to the public"—as his is not. "It's yet another disincentive to owners to open."

Certain objects—the 21 pieces of Fabergé stolen from Luton Hoo, for example—are easy to hide and to sell, even on the open market. In 1992, the National Trust decided to ban interior photography in its houses, because of a sudden rise in thefts. A hundred pieces of porcelain had disappeared from Wightwick Manor; £30,000 ($53,000) worth of small treasures was grabbed from a display cabinet at Ham House near London. "I'm afraid that photography has made reconnaissance all too easy for them," said deputy director Martin Drury. Professional thieves posing as tourists take photos of light switches, window locks, and security systems.

I posed as a tourist myself at Hatfield House just after the burglaries of May 1994. In Robert Cecil's Long Gallery, our guide apologized for the absence from its usual cabinet of the famous royal "posset set,"[4] perhaps made by Cellini, a suite of exquisite crystal vessels and utensils, all mounted on gold and set with precious stones and enamel. The house's insurers had decided the items—a gift to Queen Mary of England and King Philip II of Spain on their marriage in 1554—were too valuable and too portable to keep on display, so they had been locked away in a vault.

But not every country house owner can get by with locking his treasures away, even if he wished to. Works of art granted conditional exemption from inheritance tax *must* be made accessible to the public, in one way or another. The computerized list of such objects English Heritage now makes available may be consulted by burglars as well as art historians. Hatfield has a great number of other prizes on display. But in some cases, locking away well-known possessions might seriously diminish the tourist appeal of a country house.

It is difficult for private owners and their security providers to keep up with the level of sophistication of country house burglars. Even so, the audacity of the thieves who spirited a small Titian out of Longleat in January 1995 would have thwarted the most conscientious of owners. They drove onto the estate about 9 P.M., covered up the floodlights trained on the walls, set up an eighteen-foot aluminum ladder against precisely the window they wanted, smashed the glass (which instantly set off alarms triggered by infrared beams), ran across the drawing room with flashlights and wrenched the 18-by-24-inch painting they wanted from the wall (which set off other alarms), and managed to get back out the window, down the ladder, into their car, and off the estate before police arrived.

In addition to all these problems, the private country house owner contemplating opening to the public is faced with the same maddening vagaries as any other entrepreneur in the notoriously erratic tourist industry: location, weather, tourists' whimsical shifts in preference and their insatiable demand for novelty, as well as international travel trends and the constant threat of new competition.

Lord Romsey, at Broadlands, was delighted when 250,000 people paid to go through his spacious house in Hampshire, with its royal family and Mountbatten connections, the first year he opened in 1979. Within twelve years, the numbers were down to 70,000, and he had no idea how to improve them. Overall stately home visitors declined markedly—as did the British tourist industry in general—in 1990 and 1991. Was it the weather, owners wondered, the recession, international conditions that kept Americans at home? Were people finally growing tired of country-house visiting? Or was it the competition of too many houses (let alone other attractions) open to the public?

Owners elsewhere envy Blenheim Palace and Warwick Castle their prize location on the "Golden Triangle" for day-trippers out of London. Although they insist they would never want the hundreds of thousands of visitors such houses attract, people like Lady Victoria Leatham at Burghley (50,000), the Earl of Leicester at Holkham (30,000), and Lord Hastings at Seaton Delaval (5,000) admit that their off-the-beaten-track locations are probably responsible for the limited numbers, which they would not mind seeing slightly increased. Antony Jarvis, at Doddington Hall (12,000), seems resigned to the relative remoteness and unpopularity of Lincolnshire—the most sparsely populated county in England. The Duke of Marlborough, on the other hand, sitting pretty at Blenheim (436,000 in 1995, counting house and grounds), professes to worry about the fate of owners of houses lost in the outer darkness of Northumberland or Suffolk, let alone (heaven help us!) Wales.

Other fortunately located owners—Lord Montagu at Beaulieu, in the New Forest; Lord Arundel at Arundel Castle, on the popular Sussex coast; Lord Courtenay at Powderham Castle, in the tourist "honey pot" of south Devon, where a fresh crop of holidaymakers arrives every Saturday—are delighted that their family houses ended up located in such popular vacation spots. Arundel, with a dependable 150,000–180,000 annual visitor count, year in year out, laments the fact that his family's other house in Yorkshire, Carlton

Towers—where his brother Gerald now lives—never attracted more than 20,000, and hence always lost money.

Country house visiting has become the standard family outing when the weather turns bad—as it not infrequently does—during British summer holidays. "One of our best days," says Edward Arundel, "is when the sun shines in the morning and then it rains. They run here." Even so, only a very few houses—Longleat, Leeds, Warwick, Beaulieu—risk year-round operation, given the sensible English habit of staying close to home in the winter.

Other owners—particularly those dependent on corporate functions—gloat over their proximity to motorways and cities. Both Knebworth and Brocket Hall, near neighbors in Hertfordshire, are minutes off the M1, and—as they inevitably advertise—just half an hour from Hyde Park Corner. "It is fortunate," writes the Earl of Bradford, "that my ancestor, Lady Wilbrahim, chose to build Weston Park [in 1671] between the M6 (8 miles) and the M54 (3 miles), only 35 minutes away from the Birmingham City Centre! . . . if we were only 30 miles away on the Welsh border, we wouldn't have a hope." Everyone would love to spread the visitor numbers out more evenly, to take the pressure off summer weekends and Bank Holidays. "On a normal opening Sunday in May, when it's not a Bank Holiday, we might have twenty-five people going through," says Judith Phillips at Kentwell—which can attract up to 1,500 (mainly busloads of children) on a midsummer Sunday. "It's a disaster! We get two people on catering, just in case we are busy, one person in the shop, we have a cleaning staff in—all for an income of a hundred pounds! It's terrible." Is there any way to change people's habits? I asked. "We're racking our brains. We're losing money hand over fist."

Even a uniquely successful country house entrepreneur like Edward Montagu reminds one of the extraordinary, totally unpredictable increase in competition in recent years. "In the last ten years, forty percent of everything that's open to the public has been opened new. So the competition over the last decade has almost doubled. People have done the stately homes time and time again, and now they're looking for different things—theme parks, water parks, that sort of thing. If our numbers haven't been going up, it's because we've got so much more competition."[5]

·   ·   ·

How to Make It Work

ART AND ARCHITECTURE

Much of the cultural pretense of country house visiting is based on the premise that visitors are paying to admire your art treasures, to absorb sermons in stone from your particular three-dimensional piece of the national heritage. This, after all, is the chief justification for the government's subsidizing your expenses (and their visits) by way of repair grants, tax deferrals, and educational tours for schoolchildren.

The Duke of Bedford retired to Monaco in 1974, and left his son Robin to run the show at Woburn. But as long as he was in charge, Bedford delighted in making outspoken, iconoclastic remarks about both the aristocracy and the "heritage" they had in charge. "I get," he wrote in 1971, "more than 1,200,000 visitors a year. Of these about 800,000 come to see the Game Park alone, about five hundred are art experts, and a few thousand more are genuinely interested in the arts.... Give pleasure to people—that is why you are, or should be, in the Stately Home business, and if you can cater for all tastes, you will do well. A Rembrandt here, a slide there; a Van Dyck here, a Punch and Judy show there. . . I watched a woman who was looking round one of my rooms which contains about £800,000 worth of stuff, [and] I overheard [someone] ask her what she liked most in that room. She answered without a moment's hesitation.

"'The lino. I like it very much indeed. It's exactly what I want for my kitchen.'"[6]

It cannot be pretended that most people who go through country houses know or care much about history, architecture, or art. But it still seems important to be able to offer and advertise these in order to attract them. Most visitors are probably impressed by the rows of Canalettos on the red silk walls of the family Dining Room at Woburn, by all the Van Dycks fitted into the painted and gilded Double Cube Room at Wilton—if only because they have some sense of how valuable and famous they are. Robin Compton still believes that what attracts people to Newby Hall is "a Gobelins tapestry room which is unique, a Statue Gallery full of highly important classical statuary and a beautifully restored Adam House."

But it is clear to anyone who watches and listens to them as they make their way through a country house that most contemporary tourists care very little for such things, except as an element in the opulent decorating schemes they have come to expect. An old-fashioned gallery full of old master paintings, like that at Corsham Court in Wiltshire, is lucky to attract 10,000 people a year. Among the acres of more serious works, I would guess that the colossal Greek foot and the clever trompe l'oeil violin painted on a door are the most popular works of art at Chatsworth.

Some of the top-drawing houses, such as Chatsworth and Woburn, possess major art collections. Others, such as Beaulieu and Blenheim, do not. There is probably a point at which denuded long galleries and rooms empty of furniture cease to have appeal. But my guess is that many of the major country house art collections could be considerably reduced, with no noticeable impact on the appeal of the house to visitors.

Houses of singular architectural merit, such as Robert Adam's Syon House and Osterley Park in west London, Holkham and Houghton in Norfolk, the perfect ensembles of Stanway and Broughton Castle, rarely attract more than twenty or thirty thousand visitors a year; while any number of pseudo-Gothic Victorian castles, overwrought piles like Osborne House and Knebworth, and a giant modern mistake like Castle Drogo go on drawing 100,000 or more year after year. At the time they were reopened by commercial entrepreneurs, both Warwick and Hever Castles had been stripped of most of their contents of worth. But this has done nothing to reduce their tourist numbers. Beautiful architecture, like an important art collection, may be an admirable thing. But neither seems to be an essential determinant of success in opening a house to the public.

. . .

Considering country house opening as a business, rather than a statutory obligation or a charitable act, how one goes about *selling* a house is at least as important as what one has to sell. All things considered, Beaulieu, Knebworth, Bowood, and Leeds Castle cannot, I think, be counted among the most important of English houses, artistically or historically, despite the obvious attractions of all four, and the handsome settings of the latter two. But the owners (in the case of Leeds, the managers) of all of these houses are master marketers—as of course are the commercial entrepreneurs who own Warwick. This, as they will be the first to acknowledge, has had a great deal to do with their remarkable visitor numbers.[7]

Lord Montagu, the master salesman of the Stately Home business, was working in public relations when he inherited Beaulieu in 1951. After his first open season in 1952, he spent three months in the New York office of Ben Sonnenberg studying American-style public relations, then another three months practicing it. He gave lectures in 22 states, made fourteen radio or television broadcasts, and displayed his family's Coronation robes in American department store windows, all the while touting Beaulieu. Like the Duke of Bedford before him, and Lord Bath at Longleat today, Montagu has always maintained such a high profile—chairing national institutions, speaking out in the House of Lords, entertaining celebrities, driving his own cars in races and rallies—that he is himself an essential advertisement for his house. He has been selling Beaulieu in the states now for forty years—he admits to having learned a great deal from Disneyland—and doing television commercials since 1980. After 1980, the British tourism industry grew so competitive that Montagu felt obliged to shift from opportunistic jolts of publicity, which worked well enough in the 1950s and 1960s, to a long-term, carefully targeted, fully professional marketing strategy. He comes up with new sales and promotion ideas every year. He gives advice (for a fee) to other owners planning to open, or hoping to increase their numbers, and liberally criticizes those he thinks are going about it the wrong way.

Lord Shelburne first moved into his father's country seat in 1972, and decided to open it three years later. He realized that, with the 'Big House' demolished, Bowood had (in both senses) too low a profile to sell itself. His only hope was to push the parkland, pitch it to families, and market aggressively. He first hired an advertising agency in 1982, and almost immediately experienced an increase in visitor numbers. He explains,

> I learned the only way to get your numbers up is through television advertising. I can show you on a graph, the moment we started using television, the line just shot up. We just do it regionally, a forty-mile radius all around, which makes it a day trip. It hits the Newbury/Basingstoke area, and just touches south Wales and Bristol and Somerset. We spend a lot of money doing it—two-thirds

of our advertising budget. But by booking our television time far in advance, we can get a good rate.

We use three different length films—some ten second, some twenty, and some thirty. The ten-seconder is just the drip, drip syndrome, so they won't forget the name. During the summer, obviously, we will show the adventure play area, and the ice creamery and nonsense like that. In May we will be pushing our red rhododendrons, for the gardeners. And if it's going to be on late, we'll run the one for adults, which will have more to do with culture.

Asked to describe the 30-second commercial, he replies, "Well, unless we're pushing the Adventure Playground, it will have a bit of the house—the Library, the Orangery; cascade, lake, fountains, roses, peace, quiet, background music, restaurant, people eating lovely food—that sort of thing."

At Longleat, the Marquess of Bath confessed that his own colorful way of life—on display throughout the house by way of photos and his own gaudy murals, and throughout the nation thanks to the press—was probably his best advertisement. (The Duke of Bedford has said much the same thing about his success at Woburn in the 1950s and 1960s.) "The press and TV took note of me before without my having to work at it, so I decided I might as well make use of it as a policy. It's inescapable, in any case." After polling visitors as to what drew them to Longleat, he found that far more of them were drawn in by the inexpensive leaflets he distributes than by costly television commercials, so he ended up dropping the latter.

In 1978 and 1985, Lord and Lady Cobbold made trips to the United States promoting Knebworth to travel agents and the general touring public. Lady Cobbold made a similar trip to Australia and New Zealand in 1983. Although both are energetic, promotion minded, and ready to try almost anything going, from the start they concentrated on functions and events more than day visitors, whom the house seemed to attract in any case. News stories generated by the former (from Dickens Evenings in early days, through their 1977 skateboard park, to their giant rock concerts) have no doubt helped to attract the latter. To draw functions, John Hoy, their manager since 1985, shares ideas at meetings of event organizers and the convention industry, and collaborates with his opposite numbers at houses with similar goals and numbers.

Tim Faulkner, the manager at Powderham Castle, tries to target specialized groups and coach parties in the "off months" of April-May and September-October, and (like all entrepreneurial country house marketers) keeps thinking up new occasions for press releases. Despite the high expense, Powderham Castle first risked television advertising in the summer of 1992, and found it made a considerable difference. They aim it at people already on vacation in Devon, in the hope of pulling them in on impulse. "They've all got television, whether they're in caravans or guest cottages or self-catering. Just because they're on vacation doesn't mean they stop watching their favorite programs. The great thing about television advertising is that you can actually see the result, whereas with anything else you're never quite sure—it takes so long to get through. Television is instant impact: they see it and they come. And the mere fact that you're on television seems to say something about the quality of the place: this must be an attraction that's worthwhile, that gives value for money."

Patrick Cooke at Athelhampton says, "Promotion's the most important thing about the whole place. But it's just directed to local people, through radio and the press. A simple notice in the Historic Houses guide is nothing like good enough. You've got to do a lot more than that."

Victoria Leatham hired a full-time marketing manager almost as soon as she and her family moved into Burghley in 1980. "And she is absolutely marvelous at getting Burghley mentioned in newspapers and on television. We get a great deal of editorial coverage throughout the year," says Lady Victoria. It seems to her far more valuable than paid advertising. "We had a man out today taking background shots for Anglia Television. He won't pay us anything, but we'll get excellent coverage."

Many owners of open houses agree that the wisest approach is to concentrate on obtaining free editorial coverage—which will seem more honest (and be much cheaper) than paid advertising—by way of press releases distributed to the local and national media. To justify these, they stage special events or exhibitions, schedule "themed" weekends, and draw attention to ancestral anniversaries or their restorations in progress.

I confessed to William LeBlanc-Smith, the administrator of Sudeley Castle, that the house had only come to my attention around 1990, when full-page, back-cover advertisements in the *Historic Houses* guidebook led me to believe I had been ignoring an important site. He admitted that they had changed their marketing strategy at just about that time; his predecessor, he thought, had not been promoting Sudeley Castle aggressively enough. Despite its antiquity, the fact that the house had been abandoned for 150 years, then purchased and restored in relatively recent times meant that one had to work harder to impress it on the public imagination. After Sudeley began to advertise itself more assertively, visitor numbers rose to nearly 100,000, although there has been some falling off since 1991. LeBlanc-Smith and his young marketing manager are now working hard to break into the fixed tourist pattern. "I mean, the coaches from London roar up and down the A40 to Warwick, Blenheim, Stratford. We don't get a look-in." At the same time, he's lobbying for a relaxation in the government regulations that determine what may be the most valuable advertisement of all—your own official direction sign off the motorway. As of 1994, a minimum visitor count of 150,000 was required to obtain one of the precious brown placards bearing the white "Stately Home" symbol.

Joanna Oswin, formerly marketing manager at Leeds Castle, is a consummate marketing professional who knows precisely which audiences to target, when, and how. Together with a few other enterprising Stately Home salesmen, she has held special promotional events for Japanese and other overseas agents at the House of Lords. She mailed out volleys of leaflets to flower arranging societies before a Flower Festival, to wine tasting clubs before a Wine Festival, all designed to build up the off-peak trade. She regards regular meetings with tour operators as crucial for attracting overseas visitors—now 47 percent of the total at Leeds Castle, thanks in part to their nearness to the Channel ferry ports and

Sudeley Castle, Gloucestershire.

the Tunnel: their brochures are printed in six languages. "We offer excellent commission levels," she says, "which enables us to be packaged into just about every kind of tour program worldwide." To attract cross-Channel tourists, she doesn't bother advertising on the Continent. "It's just a matter of hotting up all the people who are involved with inbound traffic to Britain. We're working very heavily with the ferry companies. P&O have fifty sailings a day. Even with the Channel Tunnel, we should be the winners." Leeds Castle is about about 25 direct motorway miles from the English tunnel exit.

Norman Hudson's annual *Historic Houses and Gardens* guide—which charges private houses a fee to be included (£545 for a full-color page, in 1996), and is then distributed free to the travel trade—has become an efficient means for private owners to make their attractions and facilities known to British and overseas tour operators, as well as those who organize group outings.

· · ·

Gardens

It is impossible to overestimate the value of a handsome, well-maintained garden, and the open acres of green parkland beyond it, to the aesthetic value of an English country house. In fact, except for small manor houses—which should have at least a couple of acres to set them off—it is hard to imagine a self-respecting country house without them. Houses that have been shorn of their surrounding acres in the process of conversion to hospitals, offices, flats, museums, and the like, or in order to "develop" the grounds commercially, are usually so denatured in the process that they lose most of their aesthetic and historic identity.

This is one case where the general British public agrees with the hard-to-please expert, whether aesthete or architectural historian. Although British tourists enjoy going through grand or historic houses, they take at least as much—and probably more—pleasure in strolling through, or just looking at, vast stretches of rolling parkland studded with clumps of old oak, ash, and cedar, broken up by artificial lakes reflecting the sky. This might have something to do with the extraordinary density in which most English people live, whether in villages or cities. The protected farmland and legally mandated green belts between towns and cities in England are unusually important, I believe, to the emotional well-being of the English, packed as they are 915 to the square mile.[8]

But even more precious—because *so* open, so accessible, unused even for cattle or crops, such a pure blissful amenity—are Elysian fields like the Lancelot Brown- or Humphry Repton-designed landscape parks at so many country houses open to the public. At properties where separate tickets are sold, from 60 percent to 80 percent of visitors choose to go round the park or garden, but not the house.

The unique English climate, which combines a moderate hot-to-cold range with the variable days and seasons of a temperate-zone island, and a higher-than-average degree of moisture (something visitors to England often notice) allows a great variety of colorful flowering plants to thrive in most parts of the country. For this reason probably more than any other—along with what has become a matter of simple pride, of maintaining face among one's neighbors—the English have become the most dedicated amateur flower gardeners on earth. Gardening is the number one English hobby. And next to keeping up their own gardens, however small—or their allotments, their window boxes, their greenhouses—the English love to look at other people's.

More than 200 private houses, from modest cottages to stately homes, now open their gardens to the public from one to four afternoons a year, the entrance fee—typically £1— usually devoted to charity. Many other proud country house gardeners offer to show fellow-

Leeds Castle, Kent. French schoolchildren on tour.

gardeners round by appointment. On open days, these otherwise-private people may sell plants from their property, as well as cream teas.

Other large private and National Trust properties, where the house is either gone or not open, allow people to wander about their gardens, parks, and woodlands more frequently—from once a week to every day—for a fee. The most popular of these—Bicton Park in Devon, Biddulph Grange in Staffordshire, Exbury in Hampshire, Hidcote Manor in Gloucestershire, Nymans and Sheffield Park in Sussex, Sissinghurst Castle in Kent— sell more than 100,000 tickets each season.

At a few major country houses open to the public—Rousham, Stourhead, Stowe—the historic, picturesque landscape gardens, with their ponds and statues and temples and fol-lies, are the major attraction. At other great houses, such as Hatfield and Penshurst, house and garden are equally important. Recent color advertisements for well-known historic houses focus almost entirely on the gardens, as if acknowledging that they have become the major draw. Ads for the more magnificent or ambitious spreads inevitably make use of long-range or aerial views, in order to show them in their extensive, elaborately planned settings, apart from which they are hard to imagine. A "garden experience" of some sort, including if possible the satisfaction of mown greensward and woodlands stretching as far as the eye can see, is invaluable to any house that is trying to attract visitors.

Particularly, as I say, English visitors; and more particularly repeat visitors, which is an issue almost every owner in search of paying customers eventually has to face. For some reason, English people on an outing are willing to go through the same museum or cathe-dral again and again. But many seem to feel that once they've been through a stately home, they've done it, and they aren't likely to return until Aunt Sarah comes out from New Zealand and needs to be entertained.

Some owners try to overcome this tendency by way of changing exhibits or special events. But the best solution seems to be maintaining a good April-to-October garden, which will alter naturally from season to season. "I still cannot come up with a satisfactory explanation why I should be allowed to spend two and a half times as much on the gardens as my wife can spend on the house," says Antony Jarvis at Doddington. "But we do both accept that a beautiful setting for the house is a vital part of its public image, and an excit-ing garden will help to generate repeat visits."

One important function of a good garden and park, in smaller or very popular places, is to disperse people out of the house and about the grounds during their visit, to avoid crowding and queues, and keep visitors content. A country park provides wooded walks and open stretches of lawns, attractive to families with children, picnickers, strollers, and people with dogs, where dogs are permitted. Many houses sell plants and other items from a nursery or garden center on the grounds, which affords yet another source of income. The garden center at Syon attracts more than ten times as many customers as the Duke of Northumberland's spectacular Adam rooms.

· · ·

Luxury

The appeal of simple "luxury"—gold and silver plate, intricate carving, marble, precious stones—is obviously one of the major attractions at some country houses. At certain places, such as Chatsworth and Waddesdon, the sheer glitter and opulence, the over-whelming evidence of craftsmanship and expenditure form a major part of the tourist experience. This is an element related to, but in the end quite different from the quality of art and architecture. It is often spelled out (by attendants or in brochures) in terms of the actual cost of the imported Italian marble, the chandeliers, the tapestries; the royal prove-

Holkham Hall, Norfolk. Saloon.

nance of this or that piece of furniture; the hundreds of hours it took to carve a staircase railing or paint a ceiling.

Most country houses were built to impress, even to intimidate their neighbors and visitors; a few to overwhelm. Many still do. This brings into question what has been called "the politics of envy," the mixed, sometimes hostile feelings that visible wealth can arouse in the less wealthy. The very ostentatiousness of country houses doubtless played some part in the antagonism toward their owners on the part of politicians like Oliver Cromwell, David Lloyd George, and the leaders if the postwar Labor Party.

It is difficult to guess the feelings of ordinary visitors today, when some of the most opulent and extravagant houses of all are the property of either the government or the National Trust. Quite apart from their responses to architecture and art, I have no idea what goes through most tourists' minds as they confront spectacular carved marble chimneypieces, gilded ceilings, intricate marquetry cabinets piled with hand-painted bibelots, elaborate staircases that cost more to build than a whole street of ordinary houses. Do they ever consider the social implications of hundred-room houses designed to be run by great numbers of servants for a single wealthy family?

I can only imagine that all this glitter and glamour still has its own appeal—at least to those who choose to visit country houses, as people happily visit royal palaces in countries that no longer have kings. Whether they indulge in private fantasies of being storybook lords and ladies themselves, or simply love feasting in the glow of another family's former extravagance, I think the imagined vision of how the other half (tenth, one ten-thousandth) lives is a more important part of most visitors' country house experience than any appreciation of either history or art.

· · ·

THE "LIVED-IN" QUALITY

"The British are very inquisitive," says William LeBlanc-Smith at Sudeley Castle. "That's why they go round houses. And the great compliment we get here is, 'It doesn't look like a museum. It looks like a lived-in house.'" "Members of the public who go round are just like you and me," says Lord Arundel. "When you go into a room you immediately feel if it's lived in and loved—or if no one's been in it for ten years. And I think that the little touches which private ownership and use give, you know, people can feel—the flowers, the family photographs. I think that's the most charming way to go round, actually, because you know that the owner has just left. It's twelve o'clock and he's left five minutes ago."

Sudeley and Arundel Castles *are* lived in—at least parts of them—like most privately owned houses open to the public. But the point is more that they *feel* "lived-in": one of the single most important drawing cards of the private—as opposed to the publicly-owned and unoccupied—country house. In large houses, resident families may make little or no use of the grand state rooms their visitors troop through, except for events like charity concerts or annual Christmas parties. Many of them live in comfortable, modernized quarters away from the tourist path. But every effort is made to make even the state rooms look "lived in," and to convince visitors that they are indeed used, which is something most National Trust properties can never do.

"Do you make a point of leaving daily debris scattered around the rooms?" I asked Lord Courtenay, as he showed us around Powderham Castle, where pieces of the morning paper were still strewn about. "Oh definitely, yes. See the television there? That's one of the favorites of the guides. Proves we're not one of those 'frozen museums.'"

Many houses advertise that theirs is a "lived-in family house," to distinguish it from the "lifeless museums" of unoccupied National Trust houses. "All the rooms which are open to the public are still used by me and my family," the Duke of Roxburghe writes in the introduction to the Floors Castle brochure. "While this may make my life a little complicated it has always been my wish that the public should see the house as it is—very much a family home." A number of owners—the Earl of Harewood, the Duchess of Devonshire, the Marchioness of Salisbury, Lord St. Levan—write their own guidebooks, often in a chatty and informal style. The latest guidebook to Ragley Hall contains an album of snapshots of the handsome young owners and their children.

To *prove* that theirs is still a family home, owners purposely leave around framed family pictures, with dogs and babies—wedding and christening snaps are popular; hang up a hand-calligraphed family tree; and fill glass cases with labeled family correspondence or grandpa's military medals or household accounts from olden times. They will open up the old kitchen and servants' hall, unless these rooms are already being used as a teashop and store. Family portraits by an unknown artist are more important than Van Dycks of someone unrelated to the house. Copies of *Field, Lady, Harper's and Queen*, and especially *Country Life* magazines will be left out on coffee tables, ashtrays on end tables, books alongside state beds. There will be little watercolors of the grounds, visible telephones—perhaps even a television in the study. It is imperative to set the table in the state dining room with one's best silver, china, and glassware, and perhaps a gigantic silver-gilt tureen or salt cellar in the center—well behind a guard rope or microwave beam—as if the family were expecting dinner guests in as soon as all these tourists went home. The state dining table at Hatfield House, set for fourteen, even had buns—I presume real—alongside each plate. Every visitable room should be filled with armloads of fresh (or at least dried) flowers.

It is obvious from eavesdropping on the remarks of people going round a house that they are still fascinated by royal connections and aristocratic family scandals. Visitors to Broadlands in 1981, where Charles and Diana spent their honeymoon, tore through the house to get to the main bedroom. At the same time they like to think that people still *live* in country houses, doing ordinary things when the visitors are gone. Photographs of family members alongside members of the royal family casually positioned about the drawing room are no less important than the Wellington boots and rain-jackets left in the entry hall, the Range Rover or the tricycle parked on the gravel drive.

The guides may recall or invent all sorts of harmless gossip about the resident family, which is all most tourists ever ask them about. ("Oh yes, ma'am, the Earl and Countess use this room for dinner parties at least once a week in the season. The Princess of Wales danced in the ballroom just last December. Yes, her grace does all the flower arrangements herself. And that's where the children ride their ponies. The young lord is very keen on rugby.")

The ultimate example of this may be Ann Gascoigne at Stanton Harcourt, selling tickets in her own kiosk; or Beatriz Yarmouth, inviting the children in her daughter's play school (with their favorite toys and pedal-cars) to a birthday party in the Great Hall at Ragley, while paying tourists walk through and stare; or Alexander Bath at Longleat, letting goggle-eyed visitors into his private dining room, while he and his guests are still eating lunch. You can't get much more "lived-in" than that.

National Trust tourists at Kedleston were at first shocked, then delighted, when Lord and Lady Scarsdale opened the door that separates their wing from the public rooms, and led us—black retrievers bounding along—about the great house they still think of as theirs, unhooking ropes, fingering furniture. The paying visitors, of course, would not have been allowed to do this. But they seemed charmed by the presence of someone who could—someone, moreover, whom even the National Trust attendants still addressed as "M'lord" and "M'lady." At Melford Hall in Suffolk, another National Trust property, tourists are inevitably pleased to find that the Hyde Parkers (whose house it originally was) still live there, with their children, as the resident administrators.

As some owners offer to mingle with guests at corporate functions, others—particularly in smaller, infrequently open houses—welcome guests in person, and advertise the fact. Robin and Elizabeth Brackenbury, at Holme Pierrepont near Nottingham, serve as their own guides. "And virtually every day that we're open," says Elizabeth, "somebody will come up to Robin or me and say, 'Oh, we have enjoyed our visit. We think it's because the house is lived in.' And by this they mean it's got its own eccentricities, you know—the children's presents to you are out on the chest, maybe something doesn't match something else. That's what the public really enjoy."

· · ·

Tea Rooms and Gift Shops

Although many smaller and less-frequented houses (and fragile National Trust properties trying to keep down their numbers) have risked doing without one, the presence of a tea room, cafe, or restaurant at a country house of any size is now regarded as indispensible by most British tourists. Back in the early 1950s, Lord Montagu and the Duke of Bedford both realized that their visitors tended to head first for the lavatories, and last for the tea room; and that any owner opening to the public would be unwise to skimp on either facility. Lord Arundel only added a restaurant to Arundel Castle in 1991, after he realized that more and more people were refusing to come because they couldn't eat. "At the end of the tour, they asked, 'Where's the tea room?' and people were getting rather narked about it. We had a shop, so we thought that we really had to put a restaurant in, even though we had never really wanted to. And it worked very well." The restaurant, which seats 140, sells soup and sandwiches, cream teas, ploughman's lunches (bread and cheese with salad, basically), a couple of simple hot dishes, and a variety of cakes and desserts.

Shrewd house owners capitalize on this innate national craving, even though it has nothing to do with the nature and quality of a historic house, and may force them into a secondary business they dislike. (Many of them, in fact, let an outside concessionaire handle the catering, in return for a percentage of the take.) At Blenheim the best spot from which to look at the water gardens is the terrace café.

At National Trust houses, and English Heritage properties as well, tea rooms and cafés have become a major source of income. Since a concerted effort to enlarge this source began in 1985, catering in some 130 restaurants and tea rooms now earns the National

Trust—which makes a great point of offering home-baked breads and cakes and local cheeses—more than £1.5 million ($2.4 million) annual profit, on sales of nearly £12 million ($19 million). Houses in search of the family trade sometimes set up kiosks selling ice cream, sandwiches, and soft drinks about the grounds.

Both Chatsworth and Castle Howard have recently added spacious new restaurants, located in their grand old stable blocks. Other houses make use of historic barns or stables for their cafés, and advertise fresh local specialties, as if game pies and fruit crumbles topped with cream from the house dairy were part of the heritage on offer. In Suffolk, the environmentally conscious can have meals made with "produce home-grown or raised from Kentwell's own organic farm." Almost every house with catering facilities will prepare full sit-down luncheons or teas for coach parties that book in advance, and throw in a free meal for the driver.

Gift shops, as museums long ago realized, are valuable both as an attraction in themselves—tourists love to shop—and as a profit center in their own right. Terence Conran, the creator of the Habitat stores and other enterprises, has said that "There is no doubt that the visitor to a museum, gallery, or historic house is disappointed if there is no shop attached." Simon Howard talks of tourists' "right to shop," as if it were something God-given or constitutional. When a house has fewer than 15–20,000 visitors a year, tea rooms and gift shops may have insufficient traffic to show a profit. Even below this level, however, some owners decide to open them, absorbing the loss in order to keep from disappointing tourists. At Powderham Castle in Devon, with 50,000-plus visitors, Lord Courtenay admits that the gift shop and tea room are peripheral, there primarily because people expect them—"the tea rooms more than the shop. They make a bit of money. But people won't come if they can't have a cup of tea." With gift shops as with restaurants, the owner can decide to run the enterprise himself or to contract it out.

For many tourists, shopping for souvenirs—postcards, tea towels, keyrings, pennants, window decals, anything emblazoned with the name or image of the place they are visiting—seems to be a way of verifying that they have been there. American tourists are notorious for making a beeline for the gift shop in any museum, cathedral, national park, or similar tourist attraction, as soon as they quit their car or coach. Even if visitors buy nothing more than a $1.50 guidebook, a country house owner can make a tidy additional profit.

Some country houses open special Christmas shops to sell decorations, lights, even Christmas trees cut from their woodlands during the winter season. Others offer fresh garden produce, homemade cider or brandy, and pick-your-own fruit. Raby Castle in Durham announces that "venison, game and soft fruits" are available in season at its shop. Alnwick and Harewood advertise locally made pottery, and Woburn Abbey has its own resident potter. At Hatfield House you can buy potpourri made from dried flowers and spices from the garden. At Eyam Hall in Derbyshire, the owners make a point of selling tickets to the house in the combined gift shop and Buttery, so that visitors will be tempted both by the souvenirs and the good smells coming from the kitchen.

Just as the best way to see the water gardens at Blenheim is from the café, so the only

Knebworth, Hertfordshire. Stable shop.

way to exit is through the glossy main shop, which offers expensive crafts work for sale as well as books, cards, and souvenirs. The spacious gift shop at Chatsworth—also the last room on one's tour—fills the old sun-washed Orangery, with Wedgwood china and lion bookends and garden books and fudge, plus shelves full of jars of condiments and preserves made, it is suggested, by the Duchess of Devonshire herself. I cannot rid myself of the image of Her Grace, pinny on and sleeves rolled up, stirring away at great vats of marmalade and chutney.[9] At Woburn Abbey around 1970, Ian Bedford installed genuine old shopfronts in the stable block, and managed to persuade 40 different antique dealers to rent spaces behind them. When it reopened in 1994 after a meticulous remodeling, Waddesdon Manor included a spacious new cellar, in which one could buy wines of different vintages from the Rothschild family vineyards in Bordeaux.

The National Trust opened its first in-house shop at Saltram in 1965. In 30 years, this has expanded to a mammoth enterprise selling more than £20 million ($32 million) worth of their Beatrix Potter tea towels and Her Ladyship mugs and butterfly-patterned napkins and floral notepaper and potpourri sachets and herbal soaps and books and videos and honey each year in a total of more than 200 shops. These are typically located alongside the parking lots, or in separate stables or coach houses, to accommodate visitors who would rather shop than look at art or antiques. The Trust now also sells its Country House Collection of determinedly tasteful gifts in a few downtown shops and—like many American museums—out of mail-order catalogues.

· · ·

CHILDREN'S ATTRACTIONS

Even at smaller country houses, valued primarily for their art and architecture or their gardens, visitors insist on bringing children. This is especially true of British visitors, whether they are on holiday or coming from nearby homes. Most owners out of the top ten or twenty (where foreign and domestic coach tours may account for a large share of the clientele) find that a majority of their visitors live within a 30- or 40-mile radius of the house, which they come to regard as a kind of regional park.

Some owners (including English Heritage and the National Trust) take their responsibility to young visitors very seriously indeed, by providing special facilities for school tours, guidebooks and "treasure hunt" quizzes prepared for children, and historical reconstructions or re-enactments designed to enhance the educational nature of a visit. The Heritage Education Trust each year gives an award to historic properties that make special efforts to serve visiting school groups. Some do this by means of "total immersion" historical adventures, in which the children, dressed (like the house staff) in appropriate period costume, try to live the life of an earlier century in the house's existence—spinning, baking, making and using handcrafts, and the like.

The most ambitious such program is that conceived by Patrick and Judith Phillips at Kentwell in Suffolk. Beginning in 1978 with one week and 60 "actors," this program now takes over the 16th-century estate for a whole midsummer month, during which the Phillipses turn Kentwell into a "time-warp" experience for more than 500 school groups, with the help of more than 600 unpaid adult workers (200–350 on any given day), who move onto the site and assume the roles of estate residents and workers at some time between 1487 and 1610. A different year is chosen every season, to keep the volunteers fresh. All of them are obliged to research their roles—to learn the skills of their trades, their responsibilities on the estate, what was going on in the neighborhood in that particular year, a credible 16th-century vocabulary—and create a costume as authentic as possible: no heels, no zippers, no bras, no false teeth.

Judith Phillips then gets the word out to teachers across England and Wales, and sends those interested materials to help their classes bone up on daily country house life in (let

Kentwell, Suffolk. Schoolchildren in costume.

us say) 1593. The children, aged five to fourteen, arrive—in costume—by the busload, and set out in groups every seven and a half minutes, from 9 A.M. to 2 P.M., tours of the house alternating with tours of the farm, each tour lasting three and a half hours. (On one day a week, the children are allowed to wander at will.) Along the way, they encounter mock-Tudor citizens cooking pasties, baking bread, tending sheep, blowing glass, chopping wood, arguing in period dialect, playing the roles of household servants, farmworkers, itinerant craftspeople at work, or the Lord and Lady of the Manor.

Patrick Phillips is, not surprisingly, a keen Tudor history buff, and the Kentwell experience offers him a splendid arena in which to indulge his obsession. Apart from the summer weekdays devoted to school groups, he and his wife offer these "re-creations" for independent visitors on ten weekends between April and September, the price varying depending on the number of performers involved. In addition to restoring the house itself, as well as a genuine Tudor moat house, barn, and cottage on the estate, they have since had built a pair of octagonal oak-domed brick gatehouses (one serves as a shop, the other as a toilet), a granary, a cow byre, and a chicken house, to demonstrate to children and other visitors 16th-century building techniques.

Their efforts are in part philanthropic. The Phillipses start out of pocket £3,500 a day in high season, just to feed their volunteers. Children on school tours come in at reduced rates, spend less money in the shops than adults, and require a good deal more care. In return, they may help to get British youngsters into the habit of country house visiting, and to acquire a more accurate understanding of the nation's past.

Bowood, Wiltshire. Slide in Adventure Playground.

Other efforts directed at children are more openly commercial, with no particular educational component. "Adventure Playgrounds"—that is, large wooden jungle-gyms, which can expand into whole forts (Knebworth) or ships (Bowood) or castles (Longleat) full of ladders, slides, rope bridges, and hiding places—have become a common addition to the country house park. They are intended as a way to give kids bored with Van Dycks and Chippendale something to do while Mum and Dad circle the state rooms, and Gran has a look round the garden.

When I asked Lord Shelburne how he was able to turn Bowood into such a high-profile tourist attraction, he admitted that his impressive Adventure Playground had a lot to do with it. "You take a hundred fifty thousand visitors a year, or whatever we get, and a third, fifty thousand of them are kids. And they want to keep coming back. And they bring their parents and their grandparents. And then later they may bring their own children." Similar "children's diversions" or whole-family attractions are easy to spot in country house advertisements: deer parks, picnic areas, Shetland ponies, miniature railroads, collections of dolls, dolls' houses, models, or toy soldiers. Lord Cholmondeley guesses that the 20,000 model soldiers on display at Houghton probably "attract as many people as the house."

·   ·   ·

Duplicating a display technique frequently used by historical museums, a few country houses have taken to arranging exhibits or tableaux of lifesize wax (more likely fiberglass) models dressed in period costume, as if to emphasize the "historical" nature of the house. The most celebrated instances of this are the two multi-room displays at Warwick Castle, *A Preparation for War 1471* and *A Royal Weekend Party 1898*, elaborately staged displays as carefully executed as anything at Madame Tussaud's in London, which has owned Warwick Castle since 1978. The faces are peculiarly lifelike, the poses, costumes and accessories as convincing as such things can be. The only attributes of their audio-animatronic counterparts at the Disney theme parks they lack are voices and movements—and some of the 1471 creatures *do* move and make noises.

In this £4 million ($6 million) exhibit, installed in the medieval undercroft in 1994, blacksmiths, wheelwrights, armorers, bowmakers, seamstresses and many other costumed mannequins (including a smelly, caparisoned horse) are seen preparing in darkened castle chambers for what was to be a 15th-century Earl of Warwick's final battle in the Wars of the Roses. The second exhibit, in place since 1980, populates twelve of the Victorian public rooms and bedrooms, impeccably redecorated, with figures modeled after the 5th Earl and his Countess (the title was recreated in 1759), their family, servants, and guests at a country house party of the turn of the century. "Most of the furnishings and fittings," says the brochure, "are those that were actually here in 1898. And photographs taken at the time mean that it has been possible to put every chair, table, bed, and book in exactly the place it occupied nearly a hundred years ago."

Similar costumed tableaux of figures in period dress have been installed at various times at Beaulieu, Hever Castle, Hatfield House, and Hagley Hall. The exhibition in the restored lay brothers' house at Beaulieu Abbey includes a few unconvincing monks hard at work. Figures of 18th-century shipyard workers populate three of the houses at nearby Buckler's Hard. The Victorian Kitchens at Longleat are staffed by lifeless servants. A waxworks Edwardian house party is in progress in the public rooms of Croxteth Hall. The Long Gallery at Hever Castle contains an awkward set of 25 costumed figures, posed in scenes from the life of Anne Boleyn, whose family home it once was. Other houses make use of dummies to display the family's coronation robes or clothes worn by former residents.

One can go a step beyond this and dress the staff, or specially hired actors, in period costume. They are then directed to stand about the house or wander over the grounds in order to "add to the atmosphere" and, insofar as they can, answer visitors' questions in dialect and character. A number of houses duplicate part of the Kentwell experience, by dressing their staff in costume and providing "historic" hands-on experiences as part of schoolchildren's tours, a practice fostered by both the Heritage Education Trust and the National Trust. The National Trust also sponsors a group of touring players each year, who act out historic scenes in country house settings.

On my last visit to Hever Castle, the Tudor dummies upstairs were outnumbered by live costumed archers, minstrels, and miscellaneous servants around the gardens, "thee"-ing and "meseems"-ing the tourists. Leeds Castle has begun to hire costumed actors in the summer who sit by the lake and tell tales of the history of the castle. At Lyme Park near Stockport, the guides used to dress as family servants circa 1910. At Beaulieu, Victorian-costumed servants are stationed in the rooms, pretending to be of the same vintage as their clothes.

. . .

EXHIBITS

Houses connected with famous figures often make an effort to mount exhibits related to them. The most-visited is the very ordinary bedroom in which Winston Churchill was born at Blenheim Palace, which is preceded by and filled with Churchilliana—his wartime 'boiler suit,' a lock of his hair cut when he was five. For more Churchilliana, there is his own house at Chartwell, as well as the late Lord Bath's collection at Longleat. There are displays of Queen Victoria's things at Osborne House, Edwardian memorabilia at Sandringham, Mountbatten memories at Broadlands, other viceregal souvenirs at Bowood, Kedleston, and Knebworth; regimental regalia at Belvoir Castle and elsewhere; Wellingtonia at Stratfield Saye, John Ruskin's drawings at Brantwood, relics brought back from Egypt by the 5th Earl of Carnarvon at Highclere, William Fox-Talbot's early photographs at Lacock Abbey, and William Armstrong's energy experiments at Cragside.

In other instances, great halls, long galleries, or coach houses are given over to special exhibitions of various kinds, related or unrelated to the house, in the hope of adding to visitor appeal. In addition to the child-directed displays of toy soldiers or dolls' houses I have mentioned, these can include old kitchen implements, farm machinery, and other commonplace "bygones;" arms and armor—a major attraction at Bamburgh and Warwick Castles; historic costumes; horse-drawn carriages; steam engines; cricketing memorabilia; mechanical music machines; old musical instruments (Finchcocks in Kent is, in addition to a family home, a museum of the owner's historic keyboard instruments, which are frequently played); scientific instruments; dog collars, of all things, at Leeds Castle; and World War II spying devices. Both Barrington Court and Parnham are now partly used as furniture-making workshops: the results of their work are on display and for sale.

Astute house owners turn their own problems or marketing successes into temporary exhibitions. A major fire and restoration (Athelhampton, Uppark, Castle Howard) can provide fascinating materials, by way of photographs and other graphic displays. In 1994, Lord Courtenay cleverly installed blown-up production photographs from *The Remains of the Day* (in which one could glimpse Anthony Hopkins, Emma Thompson, Edward Fox, and Christopher Reeve) in the very rooms where they were shot.

More ambitious still are programs of changing exhibitions, like those of the more enterprising museums, designed to keep visitors coming back. The most ingenious so far are those staged by Victoria Leatham at Burghley. An art appraiser by profession, she realized that Burghley was an extraordinary storehouse of minor arts, containing thousands of pieces from numerous periods and places. In 1983, she began selecting items from the attics to create a special exhibition (European ceramics, Chinese snuffboxes, portrait miniatures, royal papers, antique toys, etc.) each year in the old staff ballroom. By seeing to it the press learned of these changing displays, she hit upon a perfectly legitimate means of creating "news items" that helped to keep Burghley's name in the public eye. Her annual exhibitions—like Antony Jarvis's textile shows in the Long Gallery at Doddington—have become a form of marketing as well as an attraction in themselves.

• • •

Side Attractions

Very early in the game, a number of country house owner/entrepreneurs realized that there were limits to the profits that their houses and gardens could earn, even with the addition of cafés and shops, and the added enticements of special exhibits or events. This is why Edward Montagu brought out his father's old cars, why Henry Bath and Ian Bedford imported wild animals into their game parks.

To the innovative sideshows of the three pioneers, who still lead the pack—Longleat *keeps* adding new attractions, and the National Motor Museum at Beaulieu is in a class of its own—may be added such things as the wildlife parks at Knowsley (where the house is closed) and Port Lympne; the caves at West Wycombe; the bygones collection and pottery at Holkham; a motorcycle museum at Stanford Hall; the Bird Garden and Tropical House at Harewood; the Butterfly Houses at Blenheim Palace, Berkeley Castle, and Compton House; the Falconry Center at Holdenby House; the museum of stuffed animals and Africana at Quex Park; visitor-friendly farms at Croxteth Hall, Tatton Park, Losely Park, and especially Shugborough; the Owl Center at Muncaster Castle; the rare breeds of farm animals at Croxteth, Holdenby, Kentwell, Layer Marney, and Shugborough; the Exhibition Center (film, displays, reconstructed rooms) at Wilton House; and—until a few years ago—the great 18,000-costume collection on display that used to be on display at Castle Howard, now dispersed.

Some of of these secondary attractions have been added to the house as potential income sources. Others, like the working farms, and some of the rare breeds and bygones, have been there all along. This distinction could be extended to sites like the water mills at Cotehele, Mapledurham, and Michelham Priory, even to the much-restored shipping village of Buckler's Hard south of Beaulieu, all of which help to attract visitors to the nearby house. In recent years, the new owners of Hammerwood Park, Kentwell, and Peckforton Castle have advertised their restoration work-in-progress as an attraction in itself, in the hope of making a profit out of necessity.

Other owners, it must be said, look with horror on all such sideshows as detracting from the essence and value of their house. "Firstly, I'm just not sure that the returns are there,

Waddesdon, Buckinghamshire. Visitors at aviary.

in any of those projects," says Lord Arundel at Arundel Castle. "And from a sentimental point of view, one actually wants to keep the place as much a home as possible, not clutter it up with wildlife parks and fun fairs. Because I think that does detract from it as a home, and as a place for the public to come and see." At Holkham Hall, Lord Leicester says, "We haven't even got children's swings, a children's playground. And there are people who actually appreciate that. I know for every one who writes and says, 'How nice it is you haven't got lions and tigers there,' there are another thirty or forty who actually think the same thing. I just think that Holkham is a rather dignified place, an eighteenth-century classical palace, which might be just degraded a bit by the imposition of that sort of thing."[10] The Devonshires at Chatsworth have also consistently refused to go any further than a restaurant and a shop (albeit a rather grand restaurant and shop), as they have refused to rent their house out for functions. They do have an adventure playground and a children's farm, and rent out the opulent former stables.

· · ·

SPECIAL EVENTS

How do you get people to *keep* coming back? By scheduling special events on the grounds, in addition to the house and garden tour itself.

The scheduling of special weekend events through the tourist season at the more enterprising "tourist industry" country houses has become as complicated as planning a season at a busy urban cultural center. Some houses book special events in the grounds every

Knebworth, Hertfordshire.

weekend between June and September, in the hope of filling up the parking lots, increasing ticket sales, and persuading people to return for the house and garden once the special
events are gone: car rallies, crafts fairs, equestrian events, airplane flyover shows, fireworks
displays, concerts and operas, outdoor plays, balloon races, tractor pulls, medieval jousts;
even—if you have the space, the fortitude, and some kind of bargaining power with your
neighbors and the local authorities—giant outdoor pop concerts of the sort identified first
with Beaulieu, and later with Knebworth.

In 1994, Leeds Castle scheduled a Spring Gardens' Week in March; a Children's Easter
Egg Hunt in April; a Festival of English Wines in May; and a Balloon and Vintage Car
Fiesta in June. For the latter event, 25 hot-air balloons raced through the air, over a parade
of vintage cars. Next up were two summer open air concerts with Victoria de los Angeles

and the Royal Philharmonic Orchestra. For this, £25 ($38) bought you a seat, Royal Artillery Band cannons for the 1812 Overture, and a fireworks show to accompany "Land of Hope and Glory," which the assembled thousands are supposed to sing while holding candles and waving little flags. The souvenir programs, glasses, trinkets, and sweatshirts, the drinks and picnic supplies, the candles, blankets, and little Union Jacks cost extra. In July, the Bolshoi Ballet came for three outdoor performances—"no refunds for inclement weather"— at £45–55 ($70–85) per seat. September brought the annual Flower Festival. Special candlelit "Kentish dinners" with music and dancing were scheduled for the big restored barn near the castle every Sunday through most of the year.

The big players in the country house eventing market—which include Goodwood, Harewood, Hatfield, Hever Castle, Knebworth, Longleat, Ragley Hall, Shugborough, Stanford Hall, Warwick Castle, Wilton House, and Woburn Abbey, as well as Leeds—offer everything from three-day horse trials and celebrity concerts to massed bands and battle re-enactments. But numerous lower-profile houses host, at the very least, Craft (or "Country," or "Game") Fairs—which means a park full of rented stalls under marquees offering craft goods and food for sale, along with various demonstrations and country games to play. (Game Fairs concentrate on hunting and shooting, with falconry, clay pigeon shoots and dog obedience trials to accompany the commercial stalls.) Most of these fairs are organized by national entrepreneurs, and move from one country house venue to the next every summer weekend. An organization called Rainbow Fair Ltd. organized fairs at 24 different locations in 1994. In most cases, the house owners get a preset percentage of the gate.

Next in popularity come car rallies, typically organized by marque or type—again, a broad stretch of lawn is essential; "historic re-enactments," both amateur and professional; and outdoor concerts and plays. On Easter weekend, the traditional start of the country house visiting season, British newspapers print lists of the various egg-hunts, jousts, battle re-enactments, and the like being staged at houses all over the country.

Following the model set by the 1956–61 jazz concerts at Beaulieu, Lord Cobbold decided to risk the first open-air country house rock concert at Knebworth in 1974, where 60,000 people paid £3 each to hear the Alman Brothers, Van Morrison, the Doobie Brothers, and the Mahavishnu Orchestra. (Beaulieu had never drawn more than 10,000.) In 1975, with Pink Floyd as headliners, they drew 80,000. The Rolling Stones came the following year; a total of more than 100,000 fans packed into the park. Two less successful concerts in 1978 featured Genesis and the Jefferson Starship, and Frank Zappa and the Tubes. A pair of Led Zeppelin concerts in 1979—their last concerts in England—drew a total of more than 200,000, but sent the promoters into bankruptcy. Santana and the Beach Boys lost money in 1980. In 1981 and 1982, Capitol Radio sponsored top-name jazz festivals at Knebworth. The 1985 concert (Deep Purple, Meat Loaf, the Scorpions), for 75,000 people, ended up a soggy mess in the rain, with unruly fans and an unhappy District Council. A stabbing death during Queen's 1986 concert put an end to the series for a while, and led the Knebworth staff to work out a complex "disaster contingency" plan.

On the whole, though, these events have been peaceful, well run, and remarkably successful—to the point that Knebworth (which one critic called "the Glyndebourne of rock") is now identified on a plaque as one of the major sites in the history of British rock 'n' roll. In recent years, they attracted 120,000 people to an allstar, twelve-hour, £30 ($53) charity concert in 1990, and 70,000 to a Genesis concert in 1992. A two-night appearance by Oasis in August 1996 broke pop concert records by selling out all 250,000 tickets.

These concerts take place in a 45-acre meadow away from the house, require up to 800 policemen and 350 additional security guards, and cost up to £30 for tickets, plus £5 for parking and £8 for programs—a total of $70 or more. Special "VIP Lounge" tickets go for £500 ($750). For its pop concerts, put on by outside promoters, Knebworth operates on a straight rental fee—"I want my money before they set foot in the place," says manager John Hoy—with the upper limit on available tickets negotiated in advance with the local police and county authorities. As with their hotel and functions business, the presence of a direct exit off the M1 is essential. Events of this size would be unthinkable at most country estates, however large they may be, given the likelihood of hopeless traffic snarls and unhappy neighbors.

For a while, it looked as if upscale, high-ticket classical music concerts (with extra income from champagne and picnic sales) might provide a comparable major source of income for estates large enough to accommodate them, without the anxieties that accompany monster rock concerts. This began in a small way, with semi-amateur opera companies performing in gardens (sometimes under umbrellas) or great halls at country houses up and down the land. But promoters and house owners succumbed to a *folie de grandeur*, and tried to sell outdoor country house concerts featuring major ballet troupes and opera superstars at prices from £50 to £65 ($75–100). They soon learned that the combination of high prices, uncomfortable seats, and unpredictable weather rendered these events unlikely to return any profit. In 1994, the Bolshoi Ballet cancelled its scheduled bookings at Castle Howard and Highclere Castle, and lost money at Leeds. A major series of country house concerts scheduled for that same summer—with five international-class opera singers and a pianist, who were to appear at Castle Howard, Knebworth, Warwick Castle, Blenheim, Harewood, and Broadlands—collapsed completely. The failure was later blamed on an incompetent group of promoters, but the idea was probably wrong-headed from the start. As Simon Howard of Castle Howard put it, "The promoters thought they could see big money coming and now they've floundered. People really don't have that kind of money. It's all gone flat again."

A whole separate category is "the country house turned opera venue." It began at Glyndebourne in Sussex, which has been the home of one of the world's most important summer opera festivals since 1934. In 1994, the Glyndebourne Festival Opera opened a new 1,200-seat opera house, which now looms over George and Mary Christie's 1876 neo-Tudor brick country house. But the lakeside meadows remain, where operagoers in evening dress sit and savor their lavish picnics during the long intermission.

Leonard and Rosalind Ingrams began offering opera productions on the terrace overlooking their beautiful garden at Garsington, near Oxford, in 1989. They now produce about twenty performances of three operas each summer, to an open-air audience of 390. As at Glyndebourne, performances begin early, and pause midway for a 75-minute dinner break, when guests can either eat their own picnics in the garden, or order a catered meal in the barn. "It's a formula which audiences seem to like very much," says Rosalind Ingrams—"the midsummer feeling, with the garden all around you, the music, the meal: it all seems to add up to something greater than the sum of its parts."

If the money can be raised, and the required permissions obtained, a modern, new-built 1,150-seat opera house may be built on the grounds of Compton Verney in Warwick-shire—the Glyndebourne of the Midlands, its promoters are already calling it.

. . .

In the long run, two personal characteristics seem essential if one is to make a success of opening a country house to the public: a wholly businesslike approach, with very few concessions made to sentimentality or family pride; and a dedication so total one cannot possibly be doing very much else.

These may have little to do with historical or artistic values—the grounds on which grand old English houses are usually defended; or with a concept as intangible as "The Heritage." But heritage, in Britain and elsewhere, has been big business now for a very long time. "As the past forty years have proved," wrote Lord Montagu in 1991, "well managed tourism can do more to conserve our heritage than any other source of funds."

The matter of dedication is more one of attitude than of method. Those who open solely because of government or economic pressure, who dislike the "invading hordes" and begrudge the time they take away from their more serious work at the bank or on the farm are almost doomed to fail. The most successful are those who have made opening their family estate to the public as important a part of their lives as maintaining the estate in the first place. Not surprisingly, a large number of them started in the business early, before they had a chance to become deeply committed to other occupations. In the ordinary course of events, a son or daughter might expect to take over the family business sometime at the age of 40 or 45. As of 1995, Althorp, Arundel Castle, Athelhampton, Beaulieu, Bowood, Burghley, Castle Howard, Chatsworth, Duncombe Park, Hagley Hall, Knebworth, Powderham Castle, and Ragley Hall were all being run by men or women who had taken charge before they were 33. There are no doubt many more such stories, in which the energy, imagination, and perhaps something of the foolhardiness of youth played a part.

Once his eldest son was the same age (33) that he was when he took over Knebworth ("I would never dream of doing all I did now!"), Lord Cobbold grudgingly admitted that the time might be coming soon to consider moving aside. The Duke of Norfolk handed over his two larger estates, Arundel Castle in Sussex and Carlton Towers in Yorkshire, to his two sons before they were 30, then retired to a smaller house at Henley. "I think he's been terribly clever," said his elder son. "And of course very generous. He managed to get both of us interested young, and wedded to the properties."

Some owners open grudgingly or minimally, still farmers or city businessmen at heart. Some spouses hate the very idea of all those damp Mrs. Tiggywinkles tromping through their rooms. For every enthusiastic, enterprising Chrissie Cobbold or Deborah Devonshire or (until her divorce) Penny Cobham, there are many spouses of the heirs to country houses who are less than enthusiastic about working seven months a year enticing and entertaining tourists and conference-goers.

Most country home owners are already businessmen to one degree or another: medium-scale farmers and woodsmen, landlords to the farmers and other householders or merchants on their estates. They may regard opening their house and gardens to paying visitors as just adding one more business operation to the others. The most impressive success stories in the private sector are those where the owner has treated house-opening as if it were his primary business, or at least one no less important than his farms and rental properties—Arundel, Blenheim, and Beaulieu, for example, in their very different ways. "Some people are natural entrepreneurs, and some aren't," says Montagu.

The Earl of Leicester was quite candid about the business aspects of opening his house. In 1976, he had bought out his father—who lived in South Africa, and died in 1994—and has been running Holkham Hall and its 26,000 acres ever since. Turning pages of a ledger in his estate office, he called the income from visitors totally inadequate to maintain the vast house, but all the same "very useful money indeed. Of course we set everything that the tax inspector possibly allows against the house openings—the security staff, the administrator, the gardeners, the cleaning ladies and so on."

Which makes opening more useful as a tax deduction than as a profit center?

Yes indeed. The inspector of taxes is very reasonable. We do everything we legally can to avoid taxes, of course. If we think there is anything that the inspector might be a little bit cagey about, our accountant goes to him and explains our position. And more often than not, because we have actually taken the trouble to go and see them, and laid our cards on the table, they're very accommodating. I mean, since we're only open seventy-eight days a year, the inspector could say, "Well, you can only deduct seventy-eight three-hundred-and-sixty-fifths of your gardening expenses." But our argument is, What would the gardens look like if we didn't maintain them the other hundred and eighty days?

From thirty thousand people last year we took in one hundred thirty two thousand pounds, not counting the gift shop and tea shop. And the direct costs attributable to the house opening are only about thirteen thousand. So it's very useful. It pays for nearly everyone, and it goes quite a way towards looking after the house itself. But inevitably it's not enough.

CHAPTER EIGHT

Separate Quarters

One into Many: Residential Conversions

ONE CURRENTLY POPULAR WAY to preserve an outdated country house as a lived-in piece of property is to divide it into separate apartments, or a number of normal-sized houses. If a house must depart from single ownership, preservation and owners' groups tend to favor this approach, since it keeps the building "alive" and lived in as a home. There are justified fears, however, that the quality of a fine old house may be destroyed by avaricious and insensitive conversion—in particular one that tries to cram a great many new apartments into an historic mansion, "restores" its original decoration on the cheap, and then diminishes the beauty of the big old house by surrounding it with a profitable tract of smaller new houses.

Despite planning constraints, there is always a danger that the purchaser of a big old country house, given up by a family or an institutional owner, will be a property developer more interested in the land than the house. He may be able to persuade local planning authorities to let him "develop"—that is, build new houses or condos—on larger and larger chunks of the estate, in return for "preserving" the mansion. In too many such cases, the great house—which the developer may never have got around to restoring, converting, or reselling, and which may be growing more derelict every month—is hemmed in by tacky new bungalows or an industrial park, and ends up far less attractive or desirable than it was before he got it.

. . .

One hopeful story of multiple-residence conversions in England is that of a registered charity now called the Country Houses Association (CHA). In 1955, Rear Admiral Bernard Greathed wrote a letter to the *Observer* suggesting that large country houses that could no longer be maintained by a single family might be taken up by a group of like-minded people. The sort of people he had in mind were retired armed forces officers (like himself) and their wives returning from overseas, where they had grown accustomed to a servant-eased way of life they could no longer afford at home.

In the case of the houses purchased by the association which Admiral Greathed went on to found, these people turn out to be retired people of sufficient means to lend (1995 figures) from £20,000 to £85,000 ($32,000 to $136,000) to the CHA, depending on the size and grandeur of their apartment. They bring their own furniture, choose their own decorating scheme, and pay a monthly charge ranging from a low of £750 ($1,200) for one person to a high of £1,850 ($2,960) for a couple, which also depends on the size of the unit. This charge covers three meals a day in the dining room (apartments may have a "tea-making corner," but no kitchens), utilities, maintenance, and cleaning. When one of the members leaves (or dies), the loan is repaid, less 3 percent a year and the cost of redecorating. As of 1992, the Country Houses Association had acquired and restored nine country houses together with their gardens. These were home to more than 300 residents (most of them between 75 and 85 years old; the houses all have lifts). All in the south of England, they include two Elizabethan manors, a 1725 Palladian mansion, two John Soane houses, Victorian and Edwardian estates designed by Norman Shaw and Edwin Lutyens, and Admiral Greathed's own 1868 house in Surrey.

Given the economics of their operation, the CHA can now only afford to take on houses that will yield room for at least 30 or 40 residents—which, presuming the average couple wants a two-room apartment, implies at least that number of bedrooms in the original house. The public rooms downstairs—which are often quite grand—are furnished and maintained by the association, and open to all residents and their guests, as well to paying visitors two afternoons a week. The gardens are staff-maintained, although some residents enjoy tending parts of them.

My wife and I stopped at Aynhoe Park in Northamptonshire, a fairly posh historic house in which three matching, pedimented wings face one another around a courtyard, remodeled by Thomas Archer and John Soane between 1710 and 1805. For so large a house, it lies unusually close to the village road; but walking access to a village is something the CHA looks for in the properties it buys. In any case, a handsome garden and impressive remnants of a Capability Brown landscape stretch out behind the house. Aynhoe Park had been the home of the Cartwright family from 1616 to 1954; in 1954, both the owner and his only son were killed in a car crash. The burden of double death duties obliged the family to sell. In 1959 it became the second acquisition of the new Country Houses (then called 'Mutual Householders') Association, which was able to buy it for only £10,000, or $28,000.

We had lunch in the private dining room (the main dining room is in the old conser-

Aynhoe, Northamptonshire. Private dining room.

vatory) with David and Malvina Donen, the resident administrators, then moved to the Soane drawing room overlooking the garden for coffee with a few other residents. The residents form an interesting community of upper-middle-class ladies and gentlemen, well-travelled and well-educated, who share a respect for gardening and field sports. Most of them moved here from nearby period houses of their own. With increasing years and decreasing help, they were finding their own houses too much of a burden. They professed themselves comfortable with their neighbors, loved sharing gossip about country house owners we had met, and seemed contented with their elegant, if shared, surroundings. They miss their kitchens and pets.

"We had a large Georgian, in Oxfordshire," one woman told me. "When we bought it it was a wreck. We were the first people to own it after the Church sold it. So we immediately had to put in a damp course, and new gas central heating. And it had a wonderful garden that had also been neglected. So we had ten or fifteen years, lovely years, putting it back to rights. We really enjoyed it. But then it all got a bit too much for us, so we decided to come here. You can't get gardeners, you know. People have taken such an awful punishment in the last two years—the recession, of course. Several apartments here are vacant, because people have not been able to sell their houses; they can't sell their house, so they can't afford to come."

The CHA's houses are historic, elegant, and well-maintained. Their potential clientele is limited by the investment required—although anyone who could sell a house elsewhere, and had a reasonable pension, could probably afford to join them—and by the stipulation that residents must be ambulatory and in good physical and mental health. In the spring of 1995, there were more than two dozen apartments available in their nine houses, several of which sounded quite tempting. But the difficulty of attracting tenants in recent years may define a limit to the potential of the CHA scheme for "saving" fine old houses.

·   ·   ·

A similar but more expensive arrangement is to buy, lease, or rent a fraction of a large house, sometimes from the architect or developer who first bought it, then converted it into self-contained apartments or private residences; sometimes from the estate agent who succeeded him. The house may now be divided into between four and 30 units, each with its own entrance—sometimes from the outside, sometimes off the Great Hall or grand staircase; or off a corridor, in older conversions.

In early years, such subdivisions were often crude and degrading, reducing great houses to little more than period-style apartment houses in the country. Planning permissions had sometimes been granted only as a last resort, to save the houses from demolition. But the end result was often less than "salvation": fine detailing and proportions were often lost, as interiors were chopped up into the maximum number of undistinguished flats.

In recent years, the best multiple-residence conversions have resulted in solutions at once grand and harmonious. Sensitively handled, a historic country house can retain almost all of its original architectural quality in the course of being divided into independent houses and apartments.

Ideally, the state rooms remain intact and undivided, and the exterior of the manor goes on looking as it originally did. Garages are discreetly added, or fitted into existing stable blocks or carriage houses. (New garages, in fact, are sometimes built to *look* like old stable blocks or carriage houses.) Everyone contributes on a pro rata basis to the maintenance of the house and garden and to necessary repairs, which can cost each owner £500–1,000 ($800–1,600) a year or more.

A London estate agency called Period and Country Houses Ltd. specializes in the conversion and sale of such quarters. Its founder, Christopher Buxton, lives in considerable splendor in the central wing of Kirtlington, an 18th-century mansion in Oxfordshire he converted into seven units. Since 1954, Buxton has done over more than 25 country houses in this fashion, and been the advisor for several others. Among these are Charlton Park in Wiltshire, the Jacobean/Georgian seat of the Earl of Suffolk, who now lives in one of the nineteen units; Shillinglee Park in Surrey, a 1733 house with Tudor and earlier out-buildings, restored from a ruinous state; and Compton Verney, a Grade I 1714–60 estate near Stratford, whose designers included John Vanbrugh (possibly), Robert Adam, James Gibbs, and Capability Brown. At Compton Verney, the Gibbs coach house and stable block were converted into ten residences, but the main house was never subdivided. There was talk of turning it into a hotel, but in 1993 it was sold to a private trust, which is now converting it into a museum.

Since 1965, Buxton's firm has often taken on the ownership or lease of the properties he plans to divide, which increases his risks. In addition to coming up with saleable designs, they must worry about persuading suspicious bankers into loans and perservation watchdogs into planning permission ("English Heritage have become the biggest menace of all," Buxton once declared); maintaining sufficient cash flow during the rebuilding process; predicting the course of the economy; and seeking out home buyers willing to experiment with a new way of life. A number of projects that have passed out of their hands have been abandoned by others, or dealt with in disappointing ways.

Whatever the problems he has had to confront in 40 years, Buxton still believes that implanting new residential communities is the best way to reuse medium-sized country houses—houses that are unlikely to attract a large number of fee-paying visitors. These houses, he argues, were originally designed to house residential "communities," with sepa-rate accommodations for parents, children, guests, house servants, and estate workers. His conversions, as he sees it, involve no particularly radical change. The old owner, if he desires, can live on in the main part of the house (as Lord Suffolk does at Charlton Park), and grant long leases on the secondary units.

Buxton regards the multiple-residence solution as more sympathetic than institutional use, and less risky than hotel conversion. Having several owners instead of one responsi-ble for maintaining and administering the property decreases, he believes, the likelihood of failure.

You can purchase a substantial slice of such a house, with three bedrooms, a modern kitchen, at least one stately room, a walled garden, and access to the grounds beyond, for (1995) about £250,000–400,000 ($400,000–640,000). Smaller flats, and outbuilding con-versions, go for about half that, and can frequently be found listed for resale. In addition to the variable annual maintenance fee, the management company (typically set up by the householders themselves) may vote additional assessments to repair a roof, say; or to buy up additional land.

Throughout the 1950s and 1960s, advertisements for country houses with more than ten bedrooms inevitably insisted that they were "eminently suitable for conversion" to multiple residency, and stories of successful conversions were frequently printed in the hope of attracting buyers. In more recent years, notices in the "Property Market" columns often mention that a slice of one great house or another has come up for resale. But I have found no way of estimating the total number of country houses that have found new life in this fashion.

Shortly after the 1974–75 Victoria and Albert Museum exhibition, Marcus Binney and others created SAVE Britain's Heritage, a pressure group whose purpose was to persuade individuals and government agencies to preserve, restore, and find new uses for historic buildings that had been abandoned and, in many cases, left to decay. Beginning in 1978, SAVE (as it is popularly called) began publishing illustrated catalogues of abandoned or endangered country houses, hoping either to shame their owners into repairing them, or to persuade developers to take them on as reconversion projects. Many of these houses had interesting earlier histories, when they were still in private, single-family hands (more often Victorian plutocratic than Georgian aristocratic), and real estate correspondents enjoyed writing about them. Their articles may have helped foster the postwar British dream not of owning your own house, but of owning your own share of a stately home, with a long entry drive and unbroken vistas over private parkland—which someone else has to maintain. One woman sharing a Queen Anne mansion in Sussex said, "It sounds ridiculous, but once you've got used to living in ballroom-sized bedrooms and having everything in spacious proportions, including the loos and hallways, you can't imagine living in normal-sized rooms again."[1]

Like most schemes to find new uses for large and archaic country houses, this one has turned out to have its problems. In 1987, the *Financial Times* warned developers of the astonishing, unexpected costs that a responsible restoration job could involve. "For every historic house bought, developed, and resold in parts, there have been as many that have landed enthusiastic amateurs in the bankruptcy courts. As inspection of the standards of historic building renovation works has become more efficient no developer tackling a formally listed property can hope to cut corners anymore. So it is only rising house prices, and second home buyers' consequent willingness to pay more for quality, that has saved this specialised form of residential development from extinction."[2] In 1992, *Chartered Surveyor Weekly* suggested that the fad for country house multiple-residence conversions may already have peaked. It listed six such projects that had recently come to grief, leaving their developers either bankrupt or suffering a considerable loss.

Several country house conversions were in the hands of receivers, who were selling off unfinished shells of houses and apartments at half or less their original prices. One of these unfortunate projects was Sheffield Park in Sussex, a 16th-century house bought in the 1770s by the Earl of Sheffield, who then had James Wyatt redo it in neo-Gothic. Made over into eleven flats and two houses, it stands in the middle of a 100-acre parkland designed by Brown and Repton, today the property of the National Trust. In early 1992, a number of failed or struggling developers found themselves burdened with unsellable pieces of the country houses they had taken on, as the upper-end housing market collapsed. These unhappy entrepreneurs blamed their plight (variously) on the extraordinary costs of refurbishing, the result of listed building restrictions as well as of soundproofing and fire safety provisions; on local authorities' refusal to let them add enough new houses on the property to make a profit; on the high interest rates of 1990–92, and the related unwillingness of home buyers to pay high premiums for elegance and amenities; on the difficulty willing buyers had in finding purchasers for their own houses; and on buyers' fears that a declining market would leave them with "negative equity."

But as the recession began to change course, and interest rates to decline, new buyers began to emerge. Week after week, one read again of successful, or at least hopeful residential conversions. Dene Park, an enormous 1878 Victorian house in Kent, was divided into nine spacious apartments, with additional units in the dower house, coach house, gatehouse, and around a court. One of my favorite offers was for a 7,600-square-foot slice of 24-unit Ottershaw Park (ca.1900, with a thirteen-acre park) in Surrey—the preferred county in England for such projects. This single unit came with sixteen-foot ceilings, a ballroom, a great hall measuring 46 by 27 feet, a 32-foot-long drawing room, a dining room seating twenty, five bedrooms, a terrace running the length of the house, a wine cellar, and use of the pool. In 1994, it was offered for resale for £800,000 ($1,200,000).

One of the more controversial recent multiunit developments is that of Northwick Park, a Grade I 1686-plus Palladian mansion in the Cotswolds, partly redesigned by Lord Burlington in 1732. After the death of the last Lord Northwick in 1914, and its sale by his Spencer-Churchill descendants, the house deteriorated for a decade or two, until it was bought in 1986, with nineteen acres, by a local developer. It has since been passed on to two other property developers.

In order to compensate him for the £1.5 million (about $2.3 million) expense of preserving the rotting, beetle-ridden house (on top of its £2 million cost), local authorities granted the second developer permission to build 68 new houses and apartments on the property, now expanded to 54 acres, along with ten blocks of garages, which considerably upset the heritage lobby. The first nine units were fitted into the gallery and coach house; then sixteen more (all 25 were sold at freehold) were made out of the stables, granaries, orangery, dovecotes, and wings. After months of work by stonemasons, restoration carpenters, and slate roofers, the house itself was divided and sold as six luxurious condos for about £400,000 ($600,000) each.

When I looked around in 1994, yet another developer was building eleven units on the site of the old kitchen garden (part of it now a "croquet lawn"), with tennis courts and a promised swimming pool available to all, on offer from £75,000 (for a studio flat) to £250,000, or $115–380,000. All these new residences were inoffensively neo-Georgian, faced with brick or even Cotswold stone, with traditional windows and details. The new winding, mile-long private drive approximates that of a genuine country house. But the ensemble struck me as banal and overcrowded, one pseudo-period condo jammed up against another—all the new units had to fit within the "footprint" of the original estate buildings—which is precisely what early opponents of the scheme had feared all along.

This may once have been the site of an important country house. But today the Northwick mansion is swamped by new buildings, and what is left of its estate looks like just another upscale housing developer's project.

More recently, Wardour Castle, an immense Palladian house near Salisbury designed (1768–76) by James Paine for the Earl of Arundell, shut up shop as a girls' boarding school, and was bought by London developer/ecologist Nigel Tuersley in 1992 for a bargain £1 million ($1.77 million). While converting the great house into his own home and eight additional luxury apartments, the new owner is also preserving one of the most spectacular interior spaces in England: a 60-foot-high Pantheon-like rotunda in which two cantilevered, semicircular stairways converge on the main floor gallery, where eight Composite-order columns support a skylit dome. Tuersley and his wife moved into the grandest rooms of the house, while redecorating a few spacious apartments around them to something like their original splendor—which he then rented, leased, or sold. In addition to reconstructing ceilings, doorways, lighting fixtures, and other features according to Paine's original plans, he also plans to build a "stable block" and an "orangery," following recently discovered 18th-century plans, to house 16 more units and a swimming pool, although objections have been raised to these plans; and restoring the Capability Brown park, tree by individual tree.

· · ·

An architect named Kit Martin (son of Sir Leslie Martin, chief designer of Royal Festival Hall) has since 1976 bought, converted, lived in, and sold sections of several large country houses, including some that were totally derelict before he got them. Along with Marcus Binney of SAVE—who has served as Martin's chief publicist—he has proposed plans for saving a good many others.[3]

Of Martin's first project, Binney wrote in *Country Life*, "Dingley was a wreck. Panelling, doors, doorcases, chimneypieces had been stripped out, the stone flags of the main ground-floor rooms had gone, slates had been torn from the roof, followed by the removal of almost all the internal walls, floors, and ceilings. Whole chimneystacks were collapsing as a result of the loss of lateral support, bringing down large sections of the roof as they fell."[4]

Martin, a young man at the time, rose to the challenge. Since restoring Dingley, a 16th-17th-century house in Northamptonshire, by converting it into ten houses between 1976 and 1980, he has taken on six more unwanted or endangered country houses in England and four in Scotland, including houses in remote areas that were candidates for demolition. Sometimes he was able to acquire them, and their adjacent acres, for a token price. He divides them into self-contained two-to-four-story residences (*never* apartments), each, if at all possible, with its own outside entrance and private garden. As a rule, he undertakes his restorations in successive stages, using the proceeds from one completed house to pay for work on the next. The stable and service blocks and other outbuildings are converted into private cottages, smaller houses, and flats. The exteriors tend to look exactly as they did—sometimes better than they did—in their prime. By creating substantial "vertical" houses in the mansion, some as large as 5,000 square feet, he is able to keep the great public rooms intact and undivided, one or more to a house. Not surprisingly, it is easier to find purchasers for a 3,500 square-foot house (the largest unit at The Hazells, in Bedfordshire, his second project) than for the whole original 27,500-square-foot building. Historic chimneypieces, door cases, stairways, carved moldings and wood paneling are preserved, or when missing either recreated or imported from other houses he has restored.

Typically, Martin engages a local architect to oversee construction, but maintains his own team of workmen who move from house to house. He makes a point of acquiring, along with the house and its outbuildings, a largish piece of ground (twelve, fifteen, 60 acres—more, in the unique case of Gunton Park), and then establishing ownership or covenants in such a way that the setting, shared by all owners, cannot be misused—a problem that has bedeviled many speculative country house purchases and conversions. New garage blocks are deceptively well integrated. In most cases the residents become partners in a company that keeps up the grounds. They can vote, at annual meetings, to do things like plant new trees or add a pool. Like Christopher Buxton, Martin has had little trouble selling these semistately homes at respectable prices.

Eleven country houses salvaged and resuscitated out of the hundreds at risk is not a great many. But Martin's elegant conversion jobs have been well publicized in books, magazines, and newspapers, which may lead them to serve as models for others. Unfortunately, a considerable amount of both genius and idealism is required, which not all country house converters possess to the same degree that he does.

Since restoring and populating Gunton Park in Norfolk between 1981 and 1984, Martin and his wife have sold and moved out of the central portion of the big house (1742), into a smaller, more informal farmhouse on the estate. It is here that he displays plans and photographs, and tells me tales of Gunton and other projects.

The last Lord Suffield to live at Gunton Park died childless in 1945, and left the house to his sisters, one of whom was living alone in a couple of rooms when Martin first saw the house in 1979. He was able to buy the whole tumbledown estate for £100,000 ($232,000) a year later. What excited him about Gunton Park was that, despite its shabby condition (one large piece of the front had been burnt out in 1872, and left as a roofless shell), it retained a great number of Georgian estate buildings, including an Adam-designed church and a working sawmill as well as James Wyatt stables, lodges, a tower, and other structures—far more, in fact, than a house of its size (it was once intended to be much larger) would normally have required. He immediately saw the possibility of developing these buildings into a self-contained village, which is what Gunton Park has become—a thriving home to more than 100 people.

"So we did the absolutely standard Martin maneuver, which is to do a vertical division. What amazes me is that nobody else does it. You wouldn't believe it, really, because it's so obvious. If you have a wing like that"—he points to the plan—"everyone gets a share of the grand rooms, the grand bedrooms, and the attic bedrooms. What many people don't seem to understand is that there is still a demand—has been from the time I started—for *large* houses within a country house, as well as cottages. I started trying to do over a house without dividing up the principal rooms—and then I found that there were customers."

He points out the series of four very large houses into which the main block is divided, in one of which—where he left the burned-out bit as a kind of romantic ruin, and enjoyed twelve acres of private garden—he and his family used to live. "It competed in price with a good local manor house [in fact, he put it on sale in 1993 for £525,000, or $788,000]; but it had much grander rooms than a manor house of the same size."

He makes a point of trying to provide a wide array of house sizes (there are 30 units altogether within the park at Gunton), from a 500-square-foot, one-bedroom cottage built into a gardener's shed, or a remote kennel-man's cottage hidden in the woods; through five small family houses in the stables; to the row of 5,000-square-foot mansions. Unlike almost all other country house developers, he never introduces new buildings, and has (so far) managed without government aid. He believes that a mix of house sizes makes the whole array easier to sell—and ends up populating the new estate/village with a wonderfully heterogeneous mix of inhabitants: in the case of Gunton Park, commuters from Norwich, young couples with children, gay professionals, retired people, second-home owners from London or Edinburgh, people living together as they did on a great working estate two centuries ago. Although most residents have gardens of their own, and are generally free to decorate as they wish, the estate is protected by restrictive covenants—which forbid owners, for instance, from altering the exteriors of their houses—overseen by a committee made up of Martin, the local surveyor, and the regional director of the National Trust. This, Martin admits, is a more "autocratic" system of management than that which prevails at most of his other projects, where gardens are held in common, and authority resides in a management company formed by the residents. But he had special plans for the landscape here, which a "democracy" of thirty individual owners might have blocked.

Most recently, Kit Martin has taken on two formidable challenges. Both were made more than usually complex because others before him had attempted to convert large, historic, artistically important houses into new and profitable enterprises, and failed miserably at the task.

The recent history of Burley-on-the-Hill, in Leicestershire (formerly Rutland County: the house faces Rutland Water, a large, lake-sized reservoir), involves not only poor planning, but also a scandal of no small dimensions. The 250-room hilltop seat (1694–1704) of the Earls of Nottingham, with a curving, two-armed colonnade that mimics St. Peter's in Rome, Burley was burned in 1908, abused during World War II, stripped of its contents after the war, and finally abandoned by the family. In 1991, it was purchased for £7 million (plus another £2 million for 750 surrounding acres—total about $16 million) by a free-spending Turkish Cypriot entrepreneur with big plans.

Asil Nadir, who had turned an East End clothing business into an international conglomerate, while making generous donations to British charities and the Conservative Party, wanted to turn Burley into a luxury hotel surrounded by two eighteen-hole golf courses, to the dismay of appalled preservationists. In 1990, Nadir, his enterprises revealed as a giant bubble, was arrested on charges of theft and fraud, and forced into bankruptcy. Two years later he jumped a record £3.5 million ($6.4 million) bail and fled home to north Cyprus, leaving behind debts estimated at more than a billion pounds.

Kit Martin was able to repurchase Burley and 67 acres of parkland in 1992. Joss Hanbury, the wealthy sportsman/landowner who had sold Burley to Nadir in the first place, bought back the surrounding acres, which will help to keep the estate intact, and allow new homeowners at Burley to roam or ride or walk their dogs at will through 400 acres of parkland and woods.

At Burley-on-the-Hill, Kit Martin and his team proceeded to divide the big house into seven large and luxurious individual houses (one wealthy buyer bought two, which gave him the whole flamboyantly painted Great Staircase, spared in the 1908 fire). The four largest houses have four stories and at least sixteen windows each; the windows on the two main floors each have eighteen large panes. The vaulted basement, the Great Hall and Saloon, and the vast two-story Ballroom upstairs are all spaces held in common, which can be used for concerts or social events. All the houses have outside entrances of their own. Those on the two ends have fairly spectacular sets of Baroque horseshoe steps that lead into private hedge-enclosed gardens. Four cottages with walled gardens were fitted into the kitchen block, four more into the laundry block; others into the stables and coach house at the ends of the colonnade and into service buildings about the estate. By 1995, all the houses had been sold at freehold (most of them before completion) for prices ranging from £150,000 to £600,000 ($240,000–960,000).

What makes Martin's dream-scheme for Stoneleigh Abbey in Warwickshire unique is not only the size and importance of the house, but also the fact that he is attempting to combine, for the first time, a "Country House Open to the Public" (the grand rooms at Stoneleigh are so huge they must become public spaces, or be divided up) with one of his typical stately home reconversions. In this case the home is more "stately" than any he has undertaken so far.

The home of Lord Leigh (largely designed by Francis Smith of Warwick and built in 1714–26, on a visible medieval-through-17th-century base) had also been badly damaged by a fire, this one in 1960. It took off the roof, ate through a number of rooms, and left others badly damaged from a burst water tank on the roof. Desperate to save his ancestral seat, Lord Leigh vested it in a new charitable trust before he died in 1979. The trust took five years to complete the repairs. His successor, the 5th and present Lord Leigh, planned to lease the rather crudely restored second and third floor rooms (the restored state rooms are on the first, or ground floor), which had been most severely damaged, for use as offices—an unpromising scheme for a huge house in a remote rural location.

In ten years not a single tenant showed up, and the Stoneleigh Abbey Preservation Trust found itself buried under a growing mountain of debt. The State rooms (which had been open to the public) were closed, much of their furniture sold off. The roofs of the grand Regency stables caved in. In the hope of getting clear, the trust went into partnership with a developer who planned to convert the house into a hotel, build a whole village of new houses (on a site near that of the annual Royal Agricultural Show), and transform estate farmland into a pair of golf courses.

After the golf-and-hotel deal collapsed in 1993, Martin came on board. The solution he and the Stoneleigh Trust eventually arrived at was for the latter to go ahead with the planned clusters of new houses, in order to pay off its debts. These are being designed by Andrew Brookes of Rodney Melville and Partners of Warwickshire, one of Britain's most active firms of restoration architects, and will be located well away from the mansion. A new hotel may eventually be built in the same area. But the Preservation Trust will retain and preserve the rest of the parkland—no golf courses, no more farms, no more Royal Show sheds.

In the mansion, the basement and ground floor of Francis Smith's west wing will be maintained by the Trust. This space—about a quarter of the house—includes all the Baroque state rooms (and now a tea room), which will once again be open to the public. Apartments will be added for a caretaker and custodian. Visitors will also be able to see the remaining medieval-to-Elizabethan fragments in the old abbey courtyard, and walk through the walled gardens and grounds. Behind and above the public areas will be the new private accommodations.

At Stoneleigh, Martin found an even larger and more heterogeneous complex of possible living spaces than at Gunton Park or Burley. Altogether, they will enable him and Andrew Brookes to implant some 35 different houses in existing buildings of the estate, from five- or six-bedroom vertical mansions (six of these, built around six existing staircases) in the vast mother mansion, to houses in the kennels and cottages on the home farm—all with the usual restrictive covenants to protect the ensemble. Everything will remain the property of the Preservation Trust, which, together with Martin, will sell 125-year leases for the houses.

The beauty of the scheme, if it works, is that the Preservation Trust will maintain control over the entire estate, but be responsible for maintaining only two floors of public rooms in the wing open to the public, which reduces its need for endowment income. At the same time, residents and tourists can wander about the grounds, secure in the knowledge that both the land and the buildings are protected in perpetuity by a charitable trust.

.   .   .

We ended our visit to Gunton with a wild drive in Martin's car, bumping over meadows, sailing through seas of grass as high as the windshield, so he could show us not only the various buildings on the estate (and describe their owners), but also his newest dream: to restore the parkland at Gunton, the creation of turn-of-the-18th-century landscape architects William Gilpin and Humphry Repton. "The whole point of these estates," he says, as we bounce and careen around, "was that they were once a whole world within a great park. And this particular park was fifteen hundred acres. It was designed by great landscape architects, and I thought it would be interesting to restore it as it was intended to be."

Shortly after buying the big house and 60 acres around it, Martin realized that neighboring landowners were unlikely to go along with his dream. Even Gunton Park residents might consider farming a more rational use of their land than empty, picturesque grassland, full of deer and big trees. He had showed me a photo of how the park looked when he had bought it, with sugarbeets planted right up to the door of the mansion, and ancient trees felled to make room for farm tractors and wide rolling sprinklers. Within his own property, he set about converting arable farmland back to grass. But despite pious talk of preserving hedgerows and field trees (some of the estate trees were temporarily protected by preservation orders), he realized that the farmers around Gunton were more likely, as farm prices improved, to cut down more trees and plow up more land for cash crops. "And there's no point in restoring all these buildings and then just having them surrounded by a thousand acres of sugar beets, is there?"

So, together with two like-minded neighbors, Martin began buying up as much as he could of the 1,500 acres that surrounded his restoration project. As prize 'Grade I' farmland in one of England's most fertile agricultural counties, it did not come cheap. But soon the three of them owned nearly 1,000 acres, replanted in grass and free of fences, as it had been 200 years before. The little Robert Adam church on the grounds, in the shape of a Doric temple, was restored. The Norfolk Windmills Trust took charge of a water-driven estate sawmill of the 1820s, which is operating once again. Every one of the 6,000 new trees he has planted is of the same species, and is located in the same place, as a tree on the original landscape architects' plan. We drive past clumps of saplings, fenced off against the new herds of deer he has imported to the park—trees that won't reach maturity until a century or more from now, when other eyes can admire Martin's backward-and-forward-looking vision.

In July of 1992—Martin has friends in high places—the Queen Mother helicoptered over from Sandringham to declare the park officially open. In a speech he gave in November 1993, her eldest grandson singled out Gunton Park as "a wonderful example of what private sector initiative can do with a hopeless case."[5]

· · ·

Rooms for the Night: The Country House Hotel

Many owners of country houses are willing, perhaps obliged to take in paying guests, like proprieters of upscale bed-and-breakfasts. About 230 homeowners in Britain are members of a group called Wolsey Lodges, founded in 1981. They make available bedrooms and (in most cases) meals—often taken with the family—for from four to eight paying guests. The owners of another 194 "Mansions and Manors" had, as of 1995, signed on with Andrew Grieve's Worcester-based agency called Discover Britain, Inc., which advertises only through overseas tour operators, partly to attract what they imagine will be a higher level of clientele, partly to reduce the danger of burglary from unsavory British types who might make use of an overnight stay to evaluate the contents and the security system. "Many of our owners are nervous about offering their accommodation to the criminal fraternity,"

Mr. Grieve writes. "Touch wood, to date all our clients from North America and other parts of the globe have been entirely trustworthy."

Although most of the Wolsey Lodges and Discover Britain houses are comfortable, some elegant, and a few genuinely historic, they are, as a rule, too small or unpretentious to meet my working definition of a country house. They tend to come closer in size to one's image of an old rectory or old vicarage—which, in fact, many of them are; or to a lesser manor or a substantial farmhouse. Those I have stayed at were handsome, solid houses of a certain age with a few spare bedrooms and added creature comforts. The few that could be called genuinely historic tend to be owned by people—often single or widowed ladies—who take pride in their antiques and gardens as well as their swimming pools and meals, and offer the curious traveller the chance to spend a few days in a listed historic house. Perhaps ten Wolsey Lodge properties are grand enough, and possessed of sufficient surrounding acres, to be considered traditional country houses, including a Palladian mansion in Northumberland designed by James Paine in 1740, and still owned by the builder's family; at least two Wolsey Lodges have been in the same family for more than 500 years. On Andrew Grieve's Discover Britain list, a similar number of substantial historic houses offer rooms for the night, including two 19th-century Scottish castles, beautiful Delbury Hall (1753) in Shropshire, and Hammerwood Park (1792) in East Sussex, bought by young David Pinnegar in 1982, and painstakingly restored by him since.

The National Trust offers vacation rentals by the week at 190 cottages, small houses, or flats scattered about its various landholdings in England (plus another 31 in Wales and Northern Ireland), more than half of them along the southwest coast. Several of these are former workers' cottages or gatehouse lodges on large country estates, including two very appealing Thameside cottages for rent at Cliveden. In five cases—at Cotehele in Cornwall, Compton Castle in Devon, Standen in Sussex, Hanbury Hall in Worcester, and Ightham Mote in Kent, one can actually rent a flat within or facing the main house.

A similar service is offered by the Landmark Trust, a charity established in 1965 in order to rescue unusual small buildings of historical significance—cottages, disused forts, castle towers, gatehouses, garden buildings, and follies—and turn them into vacation accommodations. They rent out two apartments at Hampton Court Palace, the top two floors of the tower at Canons Ashby, and a triangular Gothic Temple (James Gibbs, 1741) in the gardens at Stowe, where a tiny kitchen, a bathroom, two minimal bedrooms, and a stairwell have been squeezed into the three cylindrical corner towers; the circular central gallery is gloriously vaulted. "It does have all the modern conveniences," the Landmark Trust notes, "if in rather surprising places, and the heating has to work hard to be noticed; but we hope that the splendour of the temple and its surroundings will compensate those who stay here."[6]

At least eighteen Landmark Trust properties are on the present or former grounds of English country estates. But the only "whole" English country house in their current catalogue is Wortham Manor in Devon, a medieval/Tudor house near (and not unlike) the National Trust's Cotehele. It accommodates fifteen, and was going, in 1996, for £1,100 to

£1,900 ($1,760–3,000) a week, depending on the season. "Those who stay here," says the Trust, "have an unrivalled opportunity to experience the life of a prosperous, and quite sophisticated Tudor gentleman...."[7]

Norman Hudson's 1994 *Historic House & Garden Directory* listed 25 major country houses—including places such as Blairquhan Castle, Duns Castle, and Manderston in Scotland, and Kingston House and Weston Park in England—which offered overnight accommodations, either in the main house or in self-catering (i.e., kitchen-equipped) out-buildings on the estate. At Weston Park, the Earl of Bradford, who used to be in the restaurant business in London, offers a good dinner-bed-and-breakfast deal (primarily for groups) in the mansion's 28 spare bedrooms. Cobham Hall and Stowe, both now boarding schools, can sleep hundreds of guests outside of term time, for summer courses or other events. Leeds and Hever Castles, Castle Ashby, Brocket Hall, Catton Hall, Chicheley Hall, Noseley Hall, Oakley Hall, and Somerley all offered overnight rooms as well, but only for people attending special functions (primarily conferences) taking place in the house—although Castle Ashby has occasionally offered weekend "house parties" for up to 40 individual guests as well, at about £280 ($420) per person. Before it was sold to an American, one used to be able to rent *all* of Allerton Park, Lord Mowbray's ancestral home in Yorkshire—along with his staff—for £15,000 ($25,000) a week, plus expenses, for up to eight people. ("The Owner will not be present.") All of Blairquhan can be similarly rented, as can a number of shooting and fishing estates in Scotland and the North of England. Several large houses not normally open to the public will rent rooms and serve meals for classic grouse- and pheasant-shooting weekends in season, for a single negotiated price.

· · ·

One solution that has been frequently chosen as a means of providing a viable future for a large and archaic country house is that of turning it into a full-time, full-scale commercial hotel.

The conversion of grand private houses into public hotels is not a new or exclusively a British idea. The resident owners of at least 66 private chateaux in France are willing to accommodate, and sometimes to feed, overnight guests. Three hundred ten independent commercial chateaux-hotels (and *"hostelleries d'atmosphère"*) in France were listed in a recent guide. Converted castle-*paradores* in Spain and *schlossen* on the Rhine, palazzi in Rome and Venice have been taking in paying guests for many years. It's a reasonable way to recycle a big, showy house that has grown too large for the members of one family, and too costly for them to maintain: a house, typically, with a grand dining room and two or more sitting rooms on the main floor, a dozen or more bedrooms upstairs, servants' quarters, and kitchens and other work spaces equipped to handle 18th- or 19th-century balls, banquets, and house parties. It may have a coach house, stable block, and other outbuildings that can be converted into additional bedrooms or recreation areas, as well as secluded gardens and park or woodland for strolling and sports.

Just as the country house way of life took root more naturally and pervasively in Britain than anywhere else, so the concept of the country house hotel has become—especially in the last thirty years—a phenomenon almost unique to this island. Many country house hotel owners make a point, in their advertising, of pretending that a stay at their establishment will feel exactly like a visit to Lord and Lady So-and-So's private country house party a hundred years ago—the only difference being that, sometime before you leave, you will be expected not simply to tip the staff, but to settle up (discreetly) a fairly substantial bill.

The first country house owners to opt for hotel conversion as a means of survival hit on the idea soon after World War II, at almost exactly the same time that the first peers decided to open their houses to day-trippers. The growing ownership of private cars after the war, and the end of petrol rationing in 1950 contributed to the success of both ventures. Francis Coulson opened his big Lake District house, Sharrow Bay—a place of no particular importance historically or architecturally—as a hotel in 1949, the same year that the Marquess of Bath opened Longleat to paying tourists. "It was the teas wot made us famous, that put us on the map," Brian Sack, who joined him there in 1952 recalled to a reporter. "Half-a-crown teas, 12.5 pence; people used to queue."[8] Dinner, bed, and breakfast at Sharrow Bay—which was apparently the first establishment to call itself a "country house hotel," in 1952—currently runs about £250 ($400) for two. Lord Bath died at 87 in 1992, but Coulson and Sack—and both pioneering country houses-become-businesses—were still going strong, after 46 years. By the late 1960s, a country house-turned-hotel might still be offering austere, unheated bedrooms; a single bathroom and WC for up to twenty guests; and a very basic dinner of soup, roast-potato-veg, and fruit pie with custard—which is pretty much what guests had been offered before the house became a hotel, give or take a few servants. Early entrants at what is now the top of the line included Peter Herbert at Gravetye Manor (for which he paid £28,000 in 1957; a single room then cost £2 a night), Martin and Trevor Skan at Chewton Glen (£50,000 in 1966), Paul and Kay Henderson at Gidleigh Park (£100,000 in 1977), and Tim Hart at Hambleton Hall (£110,000 in 1980). Fortunately for them, large country houses were unpopular and difficult to sell in the years before 1980—hence the bargain prices. Conversion costs, of course, add a great deal more to these figures, and improvements continue to multiply the capital investment. Between 1980 and 1990, Paul Henderson figures, the number of English country house hotels in the Egon Ronay guide with a rating of 75 or more (out of a possible 100: the crème de la crème, presumably) increased from eighteen to 86.

Most existing country house hotels were purchased during the 1980s by enterprising couples (a few of them Americans) from the hard-pressed gentry whose homes they once had been. A few have become part of hotel chains. Others have joined upscale marketing groups of their own. An astute entrepreneur named Richard Broyd has successfully rebuilt into luxury hotels two country houses which had formerly been schools—Hartwell House in Buckinghamshire, a Grade I Jacobean/Georgian house that was for five years the home-in-exile of Louis XVIII of France; and Middlethorpe Hall in York, an elegant William and Mary house once inhabited by the formidable diarist and traveler Lady Mary Wortley

Montagu. Broyd's company, called Historic House Hotels, also owns Bodysgallen Hall, a 17th-century manor on the north coast of Wales.

A small number of old-line country house owners have retained ownership of the family manse, while allowing it to be converted into a commercial hotel. Thornbury Castle near Bristol, and Alexander House in West Sussex, used to remind paying guests that their premises were the property, respectively, of Lord and Lady Portlethen, and the Earl and Countess of Alexander—although you were not likely to find them sitting next to you at dinner.

· · ·

How many country houses have been turned into hotels? One current guide lists 188 of them in England, Scotland, and Wales; but many of these are of the small, family-run "Wolsey Lodge" dimensions. A luxurious bound catalogue I found in several upscale hotel lounges included, in a recent edition, 103 double-page color spreads on what I would call country house hotels; but the number is no doubt limited to establishments willing to pay to be included.

My notion of a proper country house hotel includes a noble approach; at least a few acres of secluded garden and parkland; a certain amount of opulence in the downstairs rooms; and a building with a past—specifically, a building that spent at least a generation or two as a private family home before it became a hotel. British journalists have put the number at anywhere between 100 and 1,000. The most respected British hotel guide, founded by Egon Ronay, listed about 220 country houses-become-hotels in England in 1995. The rival Johansens guide included even fewer. Some of these have been radically converted and enlarged from their original shape and size, with new bedroom wings and "leisure spas" and conference facilities. In a few cases, it would be hard to find traces of the house where it all began. Others, with fewer than ten bedrooms, are probably more in the vicarage class. But in most cases, a major selling point is that the hotel still retains what the Ronay guide inspectors call a "genuine country house feel." Mention is always made of remaining gardens, acres, and historic features.

Among the amenities that apparently contribute to a "country house feel," according to the guides and brochures, are long, tree-lined entry drives; a gracious, well turned-out staff, sometimes in uniform—although smaller country house hotels may be run by a husband and wife team, Fawlty Towers fashion, with no more than two or three helpers; an impressive entrance hall (never a reception desk), with a grandish staircase to the bedrooms upstairs; and in the libraries and lounges, real books, oil paintings, fresh flowers, fine carpets, reproduction antique furniture, paneled walls, sculpted plaster (or wood-beamed) ceilings, chandeliers, and carved stone fireplaces with open fires, lit even on summer days that are chilly or wet. In the bedrooms, they may offer four-poster (or "half-tester" or "crown canopy") beds, turned down every evening; more repro-antique furniture (one piece hides the TV), fresh fruit and flowers, a trouser press, free mineral water and sherry, jars of sweets or homemade biscuits. Hatton Court near Gloucester provides teddy bears on the pillow, and plastic ducks for the Jacuzzi. In the fancier bathrooms, you may find marble and gold taps and bidets and separate showers and giant towels and terrycloth robes and a little basket full of famous-name toiletries.

In the grounds, a croquet lawn and a garden to stroll in are almost mandatory. Beyond that, tennis and swimming facilities (indoor as well as out) are becoming more and more common; so are putting greens, even nine- or eighteen-hole golf courses, horses to ride, lakes or rivers to fish, million-pound spas. But these upper-end attractions usually mean that a country house hotel is seriously trawling for the conference trade, as opposed to the casual vacation traveler. For the conference trade—which has become a highly competitive market, as more country house hotels join the hunt for a decreasing number of corporate functions—lavish "resort facilities" (whether or not they are ever used) can be the determining factor in attracting profitable gatherings of business and professional people.

Many hotels in England do not make it into the Ronay or Johansens guides. In 1989, the *Financial Times* declared that "There are now just under 200 country house hotels throughout Britain." One year later, the *Times* put the total at "400 or so."[9] But however many English establishments *call* themselves country house hotels, there are probably no more than 200 that were once "real" country houses, by my definition.

According to the Historic Houses Association, almost one fourth of the 400 country houses sold between 1972 and 1990 were converted into hotels. But by 1991 the British press was reporting that a hundred or more country house hotels were either in bankruptcy or up for resale, often for less than the owners had paid for them. The international recession, the Gulf War of 1991, a surfeit of costly hostelries too far from the centers of population, interest rates of fifteen to seventeen percent, and overeager new owners who hadn't a clue about the hotel business were all being blamed for having burst the country house hotel bubble.

"The country house hotel of the 1980s," wrote one reporter, who studied the phenomenon in 1991, "seemed to be reviving a tradition, but it was really just another transient moment in marketing, a glance backwards in time, packaged by Laura Ashley, scented by Culpepper, with soft soap and sweetness by Crabtree and Evelyn.... The country house hoteliers are realising," he concluded, "what the country house owners realised half a century ago, when they gave up their homes to the National Trust, or dry rot, and moved into service flats in Mayfair. Which is that country life, even with the luxury and the servants and the food and the leisure, can be just a little bit...dull?" "The trouble with these places out in the sticks," he was told by Tim Hart, the owner of Hambleton Hall, an elegant fifteen-bedroom hotel overlooking Rutland Water, "is that if you don't keep them pretty full, they can get pretty gloomy."[10]

·   ·   ·

I have stayed at about fifteen of these places, and had lunch or dinner at several more, and I must admit they can be rather fun. You puzzle over your road atlas and the directions in the brochure, get lost once or twice on narrow country lanes. Finally you come across an impressive opening in a long stone wall, inscribed "Toad Hall" or "Blandings Castle." (If this were a *real*, still-private country house there wouldn't be a nameplate, and the iron gates would probably be locked.) You drive for half a mile through leafy woods on a one-lane road. Suddenly there looms up before you a grandiose pile, more often than not Victorian Gothic.

There are handsome Tudor-through-Georgian country house hotels as well, even a few early 20th-century. Many successful conversions have been made of compact manor houses or former hunting lodges, without the spreading acres and the long theatrical approach. But most British country house hotels were originally built, or at least radically rebuilt, in the mid- to late 19th century. Such houses, designed to accommodate large numbers of guests and servants, tend to have the biggest kitchens and serving areas and the largest number of bedrooms, which makes them the most suitable for hotel conversion.

Hotel conversion means seeing to the roof, walls, central heating, and wiring; meeting demanding new fire codes; adding a modern bathroom to each bedroom, and fitting in all the new plumbing that implies; modernizing the kitchen, and meeting all the health inspector's strict demands; hiring a decorator to install new draperies, carpets, and pseudo-antique furnishings; redoing the garden; possibly adding an extra bedroom wing; and (if you are aiming at the £150-and-up-a-night trade, and such amenities are not already in place) putting in at least a tennis court and a pool.

Once you, the guest arrive—I am describing a composite experience—your suitcases are taken in the graveled forecourt. From the lofty entry hall (which may have stained glass windows, antlers, or copies of old paintings), you are shown up a carved oak staircase to your room, which will have a name instead of a number (The Peony Room, the Duchess of Westminster Room) and—in many hotels—sufficient space and seating places to host a small reception. The room will be smothered in yards of chintz, and provided with hunting prints, squashy chairs, imperial swags or a fourposter tent over the bed, a bowl of fruit and a cut-glass carafe of sherry, and views out over the terrace, the strutting peacocks, the rose garden, the croquet lawn. You bathe, nap, change ("smart dress" is expected, and sometimes mandatory), and descend for drinks in the 18th- or 19th-century Library or Salon, where you peruse the prix-fixe menu and choose from three to five frequently changing courses, typically good British-regional—produce from the kitchen garden, fish from the local stream, game from neighboring estates—with a few French truffles and flourishes. The cooking in country house hotels—served either in hushed and elegant halls, or former conservatories—gets more sophisticated, and more expensive, every year. Perhaps ten can claim to have genuine gourmet restaurants, but the quality of these will depend on the chef, and chefs move about. After dinner, liqueurs or port and coffee are served before open fires in yet another decorator-designed period lounge—the "period" often seems to be 1930, aspiring to Georgian—where you are expected to make small talk, and perhaps exchange addresses, with the other guests. Except for a few noisy Americans

Horsted Place Hotel, Sussex. Drawing room.

we encountered at golfing hotels in Scotland and at one snobbish house outside of Bath, and an international sprinkling at the very top places, the other guests are almost always British. Some country house hotels even boast of this fact in their ads.

Your fellow guests will tend to be reasonably well off, as well as British. From a survey of the brochures of the 25 leading country house hotels (according to their rankings in the Egon Ronay guide), I reckoned the median price for a double room at one of them in 1992 to be £125–130, or one and a half times that many dollars, which often (but not always) included a cooked breakfast and the 17.5 percent Value Added Tax. Dinners ran about £20–30, with beverages and tip extra. Things like croquet, swimming, tennis, fishing in the estate's own riverfront or lake, and perhaps the use of a putting green came free. You paid extra, when such things were available, for use of the adjacent golf course, the elaborate health spas that have been added to a number of houses, chauffered drives in the hotel's limousine or river launch, clay pigeon (or game bird) shooting, horseback riding, balloon rides, luncheon hampers, and the like. The average hotel in this elite group had only 21 bedrooms—which helps to explain the prices, and to maintain the "house party" ambience—and anywhere from ten to 5,000 acres of grounds. (The larger properties go with Scottish shooting-party estates.) These 25 houses were built between 1320 and 1920, but most of them tend to look heavily Victorian on the outside, and to be decorated inside in a conservative, English-rich-people's style, with lots of overstuffed chairs and sofas piled with cushions, Oriental carpets, gilt framed mirrors, real books on the library shelves, bowls of potpourri and fresh flowers, old prints, old oil paintings, and the owner's (or decorator's) second-best antiques. By 1994, when my wife and I stayed at five of the top-ranked country house hotels, stopped by three others, and stayed at four with slightly lower rankings, the average room rate had gone up to £150 ($230) a night—from £98 ($150) at Studley Priory in Oxfordshire to £225 ($344) for one of the cheap rooms at Cliveden. In 1994, dinners at these hotels cost about £30 ($45) per person, not counting drinks. We were sometimes able to make money-saving deals for two- or three-night stays.

The difference between the interiors of such places and those of "real" country houses is sometimes difficult to discern. The wood panelling and carving, the decorative plaster ceilings and elaborate chimneypieces may be as good as those of the National Trust house or private stately just a mile away. Cliveden is a National Trust house as well as a country house hotel, and therefore as luxuriously furnished as it is impeccably maintained; but the standards are no less high at places like Chewton Glen, Hambleton Hall, Hartwell House, Hintlesham Hall, Le Manoir aux Quat'Saisons, and Stapleford Park. Country house hotels tend to have far fewer truly historic or valuable objects on display, for obvious reasons. You cannot keep your guests behind ropes, or post a guard in every room. On the other hand, most lived-in country houses tend to look more shabby than top country house hotels, because of the killing cost of maintaining real antiques—antique fabrics, in particular. Even so, the new-style squire-plus-innkeeper is warned to expect to make a £150,000 ($250,000) investment *per room* (1989 figures)—and no profits for three to five years. "As a business," wrote the *Financial Times*, "it fits the description of the California wine industry—the only way to make a small fortune is to start with a large one."[11]

They do, however, still like to pretend. The 1992 brochure of a fourteen-room hotel in West Sussex (where the overnight rates for two started at £185, or $325) invited one to

Enjoy the unique experience of being a house guest at Alexander House—one of the last private mansions in Sussex, with its own secluded park . . . Sussex has always been the special domain of families who preserve the better qualities of life, a respect for traditional values, an appreciation of comfort and the right to live privately in unselfconscious ease.

For hundreds of years, this part of England has been the bastion of a handful of houses built to preserve this style of living. Magnificent mansions peek through rhododendrons and yews at some of the most beautiful rolling countryside in the world. Neighbours travel in chauffeured Bentleys and Daimlers to cocktails and dinners in glittering, candle-lit rooms. Homes are filled with house parties of old friends and new, sharing the joy and magic that only a great English house can create.

Records trace the estate from 1332 when John Atte Fenn made it his home, to the famous poet John Shelley in the 19th Century through to the ownership by the Governor of the Bank of England at the turn of the century. Alexander House is perhaps the most special of all the Sussex mansions and is often the setting for stylish private parties and exclusive wedding receptions. The mansion is named Alexander House after the Right Honourable Earl Alexander, the present Chairman who, with the Countess, hosts many events at Alexander House throughout the social calendar.

Alexander House is renowned for its particularly delicious classic English and French cuisine, rare wines and vintage liqueurs, amongst a myriad of other pleasures you can enjoy: A cosy break-fast in bed, contemplating the pleasures of the day ahead; archery, croquet, tennis, a leisurely stroll down to the river or an invigorating walk around the park, as well as golf and trout fishing nearby. Also informal lunches in the library, sunny afternoon teas in the garden, witty conversations over classical dinners; backgammon, charades, or billiards—perhaps impromptu singing around the piano, by the glow of the log fire—and then to bed feeling snug, secure and indulged, happily distant from the rest of the world.

One great golfing hotel in Scotland—Greywalls at Gullane—was designed as a private house by Sir Edwin Lutyens in 1901. The 1992 British Open was held virtually on its doorstep. There are other Lutyens manors-turned-hotel in Hampshire and Sussex. Lumley Castle near Durham (which bills itself as "no ordinary hotel," and indeed it is not), was built by Sir Ralph Lumley in the 1390s. The famous Lumley Horseman, supposedly a statue of Edward III, used to preside from a shelf over the Great Hall (remodeled by Vanbrugh in 1722), a room used today for pseudo-medieval banquets. Thornbury Castle near Bristol was a royal house for 33 years, after Henry VIII confiscated it from the Duke of Buckingham in 1521. He and Anne Boleyn stayed there in 1535; his daughter, Mary Tudor, made it her home for several years. Today, it advertises itself as "the only Tudor castle in England operating as a hotel," which it may well be, since Lumley, Langley, Taunton, and Amberley Castle hotels are all older.

The three most distinguished country house hotels in England, architecturally and historically, could have been found listed in stately home guides or histories until just a short while ago. All three are Grade I listed.

Hartwell House, a part-Jacobean, part-Georgian (and part good imitation-old) mansion near Aylesbury in Buckinghamshire, is one of three grand houses bought and restored by Richard Broyd since 1979. After cashing out of a successful personnel business in London, Broyd has devoted his considerable fortune to rescuing endangered buildings he admires, collecting appropriate antiques and art works to furnish them, and then turning them into hotels.

After buying, restoring, and converting Bodysgallen (Bods-gat'ln) Hall in Wales in 1979–81, and Middlethorpe Hall near York in 1984–85, Broyd's company leased Hartwell House from the Ernest Cook Trust in 1986, then spent three years on its restoration. Ernest Cook, grandson of the pioneering Victorian travel agent Thomas Cook, was another rich man who enjoyed buying historic buildings "at risk," in order to save them. Cook had acquired Hartwell House in 1938 from the Lee family—related to the Lees of Ditchley Park (Oxfordshire) and Virginia—whose home it had been for more than three centuries.

The estate originally belonged to a branch of the Hampden family, whose seat in Buckinghamshire is now the headquarters of an insurance company. Portions of the existing entrance front were probably built by Sir Alexander Hampden around 1600. Hampden's sister and heiress had married Sir Thomas Lee, and in 1617 the Lee family settled into Hartwell for 321 years, barring a period of five years (1809–1814) when it was leased as the

Amberley Castle Hotel, Sussex.

home-in-exile of King Louis XVIII of France and a mob of his impecunious courtiers, who raised chickens, rabbits, and vegetables on the roof.

This and subsequent occupations resulted in considerable damage, especially a disastrous fire which broke out in the attic in 1963, when the house was leased to a girls' boarding school. The fire not only gutted the whole of the upper floor, but also destroyed some of the prize plaster ceilings below it. Because of this, architectural historians have had some trouble identifying the evolving aspect and successive designers of Hartwell. But at

Hartwell House Hotel, Buckinghamshire. Guest bedroom.

least three leading Georgian architects—James Gibbs, Henry Keene, and James Wyatt—had a hand in alterations made between 1740 and 1780.

Even so, the building that guests at Hartwell House Hotel admire today is largely the creation of Eric Throssell of Aylesbury, a skillful backward-looking architect hired by Broyd in 1986. Throssell was given virtual carte blanche to make of this sadly abused building something elegant, luxurious, and convincingly "historic."

Since the two bedroom floors (including a long gallery) had lost their fine detailing in the 1963 fire, Throssell was able to sweep them clear of the old dormitories and create 33 new bedrooms or bedroom suites with panelled doors, plaster cornices, and fireplaces, decorated in the flowered-chitz and fourposter norm of today's upscale country house hotels. All, of course, have private bathrooms.

Downstairs, he created three adjoining dining rooms. The 50-foot-long main dining room (made out of three smaller spaces), painted pale yellow, is modeled on an early 19th-century John Soane design, with shallow arches and coffered domes, and a convincing imitation of Soane's plasterwork and detail. The impressive, part-Jacobean staircase (dismantled and stored during the house's occupation by troops during World War II, then damaged in the 1963 fire) was turned around to hide a new elevator and refitted with lively carved figures on the newel posts, some of which are original. The room around it is done in clever imitation-Strawberry Hill Gothic, a late 18th-century style the original house never quite got around to. Altogether original—in addition to the facades, and the shapes of several ground floor rooms—are the bookcases, some of the panelling, and parts of the 18th-century plasterwork ceilings and carved chimneypieces of the elegant sequence of public rooms.

Broyd managed to find and buy back not only antique furnishings originally at Hartwell, then sold off in the 1938 auctions; but also hundreds of other bits and pieces sympathetic with the building and its history, including copies of appropriate paintings and memorabilia of the poor "people's king" of France. I talked to him over an elaborate, old-fashioned tea, served on silver in the Great Hall, while a private party was in progress in the rooms and lawns beyond. His spoken sentences fall naturally into a refined version of English prose style.

Historic House Hotels as a company was founded with the express intention of conservation; of providing a new use for certain categories of house which might be at risk. In those days, we pioneered the use of country houses as hotels, before the bandwagon got going in the nineteen eighties. Of course, there were other people, way back—Messrs. Coulson and Sack at Sharrow Bay, Gravetye with Peter Herbert. Then, in the new wave as it were, Tim Hart at Hambledon and the Smedleys at Ston Easton were all going before we opened Bodysgallen in July nineteen eight-one.

But we were still as it were in the vanguard, before a few foolish souls decided that running country house hotels was a way to get rich, which I promise you it isn't. They all got involved in the mid-eighties, and rather devalued the concept. A lot of them are being sorted out now, often sadly, tragically for the individuals concerned—but for the overall benefit, I feel constrained to say, of the overall market.

We look in a house for four criteria. Firstly, it's got to be big enough to provide a minimum of thirty rooms. Secondly, it's got to be Grade One or Grade Two-star. Thirdly, it has to have enough land to protect the setting. [Hartwell House came with 80 acres.] And fourthly, it's got to be in an area which can support the venture commercially once it's been converted. All three of our country houses are on the edge of large medium-sized towns or small cities. And that I think is meritorious, firstly in terms of market, secondly in terms of conservation. On the edge of a large town where there are pressures for building, you can help keep the town at bay, and be an ornament to it—as well as providing a service to it, and providing employment within it. Those are the ideas which governed the establishment of the company, and by which we run it.

Why, then, had his company only bought and converted three country houses in fourteen years? "Well, the Savoy Group doesn't expand very often. I don't think there's a place for limitless expansion. It is not an activity where, if you're doing things to this standard, you can justify by commercial criteria. You need to be able to afford to do it. You've got to assume a capital investment philosophy. After you've converted the house, if you can then cover your running costs, you've got it. You can't necessarily pay back the interest on your investment."

Then why, I wondered, would anyone do it? "Why would anyone build these houses in the first place? As I said earlier on—you'll find this on the tape—Historic House Hotels

Hartwell House Hotel, Buckinghamshire.

was founded as a matter of conservation, to try to provide a new use for certain country houses which fulfilled our criteria. We would never want to take on, for instance, a national asset like Blenheim or Woburn or Chatsworth. We would never want to take a house out of private family use. I'd be very sorry to take on a house with all its original contents intact, because you couldn't use those. These chairs we're sitting on now, these are brand new. It really doesn't matter what happens to these, we'll re-cover them, or eventually even dispose of them. What's on display can be old, but what's in use has to be serviceable."

The only expansion that had taken place at Hartwell House since 1989 was the conversion of the old coach house into a conference center, with a new Soane-esque "orangery" tacked on behind it, containing an indoor swimming pool and the usual luxury spa facilities. The old stables have been converted into sixteen additional bedrooms "for guests seeking seclusion and privacy," according to the brochure, particularly guests attending meetings in the conference center. "You don't want the place here dominated by men with briefcases," Broyd said, echoing an idea I had frequently heard regarding country house hotels that go after the conference trade. "A couple of ladies having morning coffee don't want to be surrounded by portable telephones. So the answer is to have a separate building for the business people." In the "lean winter months," he said—particularly at midweek—the whole hotel is sometimes taken over by a single corporate event.

"The weekends are for Londoners on break, or holidaymakers. Midweek is for the business trade. That crowd currently having tea on the terrace is celebrating a wedding anniversary. A small group came to stay last night, dinner for about eight; then lunch and tea for thirty today."

What amenities were essential for top-level country house hotels? "I think it's important to have more than just comfortable rooms and a nice house. At this size, I think you need the swimming pool, and the tennis courts, the spas and gymnasia. It's a club as well, we have local members who are very fond of the Hartwell Spa and Club. And then the food has to be good. I personally think that Michelin stars [Hartwell had a star in 1991, then lost it in 1994], all these ratings are a complete pain in the neck, because they're there one year and not the next. And if you're running a hotel consistently, these things follow the chef. I am extremely cynical of and irritated by award systems run by those who are busy promoting the motor industry, whether they are motoring organizations or the French manufacturers of motorcar tires. And that is on the record."

What does one do to promote a costly country house hotel then, if not depend on ratings and awards?

Well, simply opening a place like this is newsworthy. You attract a lot of publicity. And after that, you keep the pot boiling. I prefer a low profile myself; my style is not, for instance, Bob Payton's. Perhaps more like the couple at Gidleigh. Charming people. American.

One last point I would make. I think this is a suitable use for a building like this, which fulfills the fifth criterion by which we have chosen the house—that it is a suitable use. You do not get the enormous numbers of people [you would get at a house open to the public], you do not need the enormous car parks, the lavatory blocks, the cafeteria, the gift shop. But you are using every square inch of the building, you need the tack room, the boot room—without the crowds you associate with a house that's open, whether properties of that wonderful association, the National Trust, or houses like Woburn which are still privately owned. So I think this use for a house is sympathetic to its original purpose, and is not in conflict with it.

·   ·   ·

Stapleford Park in Leicestershire (pronounced 'Stappleford') was begun in 1500 for Thomas Sherard, whose descendants became the earls of Harborough. Most of the present house dates from the 17th century, although some rooms were redecorated in the Adam style in the next century, and the south front is Victorian. The 4th Earl, one reads, "attained notoriety by refusing to allow the Belvoir and Cottesmore hounds to draw the Stapleford coverts." But the Gretton family, who succeeded as owners in the 1890s, were avid hunters, and built a spectacular set of stables on the grounds. The Cottesmore Hunt still meets on the estate, and experienced horsemen who stay at Stapleford Park today are invited to ride with the Cottesmore, Belvoir, or Quorn Hunts in season. In 1987, the 3rd Lord Gretton, heir to the Bass brewing fortune—having tried and failed at the amusement park game—sold the house and grounds to an American advertising man and entrepreneur named Bob Payton, who had already made a reputation for his popular chain of Chicago-style pizza and ribs restaurants in England. Most critics praised his conversion of Stapleford Park into a hotel, with 35 spacious bedrooms decorated by seventeen different celebrity designers, a Capability Brown parkland, and a unique blend of great food, over-the-top luxury, and American-style welcome. It's one place where, one is told, a man does *not* have to wear a tie to dinner, although I never saw a man at dinner without one. There are barbecue lunches in the summer, hamburgers and hot dogs available year round, and a basketball court and horsehoe pitch as well as croquet, tennis, riding, and lake fishing. Though most journalists who wrote about it loved it ("as soon as I am a millionaire I shall go and live at Stapleford Park for ever," wrote a visitor from the *Daily Telegraph*), a few traditionalists carped. One called it "an English country theme park for adults." My own favorite sport at Stapleford was staring out my window at the sheep under the great trees, moving at their own leisurely pace as truck-driving shepherds tried to nudge them about.

In July of 1991, after just three years of operation, and an investment of more than £6 million ($10.6 million)—£600,000 for the house, the rest for remodeling—Bob Payton decided to put Stapleford up for sale for slightly more than he and his backers had put into it. A number of hotel industry observers believed that Payton had simply got too far in debt to get out, and regarded the offer to sell as a sign of the end of the inflated country house hotel bubble of the 1980s. According to the *Sunday Times*, more than 100 country house hotels were in receivership at the time.[12]

But all he wanted, Payton wrote me at the time, was to let the next owner spend the £4 or £5 million more required to put in the swimming pool, golf course (they have 500 acres, and the requisite planning permissions), leisure spa, and 30 more rooms it would take to make the hotel profitable in the long run. "Our passion," he wrote, "was actually for saving the building and establishing its reputation. I wanted to leave enough development opportunity for the next purchaser." He admitted that the Gulf War, high interest rates, the 1989 stock market crash, and the continued recession had not helped; but that his whole career had been based on inventing new concepts (including five different restaurant ideas). "My thing is not operating them forever. I like finding other people to do that. Stapleford was a one-off and doesn't fit into the My Kinda Town group of restaurants chain"—the overall name of his culinary enterprises, now a public company.

Payton sounded slightly bitter, however, when interviewed in 1991, about the very upmarket guests he had tried to attract. "They won't be satisfied with log fires and flowered chintz and a walk in the park," he said. "They want everything for ten minutes: swim, ride, sauna, exercise, massage . . ." When the house did not sell after a year, he withdrew it from the market, and continued to run it himself.

On July 10, 1994, I talked with Bob Payton—a large, hearty, self-assured man who wore a baseball cap and chain-drank Diet Cokes, on the terrace of Stapleford Park, where my wife and I were staying for three days. He explained the reasons behind his unusual venture.

"I mean, what am I? I'm an entrepreneur—I hate calling myself an entrepreneur—what it is is I'm a guy who can't work for anybody else.... I've always been big on taking build-ings and giving them a new life." He described how he had opened the first Chicago Pizza Pie Factory in a building opposite St. James's Palace and the oldest pub in London, then did the same with a Victorian department store in Bath. "I came to Leicestershire for a weekend stay with some friends. Driving through some village I found a derelict school for sale, a one-room schoolhouse, which I bought in nineteen seventy-nine for nine thousand pounds and converted into a weekend cottage for myself." (Payton had originally come to England in 1973, as creative director of the London office of the J. Walter Thompson advertising agency.)

> Because I like creating things, basically. So then lo and behold, in nineteen eighty-five I had nine restaurants and we were just about to open another one in Paris. And Stapleford Park came up for sale. I knew about the house because we hunt around here—we go fox hunting. And in April nine-teen eighty-five I pick up *Country Life* and there it is for sale. I had never been around a stately home—I'm not one for touring National Trust houses and that sort of thing. So I talked to a friend of mine, the lady who keeps my horses at livery, and she knew the Grettons. So she said I'll ring up Lord Gretton and see if you can have a look around.... I thought I'd look at it and see if there's development potential here; I thought, I've done pizza now, I want to do something else.
>
> So I came walking through the front door and it was just obvious to me, seeing the house—even in that sad state [the Grettons were using only a small corner]—what it could be. Because it was a house used to celebrate life... And I thought just, what a wonderful house! I went around to all these other country house hotels, and I hated them, because they were all stuffy and pompous, and the staff always seemed to be better than the guests, all that kind of crap. And I thought, none of them are *fun*. And these houses, when they used to be in existence, were fun, they were happy places. I mean, this was a hunting lodge, this wasn't the Grettons' big house. The big house was in Belgrave Square, or up by the brewery.... And what I've tried to do more than anything else is keep the integrity of the house, rather than the hotel.

The house had nine bedrooms and three bathrooms when he bought it. It now has 42 bedrooms, each with its own bathroom. Among many other changes, Payton's architect divided the huge Victorian ballroom in two vertically, to create more space upstairs for guest rooms. Payton cited a number of things he had done to maintain the illusion of its being a house rather than a hotel, such as refusing to have a reception desk. Other coun-try house hotels do that, he conceded.

> But, a), I also live here, and b), I decorated it myself, so it's my house. . . Have you seen the sev-enteenth-century wing with the big inscription "William Large Sherard Repaired This Building Anno Domini 1633"? And I added a little stone under it that's just this big, that says "And Bob Payton Did His Bit, 1988." To me that's the tradition and the integrity of this building. I mean I tried to do it in my own way, but in keeping with what went on here before. Because I'm sure that in 1633 everybody in Leicestershire was ringing everybody else and saying, "Have you seen what Billy Sherard had put on the side of his building?" And so I do this one little thing and the press blow it up into me desecrating all this English heritage.
>
> And the idea of getting all these designers to do the rooms, OK? The spirit behind that was

Stapleford Park Hotel, Leicestershire.

when they built this house they rang Grinling Gibbons and they said, "Hey Grin, come up with your chisel and some wood," and they said to Capability Brown, "Bring some seeds and a few trees and shrubs," and they rang Robert Adam and said "Bring some marble," and all that kind of stuff. And so what I did is I went to the craftsmen of today—the Tiffanys, the Turnbull and Assers, the people who if you will create style in their own fields.... And I said, give [it to] me in your own milieu, you know. This is a Victorian gentleman's hunting lodge, that was the brief for this, because that's what I believe it was, with the stables. And I've always seen myself as a reincarnated Victorian.

He discussed one designer, assigned to decorate the master bedroom, who missed his point.

What she did was she gave me a bedroom that looked like Cliveden! It looked like Lady Astor's bedroom. And I said, "I've seen all this stuff before. I don't want to do that. Everybody does floral chintz!" First of all, seventy-five percent of the people who stay here are men, right? It works as a corporate retreat; it works best when somebody takes the whole house. Which we do thirty, forty, fifty days a year. And the corporates like it because it is very massive. It's my house. The bathrooms are big because I'm a big guy. Right? The beds are high off the ground. It's all done with somebody's specific vision. I haven't gone to an interior designer and said, "How do I do a hotel?" I say, this is how I live my life, this is what I want in my house.

    Although it's a huge house, all the rooms are on a very human scale. Everybody walks down that staircase and says, "I could see myself living here."...My philosophy is, people are coming into the country for the weekend, and they want to hang around like they're in their own house. I've got this in-house video where for three hours a day you can see the Stapleford Park story. Another twelve hours you can watch song and dance videos, 'cause I'm a real Gene Kelly and Busby Berkeley fan. So you see what I like watching on television.

So yeah, it's very much driven by how I want to be treated, and how I want to look after other people....What they all want is, they want the comfort, they want the luxury, they want big chairs, big sofas, comfortable beds, and men want manly stuff.

While boasting of his growing repeat business, and insisting that if he can just get "the corporates" to come and and look at Stapleford they will buy it as a meeting venue ("there's not another house in the meeting business that's got sixteen-foot Georgian windows the way we do"), he admitted to the problems of his "Sunny Leicestershire" location. "If this thing was where Cliveden was we'd be full every day of the week." He envied Lord Brocket and Richard Broyd their nearness to London; but points out that his own favorite country house hotel in England—Gidleigh Park in Devonshire—is even farther from London, far off the beaten track, at the end of a long one-lane road. But its owner, Paul Henderson (another American) has made Gidleigh Park—as Payton has made Stapleford—a "destination resort," primarily because of the celebrated excellence of Gidleigh's food and wine. Payton is less generous to Richard Broyd at Hartwell, who is clearly not his kind of guy. (Even so, he concedes, "I wish I were as successful as he is.") "I once said to John Sinclair"—the former manager of Cliveden,

John, if you *gave* me this building I wouldn't know what to do with it. It's not me, it's not what I do....For me, my personality at the core is about lifestyle. Right? I want you to come to the country, feel comfortable in my house—you don't have to wear a tie to dinner. I want to serve Michelin-three-star cheeseburgers at lunchtime, I want to serve the best Caesar salad of anybody in town...My thing is about lifestyle and just trying to have a good time, and there are more people who *don't* know about food and wine than there are people who do. And the wine snobs, fine, let them go to Gravetye Manor, let them go to Gidleigh.

But what Henderson doesn't have is he doesn't have a set of riding stables, and Malcolm doing the clay pigeon shooting and the pheasant shooting, and he doesn't have the space. The space around here is incredible, wall to wall—a hundred years ago, everybody came for the hunting.

I bring him back to the subject of his putting Stapleford Park up for sale, and moving on to something else.

The next guy who comes along to buy it can put in the golf course and the swimming pool and add another thirty bedrooms, to make it a major commercial success; then it can be run by Sheraton or Hilton or whoever. But they would be nuts to come and buy it and then turn it into another Cliveden or Hartwell, OK? Because it's got such a distinct personality. This is a Gleneagles—a Gleneagles *house*, as opposed to a Gleneagles Hotel. Gleneagles [a large, legendary golf-and-sporting hotel in Scotland] would understand how to market it.

I could do more of these—'cause what I like to do is creating them. I gotta tell you, the satis-

Stapleford Park Hotel, Leicestershire. Entry forecourt.

faction I get out of this thing is all psychological. One day hopefully I'll sell it for a lot of money and I'll make a profit on it, but I didn't go into it for that. I did it because I wanted to do it, and I've had an amazing experience. I don't believe in the forseeable future anybody will do it on this scale, this quality again—the marble floors, the giant tubs, the real nickel taps.

At the time we spoke, he was doing up a substantial cottage with a walled garden into a four-bedroom independent unit, with its own living room, dining room, and kitchen, the decoration subsidized by Coca-Cola and MGM (with whose products he had deep personal connections), Range Rover, and IBM. I asked if he planned, for the time being, to keep adding on—like the 19th-century owner of Winchester House in California, who felt that as long as she kept adding rooms to her house she wouldn't die. "As long as I find a way to continue being creative, I'll keep doing it. But as to whether it will stay my home, I don't know. Do I think I'll die here? I don't know. That all depends on when I die."

One week later—in the dining room at Gidleigh Park, from his friend Paul Henderson—I learned that Bob Payton had died three days after our conversation, in an automobile accident not far from Stapleford Park.

. . .

The most famous and by far the most opulent country house hotel is Cliveden (pronounced "CLIVdn"), overlooking the Thames Valley near Maidenhead, just twenty miles west of London. It's an immense Italianate villa essentially designed by Sir Charles Barry—architect of the Houses of Parliament—between 1850 and 1851, so that the Duke of Sutherland could have somewhere to receive Queen Victoria in appropriate state. (The duke owned two larger houses, also designed or redesigned by Barry; but they were in far-off Scotland and Staffordshire.)

The present house at Cliveden replaced a manor built in 1666 for the 2nd Duke of Buckingham, which had entertained Swift, Pope, and the first two King Georges, and been leased to Frederick Prince of Wales (son of George II) from 1739 to 1751. "Rule Britannia" was sung for the first time in its garden amphitheatre, as part of a masque commissioned for the prince's daughter's birthday in 1740.

That house burned down in 1795. Cliveden II, built in 1824, also burned down, in 1849. In 1869 Barry's new house was bought by the Duke of Sutherland's son-in-law, the Marquess—later 1st Duke—of Westminster, which made Cliveden the home of three of the wealthiest dukes in British history, as well as an heir to the throne. Westminster remodeled the grand interiors in a heavy, Hearst-Castle style. There *are* bits left from the two earlier houses, notably an immense arcaded terrace overlooking the great parterre, and a number of 18th-century garden buildings. The odd clock tower alongside the stable court dates from 1861.

Its last private owners were the Anglo-American Astor family. William Waldorf (later 1st Viscount) Astor, from New York, bought Cliveden in 1893, Frenchified the interiors, added formal gardens and a great number of antique and Italian urns, statues, and sarcophagi outside (as he did at Hever Castle, his other English seat); the lascivious nudes-and-cupids fountain at the head of the main drive; a Japanese water garden; and a long 1619 stone balustrade imported whole—over the protests of the Italian government—from Cardinal Scipio's casino in the Villa Borghese (the one in Rome now is a copy). In 1906 he moved to Hever Castle, and made a wedding present of Cliveden to his son and his son's American wife Nancy. As Lady Astor, she achieved considerable notoriety both as a witty society hostess and (in 1919) as the first woman member of Parliament. Maintained by a staff that included 50 gardeners, twelve stablemen, and twelve maids before 1914, Cliveden became a haven for literary and political celebrities (Balfour, Curzon, Churchill, Kipling, James) between the wars, the gathering place of the so-called "Cliveden Set" in the late 1930s (see pp. 36–38), and the locale of a Tory party sex scandal in 1963.

Cliveden, Buckinghamshire.

The second Viscount Astor gave Cliveden to the National Trust in 1942—one of the first houses they agreed to take over—but the family continued to live there until his son died in 1966. Deciding that Cliveden was too big, too grand, and too costly to keep up as a mere tourist venue, the Trust leased it for fifteen years to Stanford University to serve as its "Education Abroad" base in England. When Stanford left in 1984, the Trust issued a call for new proposals for its use, and received about 100 responses—for schools, corporate offices, a trade union headquarters, etc. In the end, they accepted the offer of the Blakeney hotel chain. Under the terms of a 300-page 45-year lease agreement, "Cliveden Hotel Ltd.," which spent two years and £3 million ($4 million) on the roof, new bathrooms, and redecorating, is obliged not only to maintain the interiors and the private gardens, but also to allow hoi polloi access to three big rooms downstairs two afternoons a week, between April and October.

The 37 bedrooms and suites upstairs, which went for £245 to £685 ($380–1,065) a night in 1996—80 percent of the overnight guests, one is reminded, are British—are immense, individually decorated, and named after famous owners or guests of the house. Alongside the infamous Profumo, Keeler & Co. outdoor swimming pool was added, in 1990, a traditional looking garden pavillion which houses another eighteen-meter pool, plus the spa, saunas, gym, steam rooms, massage and beauty centers. Nearby are squash courts, indoor and outdoor tennis courts. The hotel keeps two horses for riding, has a four-hole practice golf course, and a billiard room downstairs in the mansion. The house Daimler will fetch you from the house heliport to the 1869 porte cochere, or drive you to Ascot. The house's 1911 motor launch will carry you, and your champagne lunch, to Henley for the races. Although they suggest black tie for dinner, the most elegantly dressed men I have encountered at Cliveden have been members of the skilled and deferential staff of 146, who play their period parts with astonishing ease.

In 1991, my wife and I stopped by for Kirs Royale in the giant hall, where we were hovered over by a fleet of footmen in morning dress, and ate excellent £30 ($50) lunches in a dining room overlooking the 17th-century terrace, the 19th-century parterre, the 18th-century beech woods, and the silvery S-bend of the Maidenhead reach of the timeless Thames—a vista, the National Trust reasonably suggests, "perhaps unequalled by any other English country house." From the dining room at lunch time, one also overlooks the plebian tourists the National Trust permits to wander about the 376-acre grounds for £2.80 ($4.30). They gape up from the terrace at the dining room windows and aim their camcorders at you like guns. An overnight stay three years later (despite the noise of arriving cars on the gravelled forecourt; the more expensive rooms overlook the quiet garden) only confirmed my original response. It may not have been Bob Payton's cup of tea; but from tales I have heard of her house parties, I'm willing to believe that the current management at Cliveden entertains its guests more graciously than Lady Astor did hers.

· · ·

Given the fact that perhaps 100 substantial country houses in England, and another 100 lesser ones, seem to have prospered in the form of hotels—and that this "prosperity" must remain uncertain for all but a handful at the top—just how viable is hotel conversion as a means of preserving country houses of importance?

First, very few country house hotels (beyond the three just discussed, and perhaps a dozen others) are buildings of real architectural or historical significance. Among those most respected as hotels, Gidleigh Park in Devon was a comfortable and agreeably situated "stockbroker Tudor" manor of the 1920s, not unlike hundreds of others. Before its new owners took over in 1966, Chewton Glen in Hampshire was an undistinguished brick eight-bedroom house of the 1890s; it has since been transformed into an American-style "country club" resort, with 58 bedrooms, a £5 million ($7.5 million) health center, and a staff of 140. Big Victorian or Edwardian houses, often ugly or nondescript, tend to slip most readily into the form of hotels. But by the time they have sprouted new bedroom wings, conference centers, and spas, had their upstairs chintzed up into suites and their public rooms redecorated to suit paying guests, one cannot always claim that even they have been "saved."

One effect of the boom-and-bust investments of the 1980s, in which (by 1989) too many new country house hotel owners found themselves scrambling for too little "leisure" trade, was to drive a great many of the survivors into the conference business. Half the pages in their brochures are now devoted to glowing descriptions, not of their historic halls or rolling parklands, but of their meeting rooms, equipped with audio-visual aids, microphones, video facilities, and phone, fax, and computer links. Photographs show pads and pencils arranged on blotters, alongside glasses and mineral waters, at every place around mahogany tables, in front of leather armchairs. Chauffered cars, helicopter pads, and secretaries are available. Morning coffee, buffet lunches, and afternoon teas are laid on during breaks. Although most such meetings are one-day affairs for perhaps twenty people (banks and law firms like these), country house hotels after the conference trade are eager to host meetings that last over one or two nights; better still, to have companies take over the whole spread, or at least the purpose-built conference wing, on an "exclusive use" basis. This way they can guarantee the delegates not only total security, but also their choice of meals, exclusive use of the pools, tennis courts, gym, spa, and grounds, and—on order—extra treats such as boating or shooting or falconry or ballooning or riding quad bikes and playing war games in the woods, designed to "bond" employees to one another and the firm. More than fifty country house hotels in the current Ronay guide, most of which have recently added new wings or separate blocks containing from 30 to 150 bedrooms, as well as purpose-built business centers and leisure centers, boast of their conference facilities for up to 1,000 delegates. Many of these are located in the home counties near to London and its airports; a number are members of large commercial chains. A fortunate few sit surrounded by their own golf courses.

In fighting for this obviously limited market, hotels that began life as country houses are in competition not only with one another—including places like Chateau Impney in Hereford and Oatlands Park in Surrey, which are now regarded primarily as conference venues. They must also compete with commercialized country houses (such as Brocket Hall or Castle Ashby) that devote themselves more or less exclusively to conferences, and with still others, such as Leeds and Hever Castles, which successfully combine mass tourism with daytime functions and overnight meetings; with private, lived-in family houses—and this now includes almost all of those open to the public, plus a few that are not—which *also* happily invite daytime meetings and conferences, sometimes (Hagley Hall, Knebworth, Goodwood, etc.) with remarkable success; and, of course, with hundreds of modern, nonhistorical hotels, which have been profitably hosting conferences, management meetings, and training seminars for years.

Meetings and retreats "away from the city environment," offering "tranquillity" and "time to think" have become firmly entrenched in the nation's corporate culture, and to some degree in the public sector as well. Country house hotel outings are often seen as prizes for top sales and marketing people, perks for board members or top executives, or settings for the seduction of overseas clients. In prosperous years, spouses may be invited as well. During the prolonged recession of 1989–92, however, many businesses felt obliged to cut back on this sort of extravagant treat, which drastically hurt the hotels' midweek and off-season business.

Today, a large number of country house hotels are heavily in debt, far from profitable, and hence in precarious financial shape. More than once (even in summer, even on weekends) my wife and I have eaten alone, or almost alone, in the elegant dining rooms of top-rated country house hotels in which we may have been the only overnight guests. The aggressive marketing techniques and cost-cutting offers of certain top-of-the-line hotels have about them a note of desperation. Except for a gilt-edged few at the top, with their faithful repeat visitors, winters and midweeks can be very hard to fill, particularly to houses far out in the country—and yet the kitchen must be kept stocked, the rooms cleaned, the gardens trimmed, the staff at the ready.

Viscount Leverhulme, grandson of the founder of Lever Brothers, writes that he cannot imagine anyone choosing to live in Thornton Manor, the large turn-of-the-century house his grandparents built in Cheshire, after he dies. "I think its future will probably be a hotel or conference centre." One remaining great house that may succeed as an upscale hotel is Tottenham House, a huge Palladian mansion located in 4,500-acre Savernake Forest in Wiltshire, a royal Tudor hunting ground that is now the private property of the Earl of Cardigan. Vacated in 1994 by a bankrupt prep school, Tottenham House is empty of contents, but sound and reroofed, and will go to its next tenant—ideally an enterprising innkeeper with £1.5 million, or about $2.25 million—with planning permission for a new golf course. Lord Cardigan is currently searching for such a tenant, but he admits that he may have to wait a few years for the market to improve.

In the spring of 1996, there were a few indications that, at least at the upper end of the scale, the country house hotel market might be improving. On the basis of several years of impressive profits, Cliveden Hotels went public, offering shares on the London Stock Exchange that were rapidly purchased and rose rapidly in value, giving the new corporation a book value of almost £30 million ($45 million), and the chance to acquire another luxury country house hotel. At about the same time, Stapleford Park was bought by Peter de Savary, a high-flying entrepreneur almost as colorful and eccentric as the late Bob Payton. De Savary, who had staked a British try for the America's Cup yacht race in 1983, then lost a considerable fortune during the recession, had recently bought Skibo Castle in Scotland (once the property of Scottish-American steel magnate Andrew Carnegie), and turned it into a luxurious, members-only resort hotel. Annual dues of £2,350 ($3,500-plus) and daily charges of about £500 ($750) cover not only accommodations and meals but also drinks, massages, golfing and fishing, and whatever else members require. Stapleford Park, according to de Savary's plans, would become one more home-away-from-home for Carnegie Club members.

At almost exactly the same time, Warner Holidays (a division of the Rank organization) bought a handsome Tudor estate in Berkshire formerly owned by de Savary, which he had run (on and off) from 1984 to 1994 as a mock-historic tourist attraction, along the lines of Hever or Warwick Castle. The new owners announced plans to convert Littlecote into a hotel and museum, which—along with other promising developments—prompted the *Times* to declare that "the market in historic country house hotels, among the worst hit sections of the property market, is witnessing a Phoenix-like revival."[13] We shall see.

CHAPTER NINE

Recycling Country Houses

SCHOOLS

DURING AND AFTER THE VICTORIAN PERIOD, many large country houses were converted into private boarding schools. Stowe, in Buckinghamshire, is by far the best known and most important, both historically and architecturally.

Since 1989, the gardens at Stowe designed by William Kent, with their four lakes and 32 listed buildings, have belonged to the National Trust, which is gradually undertaking the restoration of this historic landscape park. The 1st Duke of Buckingham's opulent palace within the park has been a boys' boarding school since 1923, when a number of British parents determined that the time had come for a new, more open, more independent-minded rival of the established public schools, the oldest of which date from 14th to 16th centuries. In 1974, Stowe began accepting girls into the sixth form; it currently enrolls about 80 girls and 500 boys.

For 44 years, Stowe School made valiant efforts to restore and maintain Kent's historic landscape. Crumbling buildings were repaired, stagnant lakes were drained, underbrush cleared (often by students), thousands of trees and new avenues planted. In the 1980s, an anonymous donation of £2 million, plus even larger sums from English Heritage and the National Heritage Memorial Fund, enabled the school governors—who by now realized the task was beyond their means—to hand over the historic garden and most of the park to the National Trust, while retaining the main house and other school buildings, together with the land adjacent. The school maintains the right to use part of the grounds for playing fields, golf, riding, hunting (Stowe used to maintain its own pack of beagles, as well as polo and equestrian teams), sailing and the like, although the increased number of tourists sometimes creates problems when they wander onto school property. No cricket field in England is as impressively located as the south lawn at Stowe, which faces Adam's mansion on one side, Kent's lake and garden temples on the other. The state rooms and gardens, long open to tourists out of term time, are now used for National Trust-sponsored concerts and summer opera productions. Student concerts are given in Robert Adam's Marble Saloon and State Music Room, the Queen's Temple in the park, and the temple-fronted Chapel of 1929.

It would be difficult to diminish the impact of the palatial main house. But it has now been extended on both sides (the north and south aspects are kept clear) by new classroom buildings, five new houses for boarders, an indoor swimming pool, a sports hall, an art school, a games pavillion, an armory, a theater, and a science block. The early buildings were built in a neoclassical style; more recent ones are defiantly modern.

In 1994, the headmaster admitted that the most obvious thing that distinguished Stowe from rival schools was "the magnificence of the environment in which we live." While going on to cite all sorts of other intangible characteristics of the school, he added, "I would hope that everyone who lives and passes through Stowe is enlightened and uplifted by the splendours of the buildings and the estate."[1]

.   .   .

Were it not for the institution of the English public (i.e., private, now usually called "independent") school, Mark Girouard once pointed out, there would be far fewer great Victorian country houses standing today. Of some 215 substantial English country houses he described in *The Victorian Country House*, 25 had been converted into schools. Ardent preservationists often profess to worry about country houses turned into schools (or nursing homes, convents, corporate retreats, hospitals, etc.); to consider them in fact as "lost." This is in part because houses so transformed almost always need to add on functional new buildings, to the point where the historic image of the great house, its very quality as a work of architectural art in a sympathetic landscape may be seriously compromised. But without these auxiliary structures, there is no way that even the grandest of Victorian country houses could accommodate 200 or more boarding students, often of both sexes.[2] Today's independent schools, struggling to maintain enrollments in an increasingly unsympathetic environment, are expected to offer science and computer education facilities, theaters and art workshops at least as up-to-date as those of the best modern day school in town; and to provide playing fields, tennis courts, indoor pools and gymnasia superior to those of most exclusive country clubs.

There is a decreasing demand in Britain today for expensive boarding schools, at both the public school and preparatory levels, and hence a decreasing need for country houses to serve them. Hawtreys, the oldest prep school in England, closed down in 1994 and moved out of Tottenham House in Wiltshire. The school's student population had dropped from 120 to 40, and Hawtreys could no longer pay its bills. The remaining pupils were invited to move on to Cheam, another famous prep school hungry for students. By 1995, only 8.3 percent of the students at private preparatory schools (eight to thirteen years) were boarders. During 1994, five other country house boarding schools in southern England had closed their doors: all five houses were once again up for sale. At one girls' boarding school where enrollment had dropped below profitable levels, the owner explained, "Parents no longer want to send their children away at eight."

In fact, fewer and fewer British parents want to send their children away to board at any age. Enrollment at boarding schools in Britain fell from 125,000 in 1985 to 115,000 in 1992, then to 105,000 in 1994—after two decades of similarly declining numbers. But even those figures are optimistically deceptive. Today more than four of every five students attending private schools in Britain are day students, an increase of 20 percent in five years. Day students don't need the extensive sleeping and eating quarters, the after-hours and weekend sports and diversions which oversized country houses are able to provide. In 1995 the Labor Party proposed—once it returns to power—ending the practice of "assisted places," according to which the government pays a portion of the fees of some 33,000 children of lower- and middle-income families attending independent schools, and using the money to improve state schools instead. Such a change in policy, however appropriate it may seem in democratic terms, could have a disastrous effect on private school enrollments. Other threats—perhaps more rhetorical than real—included removing the charitable status of independent schools, and charging VAT on school fees.

To the delight of heritage lobbyists who would prefer to see country houses remain forever country houses, a number of important houses that had served for many years as boarding schools—Wardour Castle, Brympton D'Evercy, and Duncombe Park, among others—have been returned to residential use. Others—Hampden House, Hartwell House, Elvetham—have been reconverted to new uses: in these three cases, as an insurance company headquarters, a luxury hotel, and a conference center, respectively.

My list is far from complete, but I know of at least 100 former English country houses currently being used as private schools, colleges, adult education facilities, specialized training centers, seminaries, or university facilities. Many of these once-great houses are now single buildings in the center of greatly extended campuses. As with country houses converted to other new uses, almost all of those turned into schools have, like Stowe, felt obliged to erect additional buildings around the historic mansion, which may now house a relatively small percentage of the school's activities and population.

Ampleforth College, the Benedictines' abbey school, was begun by a community of English Catholics in exile who fled France at the time of the Revolution, and were given, in 1802, a recently built country house near York in which to rebuild their monastery and school. Today that house is gone, replaced by impressive, purpose-built school and abbey buildings.

But nearby Gilling Castle, home since 1929 of the Ampleforth College Junior School, dates from 1350, with impressive Elizabethan additions. Although it was given its present exterior shape by William Wakefield in 1715, it can probably lay claim to being the oldest house in England converted into a functioning school. The picture of 160 schoolboys in gray shirts and ties and sweaters, sitting down to lunch in the oak-paneled Great Chamber of 1571 surrounded by the carved and glazed coats of arms of old Yorkshire families, offers a striking image of "adaptive reuse."

Milton Abbey in Dorset, a traditional boys' boarding and day school with strong military associations, can also claim medieval origins, built as it was on the site of a Benedictine abbey seized by the Crown in 1539. But it owes most of its current grandeur to an 18th-century mansion built about the abbey ruins by Joseph Damer, later Lord Milton. He restored the abbey church, and then demolished the adjacent village in order to clear a space for his new park and lake. In 1954 it opened its doors as an independent school for 240 students.

Like most of these schools, Milton Abbey is Church of England-affiliated, which means that the restored abbey church takes on a more than symbolic role. The mansion that extends out from the chapel houses bedrooms and dormitories, classrooms, and the "Abbot's Hall" (dining room), as well as a library designed by William Chambers and other 18th-century state rooms used for concerts and recitals. Estate buildings have been converted into houses for the staff, and the lawns surrounding the house have been shaped into playing fields and a golf course. But a whole village of modern pavilions has sprouted up behind—theatre, swimming pool, sports hall, music and art studios, technology center and the like.

Like Stowe, Cobham Hall in Kent has taken to renting out its state rooms for functions, its historic parkland for sporting events and concerts, and its dormitories and bedrooms for overnight conferences and courses out of term. Cobham Hall Enterprises was set up as a separate company in 1995, to go after the functions and conference business. "We do ask that your function is in keeping with the dignity and traditions of Cobham Hall," they write, which may rule out raves and steam-engine pulls.

Cobham is a redbrick and stone mansion of a number of periods, with 1584 Elizabethan wings and a Caroline central block of 1660–72, which may or may not have been designed by John Webb, Inigo Jones's star pupil and sometime partner. Past owners have included the dukes of Lennox and Richmond, and the earls of Darnley; the present earl is one of the school governors. William Chambers (and perhaps Webb) seem to be responsible for the elegant decoration of the two-story high Gilt Hall. James Wyatt had a hand in the Gilt Hall as well, and added the State Dining Room in 1783. Both can be rented for private functions. All new building lies behind the historic, U-shaped house, which thus preserves its aspect for visitors, who are allowed in 35 days a year.

Cobham Hall was leased and later sold for use as an independent girls' school, which moved in in 1962. The school currently enrolls 170 students, day and boarding, many of them from overseas. It makes use of the Long Gallery (which contains two grand Tudor fireplaces) and "Queen Elizabeth's Room" as study halls, the Chapel and State Dining Room for meals, and George Repton's original Library as the school's library.

Kimbolton School in Cambridgeshire was, from 1615 to 1950, Kimbolton Castle, the seat of the earls and dukes of Manchester: a fortified Tudor manor house transformed by Henry Bell, John Vanbrugh and Nicholas Hawksmoor into a castellated Georgian residence for the 4th Earl between 1690 and 1720. The state rooms are now used as staff rooms and a sixth form (i.e., senior class) center; other rooms in the castle serve as classrooms, common rooms, and library. The broad Robert Adam gatehouse now houses the school shop. There are well-restored Pellegrini murals in the staircase hall, a compact family chapel (used for morning prayers), and the boudoir of Queen Katharine (of Aragon), who died here in 1536. Montagu family portraits hang on the walls, and the 1690s courtyard is used for school plays. Boarders are now accommodated elsewhere, and the castle is now surrounded by the usual new science and sports blocks, playing fields, and other facilities.

At Langley School in Norfolk, the headmaster's wife admitted that obtaining planning consent for new school buildings was complicated by their presence in historic quarters. The new science center had to be built of brick and designed "in sympathy" with the main house, which added considerably to its cost. They were refused permission to erect a cricket pavilion, because it would "interrupt the view" from Langley Hall over the parkland. On "Daffodil Day," the one day a year the state rooms of Langley are open to the public, visitors are given a tour of Matthew Brettingham's 18th-century Library (plywood bookcases have replaced Chippendale's, but the elaborate plaster ceiling remains), Saloon (a staff common room), and Entrance Hall, the Clermont Room (named for the Frenchman who painted the ceiling) and Dining Room, and Anthony Salvin's lavish Victorian Ballroom. The school—now a boarding and day school for both boys and girls, with about 270 students, as well as a prep school—moved here from Norwich in 1946. "The pupils are mostly little aware of the privilege they enjoy by living in such a lovely environment," writes the headmaster's wife; but she expects them to value the experience later on.

Scarisbrick Hall in Lancashire was remodeled between 1837 and 1845 by Augustus Pugin, the neo-medievalist responsible for the interior decoration of the Houses of Parliament, for an eccentric art collector who owned much of Southport. When Charles Scarisbrick died in 1860, his sister and heiress hired Pugin's son Edward to redecorate and enlarge the house, most dramatically by the addition of a pointed, 170-foot-tall tower that dwarfs the 150-room house and looms over the landscape around.

When the Scarisbrick family left in 1946, the property was bought by the Church of England for use as a teacher training college, relocated out of Liverpool during the war. When the college returned to new modern quarters in the city in 1962, a property developer purchased Scarisbrick with plans to demolish the hall and build houses on the grounds. Refused permission, he sold the house in 1963 to Mr. and Mrs. Charles Oxley, who established within it an independent school for boys and girls. Today it serves 526 day students, from nursery school through high school. The east courtyard was filled in with a gymnasium, chapel, and dining room during the 1950s, and the usual range of modern classroom, science, and swimming blocks now stretches out behind the neo-Gothic pile, happily screened by dense woods.

The most precious contents of Scarisbrick Hall belong not to the school but to the Lancashire County Council. In order to prevent the sale and removal of a large 16th-century Flemish woodcarving fitted into the Gothic Great Hall, two 16th-century equestrian statues on the main staircase, the intricate carved walls in the Oak Room, and the wall paintings in two other rooms, the council locked them in place with a preservation order in 1963. When the Oxleys declined to buy them, the council was obliged to purchase them itself, which means they are now occasionally open to public view.

Westonbirt, a girls' school in Gloucestershire, was established in 1928 in the grandiose, neo-Renaissance, many-gabled rose-colored Bath stone house Lewis Vuillamy designed for Robert S. Holford in 1863–70, vaguely along the lines of Wollaton Hall. Like many huge Victorian houses, it was used as a private residence for only two generations. Once converted into a school, the main house accommodated dormitories, staff and common rooms; the orangery and stables were turned into classrooms, form rooms, laboratories, and a gym. In 1950, Westonbirt was singled out by the Gowers Committee as a model adaptation of an historic house into a school. "In these very different times," they quoted the Georgian Group, "some use must be found whereby the hall and saloons will again re-echo with laughter and conversation."[3] The orangery now serves as a theater and concert hall; the galleried Great Hall is a place of assembly.

Another huge Victorian mansion to be converted into a boarding school is Bear Wood in Berkshire, which Robert Kerr designed for John Walter, the proprietor of the London *Times*. The sprawling, busy "Jacobethan" brick and stone country house, all gables and pinnacles, cupolas and dormers, boasted a remarkable 22 toilets. The grand rooms all opened onto a large, skylighted picture gallery, now empty of pictures. These rooms, which retain some of their intricate woodcarving, have become dormitories, a masters' common room, and the sixth form study room and library. The main staircase, which so impressed Mark Girouard[4], has lost none of its impact. In 1921 the house, which had cost £120,000 to build in 1865, became the new home of the Royal Merchant Navy School, originally intended for the orphaned children of mariners. This evolved into Bearwood College in 1934, although the school retains its merchant navy connections and royal patrons.

One of the great country houses to have become a public school most recently is Richard Norman Shaw's Bryanston in Dorset, which was built between 1889 and 1894, served for a single generation as a house, and was purchased (for £35,000) for an innovative new public school in 1928, intended like Stowe to break the reactionary monopoly of the older foundations. Built of red brick banded with white Portland stone, Shaw's huge house was to have a major influence on the growing taste for "neo-Georgian" country houses early in this century. Its extravagant interiors, designed for the 2nd Viscount Portman, were so spacious that they converted easily into boarding school accommodations. Today, the upper two floors divide naturally into six "houses" for all the senior boys' dorms and study/bedrooms. The smaller ground floor rooms have become classrooms and offices. The huge Dining Room, Sitting Room, and Ballroom serve as subject-oriented library/study rooms for students working independently, Bryanston-fashion; the student dining room and chapel are in the basement. The Main Hall—sky-lighted, pillared and galleried—is now a student lounge and meeting place; off it run huge corridors that ease the flow of traffic between classes. "Even today," wrote Nikolaus Pevsner in 1972, "when the main rooms are classrooms and hundreds of pairs of feet tramp daily over the parquet, the interior gives one a sense of euphoria."[5] In early days, 200 boys could eat in Viscount Portman's Dining Room, and roller skate along the basement halls.

. . .

In addition to boarding (or mixed day and boarding) schools for children, former grand houses in England now shelter university facilities; business schools; adult education centers; county agricultural colleges (where the parkland and farms can be put to good use); teacher training colleges; staff training centers for police, army officers, post office workers, corporate workers, trade unions, and firemen.

The best-known education-and-research center located in what was once an English country house is the Ashridge Management College in Berkhamsted, Hertfordshire. Ashridge, rebuilt for the 7th Earl of Bridgewater by James Wyatt and his nephew Jeffrey in their familiar castellated, Gothic revival style between 1808 and 1821, was marked for sale after the death of the last Earl Brownlow in 1921. A campaign was undertaken to secure the Capability Brown park for the National Trust, which enabled it to purchase 1,865 acres (now enlarged to 4,000) in 1925–26. The house itself, the rest of the grounds, and many of the contents—including eleven 16th-century stained glass windows from the chapel—were sold between 1927 and 1928. The mansion, with 235 acres, was donated to the Conservative Party (to serve as an "educational and training center") by Urban Broughton, a former MP who had made a mining fortune in the United States.

Ashridge gave up its political affiliation in 1954, and in 1959 became an independent business school. The college, owned by a charitable trust, grants midcareer MBAs modeled after Harvard's, and is well known for its conferences, executive training courses, consulting, and business research. In addition to substantial alterations in 1928–29 to fit the house to its new purpose, extensive new building has been undertaken since 1972, adding 150 new bedrooms, conference and lecture facilities, library and computer rooms, a fitness center, and other facilities. Although Wyatt's Chapel, Main Hall, and Dining Room still bear traces of their country house origins, the impressive chapel spire is a fiberglass replica of the original.

Another country house—a suburban villa, really—of considerable art-historical importance owned today by a British institution of higher education is Strawberry Hill in Twickenham, southwest London, the jewel casket Horace Walpole designed and built in the years after 1749 to contain his collection of treasures, and to introduce to the world his exquisitely refined new neo-Gothic style. It was enlarged—still in neo-Gothic, if not quite so refined—by his descendant Countess Waldegrave in the 19th century, and occupied in 1925 by St. Mary's College, a Catholic institution now affiliated with the University of Surrey.

Today, Strawberry Hill is little more than a picturesque "signpost" for the modern 2,000-student campus that stretches out behind it, which St. Mary's finds an oppressive and unuseable financial burden. Assistant principal David J. Smith writes, "A conservative estimate at the moment suggests that we need about £4–5 million [$6–7.5 million] to restore the house properly. We do not have such a sum, can see no prospect of obtaining such a sum, and even if we did have such a sum we would in general prefer to spend it on education, which is what we are here for."

An even more notable educational conversion than that of Strawberry Hill was that of Mentmore Towers in Buckinghamshire—the opulent 1855 Rothschild estate the government refused to accept—into the Maharishi University of Natural Law, the British headquarters of the "World Government of the Age of Enlightenment." Although stripped of its moveable furnishings in the 1977 sale, the house retains its spectacular stone and wood carvings, 26 marble fireplaces and mirrors, and some fixed-in-place tapestries and wall paintings—most of them imported, Hearst Castle-fashion, from older houses in Europe. The posh Entrance Hall, the three-story-high Grand Hall, galleried and skylit, the extravagant double staircase, the gilt-ceilinged Gold Room, the Banqueting Hall, and a number of Frenchified boudoirs upstairs still evoke the wealth, power, and taste of the 19th-century Rothschilds.

In the 1980s, 70 resident staff members were meditating six hours a day, studying in the evenings, and tending to less important chores in between. In 1996, a new business college was announced, along with hopes for fully accredited university status by 2001. Mentmore may appear a distractingly opulent setting for Transcendental Meditation, but the institution also rents out these and other rooms, refitted with respectable, reproduction-antique carpets, chandeliers, and furniture, for non-TM conferences, exhibitions, and corporate events, as well as location filming, which in part justifies their grandeur. The last time I visited, the forecourt was filled with the vans, cars, staff, and equipment of a TV production unit, which was there to film an episode of a British sitcom called *Chef*.

Parts of two other important houses shelter educational functions. Half of Corsham Court in Wiltshire is leased until 2066 to the Bath Academy of Art, which spared the 6th Lord Methuen (who lived there until his death in 1994) the expense of maintaining it. About half the Earl of Derby's big house at Knowsley near Liverpool—he lives in a nearby neo-Georgian mansion of 1963—is let to the local police for a training college.

An unusual educational use for lavish but disused English estates that has emerged in recent years has been their transformation into "education abroad" centers for American universities. The best known of these was Stanford Univerity's takeover, first of Harlaxton in Lincolnshire, then of Cliveden in Buckinghamshire, between 1966 and 1984. For all the prestige these aristocratic venues may have shed upon sojourning Californian undergraduates, the American university decided that the expense was more than it could justify, and abandoned the use of these luxurious facilities.

After Stanford relinquished Harlaxton in 1969, the University of Evansville in Indiana—a midwestern Methodist institution that plays in a league somewhat below Stanford's—not only leased, but later *acquired* Harlaxton for its overseas study center. Harlaxton Manor (1831–38), designed by Anthony Salvin (with additions by William Burn) for Gregory Gregory, bachelor landowner and art collector, is the most astonishing 19th-century house I have seen in England. The view of the main facade at the end of the mile-long, dead-straight drive is hard to believe, and grows more mind-boggling the closer one approaches. With its intricate forest of carved golden-stone detail, it is like a Disneyland reproduction of Burghley, only bigger. For all its hyperbole and lack of refinement, Salvin's neo-Elizabethan pile cannot help but amaze, inside and out. The swollen, straining figures holding up the hall trusses, the colossal entrance hall moldings, the gross, gooey plaster-work of walls and ceilings, the hyper-baroque cedar staircase swarming with plaster giants, shells, drapery, and cherubs combine to make Harlaxton's the most over-the-top country house interior in all England.

The house, threatened with demolition, was bought by a fascinating woman named Violet Van der Elst in 1938, who sold it in 1948 to the English Society of Jesus. As their number of novices declined, the Jesuits—who had moved to Harlaxton from Wardour Castle in Somerset—leased the house first to Stanford, then to Evansville, and finally sold it for £180,000 ($345,000) in 1978 to Dr. Ridgway, a San Francisco opthalmologist who was a trustee of the latter university. After living there himself for some years—during which time the conservatory and many of the grand rooms were restored, and new student facilities added—Dr. Ridgway gave it to the University of Evansville in 1987.

From the outset, Wallace Graves, president of the university and chief promoter of the Harlaxton project, acknowledged that a major goal of the enterprise was to elevate the image of its small, 3,000-student home campus in Indiana. By 1990, he believed he had succeeded. Advertisements for the program (which accepts 120–150 students a term, from Evansville and elsewhere) featuring that awesome facade, appear on posters and in college magazines and newspapers all over the United States. "In the United States, Harlaxton College has enhanced the academic reputation and the institutional image of the University of Evansville just as the University's basketball victories in the 1950s and the 1960s put it on America's athletic map."[6]

Most recently, Queen's University in Toronto, Canada, bought in 1995 one of the best-known English Tudor castles—Herstmonceaux Castle in Sussex—as *its* overseas education center. This huge 15th-century brick fortress was in ruins by 1912. After World War I, it was romantically and imaginatively restored by a number of owners. In recent years, after serving as the home of the Royal Observatory, it was relinquished by the government, only to be sold and sold again. After having feared in the late 1980s that a developer was about to double its size, and add new time-share holiday cottages or corporate villas across the moat, preservationists breathed a sigh of relief when Herstmonceaux found a new owner as benevolent as Queen's University.

·   ·   ·

Hospitals and Nursing Homes

Several country houses that had been converted into hospital use during World War II continued to play that role after 1945, when their owners decided it would be too difficult or costly to return them to domestic use. In *The Victorian Country House*, Mark Girouard makes reference to five important 19th-century houses so converted, including Wyfold Court near Henley, where the "manic" architectural quality, he writes. "makes its present use as Borocourt Mental Hospital not inapposite."[7] In some cases, such conversions led to a serious deterioration of the house in artistic or historic terms, as rooms were subdivided, historic ceilings lowered, cheap new wings tacked carelessly on, and parking lots and service buildings allowed to surround the house, in place of gardens and parkland that were, in many cases, shorn off the estate. In *The Country House: To Be or Not to Be?*, Marcus Binney and Kit Martin write:

> An unexpected number [of country houses] have become hospitals, nursing homes, homes for the elderly, mental institutions and borstals [i.e., reform schools]. Among them are buildings that are of the highest calibre architecturally—houses like Staunton Harold in Leicestershire or Leigh Court near Bristol—and many that stand in superb grounds or fine parks....However, many of these houses were acquired not for their architectural merits, or historical associations or the beauty of their setting, but because at the time they offered a large amount of floor space for a relatively, or very, small capital outlay or rent.
>
> As the needs of such institutions constantly change many have been subsequently surrounded by a sea of additional buildings, sometimes prefabricated huts, sometimes substantial new buildings....all too often the institutions suddenly decide to move, leaving the house a still more difficult problem to resolve. Even where hospitals and nursing homes do continue in country houses there is usually constant pressure for new standards and improved services so that the houses must be frequently altered, not necessarily with satisfactory results . . ."[8]

One still sees *Country Life* advertisements for large, unwieldy country houses—"white elephants" in real estate agents' vocabulary—which suggest that they would be "ideal for conversion" to hospitals or nursing homes. But given demanding new health and safety regulations, and the more exacting expectations of both medical professionals and their patients, it becomes less and less likely that a Victorian (let alone an older) country house could be transformed into an acceptable modern medical care center.

The most interesting success story of house-into-hospital conversions is that of the Sue Ryder Foundation. Established in 1953, the Ryder Foundation was started by and named after an energetic woman who had worked for the British government in Poland during World War II, and who dedicated herself to war relief efforts and other charitable ventures after 1945. In 1959, she married Group Captain Leonard Cheshire, a war hero who had founded the Cheshire Foundation Homes for the disabled, a similar but separate charity. Both received life peerages (Lord Cheshire died in 1992) for their efforts.

A unique feature of the 21 Sue Ryder Homes for the sick and disabled in the United

Kingdom, supported in large part by second-hand shops around the country, is that all of them are located in former country houses, in most cases purchased by the foundation in run-down condition, and restored to meet its needs. Each house tends to care for a particular category of patients (people with cancer, Huntington's disease, or psychiatric problems, physically disabled children, the frail and elderly, the sick and homeless, the terminally ill), with the "tender loving care" not always available in National Health Service or commercial institutions. Sue Ryder Homes provide accommodations for between ten and 53 people—more than 600 in all of their houses—in addition to outpatients, and serve more than 2,000 people each year. Almost all are situated in listed buildings; several have coffee and gift shops outsiders can visit. Marchmont House in Scotland caters parties and wedding breakfasts. Staunton Harold in Leicestershire (with Thorpe Hall in Cambridgeshire, the most architecturally notable Ryder Home) and Hickleton Hall in Yorkshire have been, at times, open to the public.

In recent annual reports, the Ryder Foundation announced that it was seeking "*very large period historic listed Grade 1 and Grade 2-star houses at a reasonable price, as we cannot afford to pay more*"—preferably in or near London, Manchester, Birmingham, the Home Counties, and the Lake District. They asked for at least 25 rooms (as many on the ground floor as possible), and enough land for conversion to hospice/hospital use. Lady Ryder, who now lives in two rooms of the Ryder Home in Suffolk, writes that she believes Ryder Foundation patients enjoy living in its houses for a number of reasons: "They like the feel of a place which has an historic background; they take an intense interest, whatever their walk of life, in the building; and they enjoy the beauty of both the house itself and its surroundings."

. . .

Operating under motives at the opposite ethical and economic extreme from those of Lady Ryder are a number of for-profit nursing home chains, all positioned to take advantage of the increasing "graying" of the British population. In Britain, as in most developed countries, ever-more-sophisticated health care guarantees an ever-aging average population. The people at the far end of that population scale, however (the so-called "elderly elderly," past 85), for all their increased longevity, are often incapable of caring for themselves, and can no longer expect the home care once provided by extended-family members.

In Britain, the upper end of the private nursing home market has seized upon redundant country houses, with their numerous bedrooms, large kitchens and dining rooms, spacious dayrooms, gardens for sunning or strolling, and service quarters or outbuildings adaptable to new uses (physical therapy, limited nursing or medical care, crafts and hobbies) to help fill this need for thousands of new places for the aged and infirm.

One of the more interesting participants in the "nursing home industry" (regarded by investment counselors as a booming growth market) is a group called, in fact, Country House Retirement Homes Ltd., founded in 1980. Like its upmarket competitors, Country House has bought up a number of abandoned country estates, usually retaining at least a bit of their gardens or parkland. This allows for handsome photos in their brochures, adds to their sales appeal, and offers lovely gardens in which sons and daughters can wheel about aged parents during their occasional visits. The firm has converted these houses, often at considerable cost, into havens for the better-off British aged, whose families or estates can and will happily pay the fees of £500 ($750) a week or more, in order to feel that their elderly relations are living out their days in the genteel setting of a former country house.

Of the twenty retirement homes on their books in 1994 (they have since acquired more), most were were substantial Victorian or Edwardian residences. Of these at least four might once have been listed in country house guides. Their gardens, their familiar but imposing outside appearance, and the remaining traces of interior grandeur are obviously part of their appeal to families, along with the nursing care, companionship, meals, and activities that less expensive nursing homes also offer. Pirton Hall in Hertfordshire, for example, is advertised as "set in 22 acres of scenic woodland. Approached by a sweeping gravelled driveway, this elegant Victorian house has many original features including a magnificent balustraded staircase and a Wedgwood drawing room." Eastbury Manor in Surrey "is an elegant Georgian-style house surrounded by magnificent cedar trees, extensive lawns and a large picturesque lake. The House still retains its original features including mullioned windows, an ornate oak staircase and panelled reception rooms." Photos of Upton Manor near Liverpool show smiling old people (mostly women) in and out of wheelchairs knitting in the conservatory, reading in a bow-windowed, chandeliered drawing room, lunching in a mauve-and-cream dining room with Corinthian capitals and a high decorated ceiling.

One daughter, desperate to save her 90-year-old mother from a particularly grim nursing home of the standard, soul-draining sort, hit upon a converted country house in Warwickshire. She wrote of "the strange sensation that we weren't in a nursing home, but a rather grand country house hotel. Massive arrangements of flowers, antique furniture, light, colour. The great first-floor drawing room's piano was tuned for use, the lighting civilised, the wood fire roaring. The only odd feature was the big bar at the end of it. 'Oh yes,' she [the owner] said, 'our people really like their pre-dinner drink.' Chuckle. 'Drinks.'" The woman continued her tour, impressed with the genteel guests, the linen cloths and reproduction Georgian furniture in the dining room. "There was a heated conservatory with comfortable chairs, a great park with the Avon running through it, marvellously maintained and, in the woods, an 18th-century Chinese pagoda." The house asked for a £15,000 ($23,000) deposit, in addition to the usual fees. But to the daughter and her mother, it made all the difference in the world.[9]

The most luxurious retirement home in England must be Tabley House in Cheshire, the 1760 home of the Leicester-Warren family (Lords de Tabley) designed by Carr of York. After being taken over by the University of Manchester on the death of the last resident family member, and serving as a boys' school from 1948 to 1984, Tabley House was handed over in 1988 (at £1 million, or $1.8 million, for a 125-year lease) to Cygnet Health Care, which then spent another £2.75 million ($4.9 million) to restore and convert it. Rooms in the big house went (at the time) for £295–675, or $525–1,200 a week. The grandiose stables opposite the mansion were converted into 34 houses (£80–150,000, or $140–265,000) for old people who could care for themselves. The impressive de Tabley family art collection—including works by Lawrence, Turner, Wilson, Fuseli, and others—remains in the grand rooms for the delectation of residents, and is visible to the public several days a week. The house, surrounded by a 3,650-acre estate, is also a popular venue for country shows, game fairs, and similar events, which makes it a livelier retirement home than most of the competition.

Mention should also be made of the successful transformation of Shrubland Park in Suffolk into a luxurious health clinic in 1965 by Lord and Lady de Saumarez. As at comparable (if non-historic) health spas in other countries, essentially healthy, well-to-do people pay about £500 ($750) a week for a rejuvenating regime of diet, exercise, massage, and the like. "We try to avoid being too cranky," says the current Lord de Saumarez. His mother leases the house from the estate for her 45-bed clinic, the profits from which help cover the cost of its maintenance and that of Shrubland's extensive Victorian gardens.

• • •

CORPORATE HEADQUARTERS

Country houses converted into commercial precincts or corporate headquarters are not listed in guides, or normally open to the public, so they're not always easy to locate. A 1983 article in *Country Life* identified nine country houses that had recently been converted into modernized office space.[10] Whisky distillers have taken over a number of picturesque Scottish castles, both to entertain overseas distributors and to serve, like the chateaux of Bordeaux, as images for their labels and ads.

Heythrop Hall, a grand early 18th-century mansion built for the 12th Earl of Shrewsbury, just off the Oxford-Stratford road, was rebuilt in 1870 after a major fire, and became the headquarters of British Jesuits in 1918. It is now used as a training and visitor center for National Westminster Bank, which bought it from the Jesuits for £1 million in 1969, and then spent another million rebuilding it. The facade, Great Hall, and main staircase of Heythrop Hall (which are all I have seen of it) remain grandiose and impressive. But the grounds around it—despite an impressive, mile-long entry drive—resemble those of a new American college more than those of a country house, with new accommodation blocks, sports fields, and parking lots built along the winding roads. Hampden House in Buckinghamshire, once the home of the 17th-century parliamentary hero John Hampden, was largely restored in crenellated, neo-Gothic style for the Earl of Buckingham in the 1750s. Having served for several decades as a girls' school, it became in 1985 the headquarters of Hampden Insurance Holdings.

Most other country house corporate offices I have seen tend to be compact, Georgian, and considerably remodeled. In 1992, Electronic Data Processing of Sheffield bought two country houses already converted into corporate headquarters, for £1.65 million ($2.9 mil-

Heythrop Hall, Oxfordshire.

lion). I learned of North Mymms Park—in 1991 an international corporate headquarters, since resold; Heckfield Place, now a training center for Racal Electronics; Fulmer Hall in Slough, now Servier Research and Development; and Bushy House, now the National Physical Laboratory, from the promotional brochures of building contractors who specialize in historic restorations.

The most famous "corporate country house," along with Heythrop, is Hursley Park near Winchester. At Hursley, if you stand in or near the big, impeccably restored 1724 mansion, and look only to the north or south—which face on open lawns or fields—or to the west—

facing the stable block and coach house—you might briefly be able to imagine that the whole estate had been handsomely preserved.

But to the east lies a gigantic sprawl of modern buildings, the headquarters of IBM UK Laboratories, an ill-coordinated British version of one of the "electronic parks" built around Stanford University or along Route 128 in Massachusetts. IBM/UK originally moved into Hursley Park temporarily in 1958, with plans to move to a new custom-built laboratory nearby. But its rapid growth in the late fifties left the planned site inadequate for its needs. When Hursley Park came up for sale, along with 105 acres of property, on the death of its owner Sir George Cooper in 1962, IBM moved in and began its expansion.

The mansion house itself—which preserves many elegant interior features installed by the Cooper family in 1902, as well as "rural" views in three directions—is now used for executive offices, conference rooms and library, personnel and other departments. The Victorian stables and coach house were restored after a 1964 fire to serve as a training center; several gardens have been revived. Parts of the 17th-century home farm (leased from the local council) were retained, when new offices were constructed around them. Parking for several hundred cars and two tennis courts, along with the giant new lab buildings, are at least partially screened by trees from surrounding roads.

. . .

CONFERENCE CENTERS

People have often proposed independent conference centers as appropriate uses for large country houses. They offer sufficient bedrooms to accommodate large numbers of conference-goers, with all the dining, kitchen, and service areas needed to meet their needs for a few days. Public rooms can easily be converted into places for seminars or conference rooms, and those not so used—along with the spacious grounds and sporting facilities—should keep delegates comfortable and contented during their free time. It is generally presumed, moreover, that a rural setting—secure, self-contained, tranquil, and elegant—is conducive to the kind of serious reflection and personal interaction that is supposed to take place during a conference.

Of course, ordinary country houses (or, for longer stays, country house hotels) can accommodate most of those needs. Some of the more aggressive entrepreneurs among them work very hard to attract conferences. Among the houses, as I noted in Chapter Six, Hever Castle and Leeds Castle offer elaborate accommodations for conference-goers, who are kept away from distracting day-trippers. The owners or managers of certain upscale hotels, like Chewton Glen, Luckham Park, Stapleford Park, and Hartwell House, are all keen to have their establishments taken over on an "exclusive use" basis for weekend or weeklong business meetings or conferences.

The only dedicated country house conference centers I know of in England are Ditchley Park in Oxfordshire, the grandest and most prestigious; Brocket Hall in Herefordshire, the newest and most ambitious; Nuneham Park near Oxford, which belongs to the University; and Elvetham Hall in Hampshire. (In 1995, there was talk of converting the National Trust's Mottisfont Abbey in Hampshire—one of several country houses used for the film *Sense and Sensibility*—into a conference center as well, at a cost of £1.4 million, or over $2 million.)

Elvetham Hall is probably the best bargain, if not the most elegant. For a flat £121 ($194) a person (plus VAT: 1995), you get breakfast, lunch, dinner, and overnight accommodation, plus the use of all the conference facilities, in a haunted-house-style Victorian Gothic mansion about an hour south of London that once belonged to the Calthorpe barons and baronets. (The family still owns the surrounding estate, as well a big chunk of Birmingham.) The 68 bedrooms are relatively spare, the meeting rooms austere. But the gardens are well-tended; darts, billiards, croquet, tennis, a small gym, and a putting green are available. The deconsecrated chapel is now a squash court. Bought in 1953 from the Calthorpes by ICI, the giant chemical company, to serve as its own conference and training center, it is now available to all comers. Elvetham Hall pushes its "warmth and tranquillity" rather than grandeur, and recommends quiet walks around the gardens after a day's work.

Ditchley Park, of 1722, is a house of major architectural and historic importance. The most important country house designed by James Gibbs (architect of St. Martin's in the Fields in London and the Radcliffe Camera at Oxford), it is Gibbs's Palladian response to Vanbrugh's Baroque exuberance at Blenheim Palace nearby. The interiors are by Kent and Flitcroft, the park by Capability Brown. On the death in 1932 of the 17th Viscount Dillon (the estate had been in his family since 1583) most of the art collections were dispersed, but the new owners—Ronald Tree and his wife Nancy (an American heiress)—restored the house in the 1930s, had the park redesigned by Geoffrey Jellicoe, and maintained at Ditchley a ducal hospitality in the dying years of the "country house way of life."

The house served as a retreat and meeting place for Winston Churchill and his American counterparts during World War II. In 1958, its last owner, Sir David Wills—of the Wills tobacco family—gave it to a newly endowed foundation. Since 1962 it has officially served as a conference center dealing with global concerns such as nuclear proliferation and disarmament, the future of NATO and the ex-USSR, and the international economy. Today, with its 2,000 acres, 29 bedroom suites, a 40-seat dining room and other state rooms, Ditchley hosts about twenty international conferences (including meetings of heads of state) each year, organized either by the Ditchley Foundation or other top-level groups. As an exclusive "summit"-type conference center, in a league with such places as Bretton Woods, Bellagio, Aspen, and Bilderberg, Ditchley has entered the vocabulary of international diplomacy and economics, thanks to the postwar "Ditchley Agreement" on nuclear weapons, and the 1982 "Ditchley Group," a consortium of 35 international banks.

Lord Brocket would have been delighted if a similar summit meeting had resulted in a "Brocket Treaty," which might have helped ensure his home in Hertfordshire a place in the history books as well. Brocket Hall, designed by James Paine in 1760, has been the home of two Victorian Prime Ministers, Lord Melbourne and Lord Palmerston. By 1977,

Lord Brocket had decided that the only way to maintain the place was to turn it into an exclusive, top-level conference center. When British banks were unconvinced by his proposals, he obtained a loan from American Express, which enabled him to proceed with the costly conversion, completed in 1980. Attracting an important European Economic Community (EEC) gathering in his opening year helped put Brocket Hall on the map. Brocket's most newsworthy catch so far was the 1992 meetings of the European Community trade council and foreign ministers. The main conference room, equipped with a booth for simultaneous translation, looks ready for a meeting of the UN Security Council. An intruder-detecting system of floodlights, and four gun-posts on the roof, help take care of security. The private airport next to the estate can accommodate 757s.

"I didn't have any money to start with," Brocket said.

I inherited this place with an overdraft. I just had to work for it. But I enjoy marketing, I enjoy selling, and I love being creative—I did my practicals as an architect: I love building and I love designing.

And I love this house. I think it's got a beautiful interior. And the park I think is, without exception, the finest and most beautiful park in this country. Not even Blenheim, not Chatsworth comes anywhere near the beauty of the landscape outside. I mean this is an absolute gem. And I think it's so special it needs looking after. Because my family roots are here, I was determined to succeed in looking after it.

There were two reasons for going down this route. One, I wanted a mechanism that would allow me to restore the building totally to its original state. The first, second, and third floors, which my grandfather had converted into apartments at the Second World War, should be restored to their former glory as the bedrooms that they were—all the passages and the arches opened up again—to have the feel it had as a house when it was built.

The interiors, particularly the domed staircase hall, and the high, cove-ceilinged 60-foot-long Saloon with its paintings, mirrors, and gilded Chippendale pelmets, give some indication of where the £10 million was spent. The eight first-floor suites are as large and lavishly decorated as Cliveden's.

"And the second part of the equation was, What use would make serious money? Opening to the public doesn't make serious money, I knew that from other houses. I didn't think twice about that route, it was obvious." Brocket, a handsome ex-army officer who could once charm the birds off the trees, warms to his favorite subject, as his butler serves tea in the sunlit Morning Room. "In a hotel, guests are treated as numbers. If you dial down for a drink, it's not sent to you, it's sent to number 363. But if your firm is in occupation here, you're the guest, you're the only important person here—or rather your company is. If you want something, you get it yesterday. Somebody wanted special socks the other day; we got a bike up to Harrod's and got them fast. Whatever they want they get, so the guests feel special, while in hotels they don't."

He describes in detail his means of persuading companies and government agencies that they must, they really must hold their meetings at Brocket Hall. He begins with chatting up junior ministers or secretaries over drinks or on the phone, he says, until he finds out

Brocket Hall, Hertfordshire. Stair hall.

who in the organization makes decisions about conference venues. Then comes a very carefully written letter to that person—"suitably apologetic, but not over-apologetic"—signed by himself. "It can't come from the Marketing Director. That's death." It's not the title that impresses, he insists; it's the fact that he's the owner. And the fact that the house is still *his*, he believes, gives him an edge over Hever or Leeds.

   "The letter must be no more than one page, or it's in the bin. But the bullet-points should be contained in a separate paragraph. This tells them *what* we are: the only place in

Brocket Hall, Hertfordshire. Guest bathroom.

the U.K. where you can have exclusive use, one client at a time; *where* we are, which is off the M1 twenty minutes from Hyde Park Corner; and *how big* we are—we've got fifty bedrooms, all with private baths." He follows this up with a phone call about a week later, to go quickly over the same points, hitting only the high spots. "Even when you talk to them they're thinking in pictures."

Taking over all of Brocket Hall is no minor proposition. Accommodation, in 1994, cost £130–175, or $200–270 (not including VAT) per person per night, on top of a flat £2,000 ($3,000) fee. Drinks and music were extra, but this figure included breakfast, tea, and dinner. Each round of golf played was another £40–50 ($60–75). Archery, croquet, canoeing or fishing on the lake, tennis, carriage rides, and clay pigeon shooting came with the territory. But there were extra charges for instructors, and for diversions such as war gaming and falconry displays, or the use of a variety of sport vehicles —go-karts, dune buggies, quad bikes, hot-air balloons, land hovercraft. Major corporations—Canon, IBM, General Motors, Olivetti—sometimes put on a two-night bash at Brocket Hall as a reward to their top salesmen of the year. For a last-night climax Lord Brocket would, for a fee, lay on a marching performance by a band of Her Majesty's Guards on the floodlit lawn, followed by a fireworks show over the lake.

Since we talked in June 1994, Lords Brocket's public image has been considerably battered, as a result of unsavory publicity surrounding his divorce, and his arrest and conviction for fraud in connection with the disappearance of four valuable Italian sports cars from his collection. He was sentenced early in 1996 to five years in prison. In 1994, he had insisted to me that his golf club was totally self-supporting, his whole enterprise remarkably profitable—it returned, he claimed, 35 percent on investment. But there is now evidence that he was desperately in debt as early as 1981. By mid-1995, the failing golf club was in the hands of a caretaker chairman. Stories in the British press told of gigantic debts, impatient creditors, and takeover bids.

Late in 1994, the Ballroom was rented for a key sequence in BBC's *Pride and Prejudice*. In July of 1995, the house played host to a meeting of the environment ministers of the seven leading industrial nations. But in September 1996, the trustees sold Brocket Hall to an international private club operator on a 60-year lease. From his prison in Cambridgeshire, Lord Brocket expressed the hope that he might get a second chance as an entrepreneur after his release. "I have enormous drive," he said, "I'm good with people, and I'm very creative."

· · ·

OTHER USES

Three of the best-known English country houses put to other uses are Chequers and Dorneywood, in Buckinghamshire; and Chevening, in Kent. All three were bequeathed to the nation—in 1921, 1943, and 1967, respectively—together with substantial endowments, so that they might serve as rural retreats for government leaders.

It was the relatively impoverished situation of Benjamin Disraeli that first alerted his well-to-do political supporters to a change in the British political culture. No longer could it be assumed that every prime minister, like Sir Robert Walpole at Houghton, Lord Salisbury at Hatfield, and Lord Derby at Knowsley, let alone lesser ministers of the Crown, would have his own country house to retire to, where he and his advisers could shape political and national policy between parliamentary sessions. In 1847, a group of Tories led by the Duke of Portland simply loaned Disraeli the money he needed to buy Hughenden in Buckinghamshire, now a National Trust-owned shrine to his memory.

But in 1917, Sir Arthur Lee MP—knighted for his service in Lloyd George's wartime cabinet, elevated to a viscountcy in 1921—decided to purchase Chequers, a historic Tudor house in Buckinghamshire he had been renting, and give it to the nation, as a country home for impecunious future prime ministers.

> It is not possible [he wrote in his deed of settlement] to foresee from what classes or conditions of life the future wielders of power in this country will be drawn. Some may be, as in the past, men of wealth and famous descent; some may belong to the world of trade and business; others may spring from the ranks of manual toilers. To none of these in the midst of their strenuous and responsible labours could the spirit and anodyne of Chequers do anything but good. In the city-bred men espe-

cially, the periodic contact with the most typical rural life would create and preserve a just sense of proportion between the claims of town and country. To the revolutionary statesman the antiquity and calm tenacity of Chequers and its annals might suggest some saving virtues in the continuity of English history and exercise a check upon too hasty upheavals, whilst even the most reactionary could scarcely be insensible to the spirit of human freedom which permeates the countryside of Hampden, Burke, and Milton.[11]

Lloyd George wrote and thanked him. "Future generations of Prime Ministers will think with gratitude of the impulse which has thus prompted you so generously to place this beautiful mansion at their disposal. I have no doubt that such a retreat will do much to alleviate the cares of state which they will inherit along with it."[12] Lord Lee also gave the agricultural estate of 1,232 acres, and an endowment of £55,000 (later raised to £100,000), which he hoped would cover the costs of maintenance, repairs, and staffing. In fact, since 1932 the government has had to top this up each year, with a subsidy now approximating £250,000, or $400,000.

Dorneywood, a 45-room Queen Anne house on 214 acres rebuilt in semi-Tudor style after a 1910 fire, was given to the nation in 1953 by Lord Courtauld Thomson for use as a second ministerial residence, in this case with an endowment so substantial that it has paid all the bills ever since. (Resident ministers need only pay for their own food and drink, and that of their personal guests.) All these "grace-and-favor" houses—legally the property not of the nation, but of charitable trusts—are in the gift of the current prime minister: Dorneywood has been assigned to foreign secretaries, home secretaries, leaders of the House of Commons, and chancellors of the exchequer.

Chevening in Kent, the most classically beautiful of the government's three country houses, was built in the 17th century according to plans by Inigo Jones, and bequeathed to the nation by the last Earl Stanhope in 1959, along with an estate of 3,500 acres. He designated it for the use of either the prime minister, another cabinet minister, or "a direct descendant of King George VI." Prince Charles made his home here between the end of his military service and his move to Highgrove in 1980, at which time it became the unofficial country residence first of the chancellor of the exchequer, then of the foreign secretary. Sir Geoffrey Howe grew so fond of Chevening that he agreed to resign as foreign secretary in 1989 only if he could stay on in the house.

One could instance a few similar "tied houses," country estates that go with particular jobs. The heads of the three national armed forces in the United Kingdom, as well as a number of their upper subordinates, live in fairly grand country establishments, maintained and staffed at national expense—a matter the British press questioned a few years ago. Some Church of England bishops still reside in historic episcopal palaces, usually in or near towns; but most of them have retreated to smaller and less costly quarters.

Beyond these uses, there are former country houses serving as convents and other religious houses—an interesting return to their pre-Henry VIII function; as army or government offices; as agricultural or industrial warehouses; and, in at least one case, as a prison for juvenile offenders. Two houses on the edges of cities have been turned into civic museums. Wollaton, a great Elizabethan house, now serves as Nottingham's natural history museum; Temple Newsam is the civic art gallery for Leeds.

Of all the alternate uses discussed in this chapter, the only one for which I can foresee a possible serious future is the "upscale" nursing or retirement home. The conversion of country houses into schools, hospitals, corporate headquarters, conference centers—and ministerial residences—has probably reached, or passed, its peak.

CHAPTER TEN

Giving Your House Away:
The National Trust Today

ONE OF THE MOST SIGNIFICANT CHANGES in the country house scene since 1975 has been the astonishing growth of the National Trust. It now owns so many country houses, and considers itself so burdened with the cost of their upkeep, that it has become increasingly difficult for desperate owners even to *give* their houses away.

By the end of 1995, the Trust owned 207 historic houses of various types and sizes open to the public, about 110 of which would meet the definition of a "country house" I have been using. In 1995, 2.3 million people (four times the number in 1975, twice that of 1981) paid £20 ($30) or more a year to be members, which allows them free access to National Trust properties. Nonmembers—more than three million paid entries to Trust properties were recorded, out of some 11.6 million total— contributed another £7 million ($10.8 million) at the gate. Sales in gift shops, restaurants and tea rooms, rentals from tenants, and returns from investments brought the Trust's annual income up to almost £116 million ($180 million), to which another £44 million ($68 million) was added by government grants, legacies, and special gifts. With more than 3,000 paid employees, and up to 27,500 volunteers, the National Trust has become one of Britain's major enterprises.

Although they may be the best known to overseas visitors, the stately homes it owns are not the National Trust's most popular properties. Among the ten most visited ticketed sites are a ruined abbey, a Victorian cotton mill, and three gardens. Even these attract fewer people than certain National Trust-owned beaches and Lake District properties where no entry fees are charged, and no visitor counts taken.

One major change in National Trust policy since 1975 has resulted from the crunching combination of inflation, the decline of agricultural revenues, and the refusal of the government to compensate it for the annual losses of underendowed properties it persuaded the Trust to take over.[1] These circumstances have forced the Trust to refuse any newly offered properties that come without a major cash endowment, sufficient to cover at least a half century of unrecovered expenses for operation, maintenance, and repair.

In 1968, Roger Chorley, a chartered accountant who was then a member of the Finance Committee (and who served as chairman of the Trust from 1991 to 1995), proposed a new method for assessing the requisite endowment when taking on a new historic house. His complex scheme—still called the "Chorley Formula"—takes into account such things as the probable cost of high-level maintenance and repairs, likely revenues from the property, an estimate of increases in workers' wages and other costs over the years, and other factors.[2]

In addition to his 1982 bequest to the National Trust of Kingston Lacy in Dorset, for example, with its extraordinary collection of Italian art—not as a tax write-off, simply as a gift—Ralph Bankes (five-times-great grandson of the builder) agreed to donate as well 16,000 acres of land, including Corfe Castle and six miles of coastline, which he hoped would enable the Trust to restore the 1665 house, then to maintain it in the style to which it had once been accustomed.[3]

The accompanying endowments demanded for recent acquisitions have been so formidable that one can only wonder how many more important houses the National Trust will find it possible to accept. The greatly increased funding available to "national heritage" projects since 1995, thanks to their share of the proceeds of the new National Lottery, may still enable it to help the Trust acquire very important houses, should these "come on the market" with no other means of preservation. But this will depend on the Heritage Lottery Fund directors' priorities, which have so far proven to be demographically and geographically very diverse. Both the National Trust and its guardian angel, the National Heritage Memorial Fund, have lately been turning down both offers of houses and requests for endowment support.

The most notorious rejection by the National Trust in recent years was that of Heveningham (pronounced "Henningham") Hall in Suffolk, an important neoclassical house by James Taylor and James Wyatt. The government accepted it from the Vanneck family, descendants of the late 18th-century builder, in lieu of £300,000 ($750,000) in taxes the family had no other way of paying. For five years the National Trust agreed to manage and open it, for a fee. But without an endowment, the Trust refused to assume ownership.

As early as 1975, the *Economist* had predicted, "The government would probably be glad to sell if a rich Arab would take it on," and that is almost precisely what happened. Retaining possession of the Wyatt-designed furniture, the Department of the Environment sold Heveningham Hall in 1981 for £726,000 ($1,466,000) to an Iraqi, Abdul Amir Al-Ghazzi, on the condition that he restore it and open it to the public. A serious fire in 1984 destroyed two valuable rooms, which were only repaired five years later. While the house was briefly opened in August 1987, thieves broke in and ripped out a marble fireplace from the Dining Room. Some £5 million was eventually spent on the house—mostly on modernizing features like seventeen bathrooms and a huge new kitchen. But historic preservationists complained that the garden was going to seed, the work of restoration was brutal and insensitive, and the public was not allowed in.

When Mr. Al-Ghazzi died in 1991, it turned out that the house had actually been owned all along by a Swiss holding company, which was itself several million pounds in debt to a bank in Kuwait. The house was empty once again, and all repair work halted. The holding company declared bankruptcy. The government, which had the right of first repurchase, declined to accept it. So did the National Trust. Despite all sorts of national pressure, it remained on the open market until June 1994, when it was finally bought again, reportedly for more than £4 million ($6 million), by a London estate agent.

Almost as much publicity was given to the National Trust's refusal to take on Pitchford Hall in Shropshire, when it came on the market in 1992. Gervase Jackson-Stops, the Trust's late architectural adviser, told me two years later that he thought the organization was prepared to be more flexible in the Pitchford case, but that the pressures of time worked against them. "We were prepared to talk to English Heritage and the National Heritage Memorial Fund," he said, "and see if a deal might not be worked out. Part of the house might be let, and there would be more of a skeleton staff, and it would be open much less." But the owners were unable to wait out all these negotiations, and in 1994 first the contents, then the house were sold.

Before that, the National Heritage Memorial Fund, created in 1980 after the Mentmore affair, had been able to aid the National Trust to acquire six important country houses, as well as the Fountains Abbey/Studley Royal estate in Yorkshire, which contains a Jacobean house on the grounds. The Drydens of Northamptonshire (and Zimbabwe)—the poet John Dryden was a member of the family—had been trying since 1940 to hand over Canons Ashby, their rotting, collapsing 16th-century family home; but they were unable to raise the funds required to restore and endow it. In 1981, just as the Drydens were about to sell off, Jackson-Stops (who lived in a restored garden pavilion nearby) helped persuade the NHMF to make an unprecedented grant of £1.5 million ($3 million), which enabled the transfer to take place. Two years later, the Fund came up with almost all of the £8 million ($12 million) required by the National Trust to purchase the park and remaining furnishings of, and to provide an endowment for, Belton House in Lincolnshire—a sum required even after the house itself, its garden, and some of its contents had been donated outright by the owner.[4] To take over Calke Abbey (which had been accepted by the Treasury in lieu of taxes) in 1985, the National Trust required an additional £7.4 million ($9.6 million) for endowment and urgent repairs, which had to be supplemented by subsequent appeals. Simply to restore the *gardens* at Stowe, which the Trust acquired in 1989, involved the raising of an additional £10 million ($17.7 million), half of it from the Memorial Fund. Before it would consider accepting Kedleston, in 1986—the National Trust's most important new acquisition in decades—Viscount Scarsdale (the donor) and his trustees had to make a cash contribution as well; the National Trust agreed to find some £3 million ($4.4 million), which led to its largest single special fund-raising appeal for a building; and the National Heritage Memorial Fund contributed a record £13.5 million ($20 million). At the same time, the Fund made a contribution of £7 million ($10.3 million) toward the acquisition by a private foundation of Weston Park in Shropshire. The complicated acquisition, in 1991, of Chastleton Hall in Oxfordshire (1603–9) first cost the National Heritage Memorial Fund £2 million ($3.5 million) to purchase the house, when the cranky old owner decided to sell it, rather than donate it to the Trust as she had promised. Then a total of some £9 million ($16 million) more was required—from the Fund, the Trust, and English Heritage—to repair and endow it. In 1986, as part of a "package deal" that helped the Trust acquire Kedleston and Weston Park, the NHMF also came up with £6 million ($8.8 million) to purchase and retain in place the prize collection of Chippendale furniture custom-designed for Nostell Priory in Yorkshire, which the St. Oswald family would otherwise have had to sell on the open market to pay its taxes.

·   ·   ·

Taking endangered country houses under the protective wing of the National Trust—even when the houses are donated to it, or ceded to the government in the first place—has clearly become an extremely expensive undertaking. Faced with an estimated £210 million ($325 million) in capital repair bills in the next five years, the National Trust may find itself saying No even more often than in the past. In any event, Lord Chorley frankly admitted that the spending priorities of the Trust had shifted away from the increasingly expensive salvation and maintenance of upper-class country houses, and back towards the preservation of open space—as well as vernacular buildings, "industrial archeology," and similar populist projects.

The only additions to its country house portfolio in the first half of the 1990s have been Chastleton House in Oxfordshire, and a quaint little sixteen-sided folly called A La Ronde in Devon, where the major attraction—an upstairs gallery decorated with feathers and shells—turned out to be too fragile for visitors to inspect. The historic 18th-century landscape garden (but not the house) at Prior Park near Bath was acquired in 1992. Lyme Park—first acquired by the Trust in 1947—was taken back in 1994 from the Stockport Borough Council. "I hope we don't have to take on much more," said Jackson-Stops. "I think we're easily large enough, if not too large. The future is actually with large charitable trusts, where the owners can keep more in control."

There seems to be no question that the National Trust is trying to cultivate a more "democratic," multicultural, publicly responsible image than that acquired during its early years, when it was ruled by gentleman-amateurs more concerned about preservation than access. As recently as 1969, Robin Fedden, Lees-Milne's successor as Secretary to the Historic Buildings Committee, could declare, "The Trust has nothing to do with people." After Jennifer Jenkins—former head of the Consumers' Association—took over as chairman in 1986, a new populism ruled.

· · ·

In addition to corresponding with twelve resident donors (or donors' heirs) at National Trust houses, I talked with several others in 1994. In one letter, Richard Carew Pole at Antony in Cornwall underlined a point I referred to in Chapter Four, in discussing the earlier years of the Trust:

> The main point of sensitivity I see is that the donor, whose family has probably lived in the house for many generations, has firm and entrenched views as to how the property should be run, and will expect life to continue much as it has in the past. This may well clash with the responsibilities of the National Trust [which] has to run the property for the benefit of the public and in an historic context....
>
> Our case is a rather special one as we live in the whole house with no private family rooms apart from the kitchen and one very small sitting room. We therefore have to co-exist very closely. An insensitive National Trust which just came in, as it is entitled to do, and imposed new restrictions in, say, security, fire alarms, or changes in regime without consultation with the donors living in the house could well sour the delicate balance of the relationship, which would lead to tensions and resentments. They have never ridden roughshod over us in this way....
>
> Both sides have recognized the importance of retaining the integrity of the ambience of the house and the atmosphere which the family has created over successive generations, and the value of avoiding at all costs creating the sterility of a museum.

Lord Egremont, at Petworth House in Sussex, and Lord St. Levan, at St. Michael's Mount in Cornwall, also acknowledged that their family's relations with the National Trust had been good. Egremont, who admitted that part of the success at Petworth was due to the fact that "the house is large enough for my family to live in one end in comparative seclusion and to be fairly unaware of the public," wrote that "the Trust has always looked after the place very well and continues to show great sensitivity to the wishes and needs of my family." St. Levan—who, like a handful of other National Trust donors, still essentially runs the house himself, and contributes to its upkeep—told me that his family had always got on extremely well with the Trust, and particularly appreciated the advice of their art conservation experts. In two recent disagreements with the National Trust, St. Levan prevailed. Lord St. Oswald, who was granted similar day-to-day management and control of Nostell Priory in 1985, writes that "It all seems to work very well, but you must understand that we still look to Nostell as our home, and the National Trust is very understanding of our sentiments."

Lord Faringdon at Buscot Park and the Throckmorton family at Coughton Court share an enviable position: both families hold very long leases (250–300 years) on the donated properties, which guarantees their right to residence, and a considerable degree of control, for many generations to come. Sir Francis Dashwood still calls most of the shots at West Wycombe Park, perhaps because he pays most of the bills.

One concern of several resident owners is whether the National Trust will continue to offer the terms of their own tenancies to succeeding generations, since the usual "memorandum of understanding" has no legal force. One way of maintaining bargaining power in future negotiations, Lord Croft at Croft Castle pointed out, is for the donor of a house to retain possession of its historic contents, without which most of its public appeal would be lost. "To be a National Trust tenant," he writes, "requires almost superhuman tact and the capacity to be self-effacing in a dignified way."

The best of all possible worlds may be shared by two cousins in Kent, Lionel Sackville and Nigel Nicolson (Nigel's grandfather was Lionel's great-grandfather). They live in two of the National Trust's most popular properties: Knole, an immense village of a house which had been the Sackvilles' since 1586, and which Nigel Nicolson's mother, the writer Vita Sackville-West, grew up in and adored; and Sissinghurst Castle, the ruined fragments of an Elizabethan castle some twenty miles away, that Vita and her husband, Sir Harold Nicolson, the politician and writer, bought in 1930 and transformed into the most famous garden in England, now visited by 150–200,000 people a year. Knole gets about half as many paying visitors. But then its great 1,000-acre deer park—which still belongs to the Sackvilles—is free, unless you need to park your car. The citizens of Sevenoaks, from which an obscure lane leads into Knole, have taken to regarding it as a community playground, as their counterparts in Gloucestershire regard Lord Bathurst's Cirencester Park. Admission to Knole, for those not members of the National Trust, was £4.50 in 1996; admission to Sissinghurst Gardens £5.

Lord and Lady Sackville, attended by one live-in servant, occupy an extensive ground floor wing on one side of the second (Stone) court at Knole. The state rooms open to tourists are directly above them. Although her husband insists that they can live their lives virtually unconscious of visitors—up to 2,000 on a Bank Holiday—Lady Sackville notes how pleased they were when trainers (i.e., rubber-soled gym shoes) became almost universal footwear for Britons on holiday, as they reduced the thunder of footsteps overhead during visiting hours. Their quarters in the south front (Lord Sackville's brother Hugh has an apartment in the north front; apartments on the second floor are available for their children), where Lord Sackville has lived since 1962, are a wonderful, mazelike jumble of heavy wooden doorways and beams, stone steps and floors, with comfortable nonantique furnishings and some of the works of art they have kept for themselves. Their downstairs hall has been used for disco parties by their five daughters. For weddings and christenings, they use the Chapel and the 15th-century Great Hall. ("For a rental fee?" "Oh, no no no.")

On the five first Wednesdays of the opening months ("by my good will"), the Sackvilles have agreed to share their private 26-acre walled garden, which the Trust owns but does not manage, and which has been essentially unaltered since 1710. "We don't like it at all," declares Lord Sackville. "I was browbeaten into that by a very charming man named Jack Rathbone," Secretary of the National Trust from 1949 to 1968. On other days, visitors can try to catch glimpses of it from the show room windows, but they are usually kept curtained to protect the fabrics inside. Except for the spectacular Tudor and Jacobean furnishings of the state rooms, which the family handed over to the Treasury in lieu of taxes in 1962, they still own most of the contents and all but five of the paintings at Knole. Except for the sixteen state rooms, two painted staircases, and one wing of the big Green Court used by the National Trust for offices and accommodations, the whole of this mammoth place remains the family's to use "at a peppercorn rent," and on a very long lease. In arranging for an endowment for Knole with Lionel's Uncle Charlie, the 4th Baron Sackville, the Trust foolishly assumed in 1946 that an income of £5,000 a year would suffice. The National Trust enjoys only a "right of way" across the huge first courtyard. "I could theoretically forbid people to step off the path onto the grass," says Lord Sackville. "But of course I wouldn't."

The Sackvilles seem so contented with their lot—which they realize is the result of some very tricky negotiating between the Trust and Uncle Charlie in 1935–48 ("We were really very lucky")—that they are loathe to say anything against their docile landlord. "My main criticism of the National Trust," Lord Sackville finally offers, "is that it's a terrific bureaucracy. You never get anyone who's prepared to say Yea or Nay before it's gone through all mass and matter of committees. . . . The National Trust don't want to be seen making a mistake, so they will not make a decision. They have to go to the Building Committee, or some other committee, so it takes an awful long time to get anything done."

Cousin Nigel, meanwhile, appears to enjoy the swarms of tourists at Sissinghurst. His own cosy quarters look out directly onto the Tudor Courtyard. (The charming, and in part very old buildings at Sissinghurst—not open to the public—would fit inside one of the smaller courtyards at Knole. The famous gardens cover only six acres.) As we talk over his kitchen table, visitors keep peering in through the diamond-paned casement. Later, as he walks us around the flower gardens his parents created and he now oversees, he seems delighted with all the children about, and answers questions of anyone who asks. Unlike many owners or former owners of famous country houses, Nigel Nicolson clearly relishes the public life.

As in a handful of other special cases, the National Trust seems to have realized that no one could do a more sympathetic or dedicated job of managing a particular property than the person, or heir to the person, who donated it. For all the guides and agents and the large staff of gardeners, Nigel Nicolson remains the visible master of the manor, and he hopes that his son Adam will follow after him.

During our visit—which came the day after our visit to his cousin at Knole—Lady Rupert Nevill, the National Trust's Regional Director for Kent and East Sussex, stopped by. In a fortuitous glut of country house visiting, we had stayed at her own former house, now the Horsted Place Country House Hotel, before going on to Glyndebourne two nights before. I took the opportunity to ask her how she and the Trust got along with other

Sissinghurst Castle, Kent. The White Garden.

donor-owners in her region. "It is very difficult," she said. "It's very important to understand the owner, because I think the owner is what gives the whole quality to the property. It can be very restrictive, but you have got to install the owner in a way, because he's probably endowed the house very heavily."

In fact, Nicolson got by in 1967 by with an endowment of only £15,000 (then $36,000), plus the farm—which is all he could afford at the time. "If Sissinghurst were offered to the Trust today," he says, "they would have to turn it down. But as it is, I think I'm right in saying Sissinghurst is one of the few properties which is self-supporting." He estimates its annual take at half to three-quarters of a million pounds a year.

Nicolson is almost as pleased with the National Trust as they are with him. "They consult me on major projects and listen to what I say, even if I do not always agree," he wrote me before our visit. "There have been few disagreements, in fact, and no rows. After all, our motives and interests are identical. The only complaint I have"—and here he echoes his cousin—"is that they tend to be too bureaucratic, inevitable in any large organisation. Their wages are settled nationally, not according to local variations.... restrictions are imposed on the public which a private owner would not impose . . . it takes a long time to make simple decisions, because various escalating committees have to consider it, and they only meet quarterly, and so on. This does not amount to a grievance. I sometimes wish I had control, but then I remind myself of the enormous benefits that have accrued to me through surrendering it." On the whole, Nicolson concludes, "I don't think the Trust is insensitive. I think more often it is the donors who are."

The most enviable situation of a resident donor family in a National Trust property I encountered may be that of Sir William and Lady Hyde Parker at Melford Hall in Suffolk, a handsome redbrick manor of the mid-16th century, U-shaped and turreted, where Queen Elizabeth I was entertained in appropriate style in 1578. It became the property of the Parker (later Hyde Parker) baronets in 1786. The present owner's father valiantly restored the house after major damage caused by wartime occupation, including a disastrous fire which gutted one wing in 1942. When he died in 1951, his widow (a hardy Danish woman, who now lives in the restored north wing) finished the job. To help pay death duties, she managed the farm herself, and opened the house to the public.

What makes the Hyde Parkers' situation so attractive is that they now serve as paid administrators for their own family house. "We are in charge of the whole house, and we run the gardens, the staff, and the opening, and so on." The National Trust was at first apprehensive about the costs of opening the house, but once the Hyde Parkers proved they could manage it themselves, they were kept on as resident administrators after the transfer took place in 1960.

"We are working partners, in a way," says Richard Hyde Parker. "They are in charge of the actual structure, although I do sort of minor repairs, clean the gutters and so on. For the garden, of course"—which they are trying to restore to 17th-century style, virtually on their own—"we have a National Trust adviser. We do pay a full commercial rent, but our work—as administrators, caretakers, part-time guides, the lot—comes off the rent."

With the help of one daily from the village, Lady Hyde Parker does all the cleaning. But, she adds, "They've got a regional housekeeper now, and she's just marvelous. When the library ceiling came down"—in 1992, from the pressure of too many tourists' feet—"she had just come on. There were bits of plaster dust everywhere, and she totally took charge." It took a year to repair.

"It makes sense," says Sir Richard of the arrangement. "We are farmers by trade, we farm around the house. So we are based on the site, which makes a big difference." Like a number of serious farmers I met in my country house tour, Hyde Parker studied not at Oxford or Cambridge but at the Royal Agricultural College at Cirencester. He farms 2,500 acres himself, and leases additional farmland to tenants. Were it not for the crushing burden of death duties in 1951, he figures the agricultural estate might still be able to maintain the house, with the help of a few government repair grants and occasional special events. But the tax bill left them no choice. They paid it, in the end, by handing over Melford Hall and its principal contents to the government, which in turn passed them on to the Trust.

They have no problem with the 25,000 or so people who troop through their house, which is open weekends in April and October, and four afternoons a week during the months in between. In late autumn and winter, the whole house is theirs. They put up a family Christmas tree in the paneled two-storied hall.

"We get at most five or six hundred a day, between two and five, which is too many, really. When it gets crowded, we tell them to go round the garden first and come back. But we've been brought up to it. We were doing it long before the National Trust. It's part of our life, it's part of our children's life. They all take part—as guides, selling tickets." (They have a son and three daughters.) And in any case, their own quarters are private. So the Hyde Parkers get to live in *and* run their own ancestral home. On about 100 afternoons a year, they let strangers walk through their garden and twelve of their rooms; but they were doing that before, without the guaranteed extra income they now earn. They pay rent on quarters they once owned, but someone else takes care of all repairs. For a family willing and able to take on the job, it is hard to imagine a more satisfactory arrangement. "We do everything an outside administrator would do, and probably more, because we care more for the house. And as far as public relations are concerned, we're presumably a great help. After all, we've been here since the eighteenth century."

.   .   .

The story at Kedleston Hall near Derby, the most expensive and, along with Hardwick Hall and Knole, the most important country house ever acquired by the National Trust, is long, complex, and full of vexation. Among the recent Trust takeovers, dramatic personal stories can be told of Belton House, Calke Abbey, and Chastleton. But none of these is as significant, artistically or historically, as Kedleston; and in none of these cases has the former owner remained so vividly a part of the story.

One's estimation of Kedleston may well depend on one's response to the unique re-conception of ancient Rome by the architect Robert Adam (1728–1792), in more than 70 buildings he designed throughout Scotland and England, just as one's estimation of Blenheim and Castle Howard may depend on one's response to the earlier trumpet-fanfare style of John Vanbrugh. In the best of Adam's work—and the best includes a great deal—the shape and detailing of every room are perfectly composed; so is the sequence of rooms, the choreography of our passage through them; so is every part, every piece of furniture. Inlaid floors or carpets are specially designed to reflect the inimitable plasterwork and painting on the ceiling, ceilings more thoughtfully contrived than most people's whole houses. Chimneypieces and door surrounds become little houses in themselves. Mirrors designed to complement chimneypieces—and the custom-designed screens in front of them—are framed with Rococo double-curves that match those of plastered or painted wall panels and the sinuous candle sconces, then set precisely where they are wanted between high windows whose curtains and pelmets are *also* a part of the composition, in front of sensuously shaped console tables that seem continuations of the mirrors. Semicircular apses, oval and cylindrical halls are surrounded or divided off by neoclassical columns, and fitted with custom-designed curving bookshelves or chimneypieces or marquetry cabinets or settees. The least detail of a balustrade, a doorknob proliferating into curving bronze foliage, a sphinx or griffin-turned-candle holder is eminently sketchable; all is of a piece.

I know of no other Western architect before Frank Lloyd Wright who worked so hard to make every room—including everything *in* the room—into a complete and unified work of art. Adam often designed his own carpets, furniture, mantelpieces, ironwork grilles and railings, even his own silverware, inkstands, and birdcages. There are 42 volumes of his impeccably tinted sketches—some 9,600 of them—in the John Soane Museum in London. He was uniquely concerned about color schemes. But he also knew enough to hire the best furniture designers and decorative artists available. His collaborations with furniture makers Thomas Chippendale and John Linnell, plasterer Joseph Rose, carpetmaker Thomas Moore, and painters Angelica Kauffmann, Antonio Zucchi, and Biagio Rebecca play an essential part in the orchestral success of the spaces he designed.

This is all by way of explaining why the preservation of Kedleston Hall was a matter of such importance. Many Robert Adam country houses in England (as well as others in Scotland, and his town houses in London and Edinburgh) deserve to be saved, maintained, and opened, as the products of a uniquely British architectural genius. But there is nothing quite like Kedleston. The rooms at Syon may surpass it in splendor, the furnishings and details at Osterley may feel more engaging and complete. A single room here or there may equal or surpass any single room at Kedleston in its magical fusion of intimacy and wonder. But in no other Adam building do you have an exterior—and he only came on the scene after two other architects had laid down the essential plan—as flawless as the interior; or a whole series of rooms, with most of their original furnishings still in place, so exciting, original, and right. The landscaped setting, too, surpasses that of any other Adam house except Stowe. The north, or entrance front—Adam's improvement on Paine's original design—with its great pedimented portico and curving galleries leading to symmetrical side pavillions, has been called "the grandest Palladian facade in Britain." But Adam's own south, or garden facade—domed Roman high baroque—is even more breathtaking, with its four colossal statue-topped columns, and the grand-opera gesture of its horseshoe-curved stairs. It is hard to imagine a space more impressive than the first room one enters, after climbing to the great portico: a cove-ceilinged, top-lit Marble Hall, 40 feet high, ringed by twenty huge Corinthian columns. Between the columns stand seven copies of Roman statues in special niches, decorative gray paintings and plaster panels, and two fireplaces with intricate plasterwork and paintings above. But then you enter the cylindrical Saloon just beyond it, and all bets are off. This was Adam's response to the Pantheon in Rome, 62 feet up to the glazed eye of the huge, coffered dome, 42 feet in diameter and ringed by a gilded cornice. Between the four axial doors (shaped to fit the curve of the wall), each surrounded by a little Ionic temple-front of its own, are carved four more deep niches, which originally sheltered statues but now contain iron altars hiding stoves—something these vast, chilly spaces must have needed in a Derbyshire winter.

Like the state rooms at Blenheim, Chatsworth, or Knole, the splendid sequence of halls on the main floor of the central block were designed more as works of art than for cosy living; less for casual entertaining than as a means for Nathaniel Curzon to impress neighbors and guests with his wealth, his taste, and his devotion to Roman/Tory ideals. The family's commodious, 23-room living quarters were (and still are) located in the east wing, a substantial Palladian house of its own. The original lofty kitchen and other service areas, now open to visitors, were located in the matching pavillion to the west. Below the Marble Hall is another great hall, as large if not as high, where the 4th Lord Scarsdale was able to entertain 250 guests from the estate, on inheriting his title in 1858.

Nathaniel the builder (created Baron Scarsdale in 1761, just about the time Robert Adam took charge of his new house) was moderately active in Tory politics in the revolutionary 1770s and 1780s. But Kedleston only became a political "power house" under his great-great-grandson, the 5th Baron—one of the true grandees of a fading empire: Viceroy of India from 1898 to 1904, where he presided over the spectacular Coronation Durbar of George V and Queen Mary in 1903; leader of the House of Lords from 1916 to 1925; foreign secretary from 1919 to 1924; promoted in turn Viscount, Earl, Marquess, KG, GCSI, GCIE, PC, FRS. He married two American millionaires' daughters (in sequence) to help pay the bills, and expected to be named prime minister in 1923. But by then it had become unacceptable for a member of the House of Lords, where the growing Labor Party was unrepresented, to serve as PM, so the job went to Stanley Baldwin instead. All along, he had to put up with the popular quatrain,

> My name is George Nathaniel Curzon,
> I am a most superior person.
> My cheek is pink, my hair is sleek,
> I dine at Blenheim twice a week.

.   .   .

When Richard Scarsdale, the 2nd Viscount, died in 1977, the estate—now held by a family trust—had been reduced to the house, its contents, the garden, the park, and about 4,300 acres of farmland. The income from farming barely allowed the estate to break even in good years. But there were no liquid assets to pay the bill for the next set of death duties—a bill for £2.25 million ($3.9 million) presented by the Treasury to Richard's cousin and successor, Francis. Something drastic had to be done; interest on the tax bill alone was running at £400 ($700) a day.

A major difficulty was that Francis Scarsdale's eldest son and heir, Peter, had been made a 10-percent beneficiary of the trust. He, unfortunately, was not interested in Kedleston. Like the Prodigal Son in the parable, he wanted his share in cash, now. For a while there was talk of a possible buyer, which would have meant that the Curzon family connection to its ancestral home would be permanently and irretrievably broken. "It would have been anathema," says Viscount Scarsdale today. "If you have any pride in your family home, the very last thing you do is sell it." "I won't be the first Curzon in 850 years to sell my birthright," he had told an interviewer in 1985. "My ancestors would spin in their graves."[5]

Looking back, he admits that even without his son's intransigence, there probably would have been no way for the family to go on maintaining Kedleston on its own. "No really. Not properly. All we could have done is stagger along for a bit, as people have been doing for the last generations."

So he and his fellow trustees began looking for other options. They first considered offering the principal contents to the Treasury in lieu of taxes, with the hope that the contents would be allowed to stay where they were. But a Christie's evaluation made it clear that the principal contents alone were worth far more than the debt. Even then, Scarsdale came to realize, the family would still be left with the enormous burden of maintaining the house, gardens, and park. So, with a heavy heart, in July of 1980, he turned to the National Trust. It took nearly seven years to complete the deal.

First, the family solicitors had to draw up their formal offer to the government, of house, park, and principal contents. Then the Capital Taxes people had to make their own evaluation of the offer, which took until late 1983. As it turned out, a number of other historic house owners were doing the same thing about then, so the Scarsdales had to wait their turn in the queue. Then the trustees had to get permission from the High Court to hand it all over, since a trust cannot normally give away property under its care; that took more months to accomplish. Meanwhile, Peter Curzon kept pressing for his share in cash—which could only be achieved by selling the estate to the highest bidder. Unfortunately, it was growing painfully clear that neither the National Trust nor the National Heritage Memorial Fund had enough money to buy Kedleston from the Treasury, even if they did agree to accept the trustees' offer. And of course the National Trust would need a substantial cash endowment as well, reckoned according to the Chorley Formula at another £6 million, plus £2.5 million ($11 million total) for immediate repairs.

What broke the deadlock was Lord St. Oswald's anxious desire to hold on to the Chippendale furniture at Nostell Priory, where he needed to pay a giant inheritance tax bill of his own in 1985. He went to Lord Gowrie, the Arts Minister, and persuaded him to exert pressure on the government to increase the stipend of the National Heritage Memorial Fund, so that it could compensate the Treasury for the value of his collection.

Surprisingly, upon Gowrie's request, the Thatcher government agreed to give the Fund an additional, one-time-only sum of £25 million ($32.5 million), to distribute as it saw fit, with the hope of solving three pressing "heritage" problems at once: saving the Nostell Chippendale, helping the Earl of Bradford bail out of Weston Park in Shropshire, and doing something about Kedleston.

During another prolonged series of meetings, then, with Lord Charteris and the NHMF trustees, Scarsdale fought to get the largest part of that £25 million for Kedleston and its prize contents—which were, in terms of market value, by now far more valuable than the house itself. Kedleston intact, he argued, with its contents and surrounding parkland, was incomparably more important than Weston Park, or anyone's collection of Chippendale.

In the end, it was determined that the total cost to acquire and endow Kedleston (which also involved paying off Peter Curzon) would be something like £18.4 million, or $27 million. Subtracting the sums they would need for Weston Park and the Nostell Chippendale left the Fund (the 1985 grant had grown, thanks to interest, to about £27 million, or almost $40 million) with about £13.5 million (almost $20 million) to spend on Kedleston. Where to get the remainder?

"We all threw in a bit more," says Scarsdale. "English Heritage put in six hundred thousand. The National Trust found another million, from somewhere; they suddenly had a million. And they were going to raise another million by a special appeal, half in this country, half in America. [In the end, the Kedleston Appeal, extended to 1991, raised £2.3 million, or $4 million.] I was persuaded, for the sake of keeping everything together, not upsetting the boat and not ruining the deal, to give another million, a quarter of a million in cash and the rest in the form of more furniture. Anyway, we reached agreement in the end, and everybody fell about with relief."

When Lord Scarsdale and I first got in touch in January 1994, seven years after the transfer had taken place, it was obvious that his discontent with the National Trust had been simmering for a long time, and had finally reached a boil. Directly after we spoke in July, he went public with a vengeance. In an interview on local radio in Derby on August 10, he told the world what he thought of the National Trust's behavior, and British newspapers were delighted to spread the word.

What he wrote me in January, in response to a letter I had written some time earlier, was:

> I think I was probably inhibited from replying at the time by the daunting prospect of trying to catalogue the dramas and frustrations of "life under the National Trust" during the 6-¼ years since I gave them my family home in 1987!
>
> All I can say is that everything you have heard about their amateurishness, waste of money, lack of supervision of staff and contractors, purism and museumisation of the house, coupled with arrogance and lack of courtesy towards the "donor family" (as they call us), has been repeated and suffered by us here! The National Trust makes it clear that they regard us as some sort of thorn in their flesh which they propose to rudely ignore.
>
> The key to their behaviour really lies in the fact that they do not possess the necessary diplomacy and good manners to keep us fully informed and consulted in all the day-to-day problems, as they are *meant* to do according to our Agreement. We live here permanently, whereas their Regional Headquarters is 40 miles away, and so they are quite oblivious to the effects of slovenly management on our lives here. They are in fact trying to relegate us to the status of dumb tenant in the Family Wing, who have no right to say anything to the National Trust, who own Kedleston and know best how to run it!!
>
> We quite naturally resent and resist this attitude, and so a confrontational atmosphere exists which could be entirely avoided if they behaved in a more civilised and mature way.

Lord Scarsdale concluded with an invitation to visit next time I was in England, which I accepted. After a genial lunch prepared by Lady Scarsdale in their private quarters, we retired for coffee and drinks on the terrace, facing a view of the handsome private gardens—carefully screened from day-trippers—and some of the family's 4,000 acres beyond. And the complaints began to pour out, as if they had been bottled up and rankling for years.

Right off the bat, he remembers, Trust workers began needlessly pulling down old trees they suddenly declared "dangerous." "They love to do something, to make their mark straightaway. So they chose to take away five windblown trees that were leaning against other ones—and they took down twenty-nine! I counted the tree trunks. Opening a view of suburban Derby which my family for generations had been trying to hide! And this chap, the regional director, I wrote him a stiff letter, and got him to come along, and he admitted that he'd never thought of looking from the house to see what the effect would be."

Inside the house, he felt, they did go off on a tangent and exaggerate some of the colors—"and they swear, 'This is the way Adam painted it.' And I say, 'Well, how do you know? Were you alive in 1760?' It's all so subjective." The National Trust stripped the rooms open to the public of anything *post*-1760s, changing what had been an obviously lived-in family home into a museum to the 1st Lord Scarsdale and Robert Adam.

"And members of the public who come regularly, or who've been several times over the years, they notice these things. 'What's happened to the rooms?' they usually say. 'They look so bare. There used to be so much more furniture than this, surely. Where's it all gone? Have you sold it?' 'It's nothing to do with me,' I say. 'It's the National Trust. This is their idea of how the place should look.'

"But you know, the Trust are saying that we sold the things from the rooms," said Lady Scarscale, pouring drinks. "That's why they're so empty. But I said, 'That's not true.' I've heard it twice now, and it's they who empty the rooms. They've put it all up in the attic."

Francis Scarsdale was employed by his cousin and predecessor for eight years as the estate manager at Kedleston, so he is especially sensitive to what he regards as the National Trust's failure to maintain the grounds properly. "Some of the old-timers here say to me, 'Wish we were back in the old days, M'lord, when you knew how to run things, and keep the place tidy and good-looking.'

"Our main bones of contention with the National Trust involve outdoor work, the park and gardens, where their wardens and gardeners are idle. They don't really do things with love and feeling." At first, the Trust people wanted to clear out the gravel from his paths because they thought it "inauthentic"—i.e., non-1760s—until Lord Scarscale showed them papers to prove there had indeed been gravel paths in the 18th century. Then, when the gravel was thinning on the path to the tearoom, he suggested they replace it.

"Well, a week or two later comes a lorry and dumps twenty tons of the most awful gravel, totally out of keeping with the rest. I said, 'You really can't have this stuff here, you'll have to dig it up. This is my home, I'm not going to put up with it.' 'What's the matter with it? It's gravel.' The pieces were about half as big again, a different color. But gravel was just gravel to them. You see, you've got stupidity like that."

The Trust hired as head warden the man who used to be his third under-gamekeeper. "He's obviously a man who's used to being told what to do. He can't really think for himself, so of course they put him in charge. But he doesn't really know how to organize work. I go about the woods from time to time, and like as not the men are standing about doing nothing. Taking time off, idling. Because in this day and age you've got to supervise them on the spot.

"Likewise in the garden—the head gardener here was our under gardener. They did actually ask us if we would recommend him—'We very much value your opinion': and we said, 'Well, quite honestly not. He's not a head gardener. If he's told what to do, he gets on at the job well, and does it neatly. But he's limited, limited. I wouldn't recommend him as a head gardener, where he'd have to lead.' So they ignored that, and promoted him. And a lot of people think that as a result the garden is rather dull, there's no color there."

A few years ago, the National Trust hired as head gardener a young woman who had put in some time as a student-assistant on the estate.

> She apparently passed her final exams quite well. But I mean, you know, she doesn't have a life-time of experience. It's all through the books. I've been told she gets twenty-eight thousand a year, which is quite a lot of money. She's been indoctrinated in the modern ideas, pays a lot of attention to these trendy lobbies, the conservationists and people, pays them perhaps too much attention.
>
> Hence this idea of hers that the park should be partly mown and left to look like set-aside, and the rest left to look as if it were a bit of farmland or something. And it's a battle to try to talk to her, to get her to come round and see our point of view, the way it was always done. And I said, 'Have you seen the state of the park?' 'Looks all right to me,' she said. She'd just driven in the park, fifty miles an hour, really hadn't stopped, hadn't looked. And I said, 'Right. We're not going to have a meeting this morning, I'm going to take you round in the car. You get in.' Helene got in back, and I drove her off.
>
> We drove all over the park, and I ended up driving into a sea of thistles and nettles. And I said, 'Right. This is the worst. You can't really sit there and say that you're proud of this.'" ["This is right beside the main drive," Lady Scarscale puts in.] "I think the message got across. I think she was probably shocked, but didn't want to show it, you see. The next day, and the following week, the machines were out, and they were mowing and cutting and spraying. But why should we have to do this? Why should we have to chivvy them? They should be shown it automatically."

As we admire their own private garden, which they created themselves ten years before, he points to a great stand of Wellingtonia redwoods on the crest of a hill beyond. "There's a case in point. The National Trust want to cut down that stand of Wellingtonias, because they weren't here in 1760! They were planted in 1856 to commemorate Wellington's death. That's part of the history of the place!

"If you take this to its logical conclusion, none of us should be allowed to have cars or electricity. Why don't we wear knee breeches and tail coats and wigs? It's absurd."

His most telling complaint, however—one that he repeated to a number of interviewers in 1994—has to do with a Victorian fountain, a little circular pavilion on four iron columns that the Viceroy, Curzon of Kedleston, brought over from another estate after he inherited in 1916, and set up at the far end of the garden.

> And I remember clearly one evening about five or six years ago now. I took the dogs for a walk, down across the lawn, by the rhododendron bushes at the far end. And as I came round the corner, I stopped in my tracks: where was the fountain?

They never told me. They don't have that courtesy, you see. I was going round the corner and I thought, "Bloody hell, where's the building gone?" The columns, everything—I was absolutely staggered. Heavens above! I rushed forward: the actual sort of base of the fountain was there, the circular thing. But the columns had been cut off. I hadn't walked around that part of the garden for two or three days, and I thought, "How could it possibly vanish?" I looked all around. I couldn't even see any stone dust or chippings: I thought, "This has just disappeared magically."

I went to see the Administrator. "Oh yes," he said. "They decided to take it down." The contractor who was working on the north steps here, a stone mason, they got him to take it down, and be as quick about it as possible.

And as he couldn't release each of the four or five columns from their bases, he whacked them down with a sledge-hammer. And because that made such a mess—which I might notice—they went to a lot of trouble to clear it up. But I mean—it's sacrilege! It's vandalism. What does it matter that it was Victorian? It was rather attractive. And if a member of the family, who was head of the family at the time, wanted it to come to the family home—why not?

At that point I started keeping a log of horrors. I've got it upstairs. A list, a long list of what in my view are horrors perpetrated by the National Trust. It's quite interesting reading.

National Trust spokesmen claim that Lord Scarsdale had been consulted about the removal of the Viceroy's fountain, and agreed. No, he insists: they had discussed it, he objected, and assumed the plan had been dropped.

By October 1994, Lord Scarscale had backed off a bit, perhaps agreeing with some of his fellow-donors that, whatever his complaints, "going public" as he had may not have been the wisest course. Both Nigel Nicolson, in conversation, and Adam Nicolson, in a thoughtful article in the *Times*, while sympathizing with Scarsdale's situation, suggested he may have gone too far.[6] He had had an "encouraging" meeting with Martin Drury, the Trust's general director-designate, and decided it best to say no more. "Relations between us are much better now," he told a reporter in 1995. "The publicity I got at the time seems to have cleared the air, and they are much nicer to me now."

·   ·   ·

The hurt feelings of country house donors and their descendants may well be, as Adam Nicolson suggests, in great part due to a sense of lost authority and position. But even putting such complaints aside, and concentrating on matters more directly related to the *fate* of country houses in the hands of the National Trust, a number of criticisms remain.

One is the question of "freezing" in time to which Lord Scarsdale refers—the decision to "fix" a house and its contents, as well as its gardens and parkland, at a chosen earlier period—the time of Robert Adam and the 1st Lord Scarsdale, in the case of Kedleston—and remove traces of later periods, even if that means losing a sense of what the house may have looked and felt like when it was last in private hands. As early as 1950, the donor's nephew at Stourhead was complaining about the National Trust's "museumification" of its contents. The Duchess of Devonshire has made comments similar to Scarsdale's about what the National Trust did with Hardwick Hall, which her husband was forced to give up in 1959.

I loved it when Andrew's granny was there and she had bits of things all over the place. . . . And a lot of Victorian furniture. Because Hardwick was always a repository of things which were out of fashion here [i.e., at Chatsworth]. All sorts of things got humped over to Hardwick to get rid of them. They were never sold.

The National Trust has, according to their lights, put it back, you see, Elizabethan. So there's none of that clutter of peculiar things. There were some marvelous bits of furniture which you don't see any more. Because they're not Elizabethan and that's what the National Trust thought it should be. . . .

I think they are bound by their very being to freeze a house. They're terribly shackled in that way, I consider. Hardwick is frozen in an Elizabethan time.[7]

In the case of these two houses, I find myself on the side of the National Trust. Kedleston is, and I believe ought to be, a monument to mid-Georgian style at its finest, and to Robert Adam in particular. Hardwick Hall is one of the greatest of all Elizabethan houses, and before all else the creation of the legendary Bess of Hardwick. The fact that we can still see, at Hardwick, a great many pieces of furniture and wall-hangings that were listed in Bess's inventory of 1601, the fact that the rooms at Kedleston are still filled with the very furniture Adam & Company designed for them, is what gives them their primary importance, both historical and aesthetic. Without saying Yea or Nay to the Viceroy's Victorian fountain—which I have never seen—I think it would be sentimentally reductive to dilute the impact of the historic rooms of these houses by leaving them cluttered with 19th- and 20th-century bits, just because the Duke of Devonshire's granny, or Viscount Scarsdale's uncle left them there. However much their heirs may treasure private memories of houses that were once their property, I see far less reason to "freeze" buildings as important as Hardwick Hall and Kedleston at the way they looked in the 1920s than to freeze them at the time of their greatest glory.

This is not to say that a "fixed period" approach makes sense for all country houses. The Trust, today, quite rightly leaves some houses in a state that reveals many different stages of their past lives. As Roger Chorley points out, there's a limit to how casually "lived in" a house can look, how full of prized private possessions it can be, with 50,000 or 100,000 people trooping through it every season.

Another accusation leveled at the National Trust's treatment of its houses is that "they all look the same"—as if they were all done up in some safe, dull, decorous "museum"-style mode by rulebook-minded decorators. This is patently absurd, to anyone who has visited more than a few. Some recently acquired houses, in fact—such as Calke Abbey and Chastleton House—the Trust has decided to *leave* at (in fact, to restore to) the somewhat shabby, mixed-period jumble they were in when they were received, to make them "look as if nothing had happened." Each floor at Chastleton has a different period of window— early 17th-century diamond-paned at the top, small square-paned crown glass on the first floor, Victorian glass on the ground floor—and so it will be left, more a "romantic notion" of the 17th century than the real thing. Overbecks in Devon, a 1913 house now used as a youth hostel, is full of its last owner's junk. Snowshill, a Cotswold house more pseudo-

Tudor than real, exudes the eccentricity of its donor, who rebuilt it between 1919 and 1951 and filled it with thousands of miscellaneous things he admired, all of which are still there. At some houses, such as Erddig in Wales, the servants' quarters are more interesting than the family's. Smaller, more recent National Trust houses can look remarkably lived-in and domestic. When it gets a good Victorian or Edwardian house, the Trust goes all out to emphasize the voluptuous, even vulgar taste of the builders. A few houses—Waddesdon is one, but so are Ham House, Osterley Park, Hardwick, and Kedleston—have the good fortune to retain a great part of their original contents. On the other hand, the 16th/17th-century Treasurer's House near York Minster has been left idiosyncratically full of 18th-century French furniture, collected by a wealthy Edwardian owner. The furnishings of Wimpole Hall in Cambridgeshire, built and rebuilt between 1640 and 1840, are almost all those bought by its last owner after 1943. If the Trust is confused about what to do with a semifake Victorio-Elizabethan pastiche like Charlecote Park, so am I. Take it for what it is, I suppose—like San Simeon or Hever Castle—and then derive whatever pleasure you can from the palpable fraud.

A third kind of criticism, which reached a peak in the debate over the excruciatingly correct and costly restoration of Uppark—a beautiful brick house of the 1690s perched high on the Sussex downs, gutted by fire in August 1989—is that the National Trust is in thrall to a kind of hyperarcheological rectitude. This leads both to ontological disputes over just how "real" is the reality of any restoration, and envious snarling from the owners of private houses open to the public, who cannot possibly compete with the National Trust's resources.

Some of this can be traced to the increasing role played by outside and in-house experts in the National Trust's empire. Working under their meticulous direction, volunteers took eleven years, and spent £160,000, just to repair and restore the monumental King's Bed at Knole. During the 1960s and 1970s, the Trust made use of fashionable interior designers, who came up with new, not always authentic colors and fabrics to decorate the empty rooms in some of their houses.[8] After protest, they shifted to the other extreme of rigid academic correctness, mixing paints and laying plaster "exactly" as these were done when the house was built.

Ethical debates over the proper practice of "historic preservation" have been going on since John Ruskin attacked Gilbert Scott for what he was doing to English Gothic cathedrals and abbeys in the 19th century. What architects like Scott were doing, essentially, was filling in the collapsed or crumbling bits of medieval buildings with what they *thought* the medieval originals had looked like, then trying to make the whole appear as coherent and tidy as possible. That approach has gone out of fashion, except in a few places. Most architects no longer willingly opt for new-built, custom-made antiquities in the manner of so many 19th-century English and Scottish castles, or Colonial Williamsburg, Inc.

What the Uppark case—and, to a lesser degree, the cases of Calke Abbey and Chastleton—raised was the question of How Far to Go. At Calke, old mold stains were stippled back onto restored wallpapers in black. At Uppark, new crimson flock wallpaper was carefully tinted to recreate the "unfaded" areas that lay hidden behind pictures. "It is now a room of fuzzy-edged red rectangles," wrote Adam Nicolson, "of which Rothko would have been proud, on a subtly modulated brown wall. Of course, when the pictures are re-hung, no one will ever see those rectangles."[9] The new plaster—made from the same kind of sand and horsehair as the original—is fixed to "authentically" hand-riven oak laths, although of course the laths are invisible. Plaster affixed to metal grilles, the project architect felt, might make the room "sound different." More than half a million architectural fragments of Uppark were retrieved and computer-simulated, to give new old-world craftsmen models on which to construct replicas of the original plasterwork, moldings, wood carving, and the like.

In 1952, Coleshill in Berkshire, a "perfect" 17th-century house of major architectural significance, was burned to the ground before its planned transfer to the Trust could be effected. In November 1967, Dunsland House in Devon, a 17th-century house of Tudor origins where restorations had just been completed four days before, was gutted by a fire. In both cases, the damage was regarded as so severe that no attempt was made to restore. The remaining walls were demolished.

In the case of Uppark, however, the Trust insisted that there was no alternative but to rebuild, however high the price. There were enough fragments left to guide the restorers, and the costs were to be borne by the insurers of the contracting firm whose workmen had started the fire. According to the terms of the policy, the insurance money—some £20 million, in the end—could only be used to restore the house to its exact condition on the day the fire broke out. Hence the brand-new "sun-faded" wallpaper, with darker rectangles behind the pictures; the stains on the woodwork carefully recreated; the thousands of hours devoted to restoring embroidered fabrics to their frayed condition on August 30, 1989.

CHAPTER ELEVEN

Letting It Decay

ALTHOUGH "PERMISSION TO DEMOLISH" a listed country house is now all but impossible to obtain—whatever its current form or use may be—the owner of such a house can still try to let it decay to the point where it begins to fall down of its own accord; where vandals (or dealers in architectural scrap) feel welcome to come in and strip it of anything saleable; or where it is destroyed by fires of mysterious origin. Eventually, the owner may hope to find himself served with a "dangerous structure" notice, which may oblige him to tear the house down.[1] Then the owner is home clear, and can apply for permission to subdivide the estate into building lots.

Actually, such an owner nowadays is more likely to receive an order from the local authorities either to repair the house or to lose it—an order they are empowered to make. The owner can then either dig in his heels and do nothing, or try to set a price so high that no one will buy it. Until the 1950s, Scottish owners used to pull off roofs on purpose, which enabled them to escape paying property taxes.

The usual goal, in all these cases, is to clear the estate of its cumbersome, unwanted mansion, so that the owner can more easily develop the estate for new housing, or sell it to entrepreneurs who will. In many regions of this densely populated, greenbelted country, open space on which new houses can be built is worth diamonds.

Driving about the country in search of ruined or ruinous country houses in the 1970s and 1980s, Marcus Binney came across unroofed but substantial shells of houses that had been burned, but not quite burned *down*. He found many others that had been abandoned, even vandalized—but which, for all their dilapidation, still looked structurally sound. Discoveries like these were partly responsible for his share in the creation, shortly after the 1974–75 Victoria and Albert exhibition, of SAVE Britain's Heritage. In the exhibition catalogue, Binney noted twelve burned-out shells of country houses in England, and seventeen others in ruins. Still others, called "partly demolished," had also been left abandoned, vulnerable to wind and weather, to squatters and thieves. (There is a thriving semi-underground market for chimneypieces, wall paneling, chandeliers, doors, brass hardware, and other interior fittings pried loose from unoccupied and unguarded country houses, as well as for the valuable lead used to seal their roofs.) In 1996, Binney could write, "More than 200 fine British country houses are falling gracelessly into ruin...(The) victims of government apathy."[2]

Since then, SAVE has published a number of illustrated directories of such buildings, both to shame current owners and local authorities into preventing further decay, and to let prospective buyers know about listed country houses that may be available for purchase and restoration. So far, they have drawn attention to more than 150 empty, usually derelict country houses in England, as well as many more in Scotland and Wales. In *The SAVE Action Guide*, Binney and Marianne Watson-Smyth wrote,

> Towards the end of 1988 many people were asking: Are there still any buildings at risk? Haven't you saved them all? We knew, from our travels around the country, that there were many buildings standing empty and derelict, and we decided to start a register, firstly to try to assess the scale of the problem and secondly to try to foster interest in their repair and restoration.
>
> A letter was sent out to every planning authority asking whether there were any empty listed buildings in its district that would benefit from some publicity. We had a flood of cases: buildings of all types and sizes, of all styles and ages, but with one thing in common—they were disused and decaying and evidently in need of a new owner or a new use, as their present owners were being decidedly neglectful . . .
>
> We published the results of our survey [called *Empty Quarters*] in spring 1989.... The office was bombarded with telephone calls, letters and visitors. We had always known that there were many people looking for a historic building to restore but had not realized the extent, which was very encouraging.
>
> Two years later, we published a second edition, *Nobody's Home,* for which demand was even higher. Planning officers were keen to contribute once more, as our report clearly helped the situation. As one planner told SAVE, "A few letters from potential purchasers asking about a neglected listed building gives me the necessary ammunition to persuade my council to serve a Repairs Notice on the owner." Many of the cases included in the two reports are now on the road to recovery.[3]

Many buildings illustrated in these catalogues (like many of those in Binney and Strong's V&A exhibition catalogue) don't look particularly "historic" or worth saving to me. But SAVE insists that every listed building is a valuable and integral part of the "national heritage," and that most of the endangered domains they publicize find new owners or uses within a couple of years.

. . .

Six Cases of Arrested Decay

Barlaston Hall in Staffordshire is the most celebrated of SAVE's causes célèbres, because they ended up buying it themselves, for a pound. A stripped Palladian villa designed by Sir Robert Taylor in 1756, it was built of brick rather than stone, without the usual grand Palladian portico, and boasted a set of octagonal and diamond paned windows. The Wedgwood company bought it as part of a large new 'company town' development in 1937; but then never used or maintained it. By 1982 rain was pouring in through giant holes in the roof. The fireplaces and floors had been removed, the ceilings and staircases had collapsed. In the meantime, years of coal mining under the house had led to serious subsidence. At a hearing in October 1981, when the Wedgwood attornies defended their second application for permission to demolish, they were confronted by attorneys from SAVE. In the end, Wedgwood offered what they may have regarded as an unanswerable challenge. They would sell the hopeless house (and a scant 1.75 acres of ground) to these unworldly aesthetes for the peppercorn pound. If SAVE was unable to convert it into a lived-in, viable structure within six years, Wedgwood could buy it back for the same price.

Actually, it took SAVE eleven years: eleven years to make Barlaston Hall safe and secure enough structurally to sell it to a private buyer. It would then take the buyer at least another three years to restore the interior to a fully liveable state.

But by that time Barlaston had become such a national case—with something like £400,000 of public funds invested in its restoration—that Wedgwood cancelled its buy-back provision. After years of foot-dragging and several changes of ministries, the National Coal Board (now British Coal) grudgingly agreed to pay £120,000 plus legal fees to compensate SAVE, and the Barlaston Hall Trust it had created, for the costs of building a floating concrete raft, inserted under the house to keep it from sliding into their pits. The Historic Buildings and Monuments Commission (which, during the long-drawn-out process, had transmuted into English Heritage) and the National Heritage Memorial Fund offered a series of repair grants, first to the Barlaston trust, then—after they had bought the half-finished job for £300,000 ($530,000) in 1992—to the purchasers, James and Carol Hall, to help them rebuild the staircase and repair the public rooms.

Since 1992, the Halls (and English Heritage) have spent at least another £550,000—more than $800,000—restoring the grounds, the church, the upstairs rooms, and their private share of the ground floor rooms. Because enough of the elaborate plaster ornament and most of the exotic windows had been left intact, they were able to carry out a near-Uppark level recreation of the original house, with hand-made bricks, hand-formed decoration, and intricate "original" woodwork. As Marcus Binney wrote in 1991, "No major country house has faced a greater catalogue of danger and decay than Barlaston, with the combined problems of twenty years of rain cascading through the roof and repeated bouts of coal mining subsidence. If Barlaston can be saved, no other major country house need be forsaken."[4]

. . .

Pell Wall in Shropshire is SAVE's second most publicized rescue job. In 1995 external restoration was still incomplete, and the ad hoc preservation trust was still seeking a buyer to finish the job. In their regular announcements of the poor building's plight over the years, SAVE had made a great case out of the fact that it was one of the last (and few remaining) country houses designed by John Soane, one of Britain's most ingenious and adventurous architects. After being occupied by the original family for only about 50 years, it was let for ten years, then sold in 1891 to a Johnny Walker whisky heir, who added a swimming pool and a late Victorian wing. From 1928 to 1962 it served as a Christian Brothers school. It was bought in 1964 by Ronald Rolf of Leominster, who obviously valued the land (which he resold for modern housing development) more than he did the house—which he called "vast, unlovely, with nothing to recommend it." He allowed the empty house to deteriorate, and applied three times for permission to demolish. By 1980, the roofs had been stripped of lead; fireplaces and anything else of value had been removed. Fires of the usual "mysterious origin" had their way with the rest of the interior. Rain was pouring through the broken central dome, the plaster ceilings had collapsed, the floor timbers rotted. The North Shropshire District Council finally issued a Compulsory Purchase Order in 1988, acquired the house for a pound (Pell Wall, because of its lack of property and huge backlog of obligatory repairs, by then had negative value), and turned it over to the British Historic Buildings Trust, which spent £45,000 ($80,000) stabilizing the shell against further decay. In 1993, English Heritage offered a record repair grant of £1 million ($1.5 million) to the newly created Pell Wall Preservation Trust. Like the Halls at Barlaston, the next owners of Pell Wall will not only have to complete the restoration out of their own pockets, but also admit the public for a specified number of days a year, to compensate the nation for the liberal public grants the house has already received.

. . .

Revesby Abbey in Lincolnshire—called the whitest elephant of them all—is another SAVE horror story of a reluctant owner chained to a difficult building. A Grade I piece of "Jacobethan" flamboyance in the manner of Harlaxton—all curly gables and twisted chimneys, oriels and finials, confectionary ceilings and filigree stonework—it was designed by William Burn in 1843. Subsequently used as quarters for U.S. airmen during the war, divided into flats, and left empty since 1960, it was in the 1970s the home of Mrs. Anne Lee, who farmed the 6,000 acres around it. Having built herself a comfortable neo-Georgian house nearby, she wanted to get rid of this Victorian hulk, which was of no use to her.

Twice refused in her attempts to obtain demolition consent, Mrs. Lee refused to undertake repairs, and the house continued to decay. English Heritage stepped in, and persuaded Environment Secretary Nicholas Ridley to issue a compulsory repairs notice. As Mrs. Lee still refused to do the work (structural stabilizing, weatherproofing, arresting dry rot), EH paid for it themselves. Then—the first time the government made use of this tactic—they presented her with a bill for £119,000, nearly $200,000. She appealed against the charge, but her appeal was denied, and in 1991, four years after the repairs had been made, she was finally ordered to pay.

Meanwhile, she had sold the hated house, for £250,000 ($445,000). The purchaser spent a year's effort and, he claims, another £100,000 ($175,000) obtaining detailed planning consent to convert the house into 28 flats—all of which would share the reception rooms—with another 15 small houses in the stable block. By the time all the paperwork was finished, no bank would lend him the rest of the money he needed, and English Heritage refused him the repair grant for which he applied.

So the house was sold again in May 1992, then again in April 1993. By now the selling price had dropped to £41,000 ($62,000). Buyers were apparently frightened off by the mounting cost of repairs they would have to undertake. It was resold twice more in 1993, then again twice more in 1994. "No one seems to want it," wrote one reporter. "People keep buying it, looking at the restoration costs, and putting it straight back on the auction block."[5]

Any future purchaser will have to satisfy English Heritage's restoration demands, which could involve an extra cost of a million or more, and obtain Listed Building Consent for any alterations. Miracles may happen, but as I write Revesby Abbey appears to be a genuinely hopeless case. "All of the money English Heritage has spent seems to have been wasted," said Marianne Watson-Smyth of SAVE in June 1993.

· · ·

Ecton Hall in Northamptonshire is a fine Sanderson Miller house of 1755–56 in the Gothic Revival style, the property of Sotheby family trustees. It was abandoned in 1954 when the last occupant died, and the trustees decided they couldn't keep up with maintenance and repairs. Blocked gutters led to rotted roofs, which led to collapsed ceilings and moldy books in the library. Eventually walls and floors began to cave in; the house was hit twice by lightning, and two chimneys collapsed.

Kit Martin made an offer for Ecton Hall in 1981, which was rejected as being too low, and requiring too much property. (The trustees were hoping to save and develop the property themselves.) But Martin insisted that without the estate's service buildings, there was no way he could affect a viable residential conversion.

In response to Marcus Binney's plea that he intervene over the local council's head, Michael Heseltine (then Environment Secretary) wrote in 1982, "I naturally share SAVE's concern over the deterioration of any listed building due to lack of adequate repairs by the owner.... As a Grade II listed building, I do not regard Ecton Hall as of sufficient importance to justify my exercising my powers."[6]

After being put on the market in 1985, it was purchased, shored up with steel and concrete, meticulously restored inside, and converted into twelve handsome residential units by Period Property Investments—who helped offset the cost by converting the stables, laundry, and game larder into stylistically congenial new houses, completed by 1989.

. . .

The Grange is a strange, empty Greek temple lifted high on a podium in the open country about five miles east of Winchester, well worth the drive out of town, even though all one can see is the exterior. It is maintained, barely, by English Heritage. In the early 19th century William Wilkins rebuilt this 17th-century house into a rather large folly for the banker Henry Drummond, by adding a full-scale Doric portico to the narrow east front, atop a broad flight of steps; square-columned porticos on the north and south sides help complete the neoclassical illusion. Long abandoned and in decay, the house was scheduled to be blown up in September 1972. An important exhibition of neoclassical art had just opened at the Royal Academy in London, and a number of devotees seized the occasion to try to stop the destruction of one of England's earliest and most self-consciously neoclassical monuments by way of letters to the *Times* and to government officials.

In March 1974, owner John Baring offered to cede the house to the "guardianship" of the Department of Environment, along with a contribution toward the necessary repairs. The government accepted it (reluctantly, as it turned out—"It is not a monument we would have expected to take on," wrote an undersecretary in charge of ancient monuments in 1978); then for five years did virtually nothing either to preserve it or open it to the public, while disintegration proceeded apace. "Their tactic appeared simple," wrote Marcus Binney in 1984: "to let the building decay till costs became prohibitive and the Minister then decided it was no longer a proper use of public funds."[7]

Once again, SAVE decided to play tough. After more than four years of inaction, their attorneys demanded an explanation from the Department of the Environment. In January 1979 they threatened a writ of mandamus against the government, a legal tactic designed to force government officials to carry out their statutory duties. In February, SAVE was assured that repair work would finally proceed. In October, Secretary Heseltine announced that the new Thatcher government was reviewing its options regarding The Grange, among which were now included the possibilities of demolition or continued decay.

The heritage lobby protest that followed this announcement, in part orchestrated by SAVE, led to the official declaration in December 1979 that The Grange would indeed be at least minimally preserved, and that £500,000 ($1,060,000) would be made available for its restoration. After that, repairs proceeded with remarkable slowness: the silent, empty temple was "opened" to the public in May 1983.

. . .

Stocken Hall, Leicestershire, a big hilltop mansion in several styles built over 200 years, is another case of SAVE vs. the government—in this case, the Home Office's prison service. Taken over, like so many country houses, by the armed services during the war, it was passed on to the Home Office and became the center of a large prison farm. Its stable block was used as pig sties, 30 prison guards' houses were built along the drive, and the house was surrounded by ugly new sheds and a high wire fence. Whether by the RAF, the prison population, or vandals, the house itself was totally destroyed inside. Staircases were smashed, fireplaces and paneling ripped out.

The Home Office proposed to demolish the mansion in 1980. After "public protest," an agreement was reached between the Home Office and the Department of the Environment to put the house up for sale, but with conditions and limitations that made it very difficult to sell, even at a suggested starting price of only £25,000 (about $50,000). The house was offered with only four acres of land, and virtually no outbuildings; the Home Office refused to relocate a planned new £18 million prison and a young offender's complex adjacent to the house, which diminished its appeal; and the only access road would be through the prison grounds.

Kit Martin had come up with plans to convert Stocken into nine separate residences, but insisted he could do nothing without more land and outbuildings, and a separate approach road. Stocken Hall was finally sold in 1985, after which conversion scheme after conversion scheme failed. In 1991 it was taken over by developer Ian Moorcroft, who first repaired the roof and reinstalled windows, then converted the coach house into residences. He had obtained permission to built six new houses on the grounds. The future use of the big house itself would depend on the next buyer's needs; at the time of purchase, Moorcroft favored turning it into 19,000 square feet of offices.

· · ·

In the summer of 1995, I compiled a list of 55 additional, more or less historic country houses that had been declared endangered, at risk of collapse or decay, during the previous twenty years, and investigated their current situation. Of these, seventeen had been successfully restored: four into multiple residences, four into hotels or country clubs, three back into apparently viable country houses, three into hospitals or retirement homes, and two into offices. In another five cases, restoration appeared to be safely under way. *Parts* of three other houses (or their outbuildings) had been converted into new flats.

Thirteen were still at the "project" stage, either because planners had not yet accepted a new owner's development proposals, or because the required capital had not yet been raised. At least seven were for sale, with no particular proposal or planning consent attached. In a few of these cases, the extraordinary, million-pound-plus cost of obligatory repairs is likely to put off most buyers. The remaining eight can only be described as ruins or near-ruins, with no apparent savior in sight,

· · ·

What lessons can be learned from these 63 selected case studies of efforts to "save" decaying country houses? First, that the process of decay is regular and predictable, and belies the common image of a "crumbling pile": the last thing stately homes tend to do is "crumble," since stone and brickwork, even while gradually rotting, seem able to outlast the worst that man and nature can do. In most cases, the pattern of decay begins with an unmaintained or vandalized roof, made porous by stolen lead, slipped tiles, or blocked gutters or drainpipes. This leads to rotting roof timbers, and the separation of plastered ceilings and walls. Floor joists tend to go next, and as they collapse they naturally pull wall frames down with them. Vandalism (which can begin with the stripping of roof and window lead) takes a different path, involving smashed windows or doors, then the theft of saleable objects such as carved fireplaces, wall paneling, stair railings, portable stonework, doors, light fixtures, hinges, and the like. Fires (which may be the work of arsonists) can achieve most of these same effects all at once. At their worst, they tend to leave little more than blackened brick or stone shells, without roofs, floors, interior walls, stairways, furniture, or windows.

Since 1975, legal demolition of a listed country house, however poor its condition, has been for all practical purposes impossible. In addition to the harsh terms of the basic 1968 Planning Act (according to which unauthorized demolition—or even alteration—of a listed building is a criminal offense)[8], one has to confront the eagle-eyed minions of both English Heritage and SAVE, as well as the local protest groups that seem to spring up wherever in England someone talks of demolishing a ruinous old building.

If demolition is impossible, "conversion" to new uses is not all that easy either; a great number of proposed conversions have been rejected by local authorities. Since almost all proposed country house conversions nowadays are for commercial, profit-making purposes, new owners or developers often demand a "trade-off" in terms of estate development—that is, filling in open space with new and saleable buildings—that local councils are often unwilling to offer. The "preservationist" attitude has clearly spread far beyond the national heritage lobby, to almost every town and borough council in the land.

Virtually none of the proposed means of "saving" a country house in danger involves either preserving a traditional family home, or converting a decaying building into one: Barlaston, in this scene, is almost unique. The status of a derelict house almost by definition implies a house long abandoned by a resident family, and most often one that has passed through one or more institutional owners. Many of these 63 houses began their downward fall during World War II occupation, which lay behind the loss of so many others during the 1950s. Government ownership generally—whether by the armed forces, national ministries, health authorities, or local councils—has frequently turned out to be irresponsible and harmful.

With demolition impossible, and reconversion to family use highly improbable, three possibilities seem open, beyond simple continued decay. The first and most common is commercial development—into separate residential units, offices, old people's homes, conference centers, hotels, or country clubs. Cams Hall in Hampshire and Oulton in Yorkshire are vivid instances of ruinous country houses "saved" by massive commercial development. Derelict since 1948, Cams Hall (1771) was featured in the 1974 V&A *Destruction* exhibition. It was finally sold—for its developable acreage—for £4 million ($6 million-plus), because the purchaser had obtained planning consent to build not only two "upmarket" golf courses, but also up to 180,000 square feet of offices: 24,000 in the mansion, the rest in new and old outbuildings in a new industrial park, located near a motorway junction. This is the sort of generous "planning consent" for a disused country house of which developers dream. In 1984, the city of Leeds acquired Oulton Park, an imposing 19th-century house (formerly a mental hospital) long abandoned, vandalized, and left to decay by the West Yorkshire County Council. In 1992–93 the city sold it to DeVere Hotels for £400,000 ($600,000) on a 125-year lease. The hotel chain, insisting that a house restoration would only be viable if they were given planning consent for an additional 125 bedrooms and a golf course, obtained the requested permissions, and opened for business in 1994. They talk of making a total long-term investment of £20 million, or more than $30 million. Cases such as these involve a great deal of new building, both outside and in, and run the risk of "saving" a historic building at the expense of its soul, or (more prosaically) its historic nature.

The second means of salvation is through the injection of large amounts of public funds, whether from English Heritage, the National Heritage Memorial Fund, or the National Lottery Fund, as at Pell Wall and Barlaston. Sixteen of the 63 "country houses in danger" I surveyed have benefited from English Heritage repair grants—in six cases, very substantial grants—since 1984. Any debate concerning the propriety of such subventions might focus on the relative importance of the building preserved.

· · ·

A third means of preserving a historic house in decay is to treat it as a "stabilized" ruin, like so many old castles and abbeys. The records of the National Trust show that a number of the houses they have acquired over the decades—from Barrington Court in 1907, the Trust's first country house, to Canons Ashby and Chastleton in recent years—came to them in a decrepit state, and took a good deal of money and effort to put to rights. Several of the projects that Kit Martin has taken over for multiple-residence conversions (see pp. 208–13)—Gunton Park, Hazells, Dingley, Cullen House in Scotland—were rotting and leaking badly when he acquired them, which, by driving down the price, helped make conversion possible. At Dingley—a Grade I listed building—the paneling and fireplaces had been stripped out, and most of the walls, floors, and ceilings had gone. Yet "neither the local authority nor the Department of the Environment had been able, or indeed willing," wrote Marcus Binney, "to stop the systematic wrecking of the house."[9] At Gunton Park, Martin preserved the roofless shell of one burnt-out portion, which now surrounds a handsome open court, as a memory of an 1882 fire. Christopher Buxton's impressive restorations/conversions of Thorndon Hall in Essex and Shillinglee Park in Surrey also began as burnt-out shells.

A ruined old house is not necessarily a bad or unattractive thing. I doubt that Britain has any historic buildings more evocative than the abbey ruins of Furness, Fountains, Rievaulx, Tintern, or Whitby, or what remains of castles such as Kenilworth, Dunstanburgh, or Caernarvon. Most of the great castle and abbey ruins across the country are now

Minster Lovell, Oxfordshire.

in the care of English Heritage, and its Scottish and Welsh equivalents, since there is no way to make them liveable or whole. But ruined old houses are sometimes a major feature of intact newer houses built alongside them, as at Belsay Hall, Hardwick Hall, Scotney Castle, and Wardour Castle. The partly ruined shell of Alton Towers serves as the central landmark and logo for Britain's most popular theme park. A number of semidestroyed country houses of the post-castle-and-abbey period have been left to stand as 'stabilized ruins'—that is, ruins unlikely to fall down on visitors, or decay a great deal more. Appuldurcombe on the Isle of Wight is probably the best known—a big, beautiful house burned out in 1952, that just happens to lack windows and a roof. One may also visit with pleasure the substantial remains of Kirby Hall, Houghton House, Lulworth Castle, Sutton Scarsdale, Witley Court, and Woodchester Park. The last is a Victorian mansion in an enchanted valley in Gloucestershire left unglazed, unfloored, and unfurnished in 1870, with the workmen's tools and ladders still in place. It is now preserved as a kind of West Country Pompeii by a group of local citizens. Having acquired the impressive skeleton from the local council on a 'peppercorn' 99-year lease in 1988, the Woodchester Mansion Trust estimates it will take twelve years and £3 million (nearly $5 million) to stabilize it as a permanent monument to I'm not quite sure what.

I would never advise pulling down a good building in order to create a ruin—or purposely leaving one unfinished, as at Woodchester, or creating ruins to order, as Romantic landscape architects once did. But I can think of worse fates for an old building than to fall into ruin, and worse places to spend an afternoon than at a ruined castle or country house. Of the endangered (or once-endangered) country houses on my list of 63, this appears to be a possible future for at least three: Guys Cliffe in Warwickshire, High Head Castle in Cumbria, and Copped Hall, Essex, all buildings people have begun to grow fond of as ruins, buildings where any kind of viable "restoration" is beginning to seem foolishly expensive. Given the continued meaningfulness and popularity of handsomely preserved relics such as Appuldurcombe and Witley Court, I see no reason why the status of "stabilized ruin" might not be considered in a number of other cases, where continued decay or demolition are the only alternatives.

But the basic issues here are political and economic. Has any government the right to order an owner to restore and maintain a decrepit and ancient piece of his own property, or run the risk of enforced payment or seizure—i.e., of a compulsory repair notice or purchase order? And should any owner—or any government, for that matter—be expected to spend millions in order to shore up a house that, in the end, will be worth far less than was spent preserving it, even if it is regarded primarily as "a piece of the heritage"?

CHAPTER TWELVE

Some Tentative Conclusions

I HAD INTENDED TO CONCLUDE by offering some suggestions as to *which* country houses in England ought to be preserved; why they should be preserved; and how it might be done. But some distinctions must first be made.

Are we talking about preserving country houses all by themselves, as important pieces of architecture—like large and complex sculptures that one can walk through as well as around?

Or are we talking about preserving country houses complete with their historically related settings and contents, like Stourhead with its landscape, Nostell Priory with its Chippendale, Wilton House with its Van Dycks?

Or should we, as the Historic Houses Association would argue, make a case for preserving them *as houses*: not as unoccupied house museums, let alone as converted into nondomestic uses; but as lived-in family dwellings, which the HHA (not surprisingly) regards as their proper function?

Or, finally, ought we to make a case (as Hugh Massingberd frequently does) for the retention of historic country houses not simply as homes, but as the homes of their historic (or "traditional") families—on the presumption that, for example, Berkeley Castle would lose much of its significance if it ceased to be the home of the Berkeley family, who have lived there now for 24 generations?

· · ·

Like many country house visitors, I enjoy the imaginative exercise of contemplating the history of a house that has been owned and occupied by descendants of the same family for

200, or 400, or 600, or 900 years. My ancestors only moved to California in 1851; in my family today, it is unusual to find that three generations of adults have lived in the same house. And yet I find myself surprisingly sympathetic talking to owners who indicate that they would feel ashamed if they were unable to keep up and hand on a house that had been in their family since 1450, or 1612, or 1734. "I was brought up with the very clear belief that it was my duty above all else to keep Losely in the family," writes James More-Molyneux. "My wife's ancestors have lived here, each generation since the reign of King Henry I," said Robin Brackenbury of Holme Pierrepont, "and we intend to go on." The Earl of Leicester compared his situation with that of Patrick and Judith Phillips, who bought and restored their 16th-century house after 1971.

"I know the Phillipses, of course, they've done remarkably well. But Patrick, you know, is a clever fellow. I suspect if he came on hard times, I don't think he'd go to the lengths that, shall we say, I might go to actually preserve the place. He would get out while the going's good—and very sensibly, too. But you know, we've been here since 1610—not all that long, really, not as long as some people—but it's quite difficult to describe the sort of emotional attachment that someone like me feels to the place where my family have been so long."

From a survey of the advertisements of country houses open to the public, it would appear that most tourists are impressed, or presumed to be impressed by longevity of residence. Virtually every house that can claim continuity of single-family ownership earlier than 1815 does so in its advertisement. And yet I find it difficult to defend the notion that the nation as a whole should feel obliged to maintain old families in old family houses they can no longer afford to keep up.[1] The arguments that "tourists like it" or "it adds to the atmosphere" or "people are impressed" are too flimsy to add up to sufficient reason for the representatives of sixty million people—who would presumably be expected to bear the cost—to help a 17th earl, or a 7th baron, or the great-grandson of an ostrich feather merchant to stay on in the expensive, oversized, out-of-date house in the country one of his ancestors had built.

In any case, both history and contemporary reality contradict the claim that continuity of tenure is essential to the quality of a country house. Old English families have been selling off their ancestral homes for centuries, for a great variety of reasons: divorce, extravagance, agricultural losses, debt, inflation, labor costs, wartime damage, split legacies, the lack of (or lack of interest by) an heir. Of the 154 houses in England Michael Sayer listed as "lost" (i.e., transferred out of the family) between 1979 and 1992, 45 had been in the seller's family for 100 years or less. Many of these sellers, in other words, were a relatively short time ago newcomers not unlike the buyers they sold to in turn.[2] Among the other "lost" houses on Sayer's list are thirteen that had become the property of the National Trust, English Heritage, or private charitable trusts, which strikes me more as a salvation than a loss; eleven that had already been in institutional use; and at least seven that had been abandoned and left to decay, only to be restored by new owners.

So despite a few notorious horror stories in the newspapers of unhappy old owners forced to sell, or of insensitive and greedy new owners who stripped, disfigured, and then disposed of their purchases, the preponderant evidence suggests to me that the selling and buying of country houses should continue on its free-market course. For every tale of an Abdul al-Ghazzi at Heveningham, a Shiraz Kassam at Orchardleigh, or an Asil Nadir at Burley, whose ownership may have done temporary harm to a house, there are far more stories of buyers like Robert Cooke at Athelhampton, David Pinnegar at Hammerwood Park, Richard and Katherine Burnett at Finchcocks, the Phillipses at Kentwell, Veronica Tritton (taking over after her parents) at Parham, Andrew de Candole at Groombridge Place, Gerald Rolph at Allerton Park—all people who, in recent years, have brought an abandoned and dying historic house back to life by virtue of years of their own effort and expense.[3]

Brympton d'Evercy in Somerset, after its sale in 1992 by Charles Clive-Ponsonby-Fane, became the Poster Child of the HHA's "Save the Private Owner" campaign. Here, supposedly, was irrefutable evidence of the harm done to the national heritage by the government's grossly inadequate assistance to traditional families in traditional houses.

The house had been the property of the Fane family since 1731. It was leased to a school in 1956, when its traditional family furnishings were sold. In 1973, it had come down to Charles Clive-Ponsonby-Fane by way of his grandmother's great-grandmother's step-sister—a slightly wobbly family line, as his hyphenated surname suggests. It was in that year he decided to move back into the house, restore it, and redecorate the state rooms to show to the public. Long a favorite country house with connoisseurs, the restored gardens at Brympton won the HHA/Christie's "Garden of the Year" award in 1990.

But visitor numbers, after rising slowly to 24,000, fell back again to 10,000, which meant that the house—left with an estate of only 840 acres—was running at a loss. The Clives (he goes by the first of his three names rather than the last) had received about £350,000 in English Heritage repair grants, at unusually generous rates of 50–70 percent of the cost. But their own share—and the interest they were paying on loans—was more than they could afford, and a great deal of work remained to be done. So they were forced to put the 100-room house on the market. It was sold in August 1992 for £850,000 ($1.5 million). "It is heart-rending," Charles Clive said at the time. "There are links which go back generations between our family and local people who had connections with the estate. We are all buried side by side in the churchyard. The continuity will now be broken."[4]

The Clives still live in the neighborhood, where they presumably can maintain their local connections, and be buried in the local churchyard if they wish. With all due respect for "old blood"—and respect is not always due—I honestly can't see how "new blood" is likely to do historic houses any harm. Serious money-making skills, of the sort required today to run a large agricultural estate successfully, to make a profit out of visitors, or to earn a substantial income apart from the estate, are not distributed evenly among successive generations of the same family, however noble and ancient. "Family continuity"—powerful as it may be as an advertising tool for houses open to the public—is less significant than the vigor and value of a house's current owner and occupant.

Important houses, by and large, tend to survive, and often improve in the hands of new owners. Sales to new families do not necessarily entail a "disintegration" of the heritage, except perhaps the heritage of the family that sells—and some families consider a sale to be beneficial. Even the horror stories of mishandling so often cited—Stoneleigh, Burley, Heveningham—seem to have turned out well in the end, when a more responsible owner took over. One can feel both sympathy for Charles and Judy Clive-Ponsonby-Fane, obliged to sell Brympton d'Evercy after having put so much money and effort into restoring it; and admiration for its new owners. In August 1995, Caroline Weeks wrote me:

> We didn't mean to buy it (!) My husband and son came to see it in case it closed to the public when it changed hands, and they fell under its spell. I think you can breathe easily about its future. Its maintenance and upkeep have been helped for the last two years by the film industry—"Middlemarch" paid for the west front roof, and "Restoration" for the restoration of the canal. At the moment we are doing the roof of the old stables (*very* urgent!), and the lake awaits us.
>
> We all love it here, it's a very liveable home, swallowing up huge numbers or just me and the dogs with equal good humour. It's not open to the public at the time, but if anyone wants to make an appointment then we gladly show them round, remembering how we were sad to think that it might close altogether. . . .
>
> I sometimes think wistfully about central heating but know in my bones that it would probably activate the dry rot as well as bankrupt us, so put that thought firmly back in its box.

. . .

As to the third of my four questions—is a country house better off maintained as a family house (however new or old the family) than in some other guise, I can't honestly say. There may be a certain natural kind of "life" added to a country house when it is in fact lived in as a family home. Historic churches and cathedrals make the most sense to me when services are in progress, and a congregation is gathered; but that may be a sentimental response of my own. After all, as Bob Payton pointed out, the kind of mixed, day-in-day-out vitality his hotel guests and staff gave to Stapleford Park probably comes closer to the active energy it knew as a Victorian and Edwardian hunting lodge than any single resident family could provide it with today. If indeed a house is lived in more or less completely, its public rooms, kitchens, bedrooms, gardens, and parkland used at least to some degree as they have historically been used, then yes, single-family occupancy seems proper and desirable.

But this is clearly not the case with many large and famous houses, in which the family retreats to a single, modernized wing (or nearby building), while the historic spaces are maintained almost exclusively as show rooms for tourists, or rental space for functions. However many family photos may be left about on desks, the "lived-in" look is often largely a sham. Such places have become for the most part museums for tourists, every bit as much as a National Trust property, or corporate-owned castles like Warwick and Hever.

· · ·

Can a case be made, then, that important country houses should be preserved *along with* their contents and surrounding lands?

In a few obvious cases, yes. Some houses depend very considerably for their importance on their landscaped settings, on their custom-designed or historically relevant contents. In general—although I tend to regard architecture more seriously than I do interior decoration or landscape design—I accept the common notion that it is the *tout ensemble* of the English country house that defines its contribution to art history, the furnished house with its collections, surrounded by its garden, green park, and woods.

The ideal landscaped setting for any country house would depend on its history, size, and special features. In general, it seems desirable for a classic country house to have on all sides (or at least three out of four) an outlook uninterrupted except by the acres of its own estate, closed off only by its own woods or walls or natural hills. Much of the legendary "tranquillity" of a country house depends on this illusion of isolation, in which the only visible buildings are other estate buildings, or perhaps an historically related old church, in some cases an historically related village. If a country house worth preserving still possesses such a setting—which can be achieved in twenty acres or 2,000—it seems to me very important to try to preserve it.

On the other hand, I shrink from the idea of "listing" any gardens and landscapes except those of unquestioned national importance, such as Stourhead or Stowe. Gardens and landscapes are at once natural and man-made, regularly altered by weather, time, and the hand of man. As it would be unfair to forbid an owner to sell off needless acres (permission to develop is another matter, since community as well as private interests are involved), so it would be unwise to allow yet another official cadre of inspectors to order private landowners what they could plant and where. One can hardly "order" someone to keep up at his own expense a cascade or fountain, a topiary zoo, or a ludicrously labor-intensive bedded-out Victorian parterre, however historically important such garden features may once have been.

I feel (to use Lord Leicester's word) equally robust about restrictions on the sale or movement of furnishings or works of art—or, for that matter, about the constant cries of "Shame!" that rise from the heritage lobby whenever such objects are sold or removed from country houses.

Of course it is satisfying to have family portraits kept in a family's long gallery—until the house is sold to another family. The Reynoldses at Saltram, the Turners at Petworth, the Canovas at Chatsworth all tell a part of the history of the house. (So, of course, did the Canalettos of Warwick Castle, sold out of the castle by Lord Brooke in 1978.) Half the story of Blenheim Palace seems to be contained in three great paintings that remain there, the large Closterman, Reynolds, and Sargent groups of the 1st, 4th, and 9th Dukes of Marlborough respectively, surrounded by their elegant and unhappy families. But I would not go so far as Patrick Cormack, who once insisted that England would be the poorer if

Rockingham Castle lost its Zoffany.[5] I doubt I would have argued as aggressively as the heritage lobbyists of 1978 and 1984 to preserve the contents of either Mentmore Towers or Calke Abbey, in order to save ("for the Nation," of course) Lord Rosebery's miscellaneous collection of French objets d'art at the one, or what Lord Vaizey fairly called the "skiploads of junk" at the other.

Art collectors and owners—as I pointed out in Chapter Six—have been selling as well as buying since Day One, and it seems to me an absurd piece of culture-freezing to expect them to stop now, when old master paintings and pieces of antique furniture are often worth more than houses, and the sale of even a minor piece might pay for a new roof. Partly because of informed connoisseurship, partly because of salesroom prices, "fine art" has come to mean more to us than it did to most of its earlier owners. But, with very few exceptions (e.g., the Van Dycks "built in" to Wilton House, the rare wall hangings around which the rooms at Hardwick Hall were designed, the made-to-order furnishings at Harewood or Houghton), I have heard no irrefutable argument that paintings, in particular, are more appropriately at home in a country house whose former owner acquired them a century or two ago than they would be in a public museum—which, in fact, is where the best works from country house collections have already ended up.

The National Trust and English Heritage may establish their own standards for the proper furnishing and decoration of properties 100 percent under their control. But so, I believe, may private owners. If they choose or are obliged to open to the public, they may feel compelled to furnish and decorate to a particular high historical standard, different from the standard that would satisfy them were attracting and pleasing paying tourists not in question. But in either case, I believe, the furnishing of a house—including art collections, libraries, carpeting, draperies, wall colors, and the like—should be left up to the owner, whether of a Grade I listed country house or a semidetached in Sidcup.

Which leaves the fractious question of "export licenses" and "Waverly controls": should a work of art acquired from a Greek temple or an Italian convent or a French chateau (for which it may have first been intended) be obliged by law to remain in the United Kingdom—whether in the country house of its current owner, *or* in a public museum—as evidence of the "national heritage" of Continental collecting, or the fine taste of some Grand Touring 18th-century duke? This is a piece of contorted and chauvinistic aesthetic moralizing I am happy to leave others to unwind.

None of the preceding disputes the idea that obvious pieces of internal architecture—chimneypieces, wall paneling, molded plaster ceilings, interior columns, frescoes, carved stair railings, wall-sized screens, stained glass windows—are no less integral pieces of a treasured building than their exterior counterparts (chimneys, porches, bay windows, carved stone decoration, etc.), and should be considered no less precious and inviolate. Beyond that, however, I think conservation authorities should allow an owner considerable freedom to decide what to do with any moveable object, including chandeliers and sconces, mirrors or brasses "fixed" to a wall, statues bolted to pedestals or fixed to stairways. In many cases, a house, whatever its listed rating, is still a home. The specious claim of

SAVE Britain's Heritage that Canova's *Three Graces* was a permanent "fixture" of Woburn Abbey, and thus could not be moved or sold—after the family had paid more than £1 million in inheritance tax on it—seemed to me a particularly devious and unfriendly instance of heritage lobby obstructionism.

That said, I sympathize with the HHA's concept of a special country house "entity," in which are included—along with the house itself—integral contents that have been in a family for a long time, and the wider landholding with its garden, park, and outbuildings. Properties on William Proby's select list of houses worthy of special concern inevitably include all three of those elements. He is right to think that England would be the poorer, in the case of very important country houses, if any one of the three were to be split off from the others.

· · ·

As for the ultimate question of which *houses* deserve special protection, I will say little beyond expressing my belief that the present total of 500,000 listed buildings in England and Wales (a total more than ten times the number of any other European country's) is far, far too large.[6] At present, almost any building in Britain dated earlier than 1840 is likely to be given the protection of listed-building status, which strikes me as artistically and historically indefensible. I have scant sympathy with the claims of Marcus Binney and SAVE that *no* old building in Britain, however ratty or inconsequential, should be allowed to collapse or be demolished. Why on earth not?

It seems to me time for a new, respected, well-informed pair of national commissions to take a fresh look at what "listing" has done, what it implies for building owners, and to what degree it genuinely represents informed national values. A respected group of professional British art and architecture historians and critics—if possible, composed in such a way as to balance out stylistic prejudices—could compile a new list of the 200 or 300 most artistically important surviving country houses in England. These might include the finest intact examples of Tudor or earlier houses, the best works of important British architects throughout history, houses made uniquely attractive by reason of their settings or interiors, and buildings that, for a variety of reasons, have played an important part in architectural history.

At the same time, another group of British political and social historians might compile a list of the country houses they judged to be of the greatest *historical* importance: restored castles that served as the settings for signal events in British history; the 17th-century "prodigy" houses and 18th-century "power" houses whose builders and their descendants had so much to do with ruling and shaping the nation in previous centuries; other houses closely identified with important historical figures; or houses with no particular connection to political history, whose estates, rooms, and furnishings (including service areas and outbuildings) remain sufficiently intact to provide exemplary models of the way lives were led in earlier times.

The two lists could then be compared, to give a more meaningful indication than current (and largely occult) listing procedures of where the nation's preservation efforts in this area should most usefully be directed. The figure of 200–300 is not entirely arbitrary: it corresponds to the total of "indispensible" country houses on the list compiled by James Lees-Milne in the early days of the National Trust's country house scheme, and the number of houses that William Proby today believes it "very much in the national interest" to retain intact. It is also the approximate number of country houses singled out for special attention in Nikolaus Pevsner's 46-volume *Buildings of England* series—and that of my own private log.

Beyond this roll of Most Important Houses, of course, attention should be paid and support offered to a great many other country houses of distinction. But I would rather concentrate on a clear consensus of a few hundred than try to spread the net of national support under thousands.

·   ·   ·

Little that I have discovered will come as a surprise to most individual country house owners, or prospective owners, whether institutions or individuals. They will have already looked far more closely than I could do into whatever means exist of assuring the survival, maintenance, and liveability of these sometimes historic houses, and the potential profitability of whatever is left of their estates.

Despite the attacks it occasionally suffers, I am profoundly impressed by the work of the National Trust, which strikes me as one of the world's most beneficial and successful philanthropic organizations. Quite properly, I believe, it has redirected its resources toward education, coastal access, open space, and other amenities-for-all; demanded or established high endowments for the country houses it has already taken in charge, in order to assure their stability and accessibility forever; and concluded that its days of acquiring such luxury items are just about over. Even so, I accept the reasoning of the HHA that the large Heritage Memorial Fund grants required in recent years to transfer great (and not-so-great) houses to the National Trust have cost the taxpayer far more than the denied tax credits or exemptions that might have allowed them to remain in private hands—still open to the public, still lived in, still cared for. I sympathize with donors who are made to feel like unwelcome strangers in what they still regard as their own homes, and hope that the kind of diplomatic rapprochement described at the end of Chapter Ten (which demands sympathy, good will, and tact on the donor's part, as well as that of National Trust employees) can become the rule. Although my own interest lies more in old houses than old families, like most visitors I take considerable pleasure in the resident presence of the family at houses such as Knole, Kedleston, Sissinghurst, Kentwell, West Wycombe, St. Michael's Mount, Nostell Priory, Petworth House, Anthony House, Coughton Court, and Croft Castle; and the close and beneficent connection maintained by the Rothschild family at Waddesdon. I hope these can all be maintained.

As for the national government's proper role, it is impolitic for a foreigner to offer advice. But representing no faction or interest, I have heard from many of them, and tried to sift out reason from prejudice, the nation's interest from that of any particular individ-ual—be he or she house owner, developer, hotel keeper, headmistress, tourist industry entrepreneur, doctrinaire heritage lobbyist or conservation officer, National Trust admin-istrator, Heritage spokesman for the government or the opposition, leveling ideologue, or crusty old peer.

Elected governments find it difficult to justify offers of support or assistance to a single segment of the population (excepting the poor, sick, and disabled, the very young and the very old—i.e., those who cannot fend for themselves), unless they can argue convincingly that the whole nation, or at least region, will benefit from this aid. This is the usual defense given for state assistance to artistic or cultural endeavors, whether they are regarded as contributions to the tourist industry, or "pieces of the heritage."

The "tourist industry" argument might justify support of one kind or another to a lim-ited number of important and popular historic houses, which may indeed help to attract tourist money to Britain. But it cannot rationally be made to justify supporting them all, when most country houses are invisible to tourists, and most of those that can be seen draw no more than 10,000 or 20,000 visitors a year (generally from a 30-mile radius), and contribute little or nothing to the nation's tourism-based income. Prince Charles has called Britain's historic buildings—taken all in all—"the equivalent of the Mediter-ranean's sun, a lasting economic resource which will be with us forever, provided we look after it."[7] But half the existing country houses could disappear tomorrow with no notice-able effect on tourist income.

I fear that agencies of the British government have abused the notion of "heritage" by spreading the word so broadly and so thin, using it to define virtually anything more than a generation or two old. John Ruskin used the term "national heritage" in 1891, to describe great buildings which, he insisted, "We have no right to touch...[because] they are not ours." But then in 1920, one of the founders of the National Trust wrote a book called *The National Heritage* in which the only country house he mentioned was a ruin, and the landscapes he preferred were all wild.[8] Today, right-wing preservationists war with left-wing preservationists over whether England's "National Heritage" should refer more properly to stately homes than old workingmen's clubs, to High Church cathedrals or Methodist chapels. How you define the national heritage implies what *kind* of past you think a nation should commit itself to preserve.

Writers like Robert Hewison and Raphael Samuel have traced the spread and con-comitant devaluation of the word "heritage" in Britain since 1975. Nowadays, according to Samuel, it covers virtually anything old or nostalgia-inducing, from Adam ceilings to naked-lady lampstands, with essentially no considerations of quality involved. It attaches itself to whatever was discovered last week to be historic. "'Heritage,' writes Samuel, "is now a generic term for environments at risk," however trivial or grotty. "Instead of manu-facturing goods," complained Hewison, "we are manufacturing *heritage*, a commodity which nobody seems able to define, but which everybody is eager to sell."[9]

One can trace the growing institutionalization of the word, and the blurring of its significance, from UNESCO's declaration of "European Architectural Heritage Year" in 1975.[10] During the Mentmore affair of 1978, Norman St. John Stevas called the nation's refusal to accept the house and its contents "a grave loss to the National Heritage." In response to that crisis, a new Conservative government passed the National Heritage Act of 1980, which gave birth to the National Heritage Memorial Fund. In 1984, the National Buildings and Monuments Commission for England was officially renamed "English Heritage." Private pressure groups rose, calling themselves things like "Heritage in Danger" (1974) and "SAVE Britain's Heritage" (1975). The Heritage Education Trust, the Parliamentary Committee on the Heritage, the Heritage Co-ordination Group, and innumerable Heritage Centers and Heritage Trusts all took up the brave new word. This reached a dizzying climax with the creation of a cabinet-level Department of National Heritage in 1991, which was given responsibility for broadcasting and sport, as well as old buildings and public lands.

So what has this value-laden buzzword come to mean? During debates in the House of Lords over the establishment of the NHMF, Lord Mowbray declared that "the heritage is a memorial to everything in the past always." In the Commons, a Tory MP defined the national heritage as "that which moulders." But Lord Charteris, first chairman of the National Heritage Memorial Fund, publicly conceded that "We could no more define the national heritage than we could define, say, beauty or art." He and his colleagues decided to wait for grant applications to learn what the British people thought the term meant.[11]

Hugh Massingberd wrote in 1992, "There are those, of course, to whom the very word 'heritage' is anathema, conjuring up visions of Britain becoming an offshore adjunct of the new Euro-Disneyland, a giant theme park with everyone togged up in period attire while soliciting tips....Undeniably 'heritage' has come to be a catch-all for any naff old tat which can be flogged off to the nostalgia-obsessed Those-Were-the-Days-My-Friend ersatz history market."[12] Yet all this while, the country house, its owners and defenders were insisting on their primary claim to be a part of this valuable, government-supported new concept, whatever it meant. "The country house," wrote Robert Hewison, "is the most familiar symbol of our national heritage"[13]—a symbolism that pleased some Britons as much as it outraged others.

I have no particular sympathy with the radical critics, who write of "heritage-besotted" Britain's "unhealthy fascination" with country houses. David Cannadine, a British historian who now writes from America, regards the respect they have gained in the last twenty years as exaggerated and unwarranted, a "plague" of false nostalgia in a nation ashamed of its present and afraid of its future ("the 'Brideshead syndrome,'" he writes, "has reached epidemic proportions"); or else the result of a deceptive publicity campaign managed by private country house owners on their own behalf. "By a mystical process of association," writes Robert Hewison, "the country house becomes the nation, a love of one's country makes obligatory a love of the country house."[14]

Although I believe that official Britain has sometimes crudely overstated the case for its "National Heritage," and defined far too many buildings as precious, respect for the past, as Giles Worsley once wrote, is not a sign of weakness. "Living in an old country," in Patrick Wright's phrase, Britons have a great deal left of their tangible past, from which they can decide what to preserve and protect.[15] A decent respect for one's national past doesn't rule out a healthy concern for the present or future, although some heritage-bashers write as if it did. My admiration for the best buildings of Christopher Wren and Robert Adam in no way diminishes my respect for the best buildings of Richard Rogers and Norman Foster.

· · ·

I believe that any government, Labor or Tory, could successfully argue that preserving and maintaining buildings of important artistic or historical merit is an action that benefits the nation as a whole. We may begin by agreeing that it is important for Britain to have and preserve Stonehenge, Salisbury Cathedral, and Hampton Court Palace. We may end by conceding that the country would not have been all that greatly impoverished if every one of the 2,000 remaining red telephone booths had not been listed and preserved. Somewhere in between fall most of the surviving country houses, whatever function they may be serving today.

Once the nation has determined, more scrupulously than it has done so far, which houses are of substantial artistic or historical merit, it seems to me that the nation is obliged to help devise a fair and efficient means of preserving them. In the end, this will probably involve (as it does today) a combination of legislation regarding maintenance, alterations, and demolition; acquisition justly compensated (whether by purchase, exchange, tax write-offs, or other benefits), with a guarantee of continued care; the uniquely British solution of a handover with endowment to a nongovernmental charity like the National Trust; transfer to another willing and able owner, with requirements for maintenance and care; or grants or tax credits enabling a private owner to maintain the building at the level required by law.

It is over this last area—direct aids to individual, privately owned houses—that the greatest political controversy is likely to arise. The logic of an argument I have frequently heard raised by private owners of listed houses seems to me hard to refute:

1. If the British government (by way of English Heritage or other agencies) declares a building to be of exceptional national importance; and

2. because of that national importance, the government insists that it cannot be demolished, cannot be altered without permission, and must be maintained by its owner to a high and historically "authentic" state of repair, at a much greater cost than would be the case with a similar building *not* so designated;

3. then the government, having declared the nation's interest in the building, obligates the nation to assist in maintaining it—at least to the extent of the added costs its regulations impose.[16]

How any particular government decides to do this is a matter for its own budget crafters to decide. In a democratic state, every special interest group will insist on the "essential," the "indispensible" importance of its own favored cause: schools, health care, roads and public transport, social services, job training, support for business or industry, subsidies for agriculture or basic research or foreign trade, and so on. Just where the preservation and care of national artistic and historic treasures come on a scale of budgetary priorities will depend on the available funds, and the values of elected politicians and their leaders, responding variously to the signals they receive from the electorate, the civil service, independent experts, public pressure groups, and the press.

The proposals most often made for government support for country houses judged historic all strike me as reasonable, insofar as they would enable important cultural assets to be preserved for current and future generations (of both Britons and foreign visitors) at a relatively small cost to the Treasury. In each case, it seems to me (pace Lord Hesketh) that straightforward and easily enforcible policies could be established to ensure that it was the designated historic *properties* that obtained the benefit, and not—except indirectly—their owners or inhabitants.

That the cost of labor and materials invested in building a new house should be free of the burden of a high national sales tax (the current 17.5 percent maximum VAT), while the far greater cost of making obligatory repairs to a listed historic house remains subject to this tax strikes me as anomalous and unfair. I have never heard or read a convincing justification for this baffling distinction. If anything, the situation—which may have its origins in earlier attempts to increase Britain's housing stock (or astute lobbying from the home building industry)—might well be reversed, considering the contribution that historic house owners are making to the nation's overall cultural wealth by their expenditures. Some degree of accord among European Union partners is now required for exempting or low-rating certain categories of expense from VAT, in order to maintain price equity across borders. But considering the generous support member nations have traditionally provided to their own artistic and historic patrimony, it should not be difficult for the EU to agree that the direct costs of maintaining it might be taxed at a considerably lower rate.

The argument that the income earned by the holdings of approved Maintenance Funds dedicated to the upkeep, restoration, and repair of acknowledged historic properties should be free of taxation seems to me no less reasonable, provided that they are set up with something like the rigor and obligations of charitable trusts, which have traditionally been granted tax-free status. In return, the government has a right to insist that such funds be (by means of something like Antony Jarvis's scheme) irrevocably tied to the property, and that they cannot benefit the owner or his heirs directly, now or in the future.

Beyond these two reasonable, clear-cut, and relatively simple proposals, other budgetary policies that would effect the welfare of country houses are far too complex and vexing to be resolved with nothing but their welfare in mind. These include the proper levels (and legal escape-hatches) of capital taxation on inheritance or other transfer; the size and availability of direct repair and maintenance grants, and the appropriate "strings" to attach to them; special favors or support for agricultural (or amenity) land; and the feasibility of an annual wealth or property tax. As the HHA has long argued, income tax relief for locked-in Maintenance Funds, and Value-Added Tax relief for essential repairs, would go a long way to obviating the need for more costly interventions by the state. At the very least, it does not seem to me unreasonable to allow the owner of *any* house (not just the top 200 or 300) judged to be of artistic or historic importance to the nation to deduct the costs of essential repairs to the historic fabric—if these can be clearly distinguished and justified—from his annual income before calculating his taxes.[17] Most other private or family expenses deserve no special consideration. But keeping up—restoring, repairing, reroofing, and so on—a house that has rightly been judged to be an important national treasure *is* a service to the nation, no less than to its inhabitants, and ought at least to be granted the tax-deductible status of donations to a registered charity.

· · ·

The fate of the English country houses that remain will be, in many cases, that of eventual conversion out of single family use, in order to fulfill other functions that can make use of rooms and spaces far too numerous or grand to serve their original purpose. A few more will become house-museums, the property of either the National Trust, civic bodies, or ad hoc charitable foundations. The most likely new uses, I believe, will be as retirement or nursing homes and multiple residences, although a few more may succeed as hotels, hospitals, and educational establishments, which can make use of their many bedrooms and extensive service facilities.

In other cases, new owners will be found, as they have been through the centuries— Nicholas Ridley was, at bottom, right about the nouveaux riches and the *anciens pauvres*. A few people keep turning up each year who are willing to take on the burdensome costs of these handsome but often anachronistic dwelling places, and what is left of their estates, from old owners who can no longer maintain them, or heirs who no longer wish to. In every generation, new fortunes are made, and new people—English and non-English—are attracted to contemporary versions of the "country house way of life."

In every generation as well, a few young representatives of old families come up with ingenious schemes either to exploit their own estates (which now includes art sales and land development, functions and filmmaking as well as agriculture and tourism); to earn good money off the estate; or to elude the worst of tax bills by legal means.

In both these cases—with no special prejudice to old over new owners—it would be to the nation's advantage to assist willing and able "stewards" of properties deemed of value to the nation as a whole, particularly in ways that draw no funds from (or deny no funds to) H.M. Treasury. One of the simplest, least costly (in fact, money-saving), and I believe least controversial means of assistance would be to reduce the obstacles set in the paths of imaginative and industrious owners by local conservation officers and English Heritage inspectors. The entire process of obtaining listed building consents—now so often either inflexible or capricious, and almost always needlessly costly and time-consuming—is clearly in need of re-examination, clarification, and rationalization, every bit as much as the swollen total of listed buildings itself. Patrick Phillips makes a persuasive case for an independent architectural ombudsman, and an appeals board *outside* of English Heritage, which—in cases of disputes over alterations—would listen to evidence from amenity societies and other experts, not just the adversarial arguments of owners and planning officials.

The role played by England's country houses in the leisure and tourism industry—the means by which most of us have come to know them—is now largely determined by government mandates to owners to open their houses to the public, in return for repair grants or the deferral of capital taxation. Although burdensome, even costly to many country house owners, I cannot conceive of a future government removing the access requirement.[18] By now, some 250 owners have grown used to the intrusion of outsiders; a few profess to enjoy it. Owners who can afford to do without government aid can enjoy the luxury of privacy, and most of them do now. Others must deal with the obligation as best they can. As I tried to point out in Chapter Seven, they are usually far better off if they can undertake the enterprise of opening wholeheartedly, in a businesslike manner, and with all possible good grace.

I have no fears for the future of country houses and estates in the care of the National Trust, English Heritage, most local authorities, or sufficiently endowed charitable trusts. With a more conscientious count of the *most* important houses, and a firm declaration of support for them by all three leading political parties, I would feel confident in the future—costly though it will be—of the 200 or 300 remaining country houses I regard as an essential part of England's artistic wealth and its visible, tangible, visitable past.

Beyond that number, I am not so sure. Some few may still make it on farm income, another few on specialized or "niche" tourism. Others may be able to meet their expenses through room rentals or property development. Wealthy people will continue to spend surplus income from other sources to maintain extravagant houses they love.

But I have just about concluded that, even at 3,000 to 4,000, England probably has today more large old country houses than its people or government can reasonably afford or find fit uses for; and that the essentially absolute ban on demolition, like the overly strict rules regarding alterations, should come to an end.

The value of the houses that remain, those that can either sustain themselves or justify the nation's support, will be enhanced by an official admission that not every outdated twenty-bedroom mansion in the countryside is, in fact, an essential "piece of the National Heritage."

· · ·

One other house owner in Oxfordshire I talked to in 1991, along with the Duke of Marlborough, Lord Saye and Sele, and Mrs. Gascoigne, was Charles Cottrell-Dormer, a worried farmer who lives in a 17th-century house (the family has been here since Tudor times) which was impressively altered for his ancestor, General James Dormer, by William Kent in 1718. Kent added two neat side pavilions, designed new furniture, and repainted the ceilings. But his most inspired contribution was a 30-acre landscape garden full of artificially natural looking groves and glades and vales, cascades and classical porticoes in the manner of Claude or Poussin—perhaps the first garden of its kind in existence, and virtually unaltered since it was built. "The whole," wrote Horace Walpole later in the century, "is as elegant and antique as if the Emperor Julian had selected the most pleasing solitude about Daphne to enjoy a philosophic retirement."[19] Mr. Cottrell-Dormer was enjoying no philosophic retirement. "I'm basically a farmer," he told me.

> I have to manage entirely off agricultural income. Sixteen hundred acres, plus twenty-seven letting houses. Of course, it costs to maintain them too. Some people seem to be able to make a go of opening their houses as a tourist attraction. But I just don't know how.
>
> I inherited Rousham with a mortgage in nineteen sixty. The village was in total disrepair. Since then I've paid off the mortgage, and fixed up all the buildings. But now the stable block needs major repairs, two million pounds' worth. And the oldest ha-ha in England, it goes all round the garden, we need twenty or thirty thousand for that.
>
> We use it all, it's our home. But I can't see any way to keep it in the family as a home. No one wants to live the way we do. I got a repair grant ten years ago, so now I'm obliged to open the house to visitors permanently. We get about ten thousand a year, because of the garden. It could take twenty or thirty thousand, but I've no idea how to attract more. We're not Blenheim, after all, with all that Churchilliana. The garden is open every day, the house only two afternoons a week. We get a few bus tours, National Trust groups, Fine Arts people. There was a mention in the *Daily Telegraph* last Saturday. A piece in the *Daily Mail* last summer helped—but only for that weekend. Advertising wouldn't be cost effective, and I couldn't stand doing tearooms and gift shops. There'd be no sense, anyway, for just ten thousand people.
>
> Visitors are a lot of bother, really. You have to remember to lock every door and window every time you go out, or people will just walk in. And I can't stand the smell of the house afterwards. The entry fees only just pay for the two full-time gardeners we need (plus my wife, and a part-time girl). We can't even afford to insure the Kent garden seats and urns. [Mr. Cottrell-Dormer was pleased to have caught a notorious 62-year-old country house burglar the previous spring, a man who had already committed at least 39 burglaries.]

No, he did not want to sacrifice his independence to the interference of a charitable trust. "If all the estate income goes to a trust, what's left for the heirs?" He had no immediate intentions of selling up, but he didn't like the idea of a lifetime transfer either. "Heritage" property or no, he concluded, "I can see no way to keep it going."

· · ·

On his deathbed, the old Marquis of Marchmain—one of Laurence Olivier's last and finest roles—rambled on about what the "heritage" implicit in an old country house like Brideshead meant to him:

> Aunt Julia, my father's aunt, lived to be eighty-eight, born and died here, never married, saw the fire on beacon hill for the Battle of Trafalgar, always called it 'the New House'...the house was a century old when Aunt Julia was born . . .
>
> Aunt Julia knew the tombs, cross-legged knight and doubleted earl, marquis like a Roman sen-

ator, limestone, alabaster, and Italian marble; tapped the escutcheons with her ebony cane, made the casque ring over old Sir Roger. We were knights then, barons since Agincourt, the larger honours came with the Georges. They came the last and they'll go the first; the barony goes on. When all of you are dead Julia's son will be called by the name his fathers bore before the fat days; the days of wool shearing and the wide corn lands, the days of growth and building, when the marshes were drained and the waste land brought under the plough, when one built the house, his son added the dome, his son spread the wings and dammed the river.[20]

APPENDIX

Definitions and Numbers

The phrase "stately home" was first popularized, in solemn earnest, by Mrs. Felicia Hemans, the once-famous poet, who wrote in 1827,

> The stately homes of England,
>   How beautiful they stand!
> Amidst their tall ancestral trees,
>   O'er all the pleasant land;

This was altered by Noël Coward in 1938 to read,

> The stately homes of England,
>   How beautiful they stand,
> To prove the upper classes
> Have still the upper hand.[1]

People who lobby on their behalf, or are arguing for government grants, prefer to call them "historic houses." Instead of "stately home" or "historic house," both of which terms beg a few questions, I prefer to use the understated, self-effacing label "country house"—by which I mean a large private residence originally intended to serve as one family's home for at least several generations; a house of 20 rooms or more, which rules out most farmhouses and vicarages, however old or picturesque; a house that, ideally, still contains furniture and art works handed down in the family, and contributes to the support of the local church, village, and countryside; a house that is set in its own surrounding gardens and parkland and is (or at least originally was) in part supported by its own agricultural estate of a thousand or more acres.

Many of those acres were sold off long ago. Many of these places are no longer private residences. Of the 1,400 owner-members of the Historic Houses Association, some own houses smaller than this standard. But they are more than counterbalanced by the many country house owners—including those of several large, well-known establishments—who do not belong to the association. Add to these more than 100 large country houses now the property of the National Trust; another dozen or so belonging to the nation; and half a dozen royal houses. These, and others that now serve as museums for civic and regional authorities, are usually open to the public as well, as are some 300 HHA members' houses, and the gardens of perhaps 200 more.

That would appear to add up to a total of something under 2,000 substantial country houses that still assume at least the form of private houses, about two-thirds of them in private hands, and more than 400 open to view at least some part of the year. The numbers most often cited in books on the subject before this one—perhaps simply handed down from one writer to another—are in the 1,300–1,500 range, but then this number often refers to still-private, still-occupied houses. Country houses open to the public, or whose owners belong to a common association, are obviously the easiest to count. For reasons of privacy and security, I have found, most owners of medium-sized country houses in England, however historically or artistically important their houses may be, are not eager to have their names or locations made known.

For other reasons, it is impossible to tally up the total number of country houses in Britain that stand derelict and abandoned. The advocacy organization called SAVE Britain's Heritage guessed there were about 120 in 1985, but then discovered 140 in Scotland alone five years later. Similarly, although I know of several hundred, I have been unable to compile a complete list of those that have been transformed into hotels, private schools or training centers, hospitals or nursing homes, blocks of flats or multiple-house arrangements, corporate headquarters, conference centers, and the like.

There are numerous ways one might try to refine this definition of a "proper" country house, and obtain a more precise count of those both standing (in whatever form) and demolished. In *An Open Elite?* (1984), Lawrence and Jeanne Stone undertook a painstaking assessment of all the pre-1880 country houses built in three English counties. The British Ordnance Survey maps of 1867–82 were drawn to such a large scale that one could actually measure off the dimensions of large buildings, then compare those measurements with other drawings and plans to get a reasonable estimate of each house's floor space.

Having done that, and consulted other contemporary documents, the Stones determined that a major break occurred at the 5,000 square foot mark.[2] Below that point could be counted most farmhouses, manor or gentry houses in towns and villages, and "houses in the country," with no particular landed status. Above that point stood virtually all houses that stood at the center of substantial agricultural estates.

I do not have the time or facilities to measure the floor area of country houses in the remaining 35 (pre-1974) English counties. I am interested in the story not as of 1880, where the Stones end their story, but as of the mid-1990s. And a great many of the "country houses" I am concerned with no longer stand at the center of agricultural estates. Even so, the Stones' approach to a definition still seems to make sense. It was, after all, the 300-year-long history of English country houses as the headquarters of such estates that established most of whatever enduring historical and cultural significance they possess. So it seems to me reasonable to try to maintain, even for later, unlanded country houses, the same space distinctions—a measure of "grandeur" in both the English and French senses of the word—that Lawrence and Jeanne Stone decided typified a "true" country house of 1540–1880.

·   ·   ·

Trying to compile a master list of surviving country houses in England that met both their definition and mine, I turned to a number of sources. A key source was *Country Life* magazine, founded in 1897, which for many years has tended to "profile" one historic property in each weekly issue. The cumulative index published in December 1993 contains references to a total of 2,523 English houses outside of cities written about in the magazine during its first 96 years. Even excluding references to "cottages" or "farmhouses," as well as townhouses, I am sure that some of the remaining listings—the index includes 30 different places called "The Manor House"—are smaller than the Stones' standard for a proper country house. Subtracting those I know to have been demolished and not replaced yields a total of about 2,100 houses published so far in the magazine, which has done so much to define the English country house and to defend it as a cultural institution. Like other indices of published country houses, this still leaves room for the likelihood that there are many others that never made it into print.

Two authors have compiled lists of country houses described and illustrated in topographical guides and other books since the 18th century. John Harris drew up in 1971 (and expanded in 1979) an index of 1,751 country houses *illustrated* in any one of 107 books of country views (from the Mellon collection at Yale) published between 1715 and 1872. Michael Holmes, in *The Country House Described: An Index to the Country Houses of Great Britain and Ireland* (1986) cast his net even further, embracing an immense number of books and periodicals (including *Country Life*) in the library of the Victoria and Albert Museum. Reaching more than a century further on, he comes up with 3,675 country houses in England mentioned in print at one time or another.[3]

The "Index to the Principal Seats in the United Kingdom" appended to Edward Walford's *County Families of the United Kingdom* (1901 edition) identifies 3,321 such places in England (and 1,974 more in Scotland, Ireland, and Wales). John Bateman's *The Great Landowners of Great Britain and Ireland* (fourth edition, 1883) identifies, along with their owners' acreage and annual revenues, a total of 1,323 English estates of more than 3,000 acres, and another 617 of 2,000–3000 acres.[4] Although Bateman makes no mention of houses, it seems reasonable to assume that most of these estates contained a dwelling place of some substance.

A five-volume series on English Country Houses was published by Country Life Publications between 1956 and 1970. Drawn in most cases from house histories and descriptions that had already appeared in *Country Life*, and designed to serve as a replacement for H. Avray Tipping's monumental series of 1909–37, these books covered the years between "Caroline" (1615–1685) and "Late Georgian" (1810–1840).[5] The series can be extended backward by Maurice Howard, *The Early Tudor Country House* (1987), which covers the years 1490–1550; and forward by Mark Girouard's *The Victorian Country House* (1971), which continues the story up to 1890. To fill in the gap between 1550 and 1615, I depended on the three old volumes in Tipping's series that covered the period. Clive Aslet's *The Last Country Houses* (1982), pushes the story up to 1939. John Martin Robinson, annoyed at the presumption of Aslet's title, published in 1984 *The Latest Country Houses*, describing new houses in the country (as well as restorations, remodellings, alterations, additions, conversions, and extensions) undertaken since World War II.

Howard's, Aslet's, and Robinson's surveys treat their periods thematically rather than house by house. But for the five Country Life volumes, and Mark Girouard's Victorians, a detailed historical and stylistic overview of the period is followed by individual historical and critical analyses of about 30 surviving houses of the time the author deems especially worthy of note. The authors also list or mention 100–200 additional houses—including those no longer standing, or altered beyond recognition—built or rebuilt during their period. There is a great deal of overlap among all these lists, because houses built in one period were often significantly remodeled in another—and then another, and another; the multicentury 'palimpsest' house is an English speciality. But taken altogether, these sequential period surveys identify about 1,100 substantial country houses still standing in England.

Another important source is the 46-volume *Buildings of England* series edited by Nikolaus Pevsner and his colleagues between 1951 and 1975. Here, one must make some speculative discriminations of one's own, based on what are often very brief descriptions, between moderate-sized manor houses (of which hundreds are noted) and more substantial country houses—often simply by accepting a minimum number of bays or stories on the facade. (A three-bay, two-story house, for example, is clearly too small. At five bays and three stories, it is growing into a proper country house.) By this standard, Pevsner and his coauthors list some 2,000 country houses for England as a whole standing in the years when they were writing, of which about 200 were regarded as sufficiently important for extended descriptions.

In their inventory of country houses built between 1540 and 1880 in Hertfordshire, Northumberland, and Northamptonshire, Lawrence and Jeanne Stone came up with a total of 374 that met their minimum space standards. Either because they had been simply demolished or replaced by newer houses, only 248 of these remained standing in 1880. (At least 35 of these have disappeared since, but then a similar number may have been built since 1880 to replace them.)

Eight other counties were combed fairly closely in the second and third volumes of the Burke's and Savills *Guide to Country Houses* (1980–81), edited by the indefatigable Hugh Montgomery-Massingberd: Herefordshire, Shropshire, Warwickshire, and Worcestershire in Volume II, and Cambridgeshire, Essex, Norfolk, and Suffolk in Volume III. (The first volume was devoted to Ireland. Unfortunately, the series—originally intended to cover all England, in ten volumes—stopped after Volume III.) These extensive and illustrated inventories help one to realize how slippery the numbers game is, including as they do so many relatively small houses, totally remodeled houses, and places that are, at best, "houses in the country." Perhaps half would make the cut as "country houses," by the standards I have proposed. In all, these two volumes describe a total of 1,578 houses, 256 of them demolished, for a net total of 1,322; at the time of publication, at least 228 of these were being used as something other than family houses.

Hugh Massingberd estimated that, had the Burke's/Savills series reached completion, it would have contained about 10,000 "country seats," as he chose to call them. As he has done elsewhere in his copious and affectionate writing on the subject, Massingberd enjoyed the opportunity to focus on "the 'illustrious obscure' house, neglected by most books, not all architecturally excellent, but," he insisted, "even more than the well-known Statelies, a British specialty whose increasing loss is a real threat to our history."[6]

With the help of Pamela Johnson, I made my own effort to count all the country estates in Derbyshire, which I chose because of its impressive collection of major country houses (Hardwick, Haddon, Kedleston, etc.), and the fact that its borders remained unaltered in the 1974 rearrangement of British county lines—completely forgetting that it was as much a mining as an agricultural county, much of it occupied by what is now the Peak District National Park, which reduces its "typical" character. In the medium scale (one inch = one mile) Ordnance Survey maps, country estates are individually named, and identified by areas of dots. In the 1887 maps, we located 189 named estates; in 1923, 174. At least sixteen of these have been demolished since 1923. As with Bateman, I am rashly presuming the presence of one country house on each identified country estate.

After interfiling and amending my master list by means of all these sources, I now have a list of the names, locations, brief descriptions and histories of about 3,500 country houses that I think survive in England in one form or another. Ideally, I would now take off a few years and, packing a pile of Ordnance Survey maps, Pevsner's *Buildings of England*, local directories, and old copies of *Burke's Landed Gentry* in the back seat, drive about the backroads of all 38 (or 41) English counties checking out each entry on my list, to see whether and where it stands, and if it was substantial enough to pass the Stones' test for grandeur.

Lacking the time and inclination to do that, I return to the last-named sets of figures—the Stones' for three counties, Burke's/Savills for eight more, and my own for Derbyshire. These seem to me to come closest to thoroughness, despite the overly generous inclusiveness of the Burke's/Savills guides, my ignorance of the size of the houses on the Derbyshire estates, and the fact that the Stones only trace the status of their houses up to 1882. There is no infallible way to extrapolate a national total out of twelve counties, every region of England having different social and economic characteristics. But comparing the area and the nonurban population of England as a whole with that of these twelve counties, one might generously speculate a grand total of something like 7,000 country houses standing today, of which slightly more than half—say 3,500–4,000—might be sufficiently grand to meet the Stones' definition.

NOTES

CHAPTER TWO

1. See Appendix.

2. Flora Thompson, "Candleford Green," 1943, from *Lark Rise to Candleford*, 1945; 1973 edition, pp. 400, 403.

3. Lawrence Stone, *The Crisis of the Aristocracy*, 1965, pp. 585, 551.

4. Ibid., p. 551.

5. John Nichols, *The Progresses and Public Processions of Queen Elizabeth*, 1788; 1823 edition, vol. I, p. xxvii.

6. Nichols, vol. I, p. xxiv.

7. Godfrey Goodman, *The Court of King James I*, ed. J. S. Brewer, 1839, vol. I, p. 199.

8. Lawrence Stone, *Family and Fortune: Studies in Aristocratic Finances in the 16th and 17th Centuries*, 1973, p. 28.

9. Ibid., pp. 31–32.

10. James Lees-Milne, *English Country Houses, Baroque: 1685–1715*, 1970, pp. 9–11.

11. Ibid., p. 70.

12. Mark Girouard, *Life in the English Country House*, 1978, p. 231.

13. Ibid., p. 161

14. Christopher Hussey, *English Country Houses: Early Georgian, 1715–1760*, 1955, rev. 1965, p. 157.

15. Mark Girouard, *The Victorian Country House*, 1971, p. 6.

16. Ibid., p. 185.

17. Ibid., p. 4.

18. In *The Studio Year-Book of Decorative Art*, 1908, pp. xi-xii; quoted in Clive Aslet, *The Last Country Houses*, 1982, p. 2.

19. Christopher Sykes, *Nancy: The Life of Lady Astor*, 1972, pp. 366–67.
20. Anthony Masters, *Nancy Astor: A Life*, 1981, p. 193.
21. John Grigg, *Nancy Astor, Portrait of a Pioneer*, 1980, p. 145.
22. Ibid., p. 151.
23. Ibid., p. 149.

Chapter Three

1. Marcus Binney and Marianne Watson-Smyth, *The SAVE Britain's Heritage Action Guide*, 1991, p. 33.
2. Mark Girouard, *The Victorian Country House*, 1971, p. 27; Osbert Sitwell, "Foreword," in Ralph Dutton, *The English Country House*, 1935.
3. F. M. L. Thompson, *English Landed Society in the Nineteenth Century*, 1961, p. 342.
4. John Martin Robinson, *The Country House at War*, 1989, p. 169.
5. Evelyn Waugh, *Brideshead Revisited*, 1945; Penguin Books edition 1962, p. 330.
6. Roy Strong, in *The Destruction of the English Country House, 1875–1975*, 1975, pp. 8–9.
7. Strong, p. 11; John Cornforth, *Country Houses in Britain: Can They Survive?*, 1974, p. 19.
8. Maurice Howard, *The Early Tudor Country House: Architecture and Politics 1490–1550*, 1987, p. 27.
9. Ian Dunlop, *Palaces and Progresses of Elizabeth I*, 1962, pp. 18, 196.
10. Strong, op. cit., 1975, p. 15.
11. David Cannadine, *The Decline and Fall of the British Aristocracy*, 1990, p. 118.
12. E.g., Lawrence Stone and Jeanne C. Fawtier Stone, *An Open Elite? England 1540–1880*, 1984; F. M. L. Thompson, *English Landed Society in the Nineteenth Century*, 1963.
13. Cannadine, op. cit., p. 217.
14. Cannadine, op. cit., p. 220.
15. Cannadine, op. cit., pp. 242, 289, 292.
16. Henry Durant, "The development of landownership with special reference to Bedfordshire, 1773–1925," *Sociological Review*, 1936, p. 89.
17. Lord Newton, *Lord Lansdowne: A Biography*, 1929, pp. 127–29.
18. Cannadine, op. cit., p. 153.
19. Ibid., p. 157.
20. Ibid., pp. 26, 27.
21. "The Duke of Devonshire was spending 17 per cent of his disposible income on interest payments in 1874, but 60 per cent by 1880." Cannadine, p. 94.
22. *The Times*, October 3, 1885.
23. *Estates Gazette*, January 14, 1921.
24. *Estates Gazette*, August 29, 1931
25. Caroline Seebohm, *The Country House: A Wartime History, 1939–45*, 1989, p. 5.
26. Robinson, op. cit., p. 44. The neo-Georgian house survived the war and the schoolgirls from Portsmouth, only to be gutted by an accidental fire in April 1960. It has since been rebuilt in neo-neo-Georgian.
27. Robinson, op. cit., p. 11.
28. Quoted in Robinson, op. cit., p. 131.
29. Merlin Waterson, ed., *The Country House Remembered; Recollections of Life between the Wars*, 1985, p. 243.
30. Robinson, op. cit., p. 2.
31. Seebohm, op. cit, p. 106.

32. Robinson, op. cit., p. 166.

33. James Lees-Milne, *Prophesying Peace*, 1977, p. 182.

34. Ibid., p. 210.

35. Quoted in John Gaze, *Figures in a Landscape: a History of the National Trust*, 1988, p. 151.

Chapter Four

1. "The National Trust and the Country House," pamphlet published by the National Trust, 1980, revised 1988.

2. Quoted in Carolyn Seebohm, *The Country House: A Wartime History, 1939–45*, 1989, p. 61.

3. Quoted in Merlin Waterson, *The National Trust: The First Hundred Years*, 1994, p. 105.

4. James Lees-Milne, *Prophesying Peace*, 1977, p. 197. Lees-Milne was the sole salaried employee of the National Trust responsibile for carrying out its Country House Scheme in 1936–39 and 1941–51. He remained a half-time adviser until 1966.

5. Over Vita Sackville-West's dead body, literally and figuratively. "Never, never, never! not that little metal plate at my door! Nigel can do whatever he likes when I am dead but so long as I live no National Trust or any other foreign body shall have my darling…It is bad enough to have lost Knole but they shan't take Sissinghurst from me!" Letter to Viginia Woolf, quoted in Anne Scott-James, *Sissinghurst: The Making of a Garden*, 1974, p. 122.

6. James Lees-Milne, *Ancestral Voices*. 1975, p. 190.

7. James Lees-Milne, *Caves of Ice*, 1983, p. 168.

8. *Ancestral Voices*, pp. 269, 273, 284.

9. *Prophesying Peace*, p 167.

10. *Ancestral Voices*, p. 50; *Caves of Ice*, p. 5.

11. *Ancestral Voices*, pp. 5–6, 6, 10, 187; *Prophesying Peace*, p. 113.

12. James Lees-Milne, *People and Places: Country House Donors and the National Trust*, 1992, p. 105; *Ancestral Voices*, p. 197; *Caves of Ice*, p. 49; *Ancestral Voices*, p. 112.

13. *Ancestral Voices*, pp. 67, 94.

14. *Ancestral Voices*, p. 120.

15. A sampling of Lees-Milne's out-of-fashion opinions:

"I never expect gratitude, loyalty, affection, etc. from servants. They don't know the meaning of these qualities. From the uneducated one must expect self-interest, meanness, mendacity and guile. Of such is the kingdom of the proletariat." *Ancestral Voices*, p. 214.

"The Castle grounds [Dudley Castle, near Birmingham] are a zoo, teeming with animals and people. A ghastly place. I saw what I wanted and hurried away, sickened by humanity in the gross. The people of the Midlands are incredibly primitive." *Caves of Ice*, p. 167.

[After visiting Lower Brockhampton, a 16th-century moated manor house in Herefordshire bequeathed to the Trust in 1946]: "This evening the whole tragedy of England impressed itself upon me. This small, not very important seat in the heart of our secluded country, is now deprived of its last squire. A whole social system has broken down. What will replace it beyond government by the masses, uncultivated, rancorous, savage, philistine, the enemies of all things beautiful? How I detest democracy. More and more I believe in benevolent autocracy." *Caves of Ice*, p. 172.

16. Some owners were a bit unclear on the concept of public access. "Whatever you people do, I cannot have the public near the place," was Lady Astor's first remark to the National Trust representatives regarding Cliveden. At first, Sir Henry Fairfax-Lucy presumed that he could give Charlecote Park to the Trust to maintain, continue living in and managing it, and not admit the public at all—or at most during only three winter months, when he presumed that few people would come. Lord Sackville was opposed to

any publicity regarding the National Trust's takeover at Knole, for fear it would entice people to visit. One member of the Trust's own subcommittee on Montacute declared during a meeting, "We can't possibly let the public inside a house with valuable works of art. They smell." *Ancestral Voices*, p. 210; *People and Places*, pp. 94, 98, 181; *Prophesying Peace*, p. 160.

17. Paula Weideger, *Gilding the Acorn: Behind the Facade of the National Trust*, 1994, p. 90.

18. Ibid., pp. 87–88.

19. This is particularly the case at West Wycombe, where Sir Francis Dashwood estimates he has contributed almost a million pounds in repairs, restoration, and other contributions since 1956.

20. Reprinted in *The National Trust Magazine*, Spring 1995, p. 46.

21. Robin Fedden, *The Continuing Purpose: A History of the National Trust, Its Aims and Work*, 1968, p. 50.

22. *Prophesying Peace*, pp. 195, 125.

23. Madeleine Beard, *English Landed Society in the Twentieth Century*, 1989, p. 132.

24. The Thatcher government did in fact end the relatively short-lived Capital Transfer Tax in 1986, and reinstitute death duties, renamed (as in the United States) Inheritance Tax, with the maximum rate reduced to 40 percent. It also revived the provision for lifetime handovers, tax-exempt if concluded at least seven years before the grantor's death. But in 1989 these handovers were once again made subject to capital gains tax. Changes in British tax rates and policies occur so frequently they are very hard to keep up with.

25. Quoted in Marcus Binney and Gervase Jackson-Stops, "The Last Hundred Years," in Jackson-Stops, ed., *The Treasure Houses of Britain*, 1985, p. 74.

26. Sir Ernest Gowers et al., *H. M. Treasury: Report of the Committee on Houses of Outstanding Historic or Architectural Interest*, 1950, p. 1.

27. Ibid., pp. 4, 6.

28. Ibid., pp. 32, 34, 38.

29. John Cornforth, *Country Houses in Britain: Can They Survive?*, 1974, p. 34.

30. Every building dating from before 1700 is listed, as well as most of those between 1700 and 1840. For the period 1840–1914, buildings of "quality and character" are selected, particularly those designed by known architects. The 1986–89 resurvey added a great number of Victorian and Edwardian buildings to the list. Since then, any structure 30 years old becomes eligible.

31. The text of the 1971 Town and Country Planning Act reads, "if a person executes or causes to be executed any works for the demolition of a listed building or for its alteration or extension in any manner which would affect its character as a building of special architectural or historic interest, and the works are not authorised…he shall be guilty of an offence."

The 1971 Act also gave local authorities the power to acquire abandoned or derelict historic buildings by way of compulsory purchase orders. But local authorities have been unenthusiastic about taking them on, because of the additional burden of costs, and the problem of finding new uses or owners.

32. William Proby, "The Fiscal Climate for Country Houses since 1965," *Apollo*, December 1989, p. 404.

33. Cornforth, op. cit., p. 47.

34. *The Journeys of Celia Fiennes*, ed. Christopher Morris, 1947, pp. 69–70.

35. Fiennes, op. cit, p. 69; Daniel Defoe, *A Tour Through the Whole Island of Great Britain*, 1724–26, Dent/Everyman's edition rev. 1962, vol. II, p. 108.

36. The Duchess of Devonshire, *The House: Living at Chatsworth*, 1982, p. 86; *Chatsworth: The Home of the Duke and Duchess of Devonshire*, 1986, p. 30; Richard Warner, *A Tour Through the Northern Counties of England, and the Borders of Scotland* (1802), vol. I, p. 218.

37. Adrian Tinniswood, *A History of Country House Visiting: Five Centuries of Tourism and Taste* (1989), p. 91.

38. *The Mirror of Literature and Amusement*, February 1844; quoted in the Chatsworth guidebook cited above.

39. "This, to many, was the crowning gratification, for to see the noble Duke as well as Chatsworth, on one and the same day, was to consummate their happiness, and render that a day never to be forgotten." From an 1849 newspaper article quoted in The Duchess of Devonshire, *The House: Living at Chatsworth* (1982), p. 87.

40. Tinniswood, op. cit., p. 137.

41. Tinniswood, op. cit., pp. 157–58.

42. The Marchioness of Exeter, "The Future of Great Country Houses," *Country Life* 126, 1945, p. 813.

43. David Cannadine, *The Decline and Fall of the Aristocracy*, 1989, pp. 645–46.

44. Lord Montagu of Beaulieu, *The Gilt and the Gingerbread*,1967, p. 104

45. Montagu of Beaulieu, op. cit., pp. 109, 105, 108.

46. Ian, Duke of Bedford, *A Silver-Plated Spoon*,1959, pp. 59, 224, 218; Montagu of Beaulieu, op. cit., p. 103; from a London *Sunday Dispatch* interview of 1958.

47. Bedford, op. cit., pp. 135–36.

48. Ibid., p. 196.

49. Ibid., p. 191–92.

50. Ibid., p. 198.

51. Bedford, op. cit., p. 218.

52. John Duke of Bedford, *How to Run a Stately Home*, 1971, p. 34.

53. Montagu of Beaulieu, op. cit., p. 85.

CHAPTER FIVE

1. Michael Sayer and Hugh Massingberd, *The Disintegration of a Heritage*, 1993, p. 36.

2. At the upper end of the Stones' scale, a few country houses in each of the counties they surveyed are from 200,000 to 500,000 square feet in size. Lawrence Stone and Jeanne C. Fawtier Stone, *An Open Elite? England 1540–1888*, 1984.

3. "Report on English Heritage Section 3A Grants," Historic Houses Association, 1995.

4. Hugh Pearman, "Castles in the Air," *The Sunday Times*, August 8, 1993.

5. Her figures were questioned by the owner of a twenty-room Grade I listed manor house in County Durham, who was getting by quite nicely, he insisted, on £8,000 ($13,000) a year. Vicky Ward, "Why Alice Had to Leave Wonderland," *The Independent*, April 3, p. 19; Dr. J. Hawgood, Letter to the Editor, *The Independent*, April 11, 1995, p. 14.

6. Ann Morris, "The Burdens—and Pleasures—of Living in a Listed Property," *The Sunday Telegraph*, August 28, 1994, p. 23.

7. Morris, op. cit.

8. "Report on English Heritage Section 3A Grants," op. cit.; *Historic House*, Winter 1989, p. 5.

9. Morris, op. cit.

10. *Historic Houses Association Annual Report*, 1990–91, p. 23.

11. David Blackwell, "British Farmers Vote with their Feet," *The Financial Times*, February 6, 1991, p. 23.

12. John Young, "Earl Fights to Keep Heritage a Family Affair," *The Times*, January 2, 1992.

13. Susan Clarke, "Now Anything Goes," *The Times*, October 30, 1994.

14. Jonathan David, *Historic House*, Spring 1993, p. 35.

15. *Insurance Age*, March 24, 1992.

16. Norman Hudson, a professional consultant to country house owners, suggests that council taxes on wholly domestic properties are "not a particular burden." But business rates, which are levied on the portion of a house open to the public and presumably earning income, can vary widely. The latter, in Hudson's view, are sometimes unreasonably and unfairly assessed.

17. "The Stately Homes of England, How Wobbly They Stand," *The Economist*, July 23, 1984.

18. *The Daily Telegraph*, August 28, 1993, p. 17. Surplus silver and antiques, sold at auction in May 1996, raised more than £1.2 million ($1,930,000) for the Parham Trust.

19. The Historic Houses Association estimates that English Heritage repair grants to its own members rose to a total of £1,650,000 ($2,937,000) in 1988, then dropped to a low of £406,000 ($609,000) in 1993. The total was back up to £1,389,000 ($2,125,000) in 1994; but this represented only 23 grants, vs. 69 in 1988.

20. *English Heritage Reports and Accounts*, 1990–91, p. 4; 1991–92, p. 3.

21. The Earl of Shelburne, "Has English Heritage Lost its Way?" *Historic House*, Autumn 1991, p. 5; Lord Montagu of Beaulieu, "English Heritage and Grants to Historic Houses," *Historic House*, Winter 1991, p. 9.

22. Will Hutton, "Why the Rich Must be Forced to Hand over their Vast Inheritance," *The Guardian*, August 8, 1994, p. 11.

23. *The Observer*, June 7, 1992; David Leigh, *The Guardian*, October 8, 1992, p. 22.

24. Leigh, op. cit.

Chapter Six

1. Robert Hughes, "Brideshead Redecorated," *Time*, Nov. 11, 1985, p. 64.

2. In Gervase Jackson-Stops, ed., *The Treasure Houses of Britain*, 1985, p. 51.

3. Quoted in Jackson-Stops, p. 58. The sale lasted 40 days, and realized more than £75,000, not counting the library.

4. Considering that the best pieces had all been sold in 1848, the 1921 catalogue of 3,955 remaining lots is still impressive. Paintings by Rubens, Van Dyck, Correggio, Titian, Kneller, Velázquez, Reynolds, Lely, Gainsborough, Claude, Poussin, Hoppner, and Landseer—or so they thought—were still at Stowe to be sold, along with Grinling Gibbons woodcarvings, thirteen marble mantlepieces, scores of old guns and sabres, whole ceilings and wall panels, a throne Queen Victoria sat in, and objets d'art made of gold, silver, ivory, malachite, sandalwood, and brass. Also on offer were beds, bidets, hip baths, tons of linen, quilts, stuffed birds, antlers, kitchen coppers, fire engines, and "24 large old barrels (damaged)."

5. Gerald Reitlinger, *The Economics of Taste*, 1961–70, II, p. 236.

6. In great part because of a strong current of hostility to Earl Spencer's second wife Raine, daughter of novelist Barbara Cartland, and because of the extra attention paid to the Princess of Wales's childhood home, an angry series of articles and books appeared between 1987 and 1993 attacking the Althorp sales. These included, apparently, six Van Dycks (the first four went to the government in 1976 in lieu of death duties) and 100 other paintings, as well as furniture, porcelain, silver, drawings, rare books, and family archives.

Like all beleaguered owner/sellers, Lord Spencer defended his sales of art objects as essential to meeting the costs of running Althorp. "I inherited a million and a half pounds in death duties and another two million in estate debt," he reminded the press in 1991. Sixteen years after inheriting, he claimed, he was still paying it off.

Art world observers doubted his claim, however, and believed the continued sales from Althorp were a matter of "asset stripping" pure and simple, to subsidize a lavish lifestyle with no regard for either heritage or posterity. Robin Simon, editor of the art magazine *Apollo*, called the Althorp sales "the worst scandal that has happened to a country house in the last century. No one has ever put their hands on a collection and dealt with it so ruthlessly." Timothy Clifford, the outspoken director of the National Galleries of Scotland, called it "one of the great tragedies of the eighties." (Angela Levin, "Shame and Fortune," *The Daily Mail*, June 17, 1993, p. 51.)

7. A consortium of four British museums had unsuccessfully tried to purchase the lot for £1.65 million. It sold for almost twice that at auction; but then commissions and taxes reduced Viscount Coke's net to little more than the consortium's offer. Lord Coke—now Lord Leicester—was incensed by the furore raised by the museum directors at his trying to sell 66 master drawings to anyone else.

"When the drawings were sold, people shouted about 'The Heritage' leaving the country and so on; and it irks me. It really does irk me. Because these are the drawings bought by one's ancestor, *his* property, passed by descent through the various generations. And then a descendant decides to sell them. And then for some curious reason they become 'the property of the nation,' virtually or implied, and there are all sorts of bars put in your way.... I mean, the British Museum has got a hundred thousand Italian master drawings. A great many of them are not catalogued, and therefore the taxpayer isn't allowed to see them. Why in the name of God they want another sixty-six drawings I cannot understand—no matter how good they are."

8. In 1990, he had estimated the load of debt he took on with Broadlands, after his grandfather's assassination in 1979, at £14 million, or $25 million.

9. Letter to the Editor, *The Independent*, February 14, 1992, p. 20. Lord Cholmondeley had already ceded a prize early Gainsborough painting to the National Gallery valued at £1,750,000 in lieu of taxes.

10. Anthony Thorncroft, *The Financial Times*, March 19, 1992, p. 8.

11. In August 1996, a gigantic Guercino from Castle Howard was also "saved" from going to the Getty by post-deadline contributions. It went instead to Edinburgh, for just over £2 million.

12. Caroline McGhie, "Sales of the Centuries," *The Daily Telegraph*, Sept. 11, 1994.

13. Aubrey Chalmers, "£1/4 Million for 'Junk' in the Attic," *The Daily Mail*, Sept. 24, 1994.

14. McGhie, op. cit.

15. *Fortune*, November 20, 1978; *The Economist*, May 21, 1977.

16. Tim Jones, "Halt Called to March of the Fairways," *The Times*, June 26, 1991.

17. "Earl's Golfing Plans Land in the Rough," *The Daily Telegraph*, October 31, 1991, p. 23.

18. Hugh Massingberd, "A New Bunker Mentality," *The Daily Telegraph*, February 1, 1992, p. 103.

19. *Hudson's Historic Houses and Gardens*, 1996, p. 23. The description of Mentmore's conference facilities comes from its 1994 advertising brochure.

20. Ibid., p. 77.

21. Cryssie Lytton Cobbold, *Board Meetings in the Bath: The Knebworth House Story*, 1986, pp. 88, 100.

22. Alan Bennett, "Inside Story: King of America," *The Guardian*, February 25, 1995, p. 20. Other locations for this film included Arundel Castle, Syon House, and Wilton House.

23. Sue Birtwhistle and Susie Conklin, *The Making of 'Pride and Prejudice'*, 1995, p. 25.

24. Anthea Hall, "Action! Film-makers Put Homes in the Frame," *The Sunday Telegraph*, June 20, 1993, p. 9.

25. "You will obviously want to avoid being party to anything which is obscene or of which you would not approve eg. the dramatisation of the private life of a public person which you feel should not be publicised," advises the Historic Houses Association in its *Film and Photography* guide.

CHAPTER SEVEN

1. Altogether, the 1994 *Historic Houses* guide lists nearly 500 places that appear to be (or to have been) country houses now open to the public in one form or another, not counting hotels. *Hudson's Historic Houses and Gardens* of 1996 lists about 440.

2. Despite the legend of the "Stately Home Industry," and the substantial profits earned by a few

country houses open to the public, a majority of owners who are obliged to open insist that it is, for them, a money-losing enterprise:

"Over the last five years we have been averaging 60,000 visitors per annum, and we are currently losing about £1 for every visitor who comes here." (Alnwick Castle)

"Visitors to the house cost as much as they earn." (Burghley House)

"We have yet to come across anyone who makes money out of opening their house to the public." (Coughton Court)

On the other hand, the owners of a number of smaller houses assure me that tourist income not only covers the costs of opening, but makes a substantial contribution to the far greater cost of running the house.

3. The name is given to legal Monday holidays in Britain, when banks, schools, and offices are closed, and families throng to day-trip destinations like country houses. There are Bank Holiday weekends in April, around Whitsunday (May-June), and in August, comparable to Memorial Day or Labor Day weekends in the U.S.

4. "Possett: a drink made of hot milk curdled with ale, wine, or the like, often sweetened and spiced." *The Random House College Dictionary*, 1980.

5. Of the twenty most-visited attractions charging admission in Britain in 1995, four were theme parks, four were similar commercial nonhistoric locations, two were zoos, and three were London museums. The most popular "country house," if one can call it that, was Windsor Castle, in seventh place, with 1,212,000 visitors, against first-place Alton Towers' 2,707,000. Warwick Castle ranked eighteenth of the top twenty, with 803,000.

6. John, Duke of Bedford, *How to Run a Stately Home*, 1971, pp. 53, 49. I must admit I find it hard to imagine a room containing £800,000 worth of art with linoleum on the floor.

7. In recent years, the privately owned country houses attracting the greatest number of visitors (the numbers are an average of the 1990–1995 totals reported to the British Tourist Authority) have been:

  1. Warwick Castle (731,000)
  2. Leeds Castle (529,000)
  3. Blenheim Palace (476,000)
  4. Beaulieu Abbey and Palace House (463,000)*
  5. Chatsworth (415,000)
  6. Hever Castle (272,000)
  7. Castle Howard (210,000: no figures for 1994)
  8. Harewood (208,000)
  9. Hatfield House (162,000)
  10. Arundel Castle (157,000)
  11. Weston Park (152,000)
  12. Bowood (146,000)
  13. Longleat (145,000: 1991–1995 average)**
  14. Knebworth (134,000)
  15. Bamburgh Castle (118,000; only 1993–94 totals reported)
  16. Skipton Castle (112,000; 1990–94 average; now closed)
  17. Newby Hall (108,000)
  18. Penshurst Place (104,000)

Woburn Abbey, which does not report its visitor numbers, surely belongs on this list also. Two royal palaces (Windsor Castle and Hampton Court Palace, with 888,000 and 563,000 respectively), thirteen National Trust houses, and three other publicly owned country houses had average annual totals of 100,000 or more during 1990–94.

*As a single ticket buys admission to Beaulieu and the National Motor Museum, it is impossible to say how many of the visitors listed under Beaulieu went to one or the other.

**The safari park at Longleat attracted another 380,000 people in 1994. Its opposite number at Woburn drew 230,000.

8. The English figure is exceeded in the Western world only by the Netherlands, with 945. Globally, only Java (a part of Indonesia), with 1,509, and South Korea, with 1,130, exceed it.

9. With a stock of 3,000 different items, from a 10p postcard to a £3,000 reproduction of a Delft tulip vase, the two shops at Chatsworth take in more than a million pounds ($1.5 million) a year, and contribute £250,000 ($325,000) to estate income.

10. The dignity of Holkham Hall is apparently not compromised by the popular display of old-fashioned engines, cars, and artifacts in the former stables (for which a separate admission is charged); or the onsite sales of pottery, snacks, and garden plants.

CHAPTER EIGHT

1. Penny Chorlton, "Live Like Lords of the Manor," *The Independent (Sunday Review)*, March 10, 1991, p. 51.

2. John Brennan, "Many Houses inside the Mansion," *Financial Times*, August 1, 1987.

3. The best examples of model conversion plans and specific advice are given in Marcus Binney and Kit Martin, *The Country House: To Be or Not to Be?*, 1985.

4. Marcus Binney, "The Rescue of Dingley Hall," *Country Life*, November 27, 1980, p. 1990.

5. Prince Charles's address to the Historic Houses Association Annual General Meeting, London, November 16, 1993.

6. *The Landmark Handbook* (The Landmark Trust, Shottesbrooke, Berks.), 1995, p. 48.

7. Ibid., p. 156.

8. Michael Thompson-Noel, "A Superior Tour around England," *The Financial Times*, April 28, 1990.

9. Nicholas Lander, "Minding Your Own Business," *The Financial Times*, December 16, 1989; Harvey Elliott, "Hotels in a Huddle," *The Times*, January 19, 1991.

10. Martyn Harris, "Country House Blues," *The Daily Telegraph*, November 23, 1991, p. 10.

11. Lander, op. cit.

12. Andrew Yates, "An American Squire Sells Up for £6.5 Million," *The Times*, September 15, 1991.

13. Rachel Kelly, "From Great Houses to Country Hotels," *The Times*, April 3, 1996.

CHAPTER NINE

1. *The Stoic* (Stowe School magazine), No. 192, March 1994, p. 19.

2. Large dormitories will no longer do. The parents of current sixth form boarders—the equivalent to American twelfth grade—expect private studio apartments, or at least doubles, for their £12,000 ($18,000) annual fees.

3. H. M. Treasury, *Report of the Committee on Houses of Outstanding Historic or Architectural Interest*, 1950, p. 42.

4. "Inside and out, the most sensational feature at Bear Wood is the main staircase. It runs up to the second [i.e., American third] floor, and is of the usual substantial craftsmanship. But the surprise (and it is a startling one) comes when one raises one's eyes and finds oneself looking up past the stairs and through a remote flood of golden light to the roof of the tower, 88 feet above, painted dark blue and sprinkled with gold stars." Mark Girouard, *The Victorian Country House*, 1971, p. 124.

5. John Newman and Nikolaus Pevsner, *The Buildings of Britain: Dorset*, 1972, p. 120.

6. Wallace B. Graves, *Harlaxton College, The Camelot of Academe*, 1990, pp. 46, 69.

7. Mark Girouard, *The Victorian Country House*, 1971, p. 190.

8. Marcus Binney and Kit Martin, *The Country House: To Be or Not to Be?*, 1982, pp. 8–9.

9. Rosemary Righter, "A Daughter's Toughest Decision," *The Times*, June 11, 1994.

10. Michael Jackson, "Observing the Stately Offices," *Country Life*, February 10, 1983.

11. J. Gilbert Jenkins, *Chequers: A History of the Prime Minister's Buckinghamshire House*, 1967, pp. 68–9.

12. Ibid., p. 67.

CHAPTER TEN

1. The most troublesome "deficit properties" are six underendowed houses the government accepted in lieu of taxes between 1950 and 1975—Hardwick, Saltram, Dyrham Park, Sudbury, Cragside, and Beningborough—and handed over to the Trust, with a "gentleman's agreement" to make good any annual deficits. In 1994, the National Trust tried and failed to get the current government to "buy out" of its failed moral obligation by way of an endowment grant for these properties.

2. The Chorley Formula has come under attack from people who believe that it is over-conservative, and leads to excessive endowment demands. I was persuaded of its justice by reading a detailed report of 1994, which studied the financial history of 37 important houses the Trust had acquired since 1976.

3. The Kingston Lacy bequest, altogether, was valued at £23 million ($46 million)—the largest gift in the history of the Trust. In addition to the mansion and its estate, the art collection, and the ruined castle with all its acres, it included prehistoric stone rings, 40 farms, 327 houses, three pubs, a hotel, and a golf course. Even so, claimed Lord Chorley in 1994, "the cost of restoring Kingston Lacy was wildly underestimated." Unknown to the Trust when they acquired it, dry rot was endemic, the building was sagging and cracking, much of the projecting stone cornice was in danger of falling, and a botched job of roof leading had to be completely redone. Although never regarded as a "problem" property, the outstanding work bill for Kingston Lacy, Corfe Castle, and the rest of the estate still amounted in 1994 to more than £7 million ($10.7 million).

4. The endowment for Belton House currently provides far more income—about £600,000 a year—than the house requires, even after meticulous restoration of marginally important outbuildings. One private owner in the neighborhood was fairly bitter about this, seeing such enormous sums of public money spent on a National Trust house, when he was unable to obtain even moderate grants for essential repairs.

Ian Bollom, the National Trust's Director of Finance, argues that houses like Belton *must* build up a surplus reserve in early years, to prepare for major repair jobs that will be necessary in the future. Private owners, "however august," Bollom says, "can compromise on standards of care. At the end of the day, if they make mistakes, they can sell the whole or a part of the property." But the Trust cannot compromise, because it can never sell.

5. "Borrowed Treasures," *Life* magazine, November 1985, p. 30.

6. "By his act of enforced giving, the donor is made impotent in a place where he was once all powerful. . . . [Lord Scarsdale] has no veto and no position in the chain of command. He has become marginal to what he has given away.

"All he can do is suggest, persuade and, eventually, complain. . . . He has become a sort of cultural amputee, confronted every day with the fact of his crippledness. All the Trust can do is ease the pain of loss, pouring on a sort of courteous, anaesthetic balm." Adam Nicolson, "When an Englishman's Home is Not His Castle," *The Times*, October 22, 1994.

7. In Paula Weideger, *Gilding the Acorn: Behind the Facade of the National Trust*, 1994, p. 349–50.

8. One notable difference over redecoration arose between Lord Vernon and the National Trust over Sudbury Hall in Derbyshire, which he handed over to the Trust, only to see it "done over" in John

Fowler's idiosyncratic style. As Lord Vernon wrote to *Country Life* in the summer of 1971, "the deliberate change which has been wrought in the character and personality of the house...has resulted in the destruction of original features or of features which, if not original, had been a part of the house's history for hundreds of years."

After a fire there in 1980, the National Trust entrusted the redecoration of Nostell Priory to David Mlinaric, who introduced new colors, wallpapers, and painted chintz, and moved chimneypieces from one room to another.

   9. Adam Nicolson, "Replacing the Old with the Old," *The Sunday Telegraph*, July 31, 1994, p. 12.

CHAPTER ELEVEN

   1. "Some owners adopt a policy of deliberate neglect in the hope of incurring a dangerous structures notice requiring that the building be demolished in the interests of public safety. The owner might then reap a considerable profit by selling off the land to developers. 'Mysterious fires' and other deliberate vandalism...are still too common." Marcus Dean and Mary Miers, *Scotland's Endangered Houses*, 1990, p. 5

   2. Marcus Binney, "Sleeping Beauties of France," *The Times*, August 23, 1996. He is, of course, counting houses throughout Britain, not just in England. In this case, the unusually large number of abandoned or ruinous houses in Scotland adds significantly to the figure.

   3. Marcus Binney and Marianne Smith, *The Save Britain's Heritage Action Guide*, 1991, pp. 47–48. A third of these inexpensively photocopied, spiral bound reports, *Restoring Hopes*, was published in 1991; a fourth, *Great Expectations*, in 1992. These were followed by *Bargain Buildings*, 1993; *Stop This Rot!*, 1994; and *One Damned Building after Another*, 1996. Before this comprehensive annual series began, SAVE had already published four more polished-looking guidebooks concentrating specifically on abandoned country houses: *Tomorrow's Ruins* (1978), *Silent Mansions* (1981), *The Country House: To Be or Not to Be* (1982), and *Endangered Domains* (1985).

   4. *The SAVE Britain's Heritage Action Guide*, 1991, p. 60.

   5. Chris Partridge, *The Daily Telegraph*, December 31, 1994, p. 18.

   6. Marcus Binney, *Our Vanishing Heritage*, 1984, p. 26.

   7. Ibid., p. 48.

   8. "It is a criminal offense to carry out work involving the demolition of a Listed Building or its alteration or extension in any manner that would affect its character as a building of special architectural or historic interest, including works to its interior, unless the works are authorised by Listed Building Consent." The penalties prescribed are a fine of £2,000 or three months in jail or both. A member of parliament from Essex who had made what she regarded as insignificant functional alterations to her listed, part-Tudor house without obtaining permission was threatened in 1995 on 33 separate criminal counts (*The Times*, February 22, 1995).

   9. *Our Vanishing Heritage*, p. 58.

CHAPTER TWELVE

   1. Nigel Nicolson dismisses the notion as empty sentimentality. "There is no argument in favour of maintaining the family in the conditions to which they are accustomed," he writes, "but there is an argument for saving the house. The family will continue in one shape or another, but the house, and the architectural tradition it represents, will fade away unless steps are taken to preserve it.... The majority [of aristocratic owners] live in the past, and grumble that the State is allowing their priceless inheritance to moulder away, when what they really mean is that they have been unable to support their style of living by their own efforts.... Why should the Government pay some old squire to keep the roof over his head, just because his family has lived there since the 17th century?"

2. Of some 211 country houses treated in detail in H. Avray Tipping's seven-volume series on *English Homes* (1920–37), more than 40 had only recently acquired new owners.

Against sixteen instances of long-time family continuity in Herefordshire cited in *Burke's and Savills Guide to Country Houses* (1980–81) can be set 98 country houses in the county that were sold and often resold in this century. Of Michael Sayer's extensive catalogue in this same guide to 487 country houses in Norfolk—large and small, new and old, landed and landless, surviving and demolished—at least 60 had been lived in by members of the current owner's family for 100 years or more. At least 90 had been torn down. But more than 200 of those that survived had been sold to new owners during the 20th century, some after more than three centuries of single-family tenure.

In other words, to be demolished, sold to another family, converted into multiple units, or turned into a school or a hospital has been the most common and natural fate of the English country house for the last hundred years.

Michael Sayer's figures come from his and Hugh Massingberd's book *The Disintegration of a Heritage: Country Houses and Their Collections 1979–1992*, 1993, a work underwritten by the Historic Houses Association.

3. I do not want to give the impression that only native British purchasers can be expected to treat a historic house with care. In recent years, more than half of the larger country houses up for sale in Britain have gone to buyers from overseas, many of whom remain both conscientious and anonymous. Wealthy British expatriates and Chinese leaving Hong Kong have succeeded an earlier wave of purchasers from the Near East and continental Europe. Among the many admirable new country house owners from overseas, who have invested tens of millions of pounds in restoration, are John Paul Getty Jr., at Wormsley, in Buckinghamshire; Mahdi Al-Tajir (former ambassador to London from the United Arab Emirates), at Mereworth Castle, in Kent; and Prince Bandar bin Sultan (Saudi ambassador to Washington), at Glympton in Oxfordshire.

4. *The Observer*, August 30, 1992.

5. Patrick Cormack, *Heritage in Danger*, 1978, p. 53

6. The Grade I and Grade II* designations—a total of about 30,000 buildings—probably come closer to a reasonable number deserving special national attention. But I have no idea how many historic houses are included in these categories, or whether the standards of selection make sense.

7. Prince Charles, address to the Historic Houses Association Annual General Meeting, London, November 16, 1993.

8. Harwicke Rawnsley, *The National Heritage*, 1920.

9. Raphael Samuel, *Theatres of Memory: Past and Present in Contemporary Culture*, 1994, pp. 205, 221; Robert Hewison, *The Heritage Industry: Britain in a Climate of Decline*, 1987, p. 9.

10. Throughout this book, I have taken 1975 as a watershed year in the story of the English country house, covering as it does two essential events in the recreation of its image: the Victoria and Albert exhibition, *The Destruction of the English Country House*, and the production of the television version of *Brideshead Revisited*.

11. Hewison, op. cit., p. 136.

12. Hugh Massingberd, "Forward with the Past," *The Daily Telegraph*, March 21, 1992, p. 101.

13. Hewison, op. cit., p. 53.

14. David Cannadine, "Why the Aristocracy Sucks," *The Observer* magazine, March 20, 1994, p. 16; Hewison, op. cit., p. 53. Cannadine's article is a condensed version of several of the arguments presented in his book, *Aspects of the Aristocracy: Grandeur and Decline in Modern Britain*, 1994.

Cannadine has argued that the "cult of the country house" was created by a self-styled national élite in order to brainwash Britons into a slavish, unthinking, and undeserved respect for the aristocracy. "The idea of a 'national' heritage, which is somehow 'threatened,' and which must be 'saved,' is often little more than a means of preserving the artifacts of an essentially élite culture by claiming—in most cases quite implausibly—that it is really everybody's. . . . By re-inventing themselves as live-in cultural custodi-ans, and by persuading the Government and the public to accept this version of themselves, the British aristocracy has been extremely successful at exploiting the 20th-century cult of the country house." David Cannadine, *The Pleasures of the Past*, 1990, pp. 100, 259 .

15. Giles Worsley, Letter to the Editor, *The Independent*, October 10, 1992, p. 16; Patrick Wright, *On Living in an Old Country*, 1985.

16. "The basic underlying principle must surely be that if the nation *burdens* the individual with list-ing, then the nation should be prepared to pay something." (William Proby, President, Historic Houses Association)

"If the Government is going to list buildings as being of historic importance and is, further, going to impose conditions on the owners of those buildings with regard to repair and maintenance...then it should aim to provide the necessary support to enable owners to meet those conditions." (Lord Fever-sham, Duncombe Park)

17. This is common practice in other European countries, in which taxpayer support of the national "patrimony" (*patrimoine, patrimonio*)—apparently a less loaded word than "heritage," at least across the Channel—is generally taken for granted.

Since 1964, the French government has been especially generous in granting tax-deductible status to the cost of repairs to buildings classed as *monuments historiques*: but then it has only granted that status to some 33,000 buildings. In Austria, Belgium, Denmark, Germany, Ireland, Italy, Netherlands, Portugal, and Spain, owners of historic houses are granted various forms of tax deduction and exemption (up to 100 percent, in some cases, for houses open to the public) on wealth or property tax, income tax, VAT, or inheritance tax—in almost every case more liberal than those prevailing in the United Kingdom.

The United States, although it maintains an extensive and not particularly discriminating "National Register of Historic Places," grants no such deductions or exemptions to private owners of registered buildings.

18. As William Proby points out, "Governments are elected; they have a constituency. And there's no doubt that from their point of view, if people *see* things, the public are more inclined to think they're get-ting value for money.

"I don't mean to say that an historic house is only worth saving for the sake of the public. But it is much more difficult to make a case for public money if there is no public access."

19. Horace Walpole, *The History of the Modern Taste in Gardening*, 1780–81, rep. 1995, p. 48.

20. Evelyn Waugh, *Brideshead Revisited*, 1945, Penguin Books edition 1967, p. 317.

APPENDIX

1. Felia Hemans, "The Homes of England," in *The Poetical Works of Mrs. Felicia Hemans*, 4th edition, 1828, p. 199; Noël Coward, "The Stately Homes of England" [from *Operette*, 1938], in *Songs to Amuse*, London, n.d.

2. "The key problem is to distinguish between country houses owned by small parish gentry and those owned by members of the county elite. The first step is therefore to devise some uniform standard of measurement of house size, and the second is to establish the minimum cut-off point to qualify for elite membership."

The minimum size of a house occupied by a member of the county elite, they calculated, was one of more than 5,000 square feet. In the three counties they surveyed, houses of "parish gentry" tended to be of 3,500 square feet or more; those possessing more horses, or taxed at higher rates, owned houses of at least 5,000 square feet. This cutoff point, they insist, is not "an arbitrary one but one that corresponded in fact with a very real division of local landed society." Lawrence Stone and Jeanne C. Fawtier Stone, *An Open Elite? England, 1540–1888*, 1984, pp. 439, 441.

3. Full citations for these two useful but difficult to find directories are as follows:

John Harris, *A Country House Index: An Index to over 2,000 Country Houses Illustrated in 107 Books of Country Views Published between 1715 and 1872, together with a List of British Country House Guides* ... Pinhorns Publications, Shalfleet Manor, Isle of Wight. 2nd edition, 1979.

Michael Holmes, *The Country House Described: an index to the Country Houses of Great Britain and Ireland*. St. Paul's Bibliographies in association with the Victoria & Albert Museum, 1986.

4. There were in England, in 1883, nineteen estates of 40,000 acres or more, often made up of non-contiguous properties in several counties. The three largest were the Duke of Northumberland's, whose seat was at Alnwick Castle (181,616 acres); the Duke of Devonshire's, at Chatsworth (138,572 acres); and the Duke of Cleveland's, at Raby Castle (104,194 acres). The remaining sixteen, in descending order of size, had as their home bases Woburn Abbey, Castle Howard, Belvoir Castle, Knowsley Hall, Lowther Castle, Petworth, Welbeck Abbey, Belton House, Brocklesby Park, Londesborough Lodge, Stephenstone, Savernake, Holkham Hall, Streatham, and Wilton House.

At least thirteen of these houses are still owned and lived in by descendants of the families who owned them in 1883.

5. Individual volumes in these two *Country Life* series are:

H. Avray Tipping, *English Homes*. Vol. 1, Period I: Norman and Plantagenet, 1066–1485, 1921; Vol. 2, Period II, Early Tudor, 1485–1588, 1924; Vol. 3 [expanding on Vols. 1 and 2], Periods I and II, Medieval and Early Tudor, 1066–1558, 1937; Vols. 4–5, Period III, Late Tudor and Early Stuart, 1558–1644, 1922, 1927; Vol. 6, Period IV, v. 1, Late Stuart, 1649–1714, 1920; Vol. 7, Period IV, v. 2, The Work of Sir John Vanbrugh and His School, 1699–1736, 1928.

Oliver Hill and John Cornforth, *English Country Houses: Caroline, 1625–1685*, 1966.

James Lees-Milne, *English Country Houses: Baroque, 1685–1715*, 1970.

Christopher Hussey, *English Country Houses: Early Georgian, 1715–1760*, 1955, rev. 1965.

Christopher Hussey, *English Country Houses, Mid-Georgian, 1760–1800*, 1956.

Christopher Hussey, *English Country Houses, Late Georgian, 1800–1840*, 1958.

6. *Burke's and Savills Guide to Country Houses*, Volume II, 1980, p. vii. Massingberd is here quoting from a 1978 *Times* review of Volume I of the series.

Index